A DISPLACED NATION

Studies of the Weatherhead East Asian Institute, Columbia University

The Studies of the Weatherhead East Asian Institute of Columbia University were inaugurated in 1962 to bring to a wider public the results of significant new research on modern and contemporary East Asia.

A DISPLACED NATION

THE 1954 EVACUATION AND ITS POLITICAL IMPACT ON THE VIETNAM WARS

PHI-VAN NGUYEN

SOUTHEAST ASIA PROGRAM PUBLICATIONS
AN IMPRINT OF CORNELL UNIVERSITY PRESS
Ithaca and London

Southeast Asia Program Publications Editorial Board

Mahinder Kingra (ex officio)
Thak Chaloemtiarana
Chiara Formichi
Tamara Loos
Andrew Willford

Copyright © 2024 by Cornell University

All rights reserved. Except for brief quotations in a review, this book, or parts thereof, must not be reproduced in any form without permission in writing from the publisher. For information, address Cornell University Press, Sage House, 512 East State Street, Ithaca, New York 14850. Visit our website at cornellpress.cornell.edu.

First published 2024 by Cornell University Press

Library of Congress Cataloging-in-Publication Data
Names: Nguyen, Phi-Vân (Historian), author.
Title: A displaced nation : the 1954 evacuation and its political impact on the Vietnam wars / Phi-Van Nguyen.
Description: Ithaca, NY : Cornell University Press, 2024. | Series: Studies of the Weatherhead East Asian Institute, Columbia University | Includes bibliographical references and index.
Identifiers: LCCN 2024015909 (print) | LCCN 2024015910 (ebook) | ISBN 9781501778605 (hardcover) | ISBN 9781501778612 (paperback) | ISBN 9781501778629 (epub) | ISBN 9781501778636 (pdf)
Subjects: LCSH: Political refugees—Vietnam—History—20th century. | Vietnam—Politics and government—1945–1975. | Vietnam—Politics and government—1975– | Vietnam—History—1945–1975. | Vietnam—History—1975–
Classification: LCC DS556.9 . N4967 2024 (print) | LCC DS556.9 (ebook) | DDC 959.704/11—dc23/eng/20240605
LC record available at https://lccn.loc.gov/2024015909
LC ebook record available at https://lccn.loc.gov/2024015910

Contents

Preface vii
List of Abbreviations xiii

Introduction	1
1. Alternative Vietnams	10
2. "Refugees" on a Mission	33
3. Keeping Hope Alive	56
4. Counterrevolution	77
5. Peace in Vietnam	97
6. Estranged from the War	116
7. Lag Time	136
8. Breaking Free of the War	158
Conclusion	176

Notes 183
Selected Bibliography 253
Index 277

Preface

Who knew that I would gain a new perspective on the Vietnam wars while watching a colleague edit a TV commercial for instant noodles? Never had I imagined that whether people moved or stayed could reflect a political choice. My family came from northern Vietnam and evacuated to the south in 1954, when the Geneva ceasefire divided the country at the seventeenth parallel. After growing up in Switzerland, I returned to Vietnam to work and visit the usual tourist spots and places that were special to my parents and grandparents. This meant visiting the houses, schools, and streets of our memories, together with all the family members, in Ho Chi Minh City and Hanoi. I wanted to see the market where my grandmother tried to exchange gold without being caught in 1945 and the neighborhood to which my grandfather returned in extremis, because a nanny had kidnapped my uncle when she heard that they planned to leave in 1954. By the time of my visit, the war had long since ended, and I believed that my generation could foster a new relationship with Vietnam. I understood that due to their trauma, my uncles and aunts, still scarred by the armed conflict, questioned my desire to return. I also knew that various relatives in Vietnam begrudged that my family had resettled overseas while they had remained in the country. Our fates diverged because of a single stroke of luck, a single decision, a single connection.

But my former colleague did not share my perspective. He was roughly my age, and we worked together in advertising. His family also came from Hanoi, and he could afford an affluent lifestyle thanks to his video editing skills. Once, while we were working on the instant noodle commercial together, he expressed he had no desire to visit his family in the north. "They're all communists!" he claimed. Ever since then, I have wondered: How could a physical place have anything to do with a person's ideological choice? Can we ascribe political meaning to the act of moving or staying behind when chance events might have a greater impact on people's ability to move? Soon after this exchange with my colleague,

I ended my brief stint in advertising and spent the next fifteen years searching for an answer. In writing this book, I found snippets of answers but still have not figured it out; nonetheless, I am indebted to countless institutions and people who have helped me along this journey.

First, I acknowledge the financial support I received to write this book. I originally planned to write a short monograph on the northern Vietnamese evacuees and their mobilization in the south from 1954 to 1965. However, I was fortunate enough to have fifteen months in the Southeast Asia Program at Cornell University in which to deepen my analysis. My stay was supported by two postdoctoral fellowships, from the Social Science and Humanities Research Council (SSHRC) of Canada and the Swiss National Science Foundation, which enabled me to widen the lens. I had to return to 1945, when the end of the Pacific War spelled the end of French colonial rule, in order to determine that the partition in 1954 was a turning point in anticommunism. Extending my scope to 1975, when the Second Indochina War ended, was just as crucial, as it helped to show that the evacuees' determination to fight communism did not withstand further armed conflict. Their dream of liberating the north from communism was shattered when they were faced with the war's messiness and near-total destruction. Finally, an Insight grant from the SSHRC (435-2019-0363) and support from the Université de Saint-Boniface, which I joined in 2017, enabled me to extend my study to 1989, the end of the Cold War. Hence, I could follow the evacuees overseas to see how they reacted to the war in which Vietnam opposed Cambodia and China and to the refugee crisis across Southeast Asia. Ultimately, I was able to study the evacuees and their displacement from one Vietnam to another across three wars. Without this financial support, I could never have written the book that I wanted to.

I also owe a great deal to several scholars, who generously offered training, advice, and mentorship. The first one to mention is Chris Goscha, whom I regard as one of the best historians on Vietnam to this day. He showed me that historical interpretation requires curiosity, courage, and patient work. Andrew Barros, Edward Miller, Laurence Monnais, and Eric Tagliacozzo have been invaluable models and sources of inspiration. Countless scholars helped push this book further with their comments and criticism.

Parts of chapter 4 have appeared in the *Revue historique des armées* and I would like to thank Ivan Cadeau and Commandant Mikaël Le Gouaréguer for authorizing me to reproduce parts of this article. I also want to acknowledge that some material in this book has been discussed and explored further in other avenues. Some ideas on Catholic evacuees that appear in chapters 1, 2, and 3 were developed in an article in *Sojourn: Journal of Social Issues in Southeast Asia*, a chapter in *Refugees and Religion*, and a chapter in *Decolonization and the Remaking of Christianity*. I cannot thank enough Mike Montesano from *Sojourn*, as well as the editors and contributors of these volumes, especially Birgit Meyer, Peter van der Veer, Elizabeth Foster, and Udi Greenberg for the lively exchanges and amazing opportunity. Discussions of the number of evacuees, the rise of Ngô Đình Diệm, and the instrumentalization of refugee protection have also appeared in chapters for *Travail, migrations et culture au Viêt-Nam*, *The Cambridge History of the Vietnam War*, and *The Oxford Handbook of Late Colonial Insurgencies* for which discussions with Eric Guérassimoff, Andrew Hardy, Nguyen Ngoc Phuong, Emmanuel Poisson, Lien-Hang Nguyen, Edward Miller, Martin Thomas, and Gareth Curless have proved invaluable.

I also acknowledge the help of other scholars. They are too numerous to mention them all but among them I thank Pierre Asselin, Alvin Bui, Sean Fear, Pierre Grosser, François Guillemot, Tuan Hoang, Jérémy Jammes, Shawn McHale, Tam Ngo, Lien-Hang Nguyen, Y Thien Nguyen, Jason Picard, Mitchell Tan, Philip Taylor, Stein Tønnesson, Nu-Anh Tran, Alex Vo, and Minh Hoang Vu. I learned a lot from other scholars working on Asia. Cheow Thia Chan, Robert Crews, Aishwary Kumar, Yumi Moon, Ijlal Muzaffar, Guo-Quan Seng, Emiko Stock, and Dominic Yang helped me see how Vietnam fitted in all this. I obtained invaluable insights on Christians through working or corresponding with Le Thi Hoa, Hajin Jun, Dominique Laperle, Sandra Park, Claire Tran Thi Liên, and of course, Charles Keith. I am grateful to Andrew Barros, Chris Goscha, Edward Miller, and Ivan Small for reading the entire manuscript. I also thank the two anonymous reviewers who waded through bad prose, engaged with the argument, and understood that I needed critical feedback. Their comments were extremely insightful.

Over the years, I have relied on the guidance of countless professionals at libraries and archives. I am grateful to the archivists, librarians, and staff at the National Archives Center no. 2, the General Science Library, the Social Science Library, and the National Library in Vietnam; at the Archives nationales d'outre-mer, le Service historique de la Défense, l'Établissement de communication et de production audiovisuelle de la Défense, l'Institut catholique de Paris, l'Institut de recherche France-Asie, and la Bibliothèque nationale in France; at the United Nations High Commissariat for Refugees, the International Labor Organization, and the International Committee for the Red Cross in Switzerland;

and at the Archdiocese of New York, National Archives and Records Administration, the Vietnam Archives at Texas Tech University, Michigan State University, the United Nations Archives and Records Management Section, and, of course, the Kroch Asia Library at Cornell University in the United States. I also acknowledge the support of the librarians at the Bibliothèque et archives nationales du Québec, l'Université de Saint-Boniface, and the University of Manitoba in Canada, without whom I could not have completed this work. Last but not least, I would like to thank Đỗ Kiên from the Institute of Vietnamese Studies and Development Science at Vietnam National University in Hanoi, who helped me access archival centers and libraries in Vietnam.

I am also grateful to Quoc Thanh Nguyen, an independent researcher based in Paris, and three graduate students—Giuliano Beniamino Fleri in Geneva, Vinh Pham in Ithaca, and Benoît Gaudreau in Montreal—who helped me with data collection when I had to return to Winnipeg. Students at the Université de Saint-Boniface have also greatly helped me. Amine Tasmany developed an online database on the 1979 refugee crisis. Simon Boily, Yanko Kalem, Hannah Klos, Connor McCorrie, and Sophie Sickert collected data and contributed to the analysis. Finally, through teaching undergraduate students, I learned to focus on what matters. It was with them in mind that I wrote this book.

Professional help was needed to turn this research into a book. I benefited from the unwavering patience and efficient support of Sarah Grossman, Mary Kate Murphy, and their entire team at Cornell University Press, as well as Ariana King at the Weatherhead East Asian Institute at Columbia University. Debra Soled and Katherine Pickett contributed with hours of careful editing, turning the prose of a nonnative English speaker into something accessible. Bill Nelson designed all the maps with expert precision. Any errors, however, are mine alone. On a different note, I would like to thank Maria Stenz for authorizing me to reproduce a photograph by the late journalist Jens Nauntofte that appears in chapter 8.

Last, the most important thing that made this book possible was the gift of time, made possible by fellowships and releases from teaching. Ultimately, no one has been as generous as Hà, Lý, and Nam. For years, you have trusted me and spared no effort in helping me turn these ideas into a book. You are the anonymous producers of this book, by extending financial, moral, and emotional support to me day and night. I cannot thank you enough for this.

Unless specified otherwise, all translations are mine. Vietnamese names usually give the surname first, followed by the middle name and the first name, as in other East Asian cultures. In the text, I have sometimes used a shortened name. For example, I use Diệm, to refer to Ngô Đình Diệm, the way Vietnamese do. This order becomes more confusing when Vietnamese people live or publish in a Western context. Many use their first name, sometimes followed by their middle name, and then their surname. In my case, as I grew up with my name hyphenated, Phi-Vân corresponds to my middle name-first name and Nguyen is my surname. People know me as Nguyễn Phi Vân in Vietnamese, Van Nguyen in English, and Phi-Vân Nguyen in French.

Abbreviations

ASEAN	Association of Southeast Asian Nations
ASVN	Associated State of Vietnam
CARE	Cooperative for American Relief Everywhere
CEFEO	Corps expéditionnaire français en Extrême-Orient
CIA	Central Intelligence Agency
CICR	Comité international de la Croix-Rouge
COMIGAL	Commissariat général aux réfugiés
CRS	Catholic Relief Service
ĐMH	Đồng minh Hội (Việt Nam Cách mệnh Đồng minh Hội, Vietnam Revolutionary League)
DRV	Democratic Republic of Vietnam
FLQ	Front de libération du Québec
FULRO	United Front for the Liberation of Oppressed Races
FVPPA	Families of Vietnamese Political Prisoners Association
FTCV	Cabinet des Forces terrestres du centre Viêt Nam
FTSV	Cabinet des Forces terrestres du sud Viêt Nam
FTNV	Cabinet des Forces terrestres du nord Viêt Nam
GSA	General Student Association
HCI	Haut commissariat en Indochine
ICC	International Control Commission
ICRC	International Committee for the Red Cross
IRC	International Rescue Committee
IVS	International Voluntary Service
LLĐĐK	Lực lượng Đại đoàn kết (Greater Solidarity Movement)
NGO	nongovernmental organization
NLF	National Liberation Front
ODP	Orderly Departure Program
PAVN	People's Army of Vietnam
PLAF	People's Liberation Armed Forces of South Vietnam
PRC	People's Republic of China
PRK	People's Republic of Kampuchea

ABBREVIATIONS

PRG	Provisional Revolutionary Government of the Republic of South Vietnam
RVN	Republic of Vietnam
RVNAF	Republic of Vietnam Armed Forces
SVN	State of Vietnam
SVNAF	State of Vietnam Armed Forces
SSHRC	Social Science and Humanities Research Council of Canada
SRVN	Socialist Republic of Vietnam
UN	United Nations
UNESCO	United Nations Educational, Scientific, and Cultural Organization
UNHCR	United Nations High Commissioner for Refugees
UNICEF	United Nations Children's Fund
VNĐ	Việt Nam đồng (Vietnamese currency)
VNQDĐ	Việt Nam Quốc dân Đảng (Vietnamese Nationalist Party)
VWP	Vietnam Workers' Party

A DISPLACED NATION

Introduction

Condemned to exile twice in his lifetime, the composer Phạm Duy wrote *Cha bỏ quê, con bỏ nước* (*A Father Leaves His Home Village, a Son Leaves His Homeland*), telling a story of continuous uprooting. In 1954, when Vietnam was partitioned at the seventeenth parallel at the end of the First Indochina War, a man left his home village in the north to go to the south. More than twenty years later, in 1975, when communist troops victoriously entered Saigon, his son had to leave the country. Two generations had to move, first to the south and then to a foreign country.[1] Phạm Duy had gone through a similar process. When he was in the north before 1954, he wrote patriotic songs for the Việt Minh and, after the partition, became one of the most popular composers in the south.[2] This song was not entirely autobiographical, because when he left Vietnam in 1975, some of his children stayed behind. Yet it expressed a feeling that was all too familiar to many Vietnamese. One generation after another, people left knowing that there was no way back. If Vietnam is famous for the wars that it fought to become a united and independent country, it is also known for its refugees fleeing war and two massive waves of departure, in 1954 and 1975. Twice in Vietnam's history, the end of a war was supposed to restore peace or bring unity. However, both times, this meant departing for an unfamiliar destination. Some were displaced two or more times over a lifetime.

Asia has had its share of forced migrations and refugee flows, which had an impact on the formation of nation-states and the Cold War. The partition of India in 1947 caused the displacement and death of millions.³ Indian and Pakistani officials and religious leaders have often instrumentalized its representation for their own purposes. They have used individual cases of rape or torture as a symbol for denouncing the infringement of their nation-state's territorial integrity. The migrants' selective memories of displacement, in which innocent civilians faced a tragic and unfair destiny, also became a hagiographic narrative about the partition.⁴ Division and displacement also played a role in the Cold War. In China, the victory of the Chinese Communist Party in 1949 forced the Republic of China to relocate to the island of Taiwan. After resettling there, Nationalists felt nostalgic and hoped to return to the mainland, but they have never managed to do so.⁵ Throughout the Cold War, and ever since, Chinese who have relocated elsewhere, called overseas Chinese, engaged in a complex relationship with economic and political developments on the mainland.⁶ The Cold War, represented in Asia by the Korean War, divided Korea at the thirty-eighth parallel. The two Koreas, which exist to this day, perceived the repatriation of their nationals as a metaphor for their own legitimacy.⁷ Territorial divisions and population movements were not simply the collateral damage of decolonization and the Cold War. States and people often ascribed particular significance to population movements because it supported their own political struggle.

Vietnam split into two parts in 1954, with the end of French colonial rule and the First Indochina War. The Democratic Republic of Vietnam (DRV), led by communists, controlled the northern side of the seventeenth parallel, and noncommunist armed forces regrouped on the southern side. In its Article 14(d), the cease-fire agreement also allowed any civilian to move to their zone of choice within three hundred days after it was signed. As a result, over eight hundred thousand people, 80 percent of whom were Roman Catholic, left the north, whereas around one hundred eighty thousand went in the opposite direction. Western media painted the northern migrants as innocent civilians fleeing communist rule. Many of them resettled in the south under the leadership of their priest, setting up new villages, often named after their place of origin in the north. Saigon saw this historic resettlement as the dawn of a new nation-state, free of colonial ties and capable of resisting communism. These evacuees remembered their homeland in the north and hoped to return there one day. But, unlike the partition of India, the exile of Chinese Nationalists, or the status quo in Korea, the situation in Vietnam did not stabilize. Not once, but twice after that initial conflict, Vietnam became the epicenter of the Cold War. Three wars broke out in Indochina, encompassing Vietnam, Laos, and Cambodia, in entanglements of local conflicts with regional and global tensions.

The First Indochina War started in 1946, when the Việt Minh called upon the population to oppose the restoration of French colonial rule and defend the DRV's independence. In 1949, it became a front in the Cold War, in which coalitions supporting two competing states collided. The DRV, led by Hồ Chí Minh, received assistance from the Soviet Union and the People's Republic of China and soon afterward launched land reform, denunciation campaigns, and a general mobilization to expand its war effort. The French created the Associated State of Vietnam (ASVN), which received international recognition and support from the "free world." The competition was still ongoing when foreign powers decided to call a cease-fire in the armed conflict. The war ended at the Geneva Conference in 1954, which called for the two armies to be regrouped on either side of the seventeenth parallel. But Hanoi and Saigon still claimed to be the only government that represented all Vietnamese. In 1955 this antagonism only deepened when a new state was created in the south, called the Republic of Vietnam (RVN). Its new leader, Ngô Đình Diệm, refused to hold the political referendum envisioned in the cease-fire agreement.

Armed fighting resumed in December 1959, when communist cadres in the south rebelled against Saigon. Hanoi approved this insurrection and created the National Liberation Front (NLF), calling on all Vietnamese to join its ranks. The conflict escalated in 1963, after the assassination of Ngô Đình Diệm, the president of the RVN. The ensuing political vacuum lasted almost two years, leading the United States to intervene in March 1965, with boots on the ground. US soldiers remained until the conclusion of the Paris Peace Accords almost eight years later, in 1973, after which only military advisers and the personnel necessary to protect the US embassy remained. On April 30, 1975, the Second Indochina War ended, with Saigon's unconditional surrender. Hanoi had succeeded in unifying the country under its rule.

Only three years later, the third and lesser-known conflict broke out—with Vietnam launching a war against Cambodia and China. The main reason for this confrontation was not ideology but, rather, divisions within the communist world, which led Vietnam to see its two neighbors, Cambodia (ruled by the Khmer Rouge) and China, as its most dangerous enemies. In December 1978, Hanoi invaded Cambodia, which prompted a Chinese incursion in Vietnam's northern highlands three months later. Large-scale fighting ended in March 1979 after Beijing withdrew its troops. However, local confrontations and diplomatic pressure lasted for a decade. Only after Vietnam left Cambodia in 1989 did the Cold War eventually end in Asia.

Throughout these wars, international tensions fueled local confrontations, and local elites sought external support to gain the upper hand on the ground. However, entangling local disputes in a global conflict also enabled international concerns to take priority over Vietnamese interests. Foreign intervention and international settlement could affect the shape of Vietnam and spark population displacement, as in 1954. Those who left the north in 1954 often felt as if history was repeating. Until the late 1980s, the Cold War intersected with the contest over creating a nation-state in Vietnam several times. Every time, military interventions and international decisions had the potential to affect the country's fate and the lives of people, creating the need and possibility of crossing demarcation lines and reaching new safety zones. How did representations of the 1954 evacuation affect subsequent wars and the creation of Vietnam as a nation-state?

Although the partition of Vietnam in 1954 was not permanent, its implications were both immediate and long lasting. Because hundreds of thousands of people left the DRV, most narratives on the wars refer to them as among the most anticommunist groups in Vietnam. Archives and documents from various institutions, Vietnamese and non-Vietnamese alike, repeatedly specify whether an author, a journalist, a political leader, or a military officer in South Vietnam was originally from the north, as if this characteristic alone indicated their ideological orientation.[8] Vietnamese authors have reinforced this notion. Party historians have maintained the general narrative of a continuous struggle for independence and unity. Accordingly, those who left have obstructed this path and enabled foreign intervention.[9] Historical accounts produced in the diaspora, for their part, emphasize the importance of the civil war in tearing the Vietnamese apart. Yet they, too, insist on continuous resistance to communism, overlooking their doubts and divisions.[10] Virtually all narratives, including those that reclaim Vietnamese agency in the war, have confined those who evacuated to an ideological straitjacket.

This paradigm has not been debunked in recent literature. Often inspired by reflection on the fiftieth anniversary of the country's partition, many studies have examined the logistics and diplomacy related to the evacuation by the French, US, British, and Polish navies.[11] Studies that analyzed US nation-building programs in the RVN sometimes perpetuated the antiwar criticisms of the 1970s, which reduced Saigon to a creature of US foreign policy and regarded this project as the first step into a "quagmire."[12] The opening of Vietnamese archives offered a deeper understanding of what actually happened. Researchers produced detailed descriptions of the northern evacuees and the large proportion of them who were Catholics.[13] They also revealed that many disagreed with plans to resettle them and with Ngô Đình Diệm's policies.[14] Works about the first and second Republics of Vietnam in the south (1955–1963 and 1967–1975) highlighted their proactive role in culture and politics.[15] Finally, scholarship on the diaspora often depicted it as a tight-knit community, despite several waves of displacement and dispersion across continents.[16] These papers reveal essential aspects of the evacuees. We now understand the context that led to their departure, how they changed the religious landscape in the south, and why certain cultural characteristics endured over generations despite multiple displacements. However, we still do not understand why so many northerners repeatedly appeared to be the most anticommunist group in South Vietnamese society.[17]

Leaving that question unanswered tends to perpetuate the assumption that they remained anticommunist and never changed.[18] At first, it does not seem unreasonable to think that the evacuees opposed communism, because its expansion led to their departure. Yet to assume that they held an ongoing grudge and remained committed to fighting communism would cement the idea that they were, generation after generation, defined by their exile. Recognizing the agency of these people requires that we acknowledge all its dimensions. People have power, and they act or think with a purpose. But they also experience moments of vulnerability and indecision. Therefore, a genuine history of the evacuees must accept that their representations changed and that their self-identification remained fluid, depending on the context.

To understand the evolution in their ideological position during the war, I examine several authors, journalists, and political and religious leaders known for their public role in the immediate aftermath of their evacuation. Far from having unanimity in their opinions or political agendas, these people had unique memories of their place of origin. They also had different perceptions of the wars and different ideas about what their allies and compatriots should do. Research on this population over time fails to reveal a consistent political stance or clear continuity in their sense of belonging. Despite these caveats, the evacuees who expressed their views in the public sphere had one thing in common: they believed that the Cold War expanded the range of available political and military opportunities for the Vietnamese people.

This book argues that population displacement, when used as a weapon to reinforce or undermine the legitimacy of contesting political authorities, affects the projection of the nation-state. Population movements require humanitarian assistance and adjustments in war logistics. When political authorities compete to lead a nation-state, these movements also affect the war in three different ways. First, states use population flows as a metaphor in claiming they are the most legitimate political expression of the people. Second, this symbolic representation influences the scope of diplomatic connections, economic ties, and general support that each competing state receives from outside the country. In an armed conflict amplified by its entanglement with global tensions, this augments a state's ability to sustain the war effort. Last, representations of the movement profoundly change the displaced population's self-awareness.

State and international propaganda, which touted the evacuees as standard-bearers of the "free world," gave many political leaders and cultural activists among them a new sense of purpose. They believed that this support could create new opportunities (though over time this feeling sometimes faded), and this belief was reignited every time the Cold War intersected with local developments in Vietnam. The Cold War was paradoxical. On the one hand, states had to avoid a third world war to prevent unprecedented destruction. On the other hand, states kept preparing for a future armed conflict and sometimes claimed that this mobilization was precisely what was preventing another war from happening by deterring their opponents. Instead of fully accepting this contradiction and its implication on the unification of Vietnam, many evacuees embraced this ambiguity to adopt a new mindset. Some of them held on to distant projects and adopted an elastic conception of space and time because they thought the United States would contain communist expansion. The past and the present did not matter as much because they believed they could rely on broad support for liberating the north from communism and reuniting their country one day. The convergence of the Cold War with Vietnam and their own personal lives led many evacuees to envisage a new human condition defined by larger horizons of opportunity.

These evacuees represented a displaced nation in two ways. They claimed that they represented the Vietnamese people, forcibly removed from their ancestral territory and yearning to return. Yet they were also displaced because there was also an obvious disconnect between their aspirations and what they could realistically achieve. The Cold War convinced them that in the future anything could happen. The evacuees embraced this unique position, which they imagined only a few other people who were displaced or divided by the Cold War might also experience. They rejected the partition and blamed both Vietnamese communists and the French for negotiating an agreement on their behalf. The support and legitimation they received in 1954 persuaded them that the world would never allow this division to become permanent. As a result, they continued to deny the situation in front of them and, instead, projected themselves into the future and in alternative spaces of the Vietnamese nation. They did not see news about an upcoming war as a curse; rather, it presented an opportunity for achieving their vision of a nation-state. Only after Vietnam withdrew its troops from Cambodia in 1989 did they accept that they could not escape reality. Despite promises that the world would save Vietnam, no states were prepared to escalate and run the risk of touching off a third world war. So, they never returned to the north.

The evacuees were certainly not the only ones to advocate a vision of the Vietnamese nation. As this book makes clear, many other people, communist and noncommunist alike, imagined Vietnam, its orientation, and its contour over the course of war and peace. What made the 1954 evacuees stand out was their self-awareness as a people who were both affected by local and international events and persuaded that those events would change their future. Studying the perspective of some evacuees, albeit a literate, political, and religious elite among them, helps us understand how Vietnamese who were outside the decision-making circles engaged with the war and its political, military, and spiritual aspects.

Taking the long view is key to this analysis. As a product of the First Indochina War, the evacuees believed that their lives were intimately connected to the fate of the Vietnamese nation and blamed this tragedy on communism. In fact, the belief that their physical movements had a political impact on the war had originated in 1950, when many left zones controlled by the DRV to join another Vietnamese state created by the French. The evacuation in 1954 marked a historical moment because Western media and transnational charities brought their exodus into the limelight, leading them to believe that they were the vanguard of the "free world." This did not mean that the evacuees held this view permanently. They opposed the neutralization of the armed conflict in 1964 and applauded the landing of US troops. But they soon became disillusioned when the US strategy changed. Nixon's rapprochement with China and decision to Vietnamize the war made them realize that superpowers prioritized their own interests over their ideological commitment. The hasty departure of many evacuees in 1975 after communist troops won the war reopened old scars. Yet that alone did not reawaken their desire to liberate their homeland. Only after the international community condemned Hanoi for the "boat people" crisis and its invasion of Cambodia did some evacuees resume their mobilization against the communists. This forty-year overview shows that, with every new development in the Cold War, the evacuees kindled the hope of creating a united and noncommunist Vietnam.

The goal of this book is not to offer an exhaustive mapping of the initial and successive rounds of displacement. Many other works in the future will likely explore what I have only begun to surface. Instead, by looking at the evacuees' projections about the war, this book focuses on the political consequences of the evacuation. This approach has its own methodological problems. Most of the government archives and printed sources were destroyed by war and poor conservation. Therefore, it is impossible to imagine a history from below, considering the perspectives of all evacuees, including less vocal or underrepresented groups.[19] This book notes when evacuees identified themselves with their displacement and when they overlooked it. As a result, the analysis draws on important political, religious, and journalistic personalities who left traces in the archives and printed sources. None of them represents the average person who left the north in 1954. Their changing positions and internal debates, however, give us sufficient insight into their views, which were neither monolithic nor static.

Because of this focus on representation, "evacuation" does not refer to the actual physical experience of southward migration. In these publications, it was an idea, a memory, or a symbolic reference to a tragedy that affected individual lives and the creation of the Vietnamese nation. Another major challenge comes from the connotations of the words employed in these sources to designate the population. A "migrant" designates a person who moved from one place to another. An "evacuee" is much the same, with the additional nuance of people leaving a war zone or a dangerous situation. When sources refer to "refugees," however, another dimension emerges. Its most common definition comes from the 1951 Refugee Convention identifying a refugee as a person crossing borders to seek protection due to a well-founded fear of persecution "for reasons of race, religion, nationality, membership of a particular social group, or political opinion."[20] This definition allows refugee protection to become a diplomatic tool for undermining the state of origin as the source of danger. Therefore, a careful analysis of these representations needs to consider the "politics of refugee protection" in these documents.[21] Hence, we use "evacuee" to refer to this population and distinguish between "migrants" and "refugees," depending on how they are designated in Western or Vietnamese sources.

By the end of this book, the Vietnam wars will no longer look like three separate armed conflicts. For these evacuees, each armed conflict provided an opportunity to overturn the results of the prior one. Their ideas and initiatives spread from within South Vietnam to the other side of the seventeenth parallel and across political borders. In fact, in their minds, the war never really ended. The eight chapters in the book are in chronological order, starting in 1945, with the creation of different postcolonial states, and ending in 1989 with the end of military and diplomatic tensions. They show that the Cold War made it difficult for these evacuees to achieve peace.

Chapter 1

Alternative Vietnams

Father Georges Naïdenoff, on a ship evacuating civilians from northern Vietnam in 1954, marveled at the evacuees' moving expressions of piety. At the time, only 10 percent of the population was Catholic. But they made up 60–80 percent of the eight hundred thousand evacuees, who doubled the Catholic population in the south after 1955.[1] Most left in a hurry, carrying nothing but a religious object. A photograph accompanying the priest's report showed a man lying down in the sun, holding a crucifix. "A true sign of faith. In the deepest sleep, they hold a crucifix, which has become an identity card in this exodus to freedom," reads the caption. Naïdenoff had fled from Russia to France after the 1917 Bolshevik revolution.[2] However, unlike him, these evacuees wanted to fight back:

> These refugees had a long experience in the Việt Minh zone. They discussed going on a crusade. Someone asked my opinion.
> As a Westerner attached to the separation of church and state, I disagreed. It was unacceptable to hold such ideas in the twentieth century. And to find some support, I turned to a man who had received the highest honors from Hồ Chí Minh himself. This person, respected by everyone for his wisdom, remained silent.
> I asked him: "And you! Would you call a crusade?" He lowered his head and declared with a serious look: "Yes." This was all he said.[3]

Given that the overwhelming majority of evacuees were Catholic, religion seemed to be the central reason for departure. The involvement of US military operatives in psychological operations to encourage departure, and communist propaganda claiming that Catholics were falling for tricks enabling a statue of the Virgin Mary to weep and wave her hand at the faithful, paved the way for a myth that persists to this day.[4] Accordingly, American propaganda had persuaded Catholics that the Virgin Mary had gone to the south.[5] Secular observers considered this religiosity a sign of Vietnam's attachment to the past or to a Church from the Middle Ages. Why did people leave the north in 1954 and how can we explain the importance of religion for many of them?

Trying to understand why people left the north remains a challenge. In fact, people had been moving from one Vietnam to another since 1950, when large Catholic strongholds and many Việt Minh defected to join the Associated State of Vietnam (ASVN), created by the French. This movement reflected the multiple dimensions of the armed conflict. First, the confrontation sought a decolonization from French rule. Second, it became a front line of the Cold War after 1949 as the United States feared countries surrounding China could fall like dominoes under communist rule. Third, it was a civil war opposing Vietnamese elites about the kind of postcolonial state they should establish. Lastly, this was also a religious war to determine whether the decolonization of the Church in East Asia would involve a complete separation from the rest of the hierarchy. Seen in this light, the First Indochina War not only spelled the end of French rule but marked a long and violent struggle to define postcolonial Vietnam and the future of the Catholic Church in East Asia. When international powers convened a conference along the Geneva Lake to end the armed conflict in 1954, they could not solve all the disputes entangled in the war. The cease-fire agreements signed by the French and the DRV divided Vietnam at the seventeenth parallel, and a provision allowed civilians to join the zone of their choice. Many people left the north because the war remained unfinished business. The evacuation did not reflect a definitive move to a new place. To many of these evacuees, it meant a new stage in the war, which had yet to reach a conclusive end.

Fighting for Vietnam

Although the dream of creating a nation-state, free of French colonial rule, had existed for decades, it only became clear that Vietnamese would have to fight for it in 1945. In search of support in the Pacific War, the Japanese army overthrew French authorities in Indochina and had King Bảo Đại proclaim Vietnam's independence. However, at the local level, the new state's effective presence remained nominal. Allied bombings and a famine caused by a poor harvest and disrupted communication lines threatened the lives of nearly one million people in north-central Vietnam. Local leaders, including religious groups in the north and the south, filled the void left by the collapse of the state apparatus. On September 2, 1945, when Hồ Chí Minh proclaimed the Democratic Republic of Vietnam (DRV) in Hanoi in the wake of what is called the August Revolution, he had three goals. First, speaking on the day of Tokyo's surrender, he wanted to make clear that this state was not part of the Japanese empire. Second, he hoped that, by quoting the American Declaration of Independence in his first sentence, the Allied powers would recognize this new republic. Third, this call was also an attempt to rally nationalist groups, religious organizations, and the population to support the Việt Minh, the antifascist front that Hồ Chí Minh had created in 1941. From the outset, independence went hand in hand with efforts to unite the Vietnamese under the same banner.

A few months earlier, at the Potsdam Conference, the Allied powers had entrusted Nationalist China and the United Kingdom with receiving the Japanese army's surrender on each side of the sixteenth parallel. In September 1945, war broke out in southern Vietnam when the British let local French forces expel the DRV's representatives from Saigon. In early October, the Corps expéditionnaire français en Extrême-Orient (CEFEO; French Far East Expeditionary Corps) landed in the south. In the north, the French faced more resistance from the Nationalist Chinese, who demanded the end of French privileges in China in exchange for assuming their disarmament duties. On March 6, 1946, with the French resuming control in the south and the imminent landing of CEFEO troops in the north, Hồ Chí Minh negotiated a modus vivendi, agreeing to their return in exchange for recognition of the DRV "as a free state, with its own government, parliament, army and finances, as part of the Indochinese Federation and French Union."[6] The agreement not only remained vague on Vietnam's independence but also avoided the question of territorial unity. For the DRV, unity in Vietnam meant halting division of the empire into three *kỳ*, or countries—Tonkin in the north, Annam in the center, and Cochinchina in the south—which had formed, together with Laos and Cambodia, French Indochina since 1887. In the months that followed, French reluctance to negotiate the terms of the DRV's independence further created doubt about Paris's good faith. In December 1946, shortly after war broke out in Haiphong and Hanoi, the DRV retreated into the highlands of northern Vietnam.

The DRV's hope of conducting a war against French colonial rule depended on popular support, which was necessary for its labor force, information, food, and shelter. Hồ Chí Minh relied on his leadership skills to lead the population to join the Việt Minh. The man who portrayed himself as Uncle Hồ not only appeared to be a man close to the population but also gave concrete examples of how every Vietnamese, regardless of their wealth, age, or gender, could contribute to the country. However, Hồ Chí Minh could not take this support for granted. He was widely criticized by other political leaders who had opposed Vietnamese communists for years and suspected they used the Việt Minh as a smoke screen to seize power. Hồ Chí Minh officially pronounced the dissolution of the Indochinese Communist Party in November 1945, although members continued to meet clandestinely. But this did not appease everyone. The Việt Minh would have to work harder to gain popular support.

This involved working with not just one but many small groups with different interests. Unlike China, where communists' main competitors joined together in a single party, the Guomindang (Nationalist Party), Vietnam had several nationalist political groups, which sometimes revolved around a common religious faith. Many of them had a strong command over sizable territory. The Việt Nam Quốc dân Đảng (VNQDĐ; Vietnamese Nationalist Party), the Đại Việt (Đại Việt Quốc dân Đảng; Nationalist Party of Greater Vietnam), and the Đồng minh Hội (ĐMH; Việt Nam Cách mệnh Đồng minh Hội, Vietnam Revolutionary League) all emerged as revolutionary nationalist parties in the 1920s and 1930s, opposing both French colonial rule and communists. The Hòa Hảo (Supreme Harmony), a reformed Buddhist movement led by Huỳnh Phú Sổ, a millenarian prophet, and the Cao Đài (Đại đạo Tam kỳ Phổ độ; Great Đạo of the Third Era of Universal Salvation), a syncretic religion that merged ideas from the East and the West, controlled territories in the Mekong delta and along the border with Cambodia.[7] In the north-central part of Vietnam, just south of Hanoi, two powerful Catholic dioceses in the densely populated area of the Red River delta, Bùi Chu and Phát Diệm, had tended to both Catholics and non-Catholics alike. Catholic priests took over the administrative duties to relieve the parishioners in this chaotic period. They also reached out to Buddhist monks at the local pagoda to create their own patriotic associations. Their paramilitary troops had deposed the local authorities in the town of Kim Sơn during the August Revolution, days before the Việt Minh.[8] To survive, the DRV had to win them over.

In the south, war broke out after the British transferred their duties to the French, who chased the DRV out to the countryside as early as September 23, 1945. There, the Hòa Hảo and Cao Đài fought alongside the Việt Minh. In the north, the fifteen months between the proclamation of the DRV and the battle for Hanoi compelled Hồ Chí Minh to persuade other groups in society to join the Việt Minh in a common front to resist French colonial rule and support the new state. Hence, prominent nationalists became an integral part of the state. A VNQDĐ leader signed the agreement that Hồ Chí Minh had negotiated with the French, and members of nationalist parties and diverse groups became representatives at the National Assembly. Although communists held the most important ministries, some signs suggested that the DRV could represent the interests of other groups in society.

Unlike early Vietnamese revolutionaries who despised Catholics, whose persecution gave the French an excuse to conquer Cochinchina in 1858, Hồ Chí Minh tried to build a strong relationship.[9] The leader wanted to see a decolonized Church led entirely by Vietnamese priests and bishops. He also urged Catholics to support the DRV: "For a century, Annamite heroes have poured their blood for independence! They followed, without knowing, the example of Jesus Christ who died to save humanity."[10] Catholics were thus allies and not enemies in Vietnam's independence. Hồ Chí Minh invited Monsignor Lê Hữu Từ, the bishop of Phát Diệm, to become the supreme adviser, which he accepted. In exchange, the diocese remained autonomous and continued to run its administration and self-defense militias as part of the DRV.[11] Bishops asked Rome to support Vietnam's independence, while members of the clergy attended political meetings in large numbers. Lê Hữu Từ's ordination in October 1945 sealed this alliance. DRV officials, including communists such as President Hồ Chí Minh and Finance Minister Phạm Văn Đồng, took part in the ceremony, whereas no Western representatives or missionaries were seen.[12] The election of Catholic representatives to the National Assembly, including the nomination of Father Phạm Bá Trực as chairman, confirmed the role of Christians in the DRV. Catholics had become a pillar of national independence.

However, other signs showed that this honeymoon would be short. The nationalist parties returning to the north from their exile in China paid a heavy price for criticizing communists. Claiming the communists had an unfair advantage in the elections and for heading important ministries, they faced violent repression by the DRV. General Võ Nguyên Giáp, the chief of the police and army, ordered the execution of their leaders, closed their newspapers and offices, and forced any remaining dissidents into hiding.[13] Catholics, too, knew that their alliance was fragile. The DRV did everything it could to reassure them. One publication claimed that any communists who used the Việt Minh to impose socialism would be acting against independence. In 1946, an article that appeared in an area under the control of the DRV insisted: "The Việt Minh are not communists, and anyone advocating communism, anyone calling for implementing a communist system right now, is out of step and in fact is working against the common political line of our state in the current situation."[14] Catholics in Bùi Chu and Phát Diệm dioceses also feared the Việt Minh's large associations, which aimed to organize the population along gender, occupational, religious, or age lines, would try to control them. Monsignor Lê Hữu Từ created the Liên đoàn Công giáo quốc gia (Federation of Nationalist Catholics) to serve as an alternative to the Việt Minh's Công giáo cứu quốc (Catholics for National Salvation). To ensure that communists would not have any chance of leading Catholics, he also ordered his right-hand man to infiltrate the latter with loyal faithful and take over its leadership.[15] Father Hoàng Quỳnh, who became famous for commanding paramilitary troops in the diocese, had handed in his resignation when Rome criticized the clergy's role in political and military affairs.[16] But the situation prompted him to remain in his position and ensure that the Việt Minh and communists would not control Catholics. Relationships would remain cordial, as long as their respective interests and relative autonomy remained in balance.

Two States for One Country

From the outset, the DRV's fragile unity remained its Achilles' heel. The French knew where to strike. Their war effort focused not only on holding onto cities and major roads across Indochina but also on ways to sabotage Vietnam's unity. This began as early as 1946, when French forces returned to northern Vietnam to take over from China's Nationalist Army. One easy way to pull the rug out from under the DRV was to court separatist groups. The French approached ethnic minorities in the central highlands, where colonial rule had enabled greater autonomy than under the Vietnamese empire in the early nineteenth century. They created the Montagnard Country of South Indochina (Pays montagnard du Sud-Indochinois). The same initiative targeted the rich landowners, businessmen, and white-collar workers in Cochinchina, in southern Vietnam, where French investment had created economic opportunity. An Autonomous Republic of Cochinchina would undermine not only the DRV's territorial integrity but also the Việt Minh's claim to unite all ethnic Vietnamese under one flag.[17]

Even those who had joined the Việt Minh could become turncoats with the right incentives. The French knew that ethnic and religious groups craved the ability to organize themselves. They rewarded the Nùng, an ethnic minority that was part of the French effort to regain control of the northern highlands, by creating the autonomous zone of Hải Ninh. In the Mekong delta, the French facilitated the return of the Cao Đài's pope from years of exile in Madagascar, in exchange for his support. This led France to another partnership with the Hòa Hảo, which had been at odds with the Việt Minh since its leader's assassination in 1947.[18] In this way, the French lured many of the Việt Minh's allies to their side and carved enclaves out of DRV territory. They ensured that other groups, in addition to the French, would block Hồ Chí Minh's path to independence and unity. Fueling the fire of a civil war was an efficient colonial weapon against the Việt Minh.

Doing so required a larger effort to hold on to all these regional, ethnic, or religious communities. Talks with potential leaders to create an alternative Vietnam started in 1946. King Bảo Đại, who had abdicated in 1945 after the August Revolution, remained in exile in Hong Kong when the DRV repressed nationalist dissidents. For years, the emperor had refused French invitations to return and lead an alternative state. What changed his mind was new geopolitical conditions, which put Vietnam at the forefront of the Cold War.

The imminent victory of the Chinese Communist Party (CCP) over the Guomindang, which had been predicted since its success in northern China in January 1949, brought new prospects to Vietnam. Chinese communist support for the DRV persuaded the Soviet Union to overcome its reluctance toward helping the Việt Minh, whose early emphasis on nationalism, rather than revolution, exasperated the Soviet leader, Joseph Stalin. To oppose that coalition, the French relied on the United States, which saw Indochina and Korea as twin battlefronts. In Washington's view, the two wars had to be fought to contain communist expansion. US troops intervened in Korea in June 1950. Yet Washington's policy on Indochina had already materialized a year earlier. The French fought on behalf of the Americans, and Washington bankrolled their war effort.[19] From the perspective of noncommunist Vietnamese, US involvement made the prospects of an alternative state to the DRV more promising. Bảo Đại returned from exile in 1949 to head the ASVN based in Saigon, which, together with the newly created associated states of Laos and Cambodia, formed the Indochinese Federation, within the larger French Union.

The ASVN's independence was still limited in key areas. It had handed over diplomatic and military affairs to France, which would provide training to the new Vietnamese army until full independence. Any economic decisions would involve all the associated states of the Indochinese Federation, in which France would have as much say as Vietnam, Laos, or Cambodia. But Bảo Đại succeeded where Hồ Chí Minh had failed three years earlier.[20] France halted the division of Vietnam into three kỳ, acknowledged Vietnam's unity, and recognized Saigon as its new capital. Although ethnic and religious groups maintained some autonomy, Vietnam became a single country.

The creation of associated states came with a silver lining. Other Western countries established diplomatic relations with the ASVN in response to recognition of the DRV by China and the Soviet Union. The state also became a member of the United Nations' technical organizations in order to improve its chances for recognition as the sole legitimate authority in Vietnam.[21] The armed conflict had become international and, at the same time, its rationale and rhetoric underscored its importance for the Vietnamese. General Jean de Lattre de Tassigny, who held both civilian and military power in Indochina, wanted to persuade the Vietnamese that this was their fight.[22] At a graduation ceremony, he urged high school graduates to "be men" and to either join the communists or take it upon themselves to bring freedom to Vietnam.[23] The creation of the State of Vietnam's Armed Forces (SVNAF), fighting alongside the CEFEO in the French Union forces, highlighted that this was also Vietnam's fight.

The Cold War turn, marked by Chinese communist victories and culminating with the proclamation of the People's Republic of China (PRC) on October 1, 1949, not only brought official and rhetorical changes. On the ground, people also noticed important transformations. International backing allowed Vietnamese communists to change the nature of their war effort. It was time to take socialism back into their agenda. Communists reappeared officially as the Vietnam Workers' Party (VWP) in 1951. The logistical and diplomatic support received from the communist bloc also marked a new stage in the war effort. The communists no longer sought a broad united front against French colonial rule. Beginning in

1950, the war aimed to achieve two goals: the end of colonial rule and a socialist revolution. The DRV only controlled territory divided by roads, cities, and front posts controlled by the ASVN or contested areas. Nevertheless, some areas, such as the Việt Bắc north of Hanoi, interzone IV in north-central Vietnam, and interzone V in the central highlands, remained firmly under DRV control (see fig. 1.1).[24] The VWP was determined to launch a revolution in these areas. Party members took control of the administration, the army, and the united front by imposing political courses, rectification, a Maoist technique imposing rounds of criticism and self-criticism to party members, and purging of bourgeois elements. The general mobilization for the war effort introduced land reform and a civil service. Denunciation campaigns berated landowners and rich peasants—even if they had contributed to the Việt Minh—and put poor peasants at the top of a new, revolutionary hierarchy.[25] Army officers and united front cadres who were unwilling to obey had little choice but to commit suicide, endure imprisonment, or flee.

The first group of nationalists left one Vietnam for another just at this unique moment, when two political authorities, each controlling small patches of territory and backed by international coalitions, competed over the leadership of the nation-state. Disgruntled nationalists left the DRV. Some members of the Đại Việt or VNQDĐ took positions in the new state, and so did Việt Minh defectors. For example, Dr. Phạm Văn Huyến personified Vietnam's excellence, ingenuity, and determination to fight for independence. A native of Hà Tĩnh, in north-central Vietnam, he was the first Vietnamese bacteriologist to earn a doctorate from a veterinary school in France before returning to the country and joining the Việt Minh in 1946.[26] When Phạm Văn Huyến crossed over to the ASVN in 1951, the press broke the news and highlighted his professional achievements, among them having created a laboratory in the middle of a jungle to produce penicillin. *Gió Việt* (*The Wind of Vietnam*), a monthly for Vietnamese overseas, insisted that he left the Việt Minh for political reasons: "The State of Vietnam has made substantial progress in its path for independence," he declared.[27] News of his defection made the front page of nationalist newspapers and the chronology of armed conflict for 1950 by the Royal Institute of International Affairs in London.[28] Everyone in Vietnam and elsewhere appreciated the importance of this event. Three years later, Phạm Văn Huyến took important positions in the ASVN. In early 1954, as the minister of labor and social affairs, he launched social reforms at the village level and oversaw Vietnam's membership application to the International Labour Organization.[29] Thus this was a symbolic

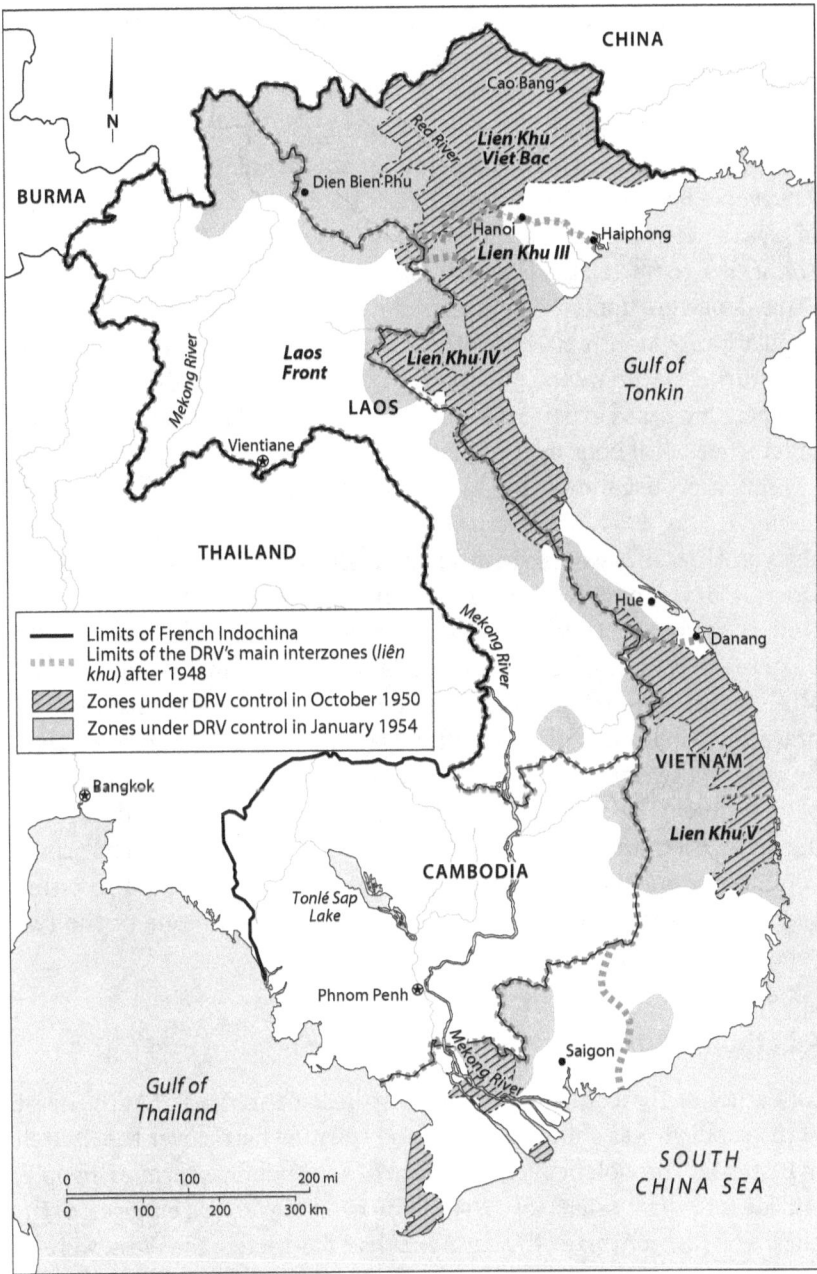

FIGURE 1.1. DRV military interzones (*liên khu*) and DRV control in 1950 and 1954. Interzones in the south and the Mekong delta do not appear in this map because their borders changed several times after 1948.

Source: Map by Bill Nelson, adapted from Christopher E. Goscha, "Une Guerre pour l'Indochine? Le Laos et le Cambodge dans le conflit franco-vietnamien (1948–1954)," *Guerres mondiales et conflits contemporains* 211, no. 3 (2003): 29–58; and Hugues Tertrais, *La Piastre et le fusil: Le coût de la guerre d'Indochine, 1945–1954* (Paris: Institut de la gestion publique et du développement économique, 2002).

victory for the ASVN, which was not an empty shell because nationalists of all backgrounds joined its ranks.

State propaganda insisted that the ASVN had received general support. One way to demonstrate the ASVN's growing popularity was the number of people who moved from one zone to another. *Gió Việt* reported that 750 people had used fishing junks to flee the DRV's military interzone IV, in central Vietnam, which the French had lost in 1946. Comments by a "returning compatriot" (*đồng bào hồi cư*) confirmed his political motives: "This departure comes from a hatred toward the Việt Minh among the population."[30] Month after month, *Gió Việt* compiled the numbers of *hồi cư* (returnees) who went to ASVN zones.[31] Bar graphs suggested that their numbers increased exponentially. The image showed the cumulative total of returnees, as if none ever returned to DRV areas.

French propaganda made great efforts to put a face on this movement. In May 1954, a theatrical troupe produced weekly skits about Nguyễn Thị Liên, a woman who not only left the DRV but also denounced the rule of a group "with no family, no homeland, and no religion."[32] Unlike Phạm Văn Huyến, this woman was no scientific pioneer. But by going over to the ASVN, she had become a heroine. Using the Việt Minh tactic of praising anonymous peasants and individuals for their brave contribution to the war effort, Nguyễn Thị Liên suggested that, by making the right decision, anyone could become the new champion of the ASVN. The war had greatly changed since its early days, calling on all Vietnamese to unite against French colonial rule. The armed conflict not only became a battlefront of the Cold War but also pitted Vietnamese against one another, urging them to join one of the two competing states.

A Catholic Struggle

For Catholics, the armed conflict had also become spiritual.[33] At the heart of the problem was a more abstract and spiritual battle over the Church in East Asia. The violent decolonization of Asia mobilized armies, people, and ideas to draw Asians into a rebellion against Western empires. Catholics, who had converted to a faith that had flowered in the West, were in a delicate position. What had happened in Vietnam after 1951 reflected an earlier confrontation that touched the entire region with the rise of Chinese communism. It would determine whether the decolonization of the Church also enfranchised their faithful from Rome and the rest of the hierarchy.

The Chinese communist victory in October 1949 demonstrated that the Church's decolonization would involve a long process regarding its scope and impact. As the historian Albert Wu has shown, Protestant missionaries imagined in 1860 that an independent church in China had to satisfy three criteria: reliance on local funding, functioning through Chinese priests rather than missionaries, and propagation with the help of both the clergy and laypeople.[34] The Three-Self principles—financial self-sufficiency, administrative independence, and apostolic autonomy—became a reality after the proclamation of the PRC in October 1949. The CCP launched a public campaign in the fall of 1950. Anyone, Chinese or foreign, who opposed the Three-Self movement would be deemed a counterrevolutionary, be stripped of their power, and lose their political rights.[35] Although Protestants joined the Three-Self Patriotic Church in 1951, many Catholics were outraged at the idea of severing ties with the Church hierarchy. The ruling from Beijing not only led to repression of lay organizations, such as the Legion of Mary in Shanghai, but also the arrest of dissident clergy and expulsion of all foreign missionaries. Catholics who wanted to remain good citizens of the PRC had to cut their ties with the rest of the Church.

The Vatican opposed what happened in China and feared that the expansion of communism across Asia would replicate those events elsewhere—in Korea, Vietnam, and other colonized countries. Rome also anticipated that the governments of countries around China could fall like dominoes—except that the outcome would split the Church. Rome insisted on the Church's unbreakable unity, the utmost respect for decolonization, and esteem for Catholics' attachment to local "tradition and civilization of the homeland."[36] It had to take positive action regarding the situation in Indochina. The Vatican recognized the ASVN on February 12, 1950, after Washington and London.[37] On April 28, 1951, an official ASVN delegation attended the pope's mass in honor of twenty-three Vietnamese martyrs at Saint Peter's Basilica.[38] This celebration of Catholics who had lost their lives in the eighteenth and nineteenth centuries allowed the ASVN to appear abroad, on its first official visit. Fifteen days later, the same delegation returned to Rome to establish diplomatic relations.[39] The head of the Catholic Church had chosen a side in the war.

The arrival of General de Lattre de Tassigny to head the French war effort further cemented Rome's commitment. During a visit to the Vatican in October 1951, the general recounted to Pope Pius XII the fierce battle putting Catholic militias in opposition to the Việt Minh in the Red River delta. According to the glorifying account of de Lattre's personal guard, the pope concluded their meeting with a benediction: "I bless the French Army which you command and represent, because it defends, over there, the Christian civilization."[40] Perhaps Rome could encourage Vietnamese Catholics to support the ASVN's war effort.

The episcopal conference gathering all bishops of Indochina issued a letter on November 10, 1951, defining the lives of Catholics in the war for decades to come. All Catholics were forbidden to participate in any activity that facilitated the rise of communist atheism (*cộng sản vô thần*). Anyone who took part in any organization related to communism, such as the DRV, would be excommunicated. This decision had little impact on Catholics living in French-controlled zones. To the Catholics who experienced confrontations with the local DRV authorities, this official stance confirmed their commitment to oppose communism. But to many Catholics who had joined the Việt Minh and remained loyal to the DRV, this announcement was heartbreaking because it meant that they had to choose between the state and the Church. The letter was reproduced in several periodicals to ensure that everyone was aware of this official decision.[41] Catholics could not remain indifferent, let alone neutral, in this armed conflict. Their hierarchy urged them not to side with communism.

Communist Party historians insist that the only reason for the Church's official opposition to the Việt Minh was the French attempt to get Rome involved. Accordingly, if it were not for de Lattre's visit and Rome's interference, Catholics would have remained united in favor of the DRV.[42] However, this view overlooks the tensions and open confrontation between Catholics and communist cadres in the Việt Minh in earlier years. In the diocese of Vinh, in interzone IV, which the DRV had held since 1946, Catholics endured the full force of socialist reforms. Farther north, Bùi Chu and Phát Diệm dioceses, which had enjoyed autonomy and had sheltered many nationalists fleeing communist repression elsewhere, also clashed with communist cadres.[43] Even Catholics who had initially joined the Việt Minh felt contempt from communist cadres. The scorched-earth tactics employed to deprive the French of any infrastructure, equipment, or building usable in their war effort also meant the destruction of religious sites and objects.[44] Monsignor Lê Hữu Từ recalls that the Việt Minh used a three-stage process. First, all dogs were killed to ensure that cadres could move around without being noticed. All houses with attics were altered so that no one could hide weapons or anticommunist soldiers. Then, the population had to practice leaving their homes, until one day, they evacuated, ensuring that fields were emptied and houses left bare.⁴⁵ Catholics did not accept that their holy sites and artifacts would be destroyed.

Rome echoed their sentiments and condemned these tactics. As early as 1949, the *Osservatore Romano* declared that the Việt Minh were not a nationalist front but a communist organization. News from Lạng Sơn revealed that priests protested the Việt Minh's confiscation and destruction of churches, and foreign missionaries had been arrested.⁴⁶ The DRV's evacuation of Bắc Ninh also left no provisions, medicine, or shelter for the population. Seven churches were burned to the ground.⁴⁷ The *Osservatore Romano* depicted "an exodus of the Vietnamese people" in referring to the persecution of Western missionaries, priests, and faithful fleeing DRV zones.⁴⁸ News about land reform and a denunciation campaign targeting Catholics amplified those fears. In January 1953, for example, a show trial condemned eighty members of the clergy and laypeople from Catholic Action, which mobilized the faithful along specific demographics or activities, holding denunciation sessions that lasted well past midnight.⁴⁹ Catholics had seemingly become enemies of the DRV.

Not all Catholics opposed communism. Many remained neutral or loyal to the DRV. Vietnamese communists tried their best to dispel those fears. Using Phạm Bá Trực, the priest elected chair of the National Assembly, as a counterpoint to the bishops, they insisted on the need to remain united with the resistance to French colonial rule. To avoid criticism that suggested communists were using the front as a cover to take over the country, the Việt Minh was replaced by another large front, the Liên Việt, whose vice chair was none other than Father Phạm Bá Trực.⁵⁰ The priest wrote public letters denouncing the Indochinese bishops' 1951 letter as an attempt to divide the Vietnamese.⁵¹ He also recounted his visit to China and Korea, claiming that religious life remained free and active.⁵² The struggle for independence did not mean the end of their religious life.

Despite these initiatives, Bùi Chu and Phát Diệm ended their initial agreement with the DRV. The two dioceses joined the ASVN and integrated their popular militia into the army under the condition that each diocese would remain a distinct province and their units would remain intact. Monsignor Lê Hữu Từ and Monsignor Phạm Ngọc Chi, the bishop of Bùi Chu, appointed priests and lay Catholics to head the civil administration.⁵³ The French called it the "mandarinal monks regime," as if the clergy had the same power as civil servants in the Vietnamese empire.⁵⁴ This was a pragmatic choice, rather than a commitment to the ASVN. Monsignor Lê Hữu Từ reminded everyone at Pentecost: "Those who want to serve France should go to France. Those who want to serve his Majesty Bảo Đại should go to Hue. Those who want to serve President Hữu should go to Saigon."[55] These Catholics had joined Saigon, but their loyalty remained with their diocese (see fig. 1.2).

The Catholic opposition to communism also gave the impression the struggle went beyond the confines of Vietnam to encompass the region. Although the expulsion of missionaries and the flight of Chinese dissident clergy felt like an earthquake in the Christian world, it became a tangible reality for the faithful in Vietnam. Catholics and missionaries from China sought shelter in the ASVN. These refugees came with stories of communist reprisal against Catholics. The testimony of N. L. H.—most probably Nguyễn Lạc Hóa, the "fighting priest" who became famous after 1954 for leading a parish fighting communism in the Mekong

FIGURE 1.2. Catholic militia in Yến Vĩ, 1950.
Source: Photograph © ECPAD/Défense, TONK 50-37 R22.

delta—described scenes of confiscation and mistreatment in China.⁵⁶ Vietnamese publications reproduced articles penned by other refugees seeking shelter in Hong Kong and elsewhere in the region. Vietnamese Catholics' awareness did not end at the borders but, rather, included the same concerns as their coreligionists threatened by communism elsewhere in East Asia.⁵⁷

Whatever Vietnamese Catholics did against communism could serve the cause of their coreligionists fleeing China. Like Chinese Catholics, they formed a Legion of Mary, which grew from one squad in Hanoi in 1948 to three others in Haiphong, Nam Định, and a small presence in Bùi Chu and Phát Diệm three years later.⁵⁸ Readers of their publication *Đạo binh Đức Mẹ* (*Legion of Mary*) learned about what had happened in China and Korea.⁵⁹ The ordination of the tenth Vietnamese bishop in 1953 did not take place in Haiphong, the diocese he would oversee, but in Hong Kong, with the consul general of France and ASVN delegates.⁶⁰ "For us Catholics, the concepts of Church and homeland are so related that one cannot exist without the other. It is impossible to serve our Church without serving our homeland. And it is impossible to serve our homeland without serving our Church," declared an ASVN representative.⁶¹ Vietnamese Catholics shared the plight of other Catholics across East Asia. This had become a spiritual war.

Seeking Noncommunist Independence

Two competing states and the firm stance of the Catholic hierarchy did not simplify the armed conflict but, instead, only made it more complicated. Two states existed, each having partial control of Vietnam, holding patches of territory cut from one another. The war not only involved local, regional, and international stakeholders but also captured power struggles, ideological divides, and spiritual matters. This created a conundrum for many nationalists who rejected the leadership of the two competing states. Despite multiple attempts to reach a breakthrough, they were still soul searching.

The population's experience in the armed conflict differed from one place to another. The sheltered life in the cities contrasted with the deprivation in some of the countryside or worse, with denunciation campaigns in areas, such as the Việt Bắc in the northern highlands bordering China and in the interzone IV, in north-central Vietnam, where parishioners in the diocese of Vinh endured socialist reforms. Despite news and rumors of political purges targeting large groups of the population, people struggled to determine what the communists intended to do. Were these policies temporary measures necessary for the war effort? Would they apply one day to the entire population? Or would Vietnamese communists, like their French counterparts in 1945, be satisfied to be the largest political party and work with others in a national assembly? No one knew for sure what to do.[62] Many people left the Việt Minh because they realized they were noncommunist, but that did not mean they were anticommunists.

Few people agreed on the overarching goal of the nationalist war effort and how it could gain leverage from the global and spiritual confrontation. Fighting against communists would be worthless if nationalists did not know what they were fighting for. The most creative responses to this critical situation came from Catholic intellectuals who found their source of inspiration in personalism, a philosophy created by the French intellectual Emmanuel Mounier, who founded the journal *Esprit*. The Vietnamese created the periodical *Tinh thần* (*Esprit*), which advocated for a different vision of a socialist revolution. Any nationalist doctrine had to acknowledge the human person and its intrinsic spirituality. From time immemorial, from Aristotle and Plato to world religions, such as Christianity, Buddhism, or Confucianism, thinkers insisted on this aspect of human nature.[63] Mounier's personalism promoted a social revolution just as radical as Marxism in its reversal of exploitation due to capital, but with a major difference. Unlike socialism, which projected a materialistic concept of human societies, personalism put the utmost priority on respect for the person, who was conceived as a human being capable of thought and spirituality. This philosophy arrived in Vietnam in the 1940s and gained traction among young Catholic intellectuals, who dreamed of a social revolution that would reverse centuries of social inequality and avoid a communist victory.

Ngô Đình Diệm, who wrote an essay in *Tinh thần* in 1949, emerged as its most prominent advocate.[64] Born to a strict Catholic family, Diệm could rely on the influence of his two brothers, Ngô Đình Thục, the third Vietnamese ever to be nominated as bishop, and Ngô Đình Nhu, an intellectual who was strongly connected to intellectuals and labor union members. Ngô Đình Diệm fiercely opposed communism. He also came with long experience as both an administrator and a political dissident opposing colonial rule. Ngô Đình Diệm had been opposed to communism, resigned from his position in the colonial administration, and spearheaded several attempts to gain, at the very least, the status of dominion from the French. In March 1945, he would have become prime minister if the Japanese military had placed Prince Cường Để at the head of the first independent state, instead of King Bảo Đại. His proximity to Japanese circles, with their history of rallying political exiles and strong connections, brought him closer to nationalists of all kinds—the VNQDĐ, the Đại Việt, the Hòa Hảo, the Cao Đài, and Catholics.[65] His public call to find Vietnam's political path at a critical juncture in the war came as a breath of fresh air, compared to the words of political leaders encumbered by their relationships with the DRV, the ASVN, and the French. The Việt Minh's order to assassinate him prompted his departure from Vietnam but did not disqualify him as a potential leader.[66] Thanks to his brother, Monsignor Ngô Đình Thục, he traveled to Europe and the United States, where he met influential people who created the American Friends of Vietnam, a lobby group that was encouraging Washington to become further involved in the country.[67] Ngô Đình Diệm was not the only contender to lead a noncommunist effort in the early 1950s. But his profile, connections, and trajectory made him a strong choice, because he could combine the struggle in Vietnam with the Cold War and Catholic networks.

Another way to create positive outcomes from these new ideas was to build or renew political alliances. Intellectuals convinced of the urgency of a social revolution promoted Christian social doctrine outside Catholic circles, to students and labor activists. The Confederation of Christian Workers, created in 1952 in the ASVN without any reference to Christianity in its Vietnamese name (Tổng liên đoàn lao công Việt Nam), raised hopes that the ASVN could introduce labor reforms.[68] Others insisted on the spiritual nature of the armed conflict. Some Catholics encouraged their coreligionists to overcome their prejudice about other religions. Readers of *Đạo binh Đức Mẹ* learned that the Cao Đài, despite its eclectic pantheon of saints, from Muhammad to Joan of Arc to Victor Hugo, shared a similar hierarchy and the belief in an Almighty God.[69] Catholics also imagined that they could "collaborate in politics with patriots of other faiths or without faith to become part of political parties that are not defined in religious terms."[70] The Đại Việt's denunciation of the Vietnamese communists' "Three Noes" (no family, no homeland, and no religion, used in the nationalist propaganda on the heroine Nguyễn Thị Liên) suggested that they could find common ground.[71] Catholics had to become creative and seek alliances elsewhere to protect their faith.[72]

However, the most pressing issue was to clarify the relationship with France and obtain an official platform in order for these discussions about spirituality or a social revolution to take place. Although the colonial authorities transferred their power to the ASVN in separate treaties (e.g., airspace, postal services, and customs), they were reluctant to grant independence, unlike the British in India or the Americans in the Philippines.[73] Military and diplomatic matters had to receive approval from Paris. France had also refused to create a parliament. Despite the organization of municipal elections in 1953, the ASVN still had no National Assembly. What led the nationalists to run out of patience was France's unilateral decision in May 1953 to devalue the piastre. Changing the exchange rate without consulting Vietnam, Laos, and Cambodia violated the core principle of the associated states created four years earlier. More than fifty intellectuals, together with political and religious leaders from all regions in Vietnam, gathered in an impromptu Congress for National Union and Peace in September 1953.[74] In their views, an association meant only a colonial kind of federalism. Most wanted total independence, but the delegates disagreed about whether to cut all ties with Paris. Vietnam still needed economic, political, and military support, especially during a war against communism. Leaders of this National Congress criticized the idea of being part of the French Union in its present state.[75] This prompted Paris to accept negotiation of Vietnam's independence and participation in the French Union's high council in separate agreements and more bilateral transfers of authority on key matters, such as customs.[76] The relationship between France and the nationalists had reached a point of no return. One day, the ASVN would become independent. Whether it would achieve it when international decisions were made about Vietnam was a different matter.

Ending the War

Nationalists had greater prospects of effectively challenging communists thanks to the support of international partners. Yet they also realized that swimming with bigger fishes in the pond could have negative effects. Their priorities could supersede promises made at any point in the war. The Cold War had brought nationalists closer to the United States and the West. But the superpowers' desire to de-escalate the armed conflicts in Korea and Indochina could very well leave the struggle for Vietnam hanging in the balance.

The two Cold War superpowers had hoped to ease tensions in East Asia. Both the Soviet Union, since the death of Stalin in March 1953, and the United States, exhausted from its involvement in the Korean War, wanted to establish a dialogue. France was also ready to abandon its hold in the Far East to better salvage what remained of its empire. Under public pressure due to the discovery of an embezzlement scheme, the Affaire des piastres, involving political and military leaders in Indochina, it realized that its inertia about granting independence might have consequences for its North African colonies. Paris had to find a way out.[77] A conference opening on the shores of the Geneva Lake in the spring of 1954 would serve these two objectives.

With this upcoming international meeting in sight, all the armies prepared for their final battle. Whereas the French believed that it would take place in central Vietnam, the confrontation in which the People's Army of Vietnam (PAVN) clashed with both the CEFEO and the SVNAF was in the northwestern highlands, in the Điện Biên Phủ valley. The victory by the PAVN, which stunned the West and electrified the colonized countries, happened the day before the conference discussed Indochinese affairs. Without a doubt, the DRV went into these negotiations from a position of strength.

The results of the battle influenced the objectives of the conference and the range of solutions imagined. Paris prioritized the safe evacuation of French forces. Hence, the conference dealt with military matters first and a political solution for Vietnam only second. The military situation was complex. French Union forces and the PAVN held separate portions of territory, involving "long lines of engagement" with the enemy. Neither the DRV nor France and the ASVN were ready to cede territory under their control. Both sides continued to fight, even as their representatives negotiated several thousand miles away. Elections to bring a coalition government seemed the most sensible solution for Vietnam, whose territory looked like a leopard skin, and where authorities governed over archipelago states controlling scattered areas.[78] Even the ASVN suggested that the United Nations (UN) oversee general elections.[79] But the need to enable the CEFEO to depart DRV zones quickly prevented this kind of complicated referendum from being arranged. Because reaching a political solution was a secondary consideration, and although France granted the State of Vietnam (SVN) independence in a treaty on June 4, 1954, the French command over the SVNAF allowed Paris to negotiate on behalf of Saigon.[80] This meant Saigon's delegates could not sit at the conference table, and whatever the French achieved at the talks would apply to the SVN.[81] Nationalists had obtained an independent and united state—but too late. It had no voice in Geneva.

The talks stalled until the DRV realized that it had to abandon the idea of territorial unity. To demonstrate the SVN's determination to reclaim a strong position at the eleventh hour, Bảo Đại appointed Ngô Đình Diệm as prime minister, responding to calls by representatives of the National Congress a few months earlier.[82] In a speech, the former king explained his reasons. Now that Vietnam had achieved unity and independence, its greatest threat was the ideology and separatism promoted by the communists. Only Ngô Đình Diệm could rally all parts of society and persuade France not to fall for the DRV's false promise of peace.[83] Hồ Chí Minh realized that the DRV could not maintain an intransigent position in Geneva forever.[84] Its representatives announced that they were ready to accept ruling over portions of territory, and not the full country, provided that peaceful provisions were included to ensure unification.[85] Now a territorial division seemed possible.

Although the talks had reached a crossroads, Paris decided that everyone had to follow one path. While negotiations continued, France ordered its troops to retreat from strategic zones in the Red River delta, affecting Bùi Chu and Phát Diệm. In the face of constant attacks by the PAVN, the French feared the loss of the eastern axis of the delta connecting Hanoi to Haiphong. General Paul Ély, the French high commissioner, ordered a strategic withdrawal to reinforce the French position on this corridor.[86] On June 29, French soldiers retreated and destroyed bridges and roads as they left.[87] Vietnamese troops and their families had no choice but to follow, and officials, in the dioceses, though they were aware that this evacuation could happen one day, at the last minute, had to board the Dakotas that would fly them to Hanoi.[88] Fifteen thousand people left on that air bridge, and thousands of others left by bus or car over just eight days.[89] The PAVN's attacks during the operation were so serious that Monsignor Lê Hữu Từ had to sail on a barge to Haiphong.[90] To these Catholics crammed in makeshift shelters, the evacuation had already started. Even though the Geneva Conference had not yet reached an agreement, Catholics in these two dioceses and others in Hanoi embarked on their journey to Saigon.[91]

This move changed the military situation and led the DRV to warm to the idea of ruling over parts of Vietnam. The DRV gained control over a large section of the Red River delta, an area densely populated and rich in paddy fields. As historians have pointed out, the meeting of Zhou Enlai with Hồ Chí Minh and Võ Nguyên Giáp at the Liuzhou Conference on July 3, days after the withdrawal, confirmed that the DRV had accepted the division of the country into two halves. Whether Chinese pressure or the DRV's obsession with avoiding US intervention prompted this decision remains a matter of debate.[92] The DRV would lose control over the Cà Mau peninsula and interzone V, in the center. But this was necessary to become sovereign over half of Vietnam.

The Western perception of the evacuation also led Washington and Saigon to gain a new perspective about the future. At first, the idea of leaving territory to the enemy seemed foolish, especially abandoning Catholic strongholds such as Bùi Chu and Phát Diệm.[93] But press depictions decrying the French evacuation showed that they could turn the situation to their advantage. The *Osservatore Romano* warned Catholics about Vietnamese faithful falling behind the "bamboo curtain" and recalled that priests had been executed by the DRV.[94] The US press also alerted its readership to this situation. Starting on June 30, the evacuation made it to the front page of the *New York Times* three days in a row. When the operation started, readers could see a map showing different colors across Vietnam, which demonstrated that neither France nor the DRV held discrete territories and that there was no clear outcome to the conflict.[95] Yet days later, after the French had retreated, the story changed. The Sunday supplement to the *New York Times* showed three maps of the areas controlled by the communists and French Union forces in 1950, 1952, and 1954. This illustration did not portray overlapping and disconnected territories. It streamlined the situation into a simplistic narrative. Using the same color for communist China and the DRV, it depicted the contraction of a nationalist zone in the face of communist expansion.[96] Articles highlighted the selfishness of the French or the powerlessness of the Vietnamese who wished for nothing but to enjoy freedom.[97] This evacuation was "a far bigger victory for Hồ Chí Minh's forces than their capture of Điện Biên Phủ," suggested one journalist.[98] Communism was winning, but the Vietnamese refused to live under this regime. According to these accounts, the West could not remain indifferent.

As the historian Philip Catton has shown, members of the US Congress reacted to this new representation of the war. Although they refused to intervene in Vietnam, they could not abandon "millions of souls to Red tyranny." So, US representatives in Geneva pushed for the cease-fire agreements to include Article 14(d), allowing civilians to join the zone of their choice during a grace period after the division.[99] That civilians and not regular troops could leave the DRV was significant. Their departure would not only signal an imminent communist expansion but, in the ongoing contest to find a state for Vietnam, it would also suggest the Vietnamese people chose the "free" world.

The Geneva Conference enabled de-escalation of Cold War tensions but left unfinished business for at least two reasons. First, Saigon and Paris still had to clarify their relationship. Second, the battle to lead postcolonial Vietnam had not reached a conclusion. Political turmoil in France, which put Pierre Mendès-France into office as the prime minister, placed the last nail in the coffin. He pledged to resign if the parties did not reach an agreement. So, the cease-fire agreement solidified in a consensus. On July 21, French and DRV representatives signed separate agreements on Vietnam, Laos, and Cambodia. The United Kingdom and the Soviet Union joined in signing the Final Declaration, expressing the willingness of the international powers to protect this outcome, but the United States refused, claiming that it had not been a belligerent in the armed conflict. To ensure that the cease-fire would hold, Vietnam would be partitioned into two temporary zones, which could not host any foreign bases or troops.[100] Cutoff dates created an agenda for delivering cities into the hands of the new ruling authorities. In the north, this meant that the DRV would take over Hanoi only eighty days after the cease-fire agreement was signed, Hải Dương after the hundred-day mark, and the French army and the SVN would fully withdraw to north of the seventeenth parallel after three hundred days.[101] This measure remained temporary, as the fate of the country would be decided in a referendum to be held two years later. However, the possibility that, under Article 14(d), civilians could leave enabled Washington and Saigon to undermine the DRV. In theory, the mass departure of Vietnamese would show that Hồ Chí Minh had not yet won the battle to lead the Vietnamese. Now this refugee flow had to begin in practice.

CHAPTER 2

"Refugees" on a Mission

Back in 1954, few people realized that the evacuation of northern Vietnamese to the south would create such high and yet contradictory expectations. After the cease-fire agreements, more than eight hundred thousand people left the north, whereas only one hundred fifty thousand journeyed in the opposite direction. English- and French-language media concluded that innocent civilians had fled communist rule. In contrast, Vietnamese newspapers reported the event as the departure of migrants (*di cư*) or northern migrants (*Bắc di cư*).[1] In the Vietnamese version, a population moved southward. The Western narrative, instead, insisted that it was the flight of victims of persecution. The two versions told the same story, but something was lost in translation.

These different interpretations did not result from a mistake. At no point did a decree command all civil servants and media outlets to use a particular translation, nor was there a clean line between the Vietnamese representations of this population movement and the French ones.[2] But the overwhelming majority of documents perpetuated this dichotomy. The "compatriots arriving in the South" (*đồng bào đã vào Nam*) in Vietnamese became the "refugees seeking shelter in the South" in English or French, and the "migrant registration" (*ghi tên di cư*) in

Vietnamese turned into a list for "refugee registration."³ Speeches by the SVN prime minister, Ngô Đình Diệm, made the same distinction. He welcomed guests in French at a ceremony, saying: "Admiral, Gentlemen, as we welcome today the hundred-thousandth refugee . . . " The Vietnamese translation, by contrast, referred to the one hundred thousandth "migrant" from the north.⁴ The agency created to provide relief and resettlement, the Commissariat Général (COMIGAL), even displayed this difference on the sign for its headquarters.⁵ The organization's name in Vietnamese, Phủ Tổng ủy Di cư Ty nạn, stated that it dealt with migrants (*di cư*) and refugees (*ty nạn*), almost suggesting they were distinct groups. However, the full name in French below it, the Commissariat général aux réfugiés, mentioned only refugees.⁶ The Vietnamese version referred to a migration and did not infer any reasons for people to move, nor did it imply that they would remain in their destinations. The Western interpretation of their movement, in contrast, insisted that victims of persecution sought protection and, therefore, could find solace in the south. By portraying different goals, these two stories also set a different agenda for the future of South Vietnam. In one case, the country's partition was temporary, whereas the other welcomed the creation of a permanent nation-state. How did the evacuees react to the partition of Vietnam and the conflicting interpretations of their departure?

In fact, the evacuation showed three different groups of the war—the SVN, the United States, and the evacuees—come together as they shared a common interest. First, the partition had many consequences for the SVN and its prospects to become a nation capable of challenging the DRV. Second, assistance in the evacuation allowed Washington to assess Saigon's potential to become a key partner in the global struggle against communist expansion. Third, whether people moved depended in part on perceptions of the reasons for this movement, as the chances of return seemed very slim. These three groups converged in opposition to communism.

Those unique circumstances led Washington to support South Vietnam, becoming deeper involved in a quagmire. However, this focus on the subsequent war and on future US military intervention should not obscure a deeper transformation happening at the same time. To fully measure the transformational power of the partition, it is essential to look beyond the ideological antagonism that brought the United States, Saigon, and the evacuees together to analyze what the evacuation fundamentally changed for the evacuees. This chapter argues that the population movement and its instrumentalization distorted the evacuees' perception of time and space and raised their hopes of one day reversing their forced departure from the north. The convergence of so many allies into the evacuation caused some of them to believe they had entered into a new human condition by which the present and the reality did not matter precisely because everything would be possible in the future thanks to their determination, state sanction, and international support. Within a year after the cease-fire agreement, many evacuees had begun to understand that most of the world viewed them as "refugees." This was a small price to pay because it allowed them to continue their struggle and, one day, liberate the north from communism.

A Meaningful Displacement

The provisions for the evacuation of civilians served a political agenda, set by Washington days before the conclusion of the cease-fire. If people left the DRV, that would mean they had rejected communism and wished to create an alternative nation-state. The movement of people fleeing communism would appear to be a human tragedy. This plan could not work, however, if the evacuation did not meet certain conditions.

The first and most important one was to ensure that international public opinion found this interpretation of the evacuation credible. So Ngô Đình Diệm called on "all other friends and allies in the free world" to help the newly independent SVN.[7] In response, on August 8, 1954, the United States sent the US Seventh Fleet, then patrolling in the South China Sea, to support the French navy. The French transported civil servants, soldiers, and materiel. Meanwhile, the US Navy moved civilians, including the families of soldiers, in its Operation Passage to Freedom.[8] Washington also changed its relationship with Saigon. Although the United States had established a partnership with the associated states soon after their creation in 1949, every dollar had to go through the French treasury. Faced with the migration of "refugees . . . who [had] 'chosen freedom' at the cost of hard sacrifices," the US Operations Mission (USOM) in Saigon realized that it had to step up to the challenge: "The Vietnam government has made promises to these refugees which must be kept for humanitarian and political reasons." Hence, in October, Washington signed a plan of action supporting the stipend distributed to every family that had regrouped in the south and their resettlement.[9] This ambitious plan for the evacuees required a governmental institution capable of carrying out the evacuation, emergency relief, and resettlement. Hence, the small program created for the evacuation within the Ministry of Labor, Health, and Social Affair was disbanded and absorbed by the newly created COMIGAL, which coordinated several ministries.

The United States alone gave $55.8 million for the exodus, of which $40 million was in counterpart funds for the purchase of goods in US dollars and more than $11 million was for transportation. Another $37 million for resettlement was added to this amount.[10] Every household leaving to the south received a stipend, transportation, resettlement, and help to sustain a new livelihood in the south. Some have claimed that this totaled $89 per evacuee, a fortune in a country such as Vietnam at the time. Considering the actual exchange rate, the amount was in fact closer to $47 per person.[11] This massive support also came from other partners. Although the United Nations High Commissioner for Refugees (UNHCR) refrained from intervening in this movement between two temporary zones, and the International Committee for the Red Cross (ICRC) doubted that the displaced population comprised "refugees," nongovernmental organizations (NGOs) that had formed to oppose fascism during World War II rolled up their sleeves to help these civilians fleeing communism.[12] They coordinated their actions at monthly meetings to help people "leaving a totalitarian regime."[13] Michigan State University added scientific expertise to this effort.[14] The success of the evacuation and resettlement became a joint venture to help Vietnam resist communist expansion.

Christian networks became the most powerful echo chamber for the prime minister's statements. On July 25, seven days before calling Western countries, Ngô Đình Diệm had contacted Cardinal Francis Spellman, the archbishop of New York, who had been involved in the Cold War in East Asia for years.[15] The prelate sat on the board of the National Catholic Welfare Council, which collected the American bishop's charity funds. After supporting Chinese and Korean Catholics, Spellman threw his weight behind Vietnamese coreligionists. As he toured camps, he declared: "Whether we are Asian, European, African or American, we are closely tied by a sacred and indestructible link: our faith in God. As soldiers of the Christ, we, members of the church have the duty to protect the faith, despite all threats and suffering."[16] Activists in the region reinforced the impression that Saigon was leading the fight in Asia against atheism. Raymond de Jaegher, a Catholic missionary, had become a celebrity after publishing his memoirs about imprisonment by the Japanese and expulsion from China. He moved to Saigon, where he ran the Free Pacific Association, uniting overseas Catholic Chinese, and wrote articles for *Free Front*, the English-language publication of the Asian People's Anti-Communist League.[17] Father Patrick O'Connor, a correspondent for the American Catholic News Service, was also based in South Vietnam.[18] Finally, Rome announced it would publish news on Vietnamese Catholics through its information agency. Its press releases in five languages reached over fourteen hundred newspapers.[19] The Catholic world clung to any new development because the Church's survival in East Asia was at stake.

Non-Christian channels reinforced the narrative of Vietnamese wanting to form a noncommunist country. News coverage and personal witness statements hammered home the idea that the Vietnamese were victims of communist persecution.[20] To the Western media, moving was a political choice: "To go South is to choose freedom," claiming that Hanoi saw this departure "as a loss." People were voting with their feet, in some kind of advance polling.[21] Thomas A. Dooley, a US Navy sailor, told the story of the oppressed Vietnamese who fled communism and sought help from the West in *Deliver Us from Evil*, which was published in *Reader's Digest* and by 1961 had been reprinted fifteen times.[22]

These accounts all became memorable because the number of Vietnamese had reached the symbolic threshold of a million. The chaotic conditions of the transportation made it impossible to obtain an accurate picture, especially because the COMIGAL's headquarters had been destroyed in March 1955. Despite the lack of reliable sources, Saigon claimed that a million "refugees ... had chosen freedom." Four years later, the COMIGAL's director explained at a conference why one could speak of a million—when rounded up, the numbers reached that figure. Among them, 768,672 had been moved by air and sea, and 109,000 went southward on their own. Without explaining how he had arrived at that number, the commissioner declared that 928,152 civilians had evacuated from the north. A significant majority of them were ethnic Kinh, who made up the majority of Vietnamese (98%), and most were peasants (76%). Unsurprisingly, an overwhelming number were Catholics (85%).[23] Critics expressed reservations about the missing data and the methods used for these calculations.[24] An analysis of the documents also suggests some manipulation in the distinction between civilians and soldiers, as well as in the composition of the population evacuated and resettled.[25] But these figures remained, and the state continued to claim that "nearly a million of refugees ... left Red Vietnam Peninsula."[26] A million resettled in the countryside to help with South Vietnam's economic development. The "Exodus of Refugees" and the "Refugee Resettlement" referred to the same story. It did not matter that they included, in fact, different populations.²⁷ At the end of the transition period following the signing of the cease-fire agreement, the parties were still negotiating an extension. Yet Washington and Saigon had already achieved their goal. The evacuation of civilians was not a perfunctory measure to guarantee respect for the cease-fire. A consensus had been reached that Vietnamese who left the DRV were victims of communist expansionism.

Setting People in Motion

None of this narrative would hold true, however, without an actual movement of population. This proved a lot harder to produce in reality. For one thing, people had to want to leave their home. Nationalists in the north did not see the point of regrouping in the south. In May 1954, French intelligence recorded almost thirty demonstrations in just two weeks in northern, central, and southern Vietnam.²⁸ In early July, political leaders and intellectuals told Ngô Đình Diệm that they rejected partition.²⁹ Some of them, such as Dr. Hoàng Cơ Bình, declared that they were ready to leave operatives behind, ready to rebel against the DRV. In response, Ngô Đình Diệm tried to show that he was on their side. He claimed that he would move the Ministry of National Defense and the National Army's general staff to Hanoi. He also used his network to organize demonstrations on July 18, 1954, to present himself as the most radical opponent to French and communist rule.³⁰ A portrait of him included a quotation made famous after the French Revolution: "If I fight, support me! If I fail, kill me! If I die, avenge me!"³¹ Unlike Henri de la Rochejaquelein, the Vendean royalist who first spoke those words, Ngô Đình Diệm was not trying to restore the monarchy. He simply believed that he was the only person who could forestall the partition. Despite the injustice, the nationalists could not continue to fight. Only one day after the cease-fire was signed, Ngô Đình Diệm insisted that the SVN was a victim of the agreement:

> Our delegation in Geneva did not sign this agreement because we do not recognize the control of Soviet China over more than half the national territory through the intermediary of its satellite, the Việt Minh. . . .
>
> Vietnam confronts a brutal fait accompli. Trying to oppose this through the use of force would only cause a catastrophe and destroy any chance to re-create a Free Vietnam from south to north.³²

Ngô Đình Diệm not only blamed others for this situation but also urged nationalists to back his leadership. Key to that support was the promise that this situation remained temporary and unacceptable.

Propaganda was needed to persuade those nationalists to join the south. In July 1954 alone, the French psychological warfare office distributed more than ten million Vietnamese-language leaflets.[33] It is impossible to determine the respective roles of the French, American, and Vietnamese operatives because of the lack of sources. But claiming that France or the United States alone pushed Vietnamese to leave the north would be inaccurate because the psychological warfare office supported both the French and the SVNAF's war effort. Aircraft dropped eight million of them, covering the countryside with propaganda. The campaign intensified when the French withdrew from the southern part of the Red River delta and continued after the ceasefire agreements. The messaging emphasized the risk of remaining in the DRV. Tracts gave contradictory information on the possibility that the French would bombard the area.[34] Fake DRV messages claimed that people would be sent to "concentration camps" and face "reeducation." The new authorities would show no mercy toward defectors.[35] People in the DRV would endure confiscation, long working hours, and taxes for wearing religious symbols or for worship.[36] Women would also have to marry the war wounded, become "female assistants" (nữ trợ lý), and satisfy their masters' carnal desires (thỏa mãn nhu cầu xắc thịt). One leaflet claimed that many women had already bitten their tongues off or jumped into rivers to commit suicide.[37] When the time came to urge people to leave the north entirely, messages claimed that China, Vietnam's historical foe, would colonize the country. The propaganda insisted that since 1949, Chinese advisers in the DRV could vote, own land, and be members of the local party committee:[38] "Northern Vietnam would become one of China's provinces."[39] Vietnam had repelled Chinese rule multiple times since the tenth century, making this unacceptable. Communism was another vehicle for achieving its conquest of Vietnam. Highlighting the "thousand years of resistance to China," leaflets conflated the Mongols, the Manchus, and the Han Chinese. They also claimed that communists had betrayed Vietnam by serving China.[40]

The greatest challenge was to persuade people that the withdrawal was not a defeat, but a tactical move.[41] Using a hand as a metaphor, the regroupment was like clenching a fist. One could hit harder with a clenched fist than an open hand.[42] Five hundred thousand copies were printed of a before-and-after image of an open hand and a fist, illustrating this notion.[43] French propagandists thus were aware that one way to make people agree to regroup was to promise not to end the fighting. Unsurprisingly, the movement to the south followed the same logic. One leaflet claimed that going south would contribute to speedier reunification of the country.[44] Another message mentioned for the first time the idea of carrying out a march to the north (*Bắc tiến*) in the future.[45] Once in the south, the SVN would have "the most powerful army in Southeast Asia to free the people from communist cruelty, reunite the motherland, and bring peace to humankind."[46] Despite all logic that said otherwise, going south pushed back communism.

The DRV reacted with counterpropaganda. Although it failed to prevent all the departures, it left an indelible mark on the evacuees.[47] The DRV realized that its opponent could rely on a vast network. So, the party took steps to appease Catholics. Hồ Chí Minh reassured them that "anyone who wanted to leave was free to do so." Cadres had to respect freedom of religion, organize mass in parishes whose priest had left, and repair religious sites or artifacts that had been destroyed or taken away.[48] Propaganda, unsurprisingly, decried the miserable conditions in the camps. It claimed that people would be forced to join the army or work on plantations in the south.[49] According to a short book published as the evacuation was still happening, the Vietnamese people did not want this evacuation and made fun of the enemy's propaganda, such as taking advantage of the lack of diacritics on a banner hanging in Haiphong to morph "Evacuating is choosing freedom" (*Di cư là chọn tự do*) into "Evacuating is burying freedom" (*Di cư là chôn tự do*).[50] From the outset, the population movement was not authentic but, rather, engineered.

Some people believe that the DRV began to criticize Washington ten years later, after US troops landed in Vietnam. But the propaganda had already denounced "American crimes" (*tội ác của Mỹ*) in 1954.[51] One pamphlet claimed that the United States had been profiteering from the war for eight years. The arrival in Saigon of General Lawton Collins suggested a new direction. Washington used Ngô Đình Diệm's "Catholic" army "to terrorize and oppress the spirit of peace and unity of our people" and turn the south into a US territory.[52] This implied that most people who left fell into different categories. They were greedy individuals, corrupted by Americans, or "lackeys" who enabled this foreign interference.[53] The DRV took pains to show that justice would be served.[54]

Seventeen cases, detailed in two volumes, revealed the deception to the public in 1955. Some of these corrupt individuals stole from the evacuees or falsified or sold travel documents, whereas others spread lies regarding the DRV or rumors about the threat of an atomic bomb attack. The worst case concerned a man who terrorized the faithful. A certain Phạm Văn Tấn pretended to be a seminarian and urged the faithful to go south, claiming that God had gone there, the new political authorities would outlaw religion, and an atomic bomb would annihilate the north. Not only did he spread fear, but he also seized and sold the property of the church in Phát Diệm, amassing over twelve million đồng.[55] Agitators took advantage of gullible Catholics.

Hanoi's representations created a stereotype, which was perpetuated by Western authors in the press at the time, such as Graham Greene. The famous British writer criticized Ngô Đình Diệm for nominating Catholics to important state positions. He blamed members of the clergy, "who had compromised themselves during the war, as prince bishops with private armies." This led "political priests" to take advantage of the faithful by declaring that "God and the Virgin [had] gone to the south, only the devil [remained] in the north."[56] By spreading the idea that Catholics in the south had become a "fourth sect," Greene not only denounced the rise of Catholics to power but also supported the idea that they were followers of a manipulative Church. In a few words, he erased the evacuees' political motivations and collapsed their history into a two-dimensional depiction of their faith.

It is impossible to assess the impact of the propaganda on both sides. The evacuation started with a large wave, consisting mostly of people who had reached Hanoi in June. It then slowed down until the last weeks with a new wave of incoming people toward the end of the grace period. A significant number of Catholics followed their priests, who were not supposed to leave their parishes. In fact, Monsignor Trịnh Như Khuê, the bishop of Hanoi, received instructions from the Vatican. Only priests with authorization from their superiors could leave.[57] Despite Rome's exhortations, bishops met in a "retreat" at the church of Chợ Quán in Saigon in September 1954. Three of them, the bishops of Bùi Chu, Phát Diệm, and Haiphong, never returned to the north.[58] Their departure was so hasty that it jeopardized French plans to organize ceremonies in Hanoi before transferring the city to the DRV.[59] Overall, almost two-thirds of the secular clergy, responsible for service to the faithful of the dioceses, departed. The highest proportion of departing priests was 87 percent in the diocese of Haiphong, whereas the secular clergy who departed the least were in the diocese of Vinh—although these discrepancies might reflect a lack of accessibility to transportation southward.[60] In all dioceses in the lowlands east of Hanoi, the secular clergy left en masse (see fig. 2.1). This often left parishes with no priest. Catholics did not leave because of propaganda. They had been deeply involved in the war and, like civil servants or families of soldiers, had good reason for moving to the south.

Events during the evacuation cemented the impression that people were voting with their feet. The CEFEO discovered that people put themselves in dangerous situations to leave DRV zones and join Haiphong. The French navy, while patrolling off the coast of Thanh Hóa, rescued people stranded on sandbanks that they had reached during low tide.[61] Another patrol sailed upstream into the Đáy River and retrieved seven hundred people over five days in October 1954.[62] The French feared that many Vietnamese Catholics had remained behind. They sought arbitration from the International Control Commission (ICC), created to monitor the cease-fire agreements.[63] Delegates from Canada, Poland, and India represented the capitalist, communist, and Third World interests. This balance would ensure the absence of further escalation.

However, India was not neutral on all matters. New Delhi was determined to prevent any foreign power, especially the West, from interfering in domestic affairs through the evacuation, as it had done in its own partition.[64] Mobile teams went to investigate both DRV claims that the French had forced people to move south and French allegations that DRV authorities had prevented people from departing. Yet the ICC almost never concluded that any side had violated provisions allowing civilians to go to the zone of their choice.[65] The ICC's hands-off approach contrasted with news of altercations between DRV authorities and people wanting to go south. In the village of Ba Làng, parishioners armed with knives, spears, and a few grenades barricaded themselves in the church.[66] They held off attempts by the local authorities to disperse for a week until the army forced its way in, claiming the lives of one soldier and three civilians and wounding over fifty people with automatic rifles.[67] In Lưu Mỹ, in the diocese of Vinh, parishioners protested against the local authorities' reluctance to issue travel documents necessary to reach assembly points. Again, the intervention of the army worsened the tensions. Two military sections intervened and opened fire. Witnesses and local authorities reported from twelve to fourteen dead and the same

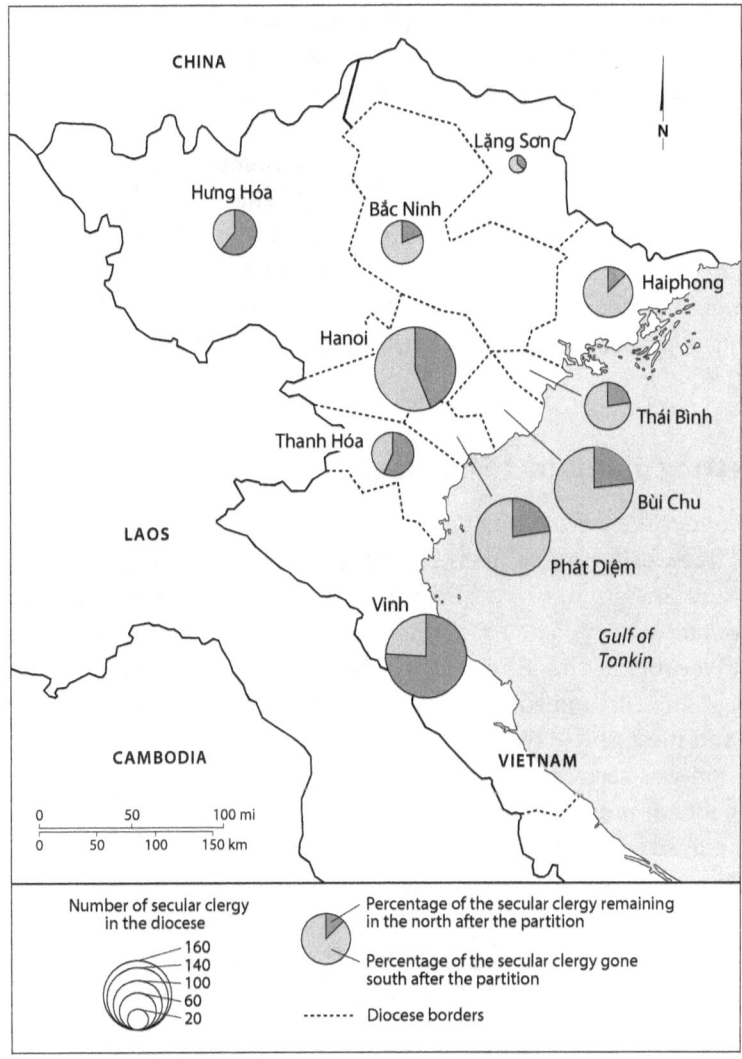

FIGURE 2.1. Proportions of secular clergy per diocese leaving the north after 1954.
Source: Map by Bill Nelson, with data from George Naïdenoff, "Vainqueurs aux mains nues, les réfugiés viêt-namiens demandent justice à l'opinion," *Missi* 5 (1955): 157–77; and George Naïdenoff, "La Triple chrétienté du Viêt-Nam dans les conjonctures présentes," *Missi* 2 (1956): 39–46.

number of wounded.[68] This time, the ICC blamed the PAVN unit for using automatic rifles in an operation involving civilians. It also recommended that an ICC team escort Catholics to the MS *Kilinski*, a merchant ship provided by the Polish navy, to make their way to the south. However, it concluded that this incident had been accidental. The DRV could not be held responsible for violating the cease-fire agreements.⁶⁹ Civilians could not rely on the ICC to ensure that they could go to the zone of their choice. But this paralysis reinforced the impression that these civilians feared communist persecution.

Altercations confirmed a narrative that numbers only weakly supported. It materialized a plan, imagined in Geneva, that the population movement could express a political choice. The political instrumentalization of the evacuation not only suggested that South Vietnam had become an alternative to the DRV but also reinforced the impression among evacuees that their fate had become intimately connected with the Cold War.

Rejecting the Current Situation

No wonder the evacuees felt as if they had reached a point of no return. The "free world" touted them as heroes, and the DRV castigated them as "traitors" or "gullible faithful." Whether they liked it or not, they could not remain neutral. Their movement conveyed a political message in the Cold War and in the legitimacy of the postcolonial state. The circumstances and the immediate decisions made did not matter. Saigon, Hanoi, and most of the West viewed them as voting with their feet. Their reaction was certainly not monolithic, nor was it a simple rejection of the political pressure coming from both sides. But many realized that they played a role in a national, regional, and global struggle. They had become agents of historical change.

Marking the importance of this historical event was essential to the evacuees. In the weeks preceding their departure from the north, journalists created a newspaper, *Lửa sống* (*The Fire of Life*), to document the evacuation. The Front-line Authors (Đoàn ký giả tiền tuyến), who pledged to fight communism with journalism, gathered at Haiphong's municipal library on April 22, 1955, to imagine how they could mark this unprecedented event.⁷⁰ Like Chopin before fleeing Poland, they wanted to collect soil from historical locations in the north and take it with them to the south. Almost four years earlier, Bảo Đại in the ASVN had also mixed soil from Hanoi, Hue, and Saigon in a ceremony to symbolize Vietnam's unity.⁷¹ The Procession of the Land, marking the departure of the last ship from Haiphong, departed on May 11, 1955. French officers, SVN representatives, and a British general laid flowers at the war memorial.⁷² The representative of the northern region collected soil in a box at the town hall, while the crowd paraded in the streets. A billboard-size map of Vietnam read: "Those who remain await the unification of Vietnam." Another sign announced: "Our flesh and bones form a defensive wall against communism." One showed a coffin with the map of northern Vietnam: "The homeland is mourning because of the Việt Cộng." A giant dummy representing China, stabbed by a pen, was at the end of the procession.[73] Nationalists rejected partition.

The arrival of this soil in Saigon days later generated the same kind of mobilization. Between six thousand and twenty thousand people, depending on the estimate, packed the docks in Saigon, awaiting the ship that would transport the "sacred earth of the north" (đất thiêng miền Bắc).[74] After a gun salute, the procession began: SVN representatives, the national guard, and religious leaders walked in silence, under the supervision of the army. Although it had begun to rain, the procession continued along Catinat Boulevard, until it reached the botanical garden. Everyone gathered solemnly at the Monument of Remembrance (Đền kỷ niệm), until the silence was broken by a cry—"We are all determined to reconquer the north!"—followed by a round of applause.[75] After several speeches, the parade left toward Norodom Palace, and the crowd dispersed in the evening.[76] People could not remain indifferent to partition. Many Vietnamese nationalists grieved their departure from the north.

Publications produced by evacuees in the south insisted that their forced departure was unfair. Vietnam's territory had been divided by two rival clans in the past. But, according to Nghiêm Xuân Thiện, a former member of parliament in the DRV and governor of the northern region in the ASVN, this partition was different.[77] The editor-in-chief of *Thời luận* lamented: "Once again, a river is used to separate the north and the south. The Bến Hải River has replaced the Gianh River in ending a grueling armed conflict. This time, however, the division was not the result of rivalry between two clans. It emerged from the confrontation of two empires: the communist and the colonial empires."[78] Two empires, Chinese in the north and French in the south, divided Vietnam. A cartoon in *Quan điểm* (*Perspective*), a weekly publication by evacuees, depicted the Geneva Conference as a dinner (see fig. 2.2). An angel sat with the American eagle, the fierce Soviet bear, the British lion, and a French rooster, which had emptied two wine bottles on its own. All of them seemed ready to share Vietnam, a minuscule dove on the table.[79] The French and the communists were feasting while Vietnam was a victim of foreign decisions. This implied that two larger phenomena, decolonization and the Cold War, had caused this division, as if nationalists had no responsibility for the war.

Several other cartoons suggested that the population did not want partition, nor did the people who remained in the north support the DRV. Drawings showed a Buddhist monk committing suicide and Catholics protesting local authorities.[80] Another cartoon depicted the population lining up to register their household, as a baby in her mother's arms urinated on a cadre's paperwork.[81] These illustrations implied that the communists and the Vietnamese were not the same. The former had seized power to enslave the latter. No one, it seemed, wanted partition or communist rule.

The media outlets publishing these cartoons blamed the communists for the situation. The cartoons highlighted the cadres' abuse of power and submission to Soviet or Chinese communists. Officers accompanying a Chinese adviser on a junk are shown abandoning citizens in flooded areas and encouraging them to "face adversity," using a well-known Việt Minh slogan used during the war.[82] In another cartoon, Hồ Chí Minh is urging skinny peasants to revere Mao Zedong and Nikolai Bulganin, the

THẦN HÒA BÌNH (trong bữa tiệc Giơ-Neo):
Có mỗi một con chim cu, thì ai ăn ai dừng ?
Nông nỗi này rồi chung đến sực cả mình mất !

Tranh hàng tuần của BÍCH-KÍCH-PHÁO

FIGURE 2.2. Criticism of the Geneva Conference in an evacuee publication in 1955.
Source: Bích Kích Pháo, "Thần Hòa bình," *Quan điểm*, August 20, 1955.

Soviet head of the Council of Ministers.[83] Depicting the communists as stooges of an empire was not enough. They were no longer even Vietnamese. A short straight line represented the cadres' eyes. Ideology had made them blind. Or this implied that they had no visible eye crease, a physical trait often associated with populations northeast of Vietnam.[84] In a different cartoon, Hồ Chí Minh is pulling Bulganin on a rickshaw, saying in Vietnamese, French, and Cantonese that his country could offer "a lot."[85] According to these cartoons, communists had become alien to the Vietnamese people.

The evacuees also created a new interpretation of history, which identified who was to blame for the partition. The historian Dipesh Chakrabarty has shown that the memoirs of Hindus who left Bengal after partition in 1947 take the narrative structure of a tragedy.[86] In their memoirs, they portray the past as ideal and their departure as an unexpected catastrophe. Their narratives not only ignore their own responsibility in the partition but also erase the notion that Muslim grievances are grounded in history. The evacuees' retelling of the war followed the same logic. The Procession of the Land presented them as the righteous heirs of a long lineage of heroes originating in the north.[87] They also rewrote the history of the August Revolution, mentioning when the Việt Minh seized power in 1945 to claim it for themselves. *Dân nguyện* (*The Popular Will*) appeared on the tenth anniversary of the August Revolution. Its editor-in-chief, Hà Thành Thọ, and one of its main contributors, Anh Hợp, both involved in the Procession of the Land, summarized their goal:[88] "The people are determined not to let August 19 fall into the bloody hands of an illegitimate proletarian dictatorship."[89] According to them, the population—not the Việt Minh—led the revolution. The "Việt Cộng" followed the Soviet Union's late declaration of war against Japan and hijacked this nationalist uprising.[90] Narratives of the war told the story of the communists' betrayal and omitted any mention of a joint struggle against French colonial rule.[91] These accounts ignore the Việt Minh's leadership in the war and in providing relief to the population during the famine.[92] They also fail to include the participation of several nationalists in the early years of the DRV. These narratives, in fact, gave the impression that from the outset, this was a civil war.

The partition helped various evacuees realize that they were part of a broader conflict. The unique situation gave the impression that they were facing a new human condition. A novelette written by Mai Thảo, a young evacuee, *Đêm giã từ Hà Nội* (*The Night I Left Hanoi*), sparked a new literary trend in the south after 1954. It described the unprecedented choices before the Vietnamese.⁹³ Mirroring André Malraux's style, the novelette weaved fiction with reality and highlighted the absurdity and tragic nature of the Cold War.⁹⁴ It told the story of Phượng's last days in Hanoi, before the city was handed over to communist authorities in October 1954.⁹⁵ Phượng was determined to go southward, but Thu, his girlfriend, refused to leave her parents. This led Phượng to reflect on the impact of international circumstances on their lives: "Two people were attached to the beauty of life and confronted with the opportunity to start anew, on their own, on the other side of the parallel. Yet the tragedy of a divided country added to the sorrow of war. It split up everyone's life. The country is divided into two zones, and destinies are going in two different directions. Like night and day. Like here and there."⁹⁶

One "felt like a German worker, or a Korean peasant." But Phượng protested: "Thu will make her own choice—like a human being free to act and choose."⁹⁷ This choice between leaving and staying had more implications than choosing where to live. It meant associating oneself with the partition of Vietnam and the Cold War. At the last minute, Thu joined him, and he understood her sacrifice.

> Phượng looked at Thu with a smile. He saw the tears of a woman who had set herself in motion, to integrate the collective ranks, the movement. Phượng knew that they were tears of confidence. A person had to fight. The struggle for freedom that had started in this place, the decisive struggle against oneself to accept the loss, the separation from one's homeland and these streets, to reach the free zone. After Thu, hundreds of others who, like her, victorious under the circumstances, left for the south. To defend their convictions. To defend their humanity. Everyone will return.⁹⁸

In real life, not all love stories ended up like that of Phượng and Thu. The memoirs of Nguyễn Công Luận recall a letter handed from a family relative to his lover, who, he hoped, would move to the south with him. Years after resettling in the United States, he learned that she never received his letter. Nevertheless, as soon as he arrived in Saigon, he joined an informal regiment, the Bắc tiến (March to the north), ready to liberate his homeland.⁹⁹

The realization of this human condition encouraged several evacuees to believe that they had to act. Mai Thảo's novel inspired the creation of a literary journal, *Sáng tạo* (*Creation*). People had to become political, "not in the defense of a party program or in becoming part of an institution, but to engage in the history of the Vietnamese nation."¹⁰⁰ Other publications exhorted every Vietnamese moved by the partition to stop being passive subjects.[101] Instead of paying the price for decisions made by others, these evacuees believed that they had to become the main protagonists in their own story.

Many understood that the new connections with international networks could support their struggle. In December, after Saigon obtained widespread support, Phạm Văn Huyến, the poster child of the ASVN during the war, was asked to head the COMIGAL.[102] He stepped up to the challenge. He represented the evacuation to the world, escorting visitors to camps and entertaining foreign officials at cocktail parties. His previous Việt Minh affiliation was not a handicap but an asset, a source of amusement for foreign representatives, who were eager to imagine the life of a rebel in the jungle.[103] Trần Thanh Hiệp, a law student who was close to Mai Thảo, took a bolder approach. He wrote to the UN in December 1954 and represented the SVN at the Bandung Conference of African and Asian countries four months later. He also exhorted his fellow Vietnamese never to give up.[104] "To turn toward the south is to believe in the capacity to restore the sacred nation. One million migrants, armed with their experience and fighting ability; a one-million-strong suicide squad [cảm tử quân] spilling their blood; one million fighters, south of the seventeenth parallel, ready to take back independence."[105] The student had not only used the magic number of a million but also embraced the idea that all evacuees wanted to return to the north and were ready to die for it. Whether the SVNAF would be no match for the PAVN in 1954 was not important. Now that the Cold War was being waged in Vietnam, some believed everything was possible.

The partition gave the evacuees a sense that they were on a mission. "Any reunification will require the participation of the migrants. Here we will need important votes if there is a referendum; there we will need a vanguard to march to the north if a war is the way to unite the country."[106] The lived experience of the conflict was not a prerequisite to the emergence of a new historical consciousness. For example, students had been relatively unaffected by the war as they remained in high schools or at the university in Hanoi. Yet they joined the literary trend set by Mai Thảo. They organized conferences to mark a Day of National Unity in Saigon on August 31, 1954. Some even took to the streets, blocking the ICC headquarters, to express their frustration.[107] Other people in the central highlands who had not experienced displacement across the country also joined the movement set by the evacuees. They, too, left DRV rule, since communist rule had departed to the north, and wanted to tell the rest of the world what they endured. *Experimenting the Dialectic* (*Thực nghiệm biện chứng pháp*) explained that, under the veneer of ideology and theory, communists claimed a monopoly on truth, reason, and patriotism and imposed a tax burden or civil service assignments on the population. This was "how an ideology is translated into practice."[108] The evacuees' self-awareness drew others into motion.

Their leadership had to become indisputable. At the general assembly in April 1955, evacuee students tried to pass a motion denouncing communism and colonialism.[109] Southern students protested, as they believed "the French and the communists had contributed, each in different ways, to the Vietnamese fatherland."[110] Two days later, the newspaper *Dân đen* (*The Masses*) criticized the southern students and rejected their position. Evacuee students left the general association, which had been created in 1936 in Hanoi and had been active in the war, in 1949, as part of the Hanoi University Student Corps.[111] They created the General Association of Nationalist Students, implying that anyone who remained in the former group was not a nationalist.[112]

This sense of superiority did not come from irreconcilable differences between the regions. Northerners did not look down on southerners only because of their place of origin, as an Orientalist perception of this divide would suggest. The evacuees' self-awareness did not target southerners because they were southerners. It defied anyone who opposed them and exonerated anyone who shared their opinion, regardless of their place of origin. On the first anniversary of the cease-fire, the demonstrators did their best to persuade the rest of the population to join them.[113] But French intelligence reported that it did not work out as planned. Among those reluctant to denounce France and the DRV were northerners established in the south in the decades before 1954. These people had little interest in pursuing the war or returning to the north.[114] Hence militants launched a new movement, called "the New Tonkinese opposing the Old Tonkinese." The fault line divided people because of their ideas and position—not because of their place of birth or experience of displacement. Unsurprisingly, the evacuees resented their forced displacement and did everything in their power to show that the cease-fire was unfair. But these claims could only become credible and become an established truth if they received external validation.

Combatants in the Free World

The evacuees arrived in the south, in near political chaos. Domestic opposition and international pressure could topple Ngô Đình Diệm at any point in the first few months. But the prime minister rose to become an undisputed leader. The evacuees' support to Diệm gained them the rank of model citizens in this emerging postcolonial state. By the end of this process, their initial rejection of the partition had become the new national rallying cry.

The largest threat came from France, which Ngô Đình Diệm blamed for the Geneva cease-fire. Paris had recognized the state's independence in June 1954, but it could overthrow this cabinet and put a new government in place that was more in tune with its interests. The CEFEO, which had now decamped entirely to the south, could mount a coup at the snap of a finger. Various competitors were ready to challenge Ngô Đình Diệm's premiership. The initial opposition came from the head of the SVNAF, General Nguyễn Văn Hình. But Bảo Đại, the head of state, sent him to France to defuse the crisis.

Henceforth, French interference was no longer merely a matter of supposition; it could become a reality. Criticizing organizations empowered by the colonial rule offered a perfect opportunity to undermine the French and deter any further involvement. The Bình Xuyên was a criminal organization specialized in violent entrepreneurship, running brothels and a casino. It had become a police force in Saigon and Cholon with the blessing of the French because of their efficient elimination of communist presence in the city.[115] Criticizing the Bình Xuyên's immorality indirectly targeted the French because they were the ones who empowered them. Local confrontations in March 1955 evolved into a full-scale battle in Saigon, which the nationalist army won. Meanwhile, the Hòa Hảo, some Cao Đài, and members of the VNQDĐ rebelled against the government, so the SVNAF launched campaigns against them in the Mekong delta and central Vietnam.[116] By May 1955, all the armed insurgencies had been put down, with most of Diệm's opponents imprisoned, executed, or forced into exile. France, with its heavy military presence on the ground, could have tipped the balance in favor of them. But at no point did they do so, out of fear that if Paris forced its way into remaining in Vietnam, North African countries would be reluctant to remain in the French Union. This violent period after the cease-fire had a significant impact. It marked an uncertain transition from a French-sponsored government to an independent state, which fiercely demanded independence from its former colonizer. For a while at least, it had overcome all opposition.

The support of evacuees during these challenging events proved crucial. Ngô Đình Diệm could use them against domestic opponents and international commitments, restraining his government. He only had to channel the evacuees' frustration against the French, their local partners, and the ICC. France was an obvious target. Paris had not only decided the fate of Vietnam at the Geneva Conference but had also long refused to grant independence. Along with protests against the cease-fire, many evacuees expressed strong resentment of the French. Ngô Đình Diệm took advantage of this anger against his domestic opponents, starting with Prince Bửu Hội. Many viewed the scientist and member of the royal family as a viable alternative. Students who organized the Day of National Unity in Saigon opposed the professor because he had declared his readiness to organize a referendum with the DRV. "A collaboration is unacceptable because the Việt Minh does not collaborate. A collaboration is nothing short of suicide," students declared in an open letter.[117] This not only supported Saigon's refusal to organize a referendum but also undermined the likelihood that Bửu Hội would become the next prime minister.[118]

The evacuees expressed frustration with the Bình Xuyên, criticizing colonial politics and strengthening Diệm's power in the SVN. Forcing a ruthless police force to deal with a floating population inevitably led to confrontation. This culminated in a demonstration on September 21, 1954. Between three thousand and ten thousand evacuees marched to Norodom Palace to express their support for the prime minister in this time of "national peril."[119] Trucks had transported them from their camps, and Ngô Đình Diệm's sister-in-law, Trần Lệ Xuân, had been spotted in strategic places, urging nationalists to turn against their French surrogates.[120] The Bình Xuyên opened fire on the crowd, which gave foreign correspondents the impression that they had repressed innocent people.[121] In fact, protestors paraded with bamboo sticks and threw bottles and bricks at police officers.[122] In the following months, French intelligence warned that members of the Cân lào (Cân lào Nhân vị Cách mạng Đảng; Personalist Revolutionary Labour Party) led by Ngô Đình Diệm's brother, Ngô Đình Nhu, had infiltrated the camps. Cân lào agents both "built on existing sentiments and launched focused and organized propaganda" against the French.[123]

This allowed Ngô Đình Diệm to remove the only person above him. He gathered influential people in a meeting dubbed the Estates General, to recall the assembly, which had called for the end of absolute monarchy in France, in the hope they would agree to demote the chief of state. His attempt to mobilize them against Bảo Đại failed. Subsequently, a more coordinated campaign portraying the former king as an indolent nobleman led the population to depose him in a referendum.[124] An overwhelming majority voted in favor of removing Bảo Đại. Ngô Đình Diệm proclaimed a new state, the Republic of Vietnam (RVN), on October 26, 1955, and assumed the position of president. Within a year, he overcame domestic opposition and eliminated the vestiges of French colonial rule. The last CEFEO troops departed South Vietnam in 1956 and transferred responsibility for training the RVNAF to the United States. The newly created RVN was finally free of French influence, only to jump into a partnership with the United States.

From the perspective of the evacuees, another, more imposing opponent remained. Large sections of society, who expressed apathy, neutrality, and even satisfaction with the cease-fire, had to be turned around. For many of them, the DRV was a nationalist state that had fought for independence, not a cover for communist activities.[125] In the south, where the Việt Minh had taken refuge in the countryside as early as September 1945, the specter of communism was even less serious.[126] Many believed there was no reason to worry about a referendum or the creation of a coalition government. Twenty-six intellectuals formed the Movement for the Defense of Peace in August 1954 to praise the cease-fire "as the ultimate recognition of the Vietnamese people's struggle for independence."[127] Saigon arrested and imprisoned them for breaching public order. In prison, they went on a hunger strike and refused to recognize Ngô Đình Diệm's legitimacy unless Saigon did the same for Hồ Chí Minh's government.[128] After being deported to Haiphong, its leaders were put under house arrest. There, they met a crowd of evacuees who awaited departure to the south, protesting in front of their house. They wanted to "expose the truth about the Việt Minh regime and living conditions in interzone IV."[129] These evacuees were ready to persuade or attack anyone who supported the DRV or expressed satisfaction with the cease-fire.

This was not an isolated movement. Its leaders returned to the south after they apologized, recognized Diệm's government, and declared that they would not engage in subversion. Thirty-nine prominent intellectuals, doctors, lawyers, and journalists demanded their "immediate freedom without restrictions," while groups of students called for the release of their professor, Phạm Huy Thông.[130] To them, the cease-fire was not a failure but a peaceful solution to the conflict. Some of the population also resented Ngô Đình Diệm's use of violence against his opponents. Sometimes, entire villages in the Mekong delta denounced these policies to the French, whom they urged to overthrow Ngô Đình Diệm and to prevent US interference in Vietnamese affairs.[131] Some denounced the expansionism of an "American empire" that had "forced compatriots in the north to move to the south," rehashing communist counterpropaganda. Interestingly, they also denounced the government's repression of the Cao Đài and Hòa Hảo and called for freedom of religion. They accused the government of the same religious discrimination for which Catholics had reproached the DRV during the evacuation. Thus, the evacuees knew that their battle to bring the population to oppose Hanoi was not over.

Last, the evacuees opposed the ICC because it symbolized the unfairness of the cease-fire. One team visited refugee camps in the south to determine whether French agents had forced people to leave. Instead, they found signs in French, Vietnamese, and Spanish that read: "Hồ Chí Minh and his gang of criminals" and "Phạm Văn Đồng and his group responsible for the partition of the country."[132] People submitted hundreds of petitions to the ICC to protest communist atrocities. They also forwarded requests from people who were still waiting to evacuate to the south.[133] The situation became so tense that the team sought refuge behind barbed wire despite the protection of Algerian soldiers.[134] The evacuees had nothing but contempt for the cease-fire.

Ngô Đình Diệm further strengthened ties with evacuees. Saigon organized the Congress of the Evacuation (Đại hội di cư) on July 8, 1955, held the day after the first anniversary of receiving his mandate as prime minister.[135] The ceremony gathered representatives of every resettlement camp in the southeastern provinces, as well as Catholic and Buddhist "spiritual leaders."[136] This gathering had special significance for the SVN. There had been no large assembly other than the National Congress in 1953 and the Estates General to depose Bảo Đại in the spring of 1955. It gave the evacuees the impression that they were the representatives of the Vietnamese nation. It also set clear expectations of their role. Saigon would train cadres, support efforts at self-sufficiency, and "prevent the Việt Minh from making trouble after July 20."[137] The people who had left the north would become the guardians of this state. Saigon joined the destiny of these evacuees with the fate of their prime minister and South Vietnam as a country, as if an achievement by one meant the success of the others. This celebration elevated the evacuees as Ngô Đình Diệm's loyal followers and gatekeepers of the nation.

The approaching first anniversary of the cease-fire offered the best opportunity for reiterating opposition to the ICC. In mid-July, evacuee students paraded in front of the Majestic Hotel in Saigon, where the delegation was staying, shouting, "Down with the ICC!" Some even painted slogans on the wall.[138] On July 20, 1955, the first anniversary of the cease-fire, a group split from the crowd and ransacked the hotel.[139] On that day, the government also launched an official publication, *Dân Việt* (*The People of Vietnam*), dedicated to the evacuees, and it served two purposes. In private correspondence, the COMIGAL's director explained that the publication would channel their frustration and persuade them to accept their displacement.[140] The publication, because of its title, also inspired them to take on a role as representatives of the Vietnamese people. This promotion came with responsibilities. The evacuees were not just victims of persecution for the West or fighters who longed to return to the north. From the perspective of the state, they had become model citizens. This reinforced the evacuees' impression that they had become torchbearers for a global struggle. They became convinced not only that they would receive the help they needed to reverse their current situation but that it would happen soon.

In fact, the 1954 evacuation was what the anthropologist Veena Das called a critical event. The lives of individuals who were previously insignificant suddenly became "invested with a new historical agency."[141] As in the French Revolution and the partition of India, people could not return to the lives that they had led before. Personal matters that previously were in the realm of individual or family choices now became a national and global issue. The anthropologist Heonik Kwon and the historian Masuda Hajimu have shown that the Cold War cannot be reduced to a confrontation of superpowers. It became an armed conflict with different objectives and implications for people around the world.[142] This critical event in Vietnam tied the evacuees to the fate of their country and larger international developments. Yet the contradictory nature of the Cold War also led them to develop a distorted perception of the reality. By ending an armed conflict while mobilizing people against a communist threat, the Cold War created the conditions for the evacuees to believe the partition was unfair, temporary, and reversible. Hence, the evacuees believed not only that they had new responsibilities in the global struggle against communism, but also that they could project themselves into the future with a united and communist-free Vietnam.

Chapter 3

Keeping Hope Alive

Although the state and the "free world" had entrusted them with a mission, the evacuees now living in South Vietnam felt as if the end of the honeymoon was near. The Procession of the Sacred Land in May 1955 did not go as planned. Ngô Đình Diệm often greeted demonstrators protesting the Bình Xuyên or the ICC when the crowd approached the gates of Norodom Palace, where he lived.[1] Yet he never came out to meet the organizers of the procession. At the botanical garden, people wanted to bring the box containing the soil to the prime minister and "express to his excellency the migrants' hope to liberate the north soon."[2] In this way, they would symbolically entrust Diệm with liberating the north from communist rule. Photographers noted that around two thousand people went to the palace, waiting for hours. Eventually, everyone left after the police dispersed them.[3] It is hard to understand why a political leader would refuse to mingle with supporters. Perhaps Diệm was simply unwilling to march to the north. Nor did the Cold War superpowers want to raise international tension. In this context, did the evacuees abandon the idea of liberating the north?

Recent literature has shown that the evacuees often opposed Diệm and posed one of his greatest challenges in the media.[4] This chapter argues that there is a fundamental reason for this relentless opposition. Not all the evacuees who opposed Diệm did so at the same time and for the same reasons. But they still had the impression they were empowered by a mission. In fact, they resisted Ngô Đình Diệm's vision for a nation-state because it contradicted their desire to reunify Vietnam and free the north from communism. This ambition had not disappeared because international developments of the Cold War revived them. Even years after the partition, many evacuees believed it was not too late to liberate Vietnam from communism.

Reluctant Resettlement

For years, the RVN had used the population movement as a metaphor for its political legitimacy to gain international recognition. At the Brussels World Expo, the Vatican Pavilion exposed the epic movement and resettlement of Catholics in the south.[5] Likewise, the United Nations never took a stand as to the legitimacy of the Hanoi or Saigon governments. Yet a pamphlet for World Refugee Year in 1959, *The Refugee Problem in the Republic of Vietnam,* implied that people leaving the north were not evacuees, but refugees.[6] The population movement demonstrated a political choice. Therefore, South Vietnam was not a temporary zone—it had become a state to which people had chosen to go.

Despite being the human face of South Vietnam, many evacuees realized that they were sidelined from power. Phạm Văn Huyến, the Việt Minh crossover, experienced this firsthand and resigned from his position as COMIGAL's director at the end of the grace period.[7] He resented Saigon's response to the Cao Đài and Hòa Hảo's dissidence and wanted the French army to remain in the south longer.[8] The same was true of the Cần lao intellectuals and labor unionists. The founders of the newspaper *Tinh Thần* held cabinet positions in November 1954. Soon afterward, they handed in their resignations to protest the handling of the opposition.[9] Most labor organizations were dissolved or forced to cancel their meetings because of government restrictions.[10] Even the Confederation of Vietnamese Workers criticized the government when Ngô Đình Nhu brought farmers and cattle raisers under state control.[11] Diệm's rise to power did not open the doors of the government to a large coalition of people with a common political vision. It meant rule by a single party, the Cần lao, which was entirely under the control of a family and its entourage.

To many other evacuees, the heart of the problem was the lack of consistency in the conceptions of resettlement. Was it temporary or permanent? Could people from the north stick together or would they have to blend into the rest of society? Despite his reassuring words while the evacuation was still underway, Diệm forced virtually all the evacuee organizations to disband, including the Nùng units in the army and the Bảo chính đoàn (Primary Defense Corps), a paramilitary group created by the Đại Việt in the Red River delta before the partition.[12] French and US protection enabled the Nùng to resettle in the area between Phan Thiết and Phan Rang.[13] But the local administration ended any autonomy or control over the materiel that they had brought from the north.[14] Saigon would not permit the existence of a state within the state.

Even Saigon's closest allies did not enjoy preferential treatment. In 1949, the ASVN gained control over immigration, including by Chinese communities.[15] Seven years later, the RVN went even further. A series of decrees in 1956 forced all Chinese born in Vietnam to take Vietnamese citizenship and a Vietnamese name and leave jobs that they had traditionally held.[16] The US secretary of state told Saigon that "nothing [should] be done to harm relations among nations of the free world." Chinese Catholics even urged Cardinal Spellman to overturn these decrees. But Saigon forced their assimilation, including refugees who went to northern Vietnam after 1949 and then migrated to the south after the cease-fire.[17] One of the few exceptions was made for Father Nguyễn Lạc Hóa, who escaped from China to join the ASVN. In the south, he persuaded Diệm to head an autonomous zone in the westernmost area of the Mekong delta, where many communists had remained. He headed the village of Bình Hưng, which became a stronghold in an area long held by the Việt Minh. The story of a priest heading both a village and a militia became so epic that the US Army shot a short documentary on this Cold War hero.[18] But that was an isolated case. Even Catholics who resettled parishes in villages whose churches can be seen today along the road from Saigon to Dalat had to scatter across South Vietnam. Monsignor Lê Hữu Từ was disappointed that Saigon did not accept his request to keep parishioners from Phát Diệm together. The protection of neither Washington nor God sufficed for them to obtain any sort of autonomy.

This applied to evacuees as well, even though the official propaganda touted them as the vanguard of the RVN. Only in their minds could they exist as a community. For all practical purposes, they were divided. In 1954, French intelligence reported that Lê Quảng Luật, a northern Catholic, asked to resettle all the evacuees in the central highlands, as close as possible to the seventeenth parallel. This would protect the south against communist expansion and form a base for the future liberation of the north. However, Diệm refused, arguing that Monsignor Phạm Ngọc Chi preferred dispersion to encourage Catholic proselytism. In reality,

Diệm's brother, Ngô Đình Nhu, and Trần Trung Dung, two key leaders of the Cần lao, "were afraid to see that a group of Tonkinese, led by a capable team, could shift the political balance to whichever camp they considered appropriate."[19] Evacuees who formed a strong community could threaten Diệm's rule. Hence, they had to spread across more than three hundred villages in southern Vietnam.

This desire to remain as close as possible to the north conflicted with Washington's and Saigon's grand plans for rural development. The Cái Sắn project, a massive compound built from scratch out of swamplands and organized around seventeen canals, was made possible through USOM, Michigan State University, and global partners.[20] But the evacuees who resettled there complained about the subpar living conditions, the difficult coexistence with other populations, and insecurity.[21] Even if this had been sold as heaven on earth, they would not have wanted to stay there.

This raised a larger issue about how the evacuation should end. To Saigon and Washington, resettlement would indicate the success of the exodus. To do so, the evacuees could not remain "migrant compatriots" forever. Ordinance 50, on August 28, 1956, ordered the integration of all the camps and marked the endpoint of their adventure (see fig. 3.1). On October 11, 1956, foreign correspondents and delegations went to celebrate when the first village, Gia Kiệm, reached this milestone. Ngô Đình Diệm lauded this achievement:

> I did everything I could and used all means available to help compatriots escape the claws of communism into the south, to contribute with free people to the reconstruction of the country.... In a time of difficulties, empty coffers, and an absence of resources, I could only rely on my trust in the compatriots' capacity to face these challenges; my trust in providence; my trust in the solidarity and mutual love of our people in general; and my trust in the spirit of self-reliance and self-determination of the group of migrants, more specifically.
>
> We can be proud of the results that we achieved in record time.... All the state's efforts, all the generous aid from governments and groups of friendly nations ... combined with the pioneering hands of the migrant patriots.... As they have established new livelihoods, migrant compatriots have effectively contributed to the development of the economy in the south and advanced the crucial struggle to lay the foundation of the republic and of democracy.[22]

Thanks to foreign support and the evacuees' efforts, South Vietnam had succeeded. However, villages struggled to achieve self-sufficiency or

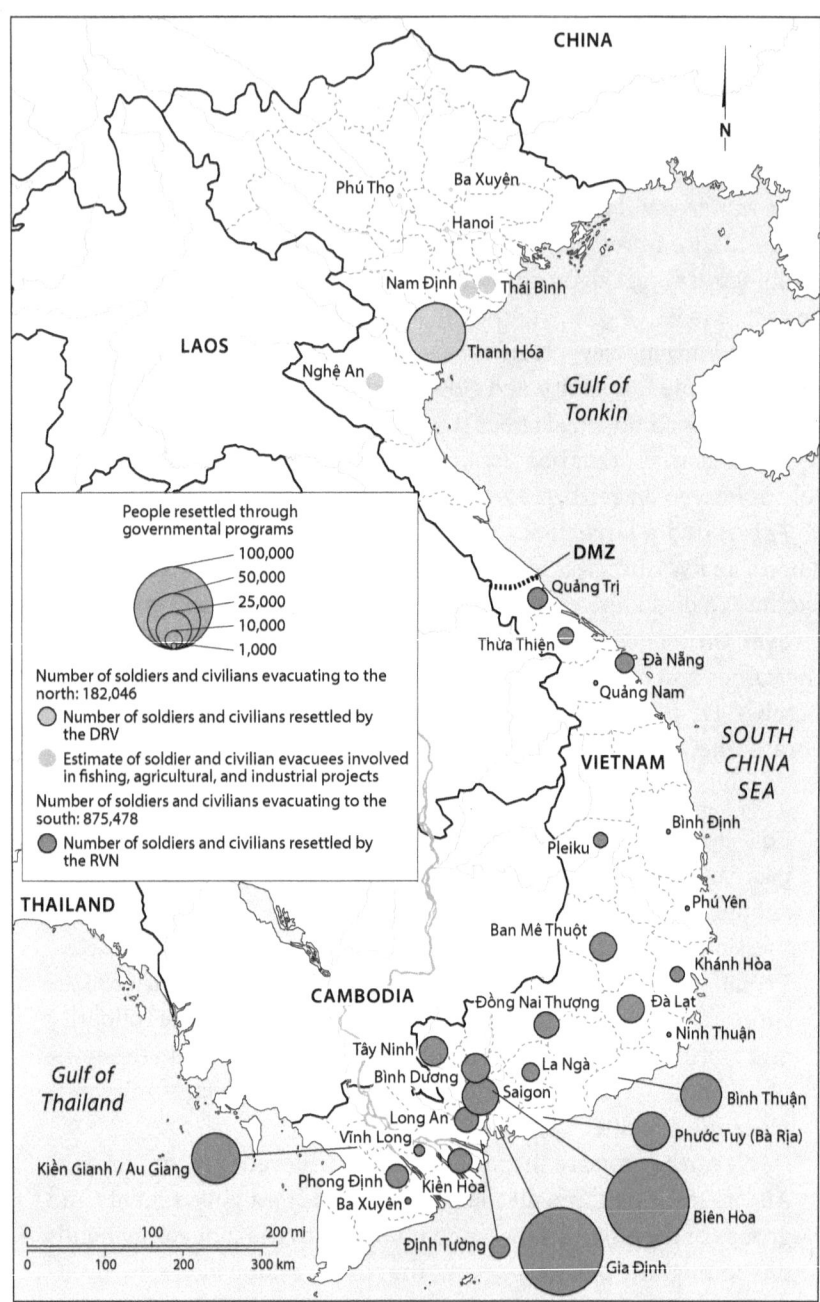

FIGURE 3.1. Resettlement of the 1954 evacuees.

Source: Map by Bill Nelson, with data from Phủ Tổng ủy Di cư Tị nạn, *Cuộc di cư lịch sử tại Việt Nam* (Saigon: Phủ tổng ủy Di cư Tị nạn, 1958), 120, 169; Phan Thị Xuân Yến, *Ban thống nhất trung ương trong cuộc kháng chiến chống Mỹ cứu nước (1954–1975)* (Ho Chi Minh City: NXB Tổng hợp T. P. Hồ Chí Minh, 2011), 78–79, 89, 92; and Quang Vũ and Duy Hưng, "Khởi công khu lưu niệm đồng bào, chiến sỹ miền Nam tập kết ra Bắc," *TTXVN/Vietnam+*, August 8, 2022.

resisted the process.²³ The deadline for dissolution of the COMIGAL was approaching in the spring of 1957, and its director explained that the migration had ended: "The word migrant [di cư] applies only to commemoration of the ignominious act committed by the communist Việt Minh, as they have conspired with the colonialists to divide our homeland. The word *migrant* is used only to keep in our hearts and minds the determination to fight against communism and unite the country."²⁴

For the state, the partition was a thing of the past—no longer either a political or an administrative reality. This foreshadowed an even bigger problem. Ngô Đình Diệm might even forget his promise to reunify Vietnam one day.

The RVN only paid lip service to the idea of reunifying the country. Saigon did not stay in touch with the groups that remained behind and even dissolved the Office for Northern Vietnam (Bắc Việt Vụ), which could have served this purpose. This office, created in November 1954, issued salaries and pensions to civil servants who moved to the south.²⁵ But Saigon closed it in July 1955.²⁶ In 1965, after the fall of Diệm, the chief of police, Phạm Văn Liễu, re-created it temporarily to coordinate sabotage operations in the north.²⁷ Unlike Hanoi, which created and maintained a Committee for Unification, Saigon did not take any concrete steps toward reunifying Vietnam.²⁸ The reason was simple. Like Taipei and Seoul, Saigon had no plan to reunify the country.

Becoming Activists

Many evacuees received funding to publish damning accounts of their experience in the north, through Saigon's campaign to denounce the communists.²⁹ But they soon realized that Diệm would not share power, maintain their unity, or organize a march to the north. This did not mean that they would give up on their dream. They took it upon themselves to make these things happen and prioritized liberation of the north.

First, the evacuees had to face losing contact with their homeland and with one another. Hanoi and Saigon sealed off their territories. People could exchange postcards, which included a preprinted text announcing births, weddings, or deaths. Only later could they send short messages.³⁰ Another concern was how to remain connected despite being scattered across South Vietnam. Most newspapers included a section to help coworkers, families, and neighbors find one another.³¹ Some tried to re-create communities in the south. Just as European settlers in

North America named new cities Cambridge, Athens, Antwerp, or Waterloo after places in the Old World, evacuees named several of the three hundred villages across southern Vietnam after their places of origin in the north. International Catholic support enabled most of these villages to build their own churches. To re-create connections across these villages sometimes spread over different regions, the evacuees formed or joined mutual aid associations among former inhabitants of a village, province, or region.[32] Although these associations in Saigon had existed before 1954, their role had changed now that returning to the north had become impossible.[33] They served as a place of remembrance and a forum for thinking about how to cope with exile.[34] Some funded the construction of a cemetery so that, even after death, members of the same community could remain together.[35] Other associations perpetuated memories of the north. They held annual meetings or published poems, memoirs, legends, or descriptions of local cultural practices.[36] Travelogues in their periodicals helped people travel back, in their minds, to their place of origin. The homeland described in the bulletins and annual celebrations did not refer to their actual place of origin. It was an imaginary place connected to a different historical time. Their native land (*quê hương*), like the German notion of *Heimat*, was an abstract reference to a homeland.[37] Its size varied from the village, the province, the diocese, the region to northern Vietnam as a whole, depending on the context. Although these communities celebrated places of different sizes, they recognized that they suffered from the same condition. They all remembered the north before the partition.

Some evacuees even imagined they could erect a memorial containing the sacred soil that they brought from the north. Their demands to the state used different names to refer to that monument. For some, it was a memorial dedicated to "those who died in the struggle against the usurper Việt Cộng." To others, it was the memorial "of the Northern land in Saigon" or a shrine to the "unification of the country."[38] Hence, the committee created for the occasion eventually called it the "Memorial" or the "Remembrance Monument" (*Đền kỷ niệm*). The memorial was never constructed. Yet every year, evacuees still commemorated the day that the Geneva Declaration was signed. In 1955, civil servants wrote to Bảo Đại, the chief of state, to declare a month of national mourning. According to a press release, over fifty thousand people took to the streets to mark this anniversary.[39] That day became the National Day of Shame (*Ngày quốc hận*), which served, year after year, as a reminder that the war was not over. The partition was not temporary. But as long as the evacuees were still separated from their homeland, they would remind everyone about this day of infamy.

Evacuees made up a majority of the newspaper industry. They comprised 4–8 percent of the entire population in the south, estimated around 12.4 million people, and most of them settled in the countryside. However, many intellectuals among them remained in the cities and became most active in the arts, the print media, the army, and politics.[40] USOM noted that, from 1954 to 1955, northerners had created twelve new dailies, nineteen weeklies, and seven monthlies in Saigon.[41] The leaders of the printed media came from all backgrounds. Some were members of nationalist parties, and others were Việt Minh crossovers. But none of them could be considered innocent refugees, as the West often saw them. They used the print media as a weapon for mobilizing the population and fighting Hanoi.

To them, merely keeping everyone unified in a fictive kinship was not enough. They had to persuade others of their worldview. The best way to do that was to make the rest of the population experience Việt Minh rule, as several evacuees had during the war. The perfect avenue for enabling people to see and feel this experience was film. One movie, *Chúng tôi muốn sống (We Want to Live)*, was the result of a joint production encompassing Bùi Diễm, an evacuee who later became the ambassador of the RVN to the United States, a Filipino crew, and American funding.[42] Their collaboration resulted in two movies, both shot in Vietnam, one with a Filipino cast and the other with Vietnamese actors.[43] The film told the story of a young man who joined the PAVN to fight colonial rule. After he returned to his village on leave, he noticed that the nationalist front had turned into an instrument of control by the Communist Party. Social peace had been shattered by land reform. His former sweetheart had become a revolutionary cadre, and his parents were condemned in a public trial. The man realized that he had sided with the wrong camp. He fled to a beach, where he boarded a raft, while others desperately swam and ended up being eaten by sharks. This was a story of betrayal, broken ties, and survival.

Location shooting, rather than filming in a studio, became a new trend in the 1950s.[44] But this Vietnamese production pushed this logic to new limits. The Vietnamese cast in the movie did not have professional actors, as the Filipino one did.[45] Evacuees were in leading and secondary roles, as well as being extras. Was this feature film supposed to transport the audience to an imaginary world? Or did it attempt to present an alternate history? *We Want to Live* did not try to tell a fictional tale—it attempted to recount a different reality.

Joining a Worldwide Uprising

Many evacuees believed that the time had come to overthrow communism. After Stalin's death in 1953, the Soviet Union rehabilitated many "revisionists" that he had sent to the gulag. In February 1956, before a closed session at the twentieth congress of the Communist Party of the Soviet Union, Nikita Khrushchev, who was then first party secretary, denounced the cult of personality. News of this speech leaked and sparked hope for change across Eastern Europe. In June 1956, workers walked out of factories in Poznań in Poland to demand better working conditions. Four months later, Bucharest students called for the replacement of the leaders put in place by Stalin with local leaders. Then, not long afterward, an uprising in Hungary prompted the intervention of the Soviet army. That the Red Army had to crush a civilian protest so far outside Soviet borders was revealing. States in Eastern Europe remained communist only by force.

Northern Vietnam also experienced upheavals. When the DRV expanded the land reform to the north as a whole after 1954, intellectuals in Hanoi expressed criticism in two publications, *Nhân văn* (*Humanities*) and *Giai phẩm* (*Masterpieces*), protesting the excesses of denunciation campaigns. Hanoi had a forceful reaction. Most intellectuals were imprisoned or were obliged to join an association in which their work was closely supervised. In the diocese of Vinh, the bone of contention was the relationship between the Church and the state, which was exacerbated by the land reform. The DRV promulgated legislation to guarantee freedom of religion, while declaring that the Vietnam Workers' Party (VWP) did "not believe in the existence of divinities and led a struggle to propagate scientific socialism and patriotism."[46] Worse still, those who feared that the party would take control over the Church, as in China, saw their nightmare become reality. In March 1955, priests loyal to the DRV formed the Catholic National Liaison Committee.[47] The denunciation campaign called on people to attack anyone who had collaborated in colonial rule—unsurprisingly, this included priests and missionaries and targeted land owned by the Church.[48]

To the village of Quỳnh Lưu in Vinh, this was nothing new. As a DRV territory since 1945, it had experienced land reform and denunciation campaigns even before the cease-fire.[49] What drove them to launch an armed uprising against local authorities was that twenty thousand people, according to French estimates, were still waiting to go to the south.⁵⁰ Not everyone had the chance to go. The ICC sent a mobile team on November 2, 1956, which received petitions complaining about unlawful arrests and confiscation. The local authorities sent cadres to educate people about their rights and duties. But parishioners resisted, formed a self-defense militia, and constructed fortifications around the village. It is hard to determine what inspired the Catholics' determination to resist. But they might have believed that the arrival of the ICC was imminent. At the time, North Vietnamese newspapers denounced plans by Saigon and the United States to march to the north, and rumors had it that Saigon and Hanoi might arrange new exchanges.⁵¹ Soon, the status quo would change. Eventually, six thousand PAVN soldiers surrounded ten villages across Nghệ An and Thanh Hóa to end this Catholic resistance.⁵² Hanoi also organized a meeting that Hồ Chí Minh attended to apologize in person. The DRV committed to spending over forty-eight million đồng for the reconstruction of religious sites and planned to train new and more compliant priests.⁵³ The uprising in Quỳnh Lưu was a crisis of Hanoi's own making in 1956.

To the evacuees in the south, these events in the north and in other countries were a sure sign that the end of communism was near. Two newspapers, *Tin bắc* (*News of the North*) and *Hà Nội*, seized on this opportunity. Their columns amplified criticisms voiced by intellectuals in *Nhân văn* or *Giai phẩm* and described the subsequent crackdown and political purges.⁵⁴ A pamphlet in 1957 publicized declarations by Nguyễn Mạnh Tường, a skilled lawyer who served in the DRV and publicly criticized the land reform. Footnotes and dramatic drawings accompanied his statements. One passage stood out: "Right now in the capital, many people complain and wish to go to the south. Many of them are simple people, such as peasants and workers. How can we explain this?" An accompanying footnote insisted that the entire population wanted to leave the north.⁵⁵ This public outcry confirmed that the evacuees had undoubtedly made the right call.

The rebellions even led some to think that the time to fight was nigh. A short story on one of their wildest fantasies was published in a periodical run by evacuees. The Republic of Vietnam Armed Forces (RVNAF) launched an attack on the north:

> H.C., Quảng Bình, August 9, 1956
> For two months, our unit has been stationed here in H.C., a small hamlet on the border.... Our intelligence service reports that the Việt Cộng have savagely put down popular resistance in the north.

They have organized public executions of hundreds of innocent people to terrorize the population.

This news has sparked outrage. In recent days, protests in the cities and in the countryside demanded a march to the north and liberation of the homeland. . . .

August 12, 1956

Today, all officers and soldiers of the 102nd Airborne Division and I send a motion to the president declaring that we are volunteering for this march to the north. . . .

August 15, 1956

The D-Day that we hoped for has finally arrived. We received the orders. GMCs full of soldiers are heading to Quảng Trị airport, our departure point. . . . Over twenty Dakotas are stationed on the airstrip, ready to take off, with their propellers spinning under the pale moonlight. In no time, we disappear into the firebird. . . .

3 a.m. We fly over the province of Kiến An. The voice of Major-General X resounds through the cabin speakers: "Brothers, Soldiers of the 102nd Airborne Division, now is the time to write history. In a few moments, you will be the first to free our homeland. Our ancestors and four thousand years of history are relying on us." . . .

—Ready!

We stand up and approach the opening door.

—Go!

I am the first to jump out of the plane. I hear my parachute go "poof" as it deploys. I float in the air, and, a few seconds later, my feet touch the ground: my homeland! . . .

3 p.m. The heavy artillery and the armored vehicles have landed in Haiphong and Đồ Sơn. Kiến An airport is being repaired in no time. All army units now have a base for operations. . . .

August 17, 1956

1 p.m. We arrive in Hải Dương, which the Việt Cộng used to call its Stalingrad. . . . Before attacking, the general commander-in-chief gives us the order. We have to seize Hanoi on August 19, so that this gang of Việt Cộng will understand that the people's will is implacable.

August 19, 1956

The flag of the republic flies over the Temple of Jade. The ancient Thăng Long has come alive again.[56]

The amount of detail and the anonymity of the village of departure suggested that this fiction could become a reality. The timing, six months after its publication, also implied that it could happen soon. However, this narrative was entirely detached from the actual military capacity of South Vietnam. Although the PAVN decreased until Hồ Chí Minh announced another general mobilization in 1960, the RVNAF also shrank, to 243,000 men, in 1960.[57] Moreover, the RVNAF used antiquated equipment, and its ill-trained divisions in the late 1950s could never be used to reconquer the north.[58] The evacuees had been so accustomed to seeing their experience turned into a story, they believed the fiction and imagined it could become reality. These plans might have formed when uprisings spread across Eastern Europe and in northern Vietnam. But they also coincided with the end of resettlement, when their villages had to integrate the local administration.

Official publications singing the praises of President Ngô Đình Diệm had implored Saigon to launch a march to the north as early as 1955 (see fig. 3.2). A special issue of *Dân Việt* marking the second anniversary

Figure 3.2. Children praising Ngô Đình Diệm and expressing their determination to march to the north in 1955. We don't know if this drawing was the original or whether it was improved by the cartoonist, but the drawing shows two signatures.
Source: Mặc Lan and C. L. Dau, "Thiếu nhi nhất định chiếm lại Hà Nội," *Văn nghệ tự do*, November 5, 1955.

of Diệm's premiership still insisted on reunifying the country. A song urged people to initiate the march to the north.[59] In Bạch Đằng, a crowd exclaimed: "Let's give a warm welcome to Ngô Đình Diệm, the great patriot! ... Let's wait patiently for Ngô's order to march to the north!" These people praised him with no reservations, but they did not let him forget what they expected from him.[60] Virtually every village celebrating the conclusion of the evacuation from October 1956 to July 1957 mentioned what they were waiting for.[61] Years after their displacement, many evacuees had not abandoned their dream of returning to the north.

One newspaper also suggested that the state had not gone far enough in its repression of communist members and sympathizers who had remained behind. Tô Văn, a former member of the Việt Minh, believed that Saigon needed to outlaw communism. Next, the government should expel the Polish delegates of the ICC. This would be the opportunity to organize people's tribunals to judge communist leaders in absentia. "After the sentence is pronounced for Hồ Chí Minh and his accomplices, the betrayers of the nation, we demand that the government create effigies and put them at street corners so that the population can put them to death."[62] The newspaper went beyond the general principle of denouncing atrocities. Tô Văn could neither make peace nor be satisfied with that situation.

Tin Bắc (*News from the North*), the newspaper, was not an opposition paper. Ngô Đình Nhu had approached Tô Văn, a journalist, to create the newspaper, and the publishing house of the Cần lao party, Nhà in cách mạng quốc gia (National Revolution Press), handled the printing.[63] But Tô Văn had good reason for hating communism.[64] His memoirs reveal that he had joined the August Revolution and followed the DRV into the countryside after December 1946. The DRV's Service for Migration to New Lands (Ty khẩn hoang di dân) resettled him in Thanh Hóa in interzone IV.[65] It did not take long for him to get into trouble. Tô Văn was imprisoned and tortured in 1947–1948 for disobedience. He lost his two sons to malaria, and a newborn died shortly after his wife was released from a labor camp. Tô Văn remained in the DRV zone after his release. He took political courses in order to work at the Department of Agriculture and became chair of the local youth movement. A year later, he crossed over to work for the ASVN's Ministry of Information, became a journalist, and eventually left for the south.[66] War and poor living conditions had caused his losses, but he saw communism as responsible for his sorrows. He would never give up his fight against communism and would even risk offending Saigon by urging the government to step up its game.

Repression was not sufficient. In fact, the evacuees needed to remember and share their war experiences. In 1958, the weekly *Hà Nội*, published in Saigon, launched a contest:

> Over the past fifteen years, many events have devastated the country! If you are a son of this land, you must have heard or seen some of them. . . . You have fought in the resistance or joined an extraordinary battle! You have been imprisoned or tortured! *You have witnessed atrocities!* You have lived through a unique story! Looking back on these fifteen years, like 150 lives, no one has attempted to record all the population's activities in this country. Perform this task, and you will deserve to win a prize.[67]

Readers responded with their stories, real or imagined, of communist crimes. Until 1954, war prisoners served as the main source of inspiration for propaganda revealing "the truth about the communist zone."[68] But hundreds of thousands of people could draw a more dramatic picture of what had happened in the war. These tales served a function similar to that of publishing Hồ Chí Minh's *Prison Diary* at a time when the DRV was calling on the population to join a new war effort.[69] Far from being asked to give an accurate depiction, they were supposed to mobilize hearts and minds.

Nothing had changed in the eighteen months since the last uprisings. Regime change in the DRV would not happen on its own. The main question was whether this transformation had to come from the north, the south, or outside Vietnam. Again, the evacuees wondered which was most plausible: World War III or a civil war sparked by Hanoi or themselves. One article concluded that the best chance for success would come from building up military and economic forces.[70] However, in both cases, many evacuees felt disheartened. Leadership from Saigon was lacking.

A Spiritual Fight in the South

Catholic evacuees reacted to the uprising in Quỳnh Lưu much more resolutely, especially those who came from that area. The RVN never considered Catholicism an official state religion. But the state elevated personalism as a guiding philosophy, and lay Catholics and priests became its thought leaders.[71] Members of the clergy provided health care, ran private schools, and created a private university in Dalat.[72] They also contributed to the training of civil servants at a personalist center. Although the Church did not officially enjoy privileges, its members had significant power and influence because of the RVN's emphasis on personalism.

Nevertheless, Catholic evacuees could not represent a diocese in exile and had to integrate the local hierarchy. Forming a native place association allowed them to maintain a sense of unity on Vietnamese terms. Catholics from Vinh gathered at the Hội tương tế Nghệ Tĩnh Bình, an association representing their provinces of origin: Nghệ An, Hà Tĩnh, and Quảng Bình, often called the Nghệ Tĩnh Bình region. As a cultural association, it did not contradict the state policy of becoming integrated into the local administration, nor the instructions from the hierarchy to join southern dioceses. Unlike other associations, which held meetings once or twice a year, this association was most active. Its monthly publication *Luyện thép, Cơ quan ngôn luận Nghệ Tĩnh Bình* (*Hardening Steel: The Discussion Organ of the Nghe Tinh Binh*), launched only weeks after the repression of the Quỳnh Lưu, left no doubt.[73] Catholic evacuees from Vinh had to mobilize in the wake of that event.

Father Nguyễn Viết Khai, the editor-in-chief of *Luyện thép*, had a long experience of communism. Ordained as a priest in 1951, he was imprisoned in Nghệ An the following year.[74] By the end of the war, he had spent more time in prison or in resisting the DRV than saying mass in church. Like many others, he viewed the First Indochina War as "ten years of cruel fighting against the Việt Cộng."[75] He contributed to a general movement criticizing the Việt Minh's manipulation of Catholics' patriotism.[76] Most important, he considered the evacuation and the uprising in Quỳnh Lưu within the context of a long history of Catholic resistance. Places and times were central in this new history of the war. *Luyện thép* formed the backbone of this chronology by describing the right events: "The people clearly see the nefarious purposes of the Việt Cộng, abusing the spirit of resistance to oppress and enslave civilian workers through a general mobilization . . . against which resistance rose everywhere, particularly in Làng Nghi (Diễn Châu, Nghệ An) in 1951, Hưng Yên (Nghệ An) in 1952, Nam Đàn (Nghệ An) in 1953, etc., where the people expressed their insubordination to Hồ Chí Minh's yoke."[77] *Luyện thép* wanted to establish a list of dates that suggested a continuous fight against communism.[78] This had to become public history.

Catholic evacuees could also help in the struggle against communism by propagating their faith. Catholicism and communism were deemed to be incompatible. Hence, religious faith could become a remedy for Vietnam's civil war, by creating a defense against communism expansion.[79] They could play a crucial role. According to an article in *Luyện thép*, "In the ongoing bloody conflict, God has saved many of us from a certain death, but he has also vested us with a mission."⁸⁰ The association sent groups of students to evangelize in the central highlands, formerly in the DRV's interzone V. Every summer, a theater company toured the new settlements and helped the local priest propagate the faith.⁸¹

Father Nguyễn Viết Khai helped to coordinate youth groups with the priests' activities in the region. He borrowed from the Marxist analysis and Việt Minh organizational principles that he had learned during the war. Mobile teams engaged in political struggle embedded in military, economic, and cultural systems. He also advised Saigon's Special Commissariat for Civic Action, which supported pacification with political education.⁸² Nguyễn Viết Khai reached out to its director and to the central highlands' Military Command to claim that the Nghệ Tĩnh Bình's youth were best suited to the task. They could teach civics and warn the population against communism because they had experienced DRV rule in interzone IV and knew how to serve as political cadres. He insisted that he could submit a list of volunteers ready to serve in the Commissariat for Civic Action.⁸³ In his view, the struggle was not only political and military but also spiritual, so the natural response to the near-collapse of communism in 1956 was to start mobilizing the population in the south.

Aside from the association, propagation of the faith also relied on Catholic evacuees, and the effort to engage them in doing so paid off. An article in *Osservatore Romano* claimed that the Church could not meet the demand for catechism in Quy Nhơn Province.⁸⁴ "Three thousand people demanded a religious education," and others kept asking when the clergy could return to see them. Because only seventy priests were scattered across four hundred fifty square kilometers to serve one hundred thousand faithful, the solution was to train "northern refugees" to proselytize. The evacuees were no substitute for missionaries, but they were, in a way, apostles of the faith during the Cold War. It is hard to tell whether their religious zeal or their state had the greater impact, but the number of Catholics in the general population grew steadily. The situation had worsened in China, and the Church was barely surviving in the north. But the vitality of the Catholic community in South Vietnam and the dramatic number of new converts were in sharp contrast to those conditions: in the south, the Catholic faith thrived.

Resuming the War against Communism

Compatriots in the north and international developments did not change the status quo, but communists in the south did. In 1959, communist cadres who had remained in the south suffered under Saigon's constant surveillance and repression. Like the evacuees, they were itching for the war to resume. Some misinterpreted instructions to continue the political struggle as a green light for resuming the armed conflict. In December 1959, communist insurgents, sympathizers, and allies, fed up with Saigon policies, took control of a few towns. In Bến Tre, they held control for weeks. The VWP's Central Committee, headed by a southerner, Lê Duẩn, agreed to end the status quo prevailing since the ceasefire and support an armed insurrection.[85] Created by the communists in Hanoi, the National Liberation Front (NLF) was born in 1960. Like the Việt Minh, it hid its communist origins and called on the population to rise up against Ngô Đình Diệm's dictatorship and American imperialism.

To many evacuees, this new creature was a stalking horse for a communist takeover and a magnet for anyone disaffected by Saigon. On March 2, 1960, Vietnamese bishops issued a letter denouncing "atheistic communism." An intercepted document detailed how communists had infiltrated the Church to "divide and rule" and "use the enemy to eliminate the enemy."[86] Any Catholic in the south who still doubted the communist intentions was told to look at China. The "patriotic associations" tried "to separate the faithful from the unity of the Church."[87] Rome also recognized the success and challenges of the Vietnamese Church. In 1958, the pope wrote a letter that praised the growth of the Church and sympathized with the hardships of the faithful in the north.[88] Communists were resuming the war, and Catholics had to stand strong.

Rome finally created a religious hierarchy in Vietnam in November 1960. This allowed its church to be on equal terms with other national churches. Gone were the days when missionaries acted as intermediaries between Vietnamese Catholics and the rest of the hierarchy. Missionaries had been expelled from the north in 1958, so by late 1959 it had only two hundred priests to look after about 300,000–350,000 souls.[89] In contrast, more than 1.2 million Catholics lived below the seventeenth parallel. Over 1,300 Vietnamese priests were responsible for 97,000 catechumens, over 54,000 adult baptisms, and 128,000 child baptisms.[90] South Vietnam was a spiritual society whose disposition toward personalism made it fertile ground for propagation of the faith.[91] Foreign dignitaries from across the West and East Asia attended Catholic celebrations in South Vietnam. Pope John XXIII even wrote a letter to congratulate the Church on this transformation. This was "an eloquent testimony of the maturity and the capacity of Catholics of this land."[92] International and national recognition were received again in 1961, when the church of La

Vang became a minor basilica. Officials, foreign representatives, and over two hundred thousand pilgrims arrived to celebrate this achievement.[93] Ngô Đình Thục, the new archbishop of Hue, announced the significance of this event on television. The shrine was a significant site both religiously and nationally. Catholics expressed their adoration of the Virgin Mary, and the Vietnamese yearned for unification of the country.[94] The articles in the periodical created for this event concurred. The basilica was a beacon of light in the "worldwide fight against communism," especially in Tibet, India, Ceylon (Sri Lanka), Burma (Myanmar), Thailand, and Cambodia.[95] La Vang had become a holy land for Vietnam, Southeast Asia, and the anticommunist world.

Compared with the buoyancy of Catholic activities, the government response was unconvincing. Another wave of repression followed a communist-led uprising. Saigon imposed limits on most individual freedoms. Instead of tamping down the insurrection, these measures inflamed resentment against Saigon. It was not until 1961 that Saigon launched a wider military and political initiative to secure its control over the countryside, in what it called the strategic hamlets program.[96] Even then, many evacuees wondered whether Saigon had completely failed at its primary task: keeping the south free of communism. Support began to dwindle for Ngô Đình Diệm and his brothers, Ngô Đình Nhu, the personalist intellectual; Ngô Đình Thục, the bishop; Ngô Đình Cẩn, who headed the Cần Lao in central Vietnam; and Nhu's wife, Trần Lệ Xuân. In recognition of the year of the rat, the newspaper *Tự do* (*Freedom*) published a cartoon showing a cracked watermelon being devoured by five mice.[97] If the cartoon was turned upside down, it looked like a depiction of Vietnam, in which the rodents represented the five Ngô siblings pillaging the country.[98] Historians have shown that many evacuees opposed Ngô Đình Diệm because of his authoritarian leadership.[99] They include nationalists writing in *Thời luận* and Catholics, such as Father Trần Văn Hiến Minh and Father Vũ Đình Trắc, who ran *Đường sống*, a newspaper that Saigon praised for its influence on Catholic evacuees.[100] Some of them had expressed resentment of Ngô Đình Diệm. But the need to repress the communist insurgency pushed critics to voice their disapproval. Growing criticism targeted both its undemocratic rule and its poor record at fighting the insurgents. A case in point is what became known as the Caravelle Manifesto. In April 1960, intellectuals and political figures, many of whom were evacuees, convened a press conference at the Caravelle hotel in Saigon and read a letter they had previously sent to the president:

> We recognize the danger of the current situation and cannot remain indifferent to the survival of our homeland....
>
> Continuous arrests have made the jails more crowded now than ever before.... Sectarian areas that were once deadly ground for the communists have become insecure and are now the guerilla zones of the Việt Minh just like other areas, which shows that the sect organizations may have been feudal but were nonetheless effective anticommunist elements. Annihilating those elements has cleared the way for the Việt Cộng, thus inadvertently lending a hand to the enemy, thus opening the gate for the communists.[101]

The situation in South Vietnam was dire. Democratic freedoms were absent. But the failure to contain communist expansion was also a prime concern.

The lack of significant results in repressing the communist insurgency through the strategic hamlets prompted evacuees to rearm. Catholics among them reconstituted armed groups. Father Hoàng Quỳnh formed self-defense militias similar to the ones that he led in Phát Diệm and mobile offensive units. The government agreed to fund and provide weapons but refused to grant these militia units autonomy from the RVNAF.[102] The priest sent young Catholics from central Vietnam to patrol in southern Vietnam, in what is now Đồng Tháp Province. According to French intelligence, on August 18, 1962, the young Catholic volunteers created the "Đồng tiến" battalion. Six months later, it defeated an entire section of the People's Liberation Armed Forces, the NLF's army, and took the weapons of two others.[103] This insurrection allowed many evacuees to resume their fight.

However, their political and military mobilization also meant that they could turn against Ngô Đình Diệm one day. This is precisely what happened between 1960 and 1963. Three attempted coups aimed to overthrow the president, the last of which succeeded, with fatal results for Diệm. Evacuees were part of two of these plots. The first was conducted by Colonel Nguyễn Chánh Thi, who was not from the north and became famous during the 1966 Buddhist uprising. Yet he was part of a group of military officers that included many Đại Việt evacuees. On November 11, 1960, in the first coup attempt, Lieutenant Colonel Vương Văn Đông, Lieutenant Colonel Nguyễn Triệu Hồng, and Colonel Phạm Văn Liễu, who was also a member of the Đại Việt, failed to seize power.[104] The VNQDĐ was behind the second attempted coup, on February 27, 1962, when bombs were dropped over the prime minister's residence, renamed

Independence Palace, killing two people. This attempt was organized by the son of Nguyễn Văn Lực, a member of the VNQDĐ who was imprisoned in 1960 on Diệm's order.[105] The evacuees were tired of Saigon's preference for eliminating enemies instead of battling communism.

The president understood that the most immediate threat to his life came not from the communists but, rather, from the remaining Đại Việt and VNQDĐ officers in the RVNAF. The seizure of an illegal publication called *For Vietnam* confirmed this concern. This publication had declared its support for fighting communism, unifying Vietnam, and assassinating Ngô Đình Nhu. Retribution came immediately. Forty-three Đại Việt and twenty-nine VNQDĐ members were arrested, and the remaining officers were forced to pledge their loyalty to the RVN.[106] Ngô Đình Nhu, the head of the Cần lào, gestured toward the evacuees, suggesting more action. In the fall of 1962, the CIA reported that Saigon had considered the possibility of having their family members create their own strategic hamlets in the north.[107] However, these initiatives could not hide the elephant in the room: nationalists, not just communists, wanted to get rid of the Diệm government.

The clergy also prepared for a leadership change. Nguyễn Tôn Hoàn, a Đại Việt leader, claimed that he had received support from the bishops Lê Hữu Từ, Phạm Ngọc Chi, and Nguyễn Văn Bình. All three declared that Catholics, except perhaps for Monsignor Ngô Đình Thục, had turned their backs on Diệm. This argument was presented to his interlocutor, Professor Wesley Fishel, so that he could convey the information to Washington.[108]

On the night of November 1, 1963, when the third and final coup succeeded, none of the officers who captured Nhu and Diệm were evacuees. However, as Ellen Hammer writes, since August 1963, six other plots had also been organized.[109] The government had begun to lose its luster in 1959. The absence of democratic freedom put South Vietnam in a bad light. Demonstrations by Buddhists protesting restrictions to their freedom of worship in May 1963 revealed to the world Saigon's authoritarian rule. In the West, public opinion was alarmed by the image of a monk setting himself on fire, raising concern over conditions there and prompting Washington to reconsider its support for Diệm. He was headed for a fall, with or without the evacuees. Nonetheless, the rocky relationship between them illustrated a disconnect in building an anticommunist state. Although both sides opposed communism, they had different goals. On one side was the United States, which drew a line at the seventeenth parallel and was committed to protecting the southern half of the country from communist expansion, and Diệm, equally focused on South Vietnam, who wanted his government to inspire the rest of the population in the north and other countries across Southeast Asia. But on the other side were the evacuees, many of whom wanted nothing less than the end of communist rule throughout Vietnam, north and south. They would not be appeased by resettlement or by the passage of time. Local and global developments only reinforced their hope that one day they would be able to achieve that goal.

CHAPTER 4

Counterrevolution

Perched on a hotel balcony in Danang in August 1964, American soldiers and Vietnamese girls jeered at passing Buddhist protesters and threw chewing gum at them.[1] Infuriated, the demonstrators burst into the hotel until the sound of automatic rifle fire, shot into the air, stopped them in their tracks. The rioters fled across the road to Thanh Bồ-Đức Lợi, a neighborhood in which Catholic evacuees had resettled ten years earlier. Believing that they were under attack, the inhabitants confronted the angry mob. People were killed on both sides, including a child crushed in the stampede.[2] Four days later, a new protest broke out in a hospital run by American staff where the wounded were being treated. Three people, together with a priest, died because of this new outburst of violence.[3] Catholics and Buddhists seemed to be waging a holy war against each other (see fig. 4.1).[4]

In 1964, South Vietnam was in total chaos because of three ongoing developments. First, the assassination of Ngô Đình Diệm and Ngô Đình Nhu on the morning of November 3, 1963, left a political vacuum in the country. Over the next few months, South Vietnam had no less than four coups and eight successive cabinets under a military junta. Political stability returned only after Air Marshal Nguyễn Cao Kỳ and General Nguyễn Văn Thiệu put down urban unrest. The second problem came from the intensifying war. Hanoi took advantage of the

FIGURE 4.1.   Rioters in Saigon in August 1964.
Source: Photograph © Mauritius Images/TopFoto, 12156301.

political instability to ramp up its war effort in the south by infiltrating larger contingents on the Hồ Chí Minh Trail. This not only intensified the armed conflict but also led some people to wonder whether Saigon should de-escalate the war and negotiate with Hanoi. Then, on November 22, 1963, the United States was shaken by the assassination of President John F. Kennedy. Presidential elections the following year precluded any US intervention. During the long period ending with the election of Lyndon B. Johnson as president, neutralization of the war in Vietnam became a real possibility. Third, in May 1963 Buddhists had begun to mobilize against the government's discrimination. These demonstrations gained momentum after Diệm was overthrown.[5] Protesters demanded retribution against members of the Ngô family, members of the Cần lao, and groups associated with Diệm, including the evacuees and Catholics. Neither group believed they had contributed to the former regime's abuse of power, nor did they feel comfortable about the political vacuum and the possibility of ending the war. What could the evacuees do in the midst of that chaos to ensure that Saigon would not pivot away from their political goals?

Scholars studying the period between the collapse of the RVN in November 1963 and the landing of US troops in March 1965 often focus on the US decision-making process and rivalry among the Vietnamese generals.[6] Some mention in passing that this period was remembered as the November 1, 1963, Revolution. But they often dismiss this designation as mere rhetoric and minimize the political change it entailed. After all, the Revolutionary Military Council (Hội đồng Quân nhân Cách mạng) had seized power from the Personalist Labor Revolutionary Party (Cần lào Nhân vị Cách mạng Đảng), so the meaning of "revolutionary" could be confusing. However, ignoring it creates another problem by failing to consider what the Vietnamese imagined they would do after Diệm was gone. In fact, the period before the US intervention was a critical juncture. People clashed in a revolution and a counterrevolution, sending shock waves across the south.

Despite its radical aspirations, the revolution was not defined by a single speech or document, in a straight line from top to bottom. Neither did one single group influence its orientation. After a period of weeks, the law and revolutionary justice established its direction, as assassinations, altercations, and discrimination determined how it was translated into practice. Buddhist demonstrators believed they led this revolutionary change because they lit the match that ended Diệm's rule. The new political leadership claimed it would conduct a revolution. But this did not mean Saigon would embrace the Buddhist activists' views.

Soon after the new regime came to power, evacuees and Catholics formed a counterrevolutionary force, limiting the scope of change. Their mobilization was triggered by three issues. First, they had to ensure that they would not be considered reactionaries. Second, they did not want South Vietnam's new direction to question the fight against communism. They knew that the political vacuum created by the revolution opened the door for foreign interference. Washington gave mixed signals, as it was dealing with the aftermath of Kennedy's assassination and an upcoming presidential election. There was no assurance that the United States would keep its promise to defend South Vietnam from communism. Third, France, several Afro-Asian countries, and the UN secretary general called for neutralization of the war in Vietnam. Many evacuees wanted the 1963 Revolution to overthrow the Ngô family—not smother their struggle against communism. Vietnam could not move toward peace.

To Be or Not to Be a Reactionary

Now that Diệm was gone, everything seemed possible.[7] Political prisoners were released. Exiles returned from France or Cambodia. Parties such as the Đại Việt and the VNQDĐ could even resume their activities. The army, now heading the state, purged people who were tied to the former regime and announced the end of rule by Cần lao.[8] "Popular militias will no longer be used for personal reasons," announced a general.[9] Unlike under the previous regime, the RVNAF controlled the state's security and administrative apparatus. What remained unclear was how generals would effect the political change wanted by the Buddhists. Should the revolution cast a wide net, or should it be limited to members of certain families and party leaders?

After revolutions, people engage in retribution in different ways, sometimes in the form of personal vendettas.[10] The 1963 Revolution also left room for maneuver. Buddhists formed a grassroots movement opposing Diệm. They believed that the RVN discriminated against them and in 1963 asked the UN to investigate.[11] The influence of Catholics and evacuees over politics remained a problematic aspect of the prior regime. This raised questions as to whether they should also become targets of the revolution.

In the days after the coup, some Catholics and even a Buddhist monk from the north believed that communists were behind sectarian violence, but soon afterward, they realized that Buddhist demonstrations continued to target Catholics.[12] Rumors spread that the new regime would allow retribution against people from northern and central Vietnam. The evacuees felt as if they had targets on their backs. Their villages created committees to lobby the provisional government not to let that happen.[13] In Biên Hòa, Catholics formed self-defense militias, armed with clubs and sticks, but then saw that they had nothing to fear. By contrast, in Tam Kỳ in central Vietnam, Buddhists allegedly destroyed thirty Catholic homes, killing six people and injuring a hundred others.[14] Local confrontations were inevitable.

Whether the government would put Catholics and evacuees on the wrong side of history was a different matter. Behind the scenes, General Dương Văn Minh, who took control of the country, was eager to maintain good relations with people who had been allied with Diệm. Saigon changed its official version of Diệm's death after a complaint by Patrick O'Connor, the Catholic News Service's correspondent.[15] The Ngô brothers had not committed suicide but had been assassinated. Dương Văn

Minh told Raymond de Jaegher, the head of the Free Pacific Association, that he regretted the death of the president and his brother.[16] But none of this was known to the public, which instead saw the government siding with the Buddhists. On December 5, 1963, the general in command of the First Tactical Region in central Vietnam declared his determination "to eliminate all remains of the former regime." The government denied that the political purge would target Catholics. It guaranteed "the equality of all religions" but sent representatives to attend the National Congress for the unification of Buddhism in Vietnam.[17] The police and the army did not stop violent Buddhist demonstrations. Worse yet, rumors circulated that a statue would commemorate the death of Quách Thị Trang, a young Buddhist student killed in the spring of 1963. This confirmed the Catholic evacuees' greatest fears. If Buddhist persecution were recognized as a force in the revolution, then Catholics would be targeted for retribution. Many could deal with the end of Diệm's rule, but a new order that would label them enemies was out of the question.

They heaved a sigh of relief on January 30, 1964, when General Nguyễn Khánh overthrew the Military Revolutionary Committee. The new cabinet included many Đại Việt members, whose commitment to the fight against communism was unquestionable. The presence of nationalist figures and the nomination of a Catholic, Nguyễn Tôn Hoàn, as the head of the Ministry of Pacification gave them some comfort.[18] But Buddhists protested because this new cabinet perpetuated the same power imbalance as the prior regime. One minister was a Catholic, and others came from north-central Vietnam. Evacuees responded that none of them had ties to Diệm. They had been imprisoned for their political views or condemned to exile overseas. Disqualifying them would be proof that the revolution was taking a wrong turn. Any reservation because of their regional or religious affiliation would lead to discrimination against Catholics and the evacuees. The general had to reassure the Buddhists that he could also lead the revolution. So the government increased the number of confiscations and arrests and organized an exhibit that denounced the Ngô family for its crimes.[19] But the Buddhist demonstrations continued, forcing the prime minister to resign on April 4. South Vietnam had become ungovernable.

Military justice judging members of the former regime could clarify the direction of the revolution. Two cases stood out: the first set an example, whereas the second determined who had become an enemy of the revolution. Ngô Đình Cẩn was the only Ngô brother who remained in Vietnam. Diệm and Nhu were dead, whereas Thục, Luyện, and Madame

Nhu had gone overseas. Ngô Đình Cẩn had also tried to flee, taking refuge at a Redemptorist monastery and then at the US consulate in Hue.[20] He was granted asylum in the United States, but the police intercepted him at the airport and arrested him.[21] Family members, the director of Catholic Relief Services, and Father Patrick O'Connor, the correspondent of the American Catholic News Service, all complained that the United States had failed to protect him, but to no avail.[22] Ngô Đình Cẩn became the highest-profile case of revolutionary justice.

The trial captivated the Vietnamese public. Hearings started on April 16, 1964, in a tense atmosphere. Less than two weeks later, Ngô Đình Cẩn, as the chief of the Cần lao, was sentenced to death for the murder of three people, the arrest of twenty others, and fraud.[23] Cẩn had hidden skeletons in his closet for a long time. In 1955, he ran a smuggling ring involving transactions with the DRV. He had to end this business, under pressure from Washington, and provoked the dismissal of several provincial leaders.[24] Cardinal Spellman demanded clemency for him. The US embassy also suggested postponing his execution because it might inflame 1.6 million Catholics living in southern Vietnam.[25] Nevertheless, Ngô Đình Cẩn and his closest associate were executed on May 9, 1964. The revolution was uncompromising.

Whether similar treatment would apply to other members of society remained unknown, until the trial of Major Đặng Sỹ. Unlike Ngô Đình Cẩn, the major was not a big shot in the Cần lao, the state, or the army, but he had led the repression of the Buddhist demonstration in May 1963, which had sparked the uprising. Much debate remains whether his order to fire MK-3 grenades or communist sabotage had been responsible for killing eight demonstrators.[26] The tribunal had to determine whether he was personally responsible for their deaths, a decision with tremendous implications. Because he was a Catholic, his indictment could lead to trials for other coreligionists.

Evacuee newspapers initially downplayed the sectarian divide.[27] But everyone was aware of the sensitive nature of the trial. Unlike the trial of Ngô Đình Cẩn, these hearings were closed to the public and not broadcast on loudspeaker.[28] Moreover, the trial was held in Saigon, rather than Hue, where the Buddhist mobilization was the greatest.[29] Buddhists continued to protest, and Catholics called for forgiveness.[30] Major Đặng Sỹ said that he had been approached with the promise of freedom, money, and a promotion twice during the trial if he would place responsibility for the repression of Buddhists on Monsignor Ngô

Đình Thục.³¹ Nonetheless, the jury decided against him, and he was sentenced to death.³² Justice was meted out.

Neither Buddhists nor Catholics were satisfied with this outcome. The former found it unacceptable that the tribunal took several days to reach that conclusion; and the latter feared retribution. Purge committees (Ủy ban Thanh trừng) in each province arrested people who were "against the supreme right of the people and the country."³³ Countless Catholics and evacuees lost their jobs. Women implored the government to release their sons or husbands who were imprisoned without trial.³⁴ Their letters decried the injustice: "The enemy of the people are the communists who are welcomed in the Chiêu hồi [a program for PAVN and NLF defectors]. The government recently freed twenty thousand of them, whereas we, anticommunist nationalists, are still being imprisoned despite being innocent."³⁵

On November 1, 1965, the new national day commemorating the anniversary of Diệm's overthrow, most of the detainees were released or had their sentences reduced.³⁶ But two years later, Father O'Connor reported that twenty-four Catholics were still being detained without trial. A witch hunt had been conducted among Catholics and evacuees.

The Church denounced this treatment. On January 20, 1964, when all the bishops but Ngô Đình Thục returned from the Second Vatican Council in Rome, they issued a statement.³⁷ If Catholics took a stance in the current situation, the Church as a whole could not become involved in it. Priests had to obey the instructions of the bishop in their diocese. The faithful had to stop fanning the flames of division: "We do not question everyone's good faith, but we perceive great danger for our country.... We strive to restore, with all our strength and at all costs, family unity in our country. Under the circumstances faced by our homeland, anyone who turns a deaf ear plays into the hands of communists. Therefore, we must recall Jesus Christ's warning: 'Any kingdom divided against itself will be ruined.' "³⁸

Catholics did not have to remain passive and could still protest and take action, but they had to respect three conditions. First, political formations, parties, and movements could not include "Catholic" or "Christian" in their name. Second, none of them could claim to speak on behalf of the Church. Third, Catholics could not join a political organization, such as the communist party, whose "doctrine and objectives [are] incompatible with the Catholic faith or whose mode of action would be contrary to Catholic values."³⁹ The same conditions applied to newspapers:

they were forbidden to spread rumors and make defamatory comments. The bishops also sent a warning to General Nguyễn Khánh: "Engaging in revolution means that you want to end whatever is wrong, to build a present and a better future. This is why the revolution must not rely on prejudice against individuals or groups.... One might wonder whether the citizens who have been arrested and imprisoned were [illegible] because they served faithfully under the prior regime or—which would be still more unjust—because they are Catholics."[40]

The bishops would not let the government punish Catholics. They authorized Father Hoàng Quỳnh to organize a movement. After leading militias in the north and a battalion in the Mekong delta, the priest now had to lead another struggle. He believed that he could mobilize three hundred sixty thousand youths. Those who were concerned about the political situation gathered as the Catholic Bloc (Khối công giáo). A smaller group recruited militants "by calling on their patriotism and faith to form the Lực lượng Đại đoàn kết [LLĐĐK; the Greater Solidarity Movement], and carry out the instructions of the Church, follow their chief Father Hoàng Quỳnh, save the nation, and eliminate communism at any time."[41] Parishes enlisted volunteers to hold protests, circulating instructions on where to walk, how to react to provocation, and which slogans to use on banners. Catholics went to war, this time against the government.

The day after Major Đặng Sỹ received his sentence, the LLĐĐK protested in most cities. In Saigon, between 150,000 and 200,000 people marched in silence.[42] Three hundred priests signed a petition.[43] The Catholic press also criticized the sentence. "This trial is unique because of the precedent it creates."[44] By condemning the officer, the court had sealed the fate of Catholics. In the Catholics' view, the court had condemned a person whom they believed to be innocent because of prejudice against a religious minority. This was the Vietnamese equivalent of the Dreyfus affair, in which a Jewish officer had been unfairly accused of treason because of widespread antisemitism in France in the late nineteenth century.

A Growing Communist Threat

Catholics also believed that far-reaching purges distracted the government from other priorities. The NLF established control of several parts of the countryside (see fig. 4.2). Shortly after the coup, communist insurgents went to an evacuee village to express their condolences about

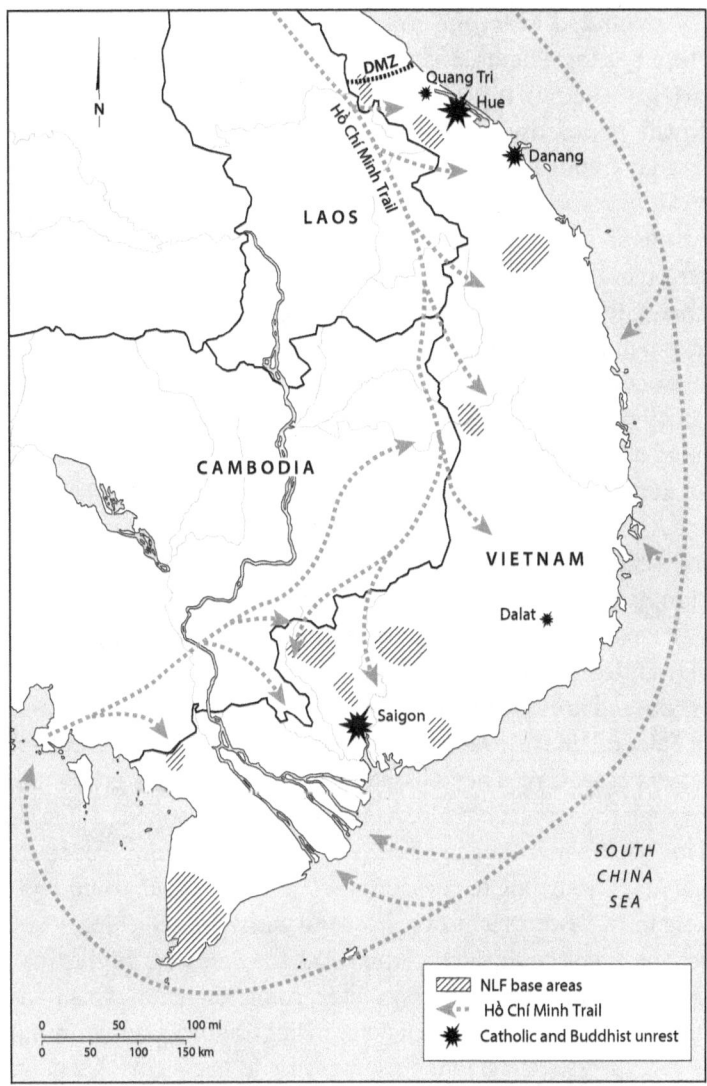

FIGURE 4.2. War in the countryside and riots in the cities in 1964.
Source: Map by Bill Nelson, adapted from the United States Military Academy, "The Enemy Situation Early 1964," accessed November 7, 2023, https://www.westpoint.edu/academics/academic-departments/history/digital-history-center/atlases/vietnam-war.

Diệm's death. They told the local priest that they would soon take over the country and recommended that they turn themselves in.[45] Catholics thought that the divisions plaguing South Vietnam only made the communists stronger and feared that the revolution would cripple the struggle against communism.

They reminded everyone that the seventeenth parallel was not a definitive border. Poems, essays, and articles in newspapers recalled memories of the north.[46] The Episcopal council sent Christmas greetings to the population on the other side of the parallel. Newspapers dedicated columns to them in their special editions for the Lunar New Year.[47] Many evacuees, including non-Catholics, also celebrated the tenth anniversary of the cease-fire. A journalist who had organized the Procession of the Sacred Land created the publication *Dân chủ mới* (*New Democracy*). It argued it was time to imagine what kind of state Vietnam needed. Communists had partitioned the country and worked as "lackeys of Chinese communists."[48] It also recalled that on July 18, 1954, about fifty thousand people had protested the partition.[49] People were reminded about this tragic past to ensure that they did not forget it.

Younger generations also commemorated the event. The General Student Association (GSA) organized a series of conferences and a new event, the Sleepless Night (*Đêm không ngủ*), in Saigon on July 20.[50] The association had changed since being re-formed in 1955. But several members of its executive committee were from the north, and others shared a similar anticommunist commitment.[51] For the Sleepless Night, almost three thousand university and high school students met at the Faculty of Arts in Saigon.[52] In the evening, the students attended talks and debated the Geneva cease-fire. They passed by the palace of the prime minister and through the streets of Saigon. At 2 a.m., they stopped to sing the national anthem to mark the moment when the agreements were signed in Geneva. After returning to the campus, the students sat around bonfires and sang until dawn in a mostly peaceful gathering. Nothing seemed to suggest the event could turn violent. Yet the Sleepless Night was not a graduation celebration. Two days later, some students explained their intention: "The spirit of the Sleepless Night allows people in cultural circles to express their belief that reason and the rightful struggles of weaker people will prevail. A Sleepless Night will awaken our comrades and compatriots to the insidious past and to reveal collaboration between colonialists and communists. The procession in the streets of the capital is an exhortation to compatriots and the government. They will show the same unshakable determination as the students."[53]

The GSA wanted to raise awareness about the gravity of the situation in South Vietnam. The communists were enemies of the country, and the number one priority remained national unification.

The government seized this opportunity to show its commitment to fighting communism. Major General Đỗ Mậu, an officer from Quảng

Bình, created a cultural program, "with roots in the nation, an understanding of culture in the present, and a direction for culture in the future."[54] Unsurprisingly, as an evacuee involved in cultural initiatives, Đỗ Mậu highlighted Vietnamese unity in his campaigns. One of the first initiatives was to celebrate the Hùng kings, the mythical royal line from which the Vietnamese people supposedly grew in the Bronze Age.[55] The Association of Confucian Studies (Hội Khổng học) and the Association of Northern Vietnamese (Hội Bắc Việt tương tế) applauded this initiative. Previous regimes did not consistently celebrate this anniversary.[56] To Đỗ Mậu, this "created a feeling of solidarity, a sense of patriotism, a reminder to the people in the south and in the occupied territories they were descendants of the Hùng kings."[57] This celebration showed that communists had "no spirituality" (vô thần) and "no country" (vô tổ quốc).[58] The current regime could also set itself apart. "Although citizens held this celebration dear to their hearts, the former administration ignored it for nine years," Saigon declared.[59] Hence, evacuees had no reason for doubt. Unlike Diệm, this military leadership pretended that it was poised to reunify the country.

On July 19, 1964, the tenth anniversary of the cease-fire, the government organized a Week of National Shame (Tuần quốc hận), with a ceremony commemorating the cease-fire as an infamy. During the ceremony, General Nguyễn Khánh approached two chests, representing the northern and southern halves of Vietnam. He took some soil from each of them and mixed them together, recalling what Bảo Đại and the evacuees had done earlier.[60] Saigon reaffirmed its commitment to the reunification of Vietnam and reused prior symbols of unity.

The ceremony was well attended, with an estimate by the official news agency of a million people.[61] That estimate may have been inflated, and the government may have asked civil servants to attend the event, as it did in later years.[62] But a majority of the crowd had attended spontaneously.[63] The newspaper Thời luận reported that the organizers did not expect such high attendance.[64] The call to march to the north expressed at the ceremony resonated with many of the evacuees, including students. The president of the GSA, an evacuee, disapproved of the disparities in the recruitment of new soldiers: "In a march to the north, there would be a general conscription, and students would volunteer for the front line."[65] Remaining members of the Cần lao urged the government to launch a military intervention.[66] Some even sent letters to the government. Proposals abounded to "make the Việt Cộng pay," "form a suicide squad," and take advantage of the rising water level in the spring to reconquer the north.[67]

"Northern migrant ethnic minorities" (đồng bào thiểu số Bắc Việt di cư) also demanded the end of their dispersion, the creation of new villages, and seats in the National Assembly.[68] They, too, offered to create a unit in the march to the north.[69] Catholics went further.[70] One group in Hố Nai submitted a petition requesting that weapons be given to the ten thousand men in the LLĐĐK and take the battle to the north.[71] For so many evacuees, fighting communism remained the absolute priority even though it had become more unrealistic than ever now that communist troops were fighting in the south. Liberating Vietnam would require a victory on both sides of the seventeenth parallel. But the idea of a march to the north remained a powerful symbol, calling on people to resist communism.

Calls for a Cease-Fire

The political instability in southern Vietnam was not the evacuees' only cause for concern. As in any other revolution, foreign powers could take advantage of the situation, in this case by diverting the country from the trajectory envisioned by them. Influential voices called for an end to the armed conflict, and the notion of a cease-fire in the region was not new. In July 1962 a second Geneva conference ended the armed conflict in Laos, which neither Hanoi nor Washington had wanted to escalate.[72] US foreign policy was hampered by indecision after Kennedy's assassination. Now, many Afro-Asian countries, the United Nations, and France all wanted to end the war in Vietnam.

Communist insurgents took advantage of the urban chaos to gain ground in the countryside. Soon, the guerrilla war escalated into a full-scale war, and still the United States did not increase its military presence. Moreover, its embassy appeared to have played an ambiguous role in the coup against Diệm and in the confrontation between Buddhists and Catholics.[73] Catholics made no secret of their suspicions. A Catholic weekly criticized the decision by the state to name the square and erect a monument in front of Notre Dame Cathedral, in central Saigon, after John F. Kennedy.[74] Some protesters criticized US ambassador Henry Cabot Lodge for having encouraged the coup against Diệm, and others vandalized the monument.[75] Saigon first dispatched guards to protect it, but then removed it, claiming that doing so would prevent internal criticism and enemy propaganda.[76] The United States was not the dependable ally that the evacuees needed.

The greatest danger came from calls to end the war. Many Afro-Asian countries had criticized the superpowers' expansionism after the

Bandung Conference in 1955. They also feared that China, which tried to lead this emerging movement, could mobilize its diaspora and destabilize governments in Southeast Asia.[77] In their view, the cease-fire declared in Laos in 1962 was a success. It eliminated a major threat to peace, prevented further Chinese expansionism, and protected a country's sovereignty. Why not do the same in Vietnam in 1964, considering what happened for Laos two years earlier?

These calls for peacekeeping were seconded by U Thant, the UN secretary general, who believed that the situation in Korea and Indochina had been dealt with in 1954 and Laos in 1962, so now it was time to organize another Geneva conference to find a solution for Vietnam. U Thant made several attempts to promote peace.[78] Articles in evacuee publications criticized these initiatives. According to them, even the ICC had recognized that Hanoi was infiltrating troops into South Vietnam through Laos and Cambodia.[79]

The third voice calling for the end of the war came from France. Charles de Gaulle had changed his country's perception of French colonies. He had hoped to re-create the French empire in 1945, but the Algerian war ending in 1962 made him realize that Paris needed support from its former colonies in the new postwar context.[80] De Gaulle understood that he had to become closer to Algiers in order to become more independent from Washington.[81] This repositioning applied to Hanoi, too. The armed conflict in Vietnam had to be disengaged from Cold War politics so that former colonies could support his own quest for independence from the United States. De Gaulle also believed that the time was right because Moscow and Beijing were growing apart in the wake of de-Stalinization of the Soviet Union sparked by Khrushchev in 1956. Rapprochement with China, with an official recognition in January 1964, assisted Paris's attempt to break free of Washington and extend an olive branch to Hanoi.[82] This could bring Paris closer to the nonaligned countries, including Cambodia, whose chief of state, Norodom Sihanouk, also called for a cease-fire. In October 1964, the second nonaligned conference in Cairo urged foreign powers to respect the commitments made at the 1954 and 1962 Geneva Conferences. They demanded a third conference to find a peaceful solution to the war in Vietnam.[83] The stars were aligning for a cease-fire. Not only was the United States nearly absent but also France's diplomatic shift converged with the UN and nonaligned countries' hopes for de-escalating the Cold War.

The evacuees immediately reacted to the French proposals. On December 23, 1963, just days after de Gaulle announced a three-step plan to end the war, two thousand people protested in front of the French embassy in Saigon. In the following weeks, people protested at the Alliance Française, at French high schools, and at the French cultural center.[84] Protesters attacked any symbols in Saigon that were reminiscent of the former colonial power. The peak of these anti-French protests came with the celebration of the tenth anniversary of the Geneva agreements. During a massive demonstration, people spotted students carrying a model of de Gaulle shaking hands with Hồ Chí Minh. A group of students desecrated the monument dedicated to French soldiers lost in the two world wars at a roundabout, steps away from the Faculty of Arts. The students shouted: "Down with the French colonialists!" "Down with de Gaulle!" and "Down with the Geneva Accords!"[85] They removed the bronze inscriptions on the statues and threw paint on them, and ten days later they dismantled them with chisels, hammers, and ropes.

The situation had in fact turned violent during the Sleepless Night, and riots targeted France because of its calls for a cease-fire. Rioters burst into the French embassy grounds, where they bashed the hood of a car and set another one on fire. They broke the windows of the main floor and tore the tricolor flag into pieces. The message was clear: France should not interfere in Vietnamese affairs. Two days after this incident, the GSA held a press conference.[86] It took responsibility for destruction of the war memorial but refused to be held accountable for what happened at the embassy. The GSA president declared: "We only dismantle symbols. . . . But later, we will use more civilized means to dismantle these shameful remains, because this statue does not represent the soldiers who fought for the independence of this country."[87] He also demanded that the government do three things: end diplomatic relations with France, nationalize all French property, and construct a memorial to Vietnamese soldiers.[88] The decolonization had not gone far enough. It was time to eradicate any remaining French presence.

Domestic Calls

Part of the population in South Vietnam supported international plans to end the armed conflict. Under the RVN, only a few people, such as Phan Quang Đán, had called for talks with Hanoi.[89] After the war escalated, large portions of society, not a handful of intellectuals, began to ask the same question: Was it time to escalate or should Saigon end the war?

People were unsure what to do with the insurgency. Overseas Vietnamese based in Phnom Penh and Paris had already tried to find an alternative to armed conflict. The two cities had always been a haven for political exiles, a forum to create a third force, different from the communists and nationalists, and, of course, a place to hold meetings under the radar.[90] But the new regime's open-door policy allowed people and ideas to spread back into South Vietnam. Some of them were calls for a cease-fire. Central Vietnam, where the Buddhist movement was influential, became another epicenter of this movement. Therefore, it is not surprising that a deadly riot opposing Buddhists and Catholics happened in Thanh Bồ-Đức Lợi, on the outskirts of Danang, along the coast of central Vietnam. Their confrontation was not merely about religion. It also concerned different views about what South Vietnam should do.

Not all Catholics were anticommunist, but the Church had become a powerful institution that opposed the spread of communism. In contrast, Buddhist activists believed that the time had come to impose a cease-fire and make peace with the north. The influential bonze Thích Quảng Liên created the Movement for Peace and advocated the end of the fratricidal conflict.[91] Although the historian Robert Topmiller has claimed that the bonze was critical of US intervention, the movement's manifesto in 1965 demanded the end of the war, the withdrawal of US and communist troops from the south, and the departure of Soviet and Chinese advisers from the north.[92] This manifesto was neither the result of communist sabotage nor merely the expression of anti-American sentiment. The movement wanted to end the human loss from the armed conflict.

Separatist movements also threatened the territorial integrity of South Vietnam. A Committee for the People's Salvation, created in Hue in August 1963, demanded political autonomy and a cease-fire in central Vietnam. France and Japan, which called for de-escalation of the armed conflict, could support a new buffer zone.[93] However, the evacuees saw this proposition as dangerous. If central Vietnam were separated from the south, then reunifying the country someday would become twice as difficult.

Some factions in the LLĐĐK attacked this movement. The leader of Tự do dân chủ (Democratic Freedom) was an evacuee who had been born in Thanh Hóa. His father had died in a DRV prison, and he went to the south in 1954.[94] To him, the threat of government repression was second only to the infiltration of communists in Buddhist circles. He saw the Committee for the People's Salvation mobilizing students in central Vietnam as a facade. Hence, he created a movement for authentic studies (Sinh viên Học sinh bảo vệ giáo dục thuần túy) targeting the student population and disrupted a rival organization's activities from Saigon to Danang. Buddhism, from their perspective, had become a vehicle for communist propaganda.

Evacuees and Catholics who opposed communist infiltration expressed their ideas in various ways. The GSA volunteered to "awaken consciousness and stand ready to take up the arms for the homeland."[95] The LLĐĐK and its radical student faction Tự dân were strictly Catholic. Many resorted to violent demonstration against Buddhists and the Committee for the People's Salvation in central Vietnam.[96] Other initiatives tried to show unity. Together with other religious leaders, Father Hoàng Quỳnh created the Interreligious Committee against Communism and Neutralism (Liên tôn chống cộng chống trung lập). Other movements became large, including the United Front against Neutrality, which gathered the Đại Việt, the VNQDĐ, and Catholic evacuees; and the Front for Unification against Communism (Mặt trận thống nhất chống cộng), comprising the Hòa Hảo as well as political figures, such as Nghiêm Xuân Thiện, the publisher of *Thời luận,* and Dr. Hoàng Cơ Bình, the man who wanted to leave stay-behind operatives in the north after the partition in 1954 to organize an armed rebellion against the DRV.[97] Regardless of their modus operandi, they opposed both communism and neutrality. Even after the US military intervention chose war over peace on behalf of the Vietnamese, some of these divisions remained in the National Assembly of the Second Republic of Vietnam.[98] Ten years after their evacuation, these nationalists refused to make peace with Hanoi regardless of the cost.

Defending Catholic Activism

The final and most dangerous actor that could end the war was Saigon itself. General Nguyễn Khánh's ouster in January 1965 facilitated the rise to power of a new duo. General Nguyễn Văn Thiệu and Major Nguyễn Cao Kỳ used the army to suppress urban violence and Buddhist demonstrations.[99] They formed a provisional government and organized a constituent assembly, leading to the creation of the Second Republic of Vietnam (RVN) on April 1, 1967. But before this government achieved stability, Saigon made another decision that triggered a furor among Catholics. Three days before his resignation, Nguyễn Khánh appointed the next prime minister, Phan Huy Quát, who tried to end the armed conflict and limit Catholic mobilization.

After the departure of the general and apart from the official position of chief of state, held by Phan Khắc Sửu, Phan Huy Quát was free to form his own cabinet. He had served as minister of culture in the ASVN. During the First Indochina War, he strove to find international allies in the struggle against the DRV.[100] In 1965, however, Phan Huy Quát wanted to achieve the exact opposite. Bùi Diễm, who was an old friend and held the position of secretary of state, recalled these unique circumstances. The United States started the bombing of Vietnam with Operation Rolling Thunder only four days before his nomination. Phan Huy Quát and Bùi Diễm resented the US forces for landing in Danang in March 1965, without even notifying Saigon.[101] The war intensified whether he liked it or not. The Americans had their own agenda and did not consult Saigon.

The Phan Huy Quát cabinet tried to regain control of the situation by attempting negotiations with Hanoi with the help of Trần Văn Tuyên, a lawyer who held the position of deputy prime minister for planification. In practice, the nationalist had a long experience of diplomacy as he had attended the Geneva Conference in 1954 and would explore ways to implement this new policy.[102] As a diplomat, he traveled to Rome to see the pope and to North African countries, such as Algeria.[103] He sought the support of other former French colonies before requesting the backing of Latin American and European countries for removing Vietnam from the Cold War.[104] On his way to Europe, he was also supposed to meet Monsignor Lê Hữu Từ in Rome in order to ask him to calm down Catholics.[105] These initiatives were part of a larger strategy to enable the Vietnamese to decide matters for themselves. But some evacuees regarded this as capitulation to pressure by Hanoi.[106]

This time, a cease-fire could succeed. American intervention had intensified the armed conflict, but this diplomatic campaign could de-escalate the war. On the day that Phan Huy Quát was nominated as prime minister, the LLĐĐK held a meeting to discuss its position.[107] Most were critical because Phan Huy Quát represented the ASVN's inertia and was incapable of achieving independence from Paris. It was precisely because people like him had been weak, they thought, that France negotiated on behalf of nationalists in 1954. Catholics of the LLĐĐK did not recognize his legitimacy because he had been put in office by an undemocratic government.[108]

The LLĐĐK's central committee agonized for days because the government had failed to declare its position regarding communism and neutrality.[109] But in the following weeks, their doubts vanished, as Phan

Huy Quát revealed his program. At the international level, Saigon sought rapprochement with Afro-Asian countries, perhaps including China. The second Afro-Asian Conference, to be held in Algiers in 1965, ten years after the first meeting in Bandung, could discuss peace in Vietnam.[110] Evacuees believed that South Vietnam's attendance at this meeting would be political suicide.[111] Because of China's influence over the movement, ending the war would mean recognition of Hanoi as the only government in Vietnam. This Afro-Asian summit could attract thirty states in agreement with a French general, a Cambodian leader, and a dozen nonaligned countries. Moreover, the meeting would be held in Algiers, where another National Liberation Front had triumphed, like the DRV, and ended colonial rule.

The prospect of such a meeting distressed the evacuees. In February 1965, some of them protested to prevent Saigon's participation. A student publication highlighted three reasons for their position: the inexperienced cabinet was no match for Hanoi; the government did not represent the population; and Saigon advocated "a policy of neutralization, giving an advantage to the communist side."[112] Phan Huy Quát had agreed to a cease-fire in 1954, and he might repeat that mistake if he attended this conference.

In June 1965, again, the conference organizers showed signs of weakness when they could not determine whether the Soviet Union could attend as "a great Asian power."[113] Saigon's willingness to end the armed conflict became even more concerning because its delegation stopped in France before traveling to Algeria. The evacuees repeated their opposition to the event.[114] The LLĐĐK organized a general assembly on May 9, 1965. A hundred and fifty people signed a motion denouncing communism, domestic voices that called for ending the war, and Saigon's attempts to attend the Afro-Asian Conference.[115] In fact, the conference never took place because Ahmed Ben Bella's government in Algeria was ousted in a coup. But many in the weeks and months prior to that cancellation worried an international conference could decide the fate of Vietnam again.

Moreover, the evacuees had other reasons for opposing the government in Saigon. Phan Huy Quát led the first government that was trying to restrict social and political activities of Catholics. Previous governments had feared their mobilization and demanded that police collect intelligence on the most prominent activists. But Phan Huy Quát's administration tried to prevent interreligious violence, drafting a bill regulating the activities of religious groups. Its biggest mistake was to circulate the draft for comment. It established common rules for activities by Buddhist, Catholic, and other religious groups. However, from the perspective of Catholics, this bill was a frontal attack on their freedom of religion. Their initial opposition turned into outright hostility. On May 25, 1965, Phan reshuffled his cabinet, eliminating three men whose anticommunist stance was unshakable and nominating Nguyễn Trung Trinh, a French citizen, as minister of economy. That was the straw that broke the camel's back. Catholics saw this nomination as "humiliating."[116] Phan Huy Quát had not cut his ties with France and was ready to diminish the anticommunist struggle. In June, their fury reached a peak. Catholics criticized other evacuees who remained moderate on the issue. The priests in charge of the newspapers Hòa bình (Peace) and Xây dựng (To Build) criticized other journalists like Tô Văn for supporting the government. Although they believed Tô Văn was undoubtedly "resolute and full of hatred" for communism, his position suggested otherwise.[117]

However, the main opposition targeted the government. The LLĐĐK described a three-step plan of action: mobilization of the population, street demonstrations, and a general uprising to seize power.[118] This time, the ultimate goal was overthrowing the government. On June 7, 1965, evacuee Catholics gathered en masse and then attended a political meeting to celebrate the first anniversary of the LLĐĐK's formation and commemorate six young Catholics who had been "killed in action."[119] The wording used was not accidental. These men had not died fighting the communist insurgency but, rather, in opposing Buddhist demonstrators and the government. Protests continued until June 12, when the largest one demanded Phan Huy Quát's resignation.[120]

The third step in their plan for Catholic mobilization was never reached. During the summer of 1965, the Catholics never came close to staging a coup. But the government realized that it could not govern. The head of state, Phan Khắc Sửu, and the prime minister, Phan Huy Quát, continually countered each other's moves. This suggested that there could be no progress toward political stability. On June 11, they both resigned, leaving control of the state to generals, who eventually appointed Marshal Nguyễn Cao Kỳ, an evacuee serving in the air forces, as prime minister. The election of General Nguyễn Văn Thiệu as president of the Second Republic of Vietnam soon followed in 1967, keeping Kỳ as prime minister until 1971 and remaining in power as president until April 1975. However, this political change had serious implications for those who believed in an anticommunist Vietnam. This military leadership meant that the war would continue.

As the historian Fred Logevall has shown, the "long 1964" corresponds to the time of uncertainty in US foreign policy from Kennedy's assassination to Johnson's election as president and his decision to intervene directly in Vietnam. For the population of southern Vietnam, this time was just as long, but it was a moment of revolution and counterrevolution.[121] The evacuees had spent the major part of the decade trying to ensure their return to the north. Changes in local and international conditions made them realize that the most urgent political struggle was in the south. The evacuees opposed the notion that they could become reactionaries. The prospect of losing their rights and privileges as citizens of South Vietnam was unfathomable, and it was not possible for Catholics to abandon their capacity for organizing themselves. What was the most striking, though, was their determination to fight communism. Ngô Đình Diệm was gone, and Saigon showed no sign of stability. The evacuees were the only ones forcefully calling for a war against communism. Ten years after the partition, they had not given up on the idea of a march to the north, although they recognized that it had become increasingly elusive. The battle had come to them in the south and fighting communism had become a matter of survival. The self-awareness that emerged with the evacuation had not disappeared. Activists for partition and the younger generation not only expressed a refusal to make peace but were ready to go to war with the state and fellow southern Vietnamese.

Chapter 5

Peace in Vietnam

In late 1965, Catholics around the world contemplated two very different concepts of peace. On December 8, the NLF announced that "in view of the religious beliefs of our Catholic compatriots," it would hold a twelve-hour truce starting on Christmas night.[1] The pope seized this olive branch to call for an end to the war in Vietnam. In an address at St. Peter's Square in Rome on December 19, he declared that this could pave the way for "reflection, negotiation, and finally peace."[2] Meanwhile, on the tarmac at Tân Sơn Nhứt airport in Saigon, Cardinal Spellman affirmed that peace was precisely the goal of the war effort.[3] The same discussion occurred among Vietnamese Catholics. *Xây dựng* (*To Build*), a daily newspaper run by evacuees, insisted that only victory over communism could bring peace.[4] In contrast, on January 1, 1966, a few Catholic priests published a letter demanding all parties, both north and south, end the war.[5] Vietnamese had been at war against the insurgency led by the NLF since 1960, but in March 1965 the US intervention on the ground dramatically intensified the armed conflict. How did the evacuees react now that the war they wanted had come?

Most of the literature on the period of the US intervention focuses on the creation of a Second Republic of Vietnam (RVN), its electoral politics, economic reforms, diplomatic strategy, and attempts to create, yet again, a credible alternative to the DRV in the south.[6] Recent works have underscored debates among Vietnamese intellectuals, students, and associations about the war.⁷ This chapter looks at the evacuees' reaction to the war and worldwide mobilization, through their opinions and interpretation of political events in their newspapers. Saigon was committed to war, but many realized that things were not happening the way they had hoped. Other people, especially Christians in the West, did not reach the same conclusions about a full-scale armed conflict. Although some believed communism threatened freedom of religion, others thought the DRV protected this right and fought against a foreign invasion. Central to this shift in perception was the role of overseas Vietnamese, especially Father Trần Tam Tỉnh, a Catholic priest, because he gave authenticity to international calls for peace. These discussions about the war and the role of religion in South Vietnam and abroad startled many evacuees. Not only had their dream of returning to the north become more distant, but Catholics among them also understood that Rome and Western Christians refused to support their crusade against communism.

A Disappointing War

Intensification of the armed conflict after the US intervention in 1965 did not bring about the unity sought by many evacuees. In fact, the widespread devastation brought on by this escalation caused many people to doubt the need to keep fighting. The Second Republic of Vietnam, whose Constitutional Assembly started meeting in 1966, did not change its course in the war. Two military officers held the highest positions in the government. General Nguyễn Văn Thiệu served as president, and Air Marshal Nguyễn Cao Kỳ was prime minister. This assured the representation of the army's interests in the government and the country's commitment to the war.

Washington held all the cards to repel a communist expansion. The newly elected president, Lyndon B. Johnson, had claimed in August 1964 that two northern Vietnamese missiles had been fired on the US Navy in the South China Sea. The US Congress approved the Tonkin Gulf resolution that month, allowing the president to take "all necessary steps, including the use of armed force, to assist any member or protocol state of the Southeast Asia Collective Defense Treaty requesting assistance in defense of its freedom."⁸ The White House and Congress both believed that the United States had to use military means to prevent communism from taking over southern Vietnam. Washington and Saigon dismissed the idea that people within the south had rebelled against their government.

Instead, a white paper reinforced the idea that South Vietnam was an independent state being invaded by the DRV.⁹ US soldiers and a few allied troops intervened on the ground. The world hung on any new developments of the war.¹⁰ The unique circumstances that many had hoped for finally materialized. What happened in Vietnam would determine the fate of the country and the outcome of the Cold War.

However, these evacuees faced unexpected challenges. Although the US Army had put boots on the ground, many realized that its commanders were acting like patrons, rather than partners. This was why, when US troops landed in Danang in March 1965, Phan Huy Quát, who like other evacuees came from the north-central region, saw the danger. This unannounced arrival foreshadowed an unequal relationship, rather than military support from a dependable partner.

The escalation in the war also seemed to be out of control. The US bombing of the DRV never targeted the territory too far north of Hanoi, for fear of triggering Chinese intervention. But it razed entire cities, such as Vinh, to the ground and forced the evacuation of hundreds of thousands to the countryside.¹¹ Explosives, defoliant, and napalm were dropped in the south and along the Hồ Chí Minh Trail, causing irreparable damage. On the ground, the US armed forces used a poorly trained conscription army, for which it compensated with superior firepower, technology, and mobility through air transport. Hence, patrols went on search-and-destroy missions to identify communist bases. Air support brought platoons to this invisible front line and back to safety. Meanwhile, US aviators carpet-bombed the countryside and the highlands to reveal infiltration routes. The war created immeasurable devastation, human loss, and disruption.

This unprecedented destruction led early advocates of war against communism to shift their views. In the winter of 1964–1965, floods caused major suffering on both sides of the seventeenth parallel. Fernand Parrel, a founder of Vietnamese personalism, called for a ceasefire in a letter to the National Red Cross Leagues and Pax Christi.¹² The missionary called on everyone to remember that the Church had fought for peace.¹³ Vietnam still bore the scars of an "atrocious memory," the famine of 1945, which had taken millions of lives and could be repeated in the aftermath of these floods.¹⁴ Vietnamese were all in the same country. This natural disaster raised questions about the need to continue the war effort.

A few evacuees also changed sides. Dr. Phạm Văn Huyền, the former head of the COMIGAL, cochaired the new Committee for the

Defense of Peace and demanded an end to the armed conflict in February 1965.[15] Although its members are often cast as communist agents in the literature, some ambiguity remains. Phạm Văn Huyến's daughter, Madame Ngô Bá Thành, who was a lawyer, became an important advocate of the Third Force in the 1970s and was married to a prominent NLF leader.[16] Yet Phạm Văn Huyến's statements following his arrest do not establish that he was part of the front, as some have claimed. A police inquiry identified continuity between the members of this committee and those of the 1955 Movement for the Defense of Peace.[17] But, in reality, the groups in 1955 and 1965 were different. Whereas Nguyễn Hữu Thọ, the NLF leader, was a member of the earlier one, the later one did not have high-ranking communists. The police officer responsible for the investigation was quite disappointed, as he had not caught any prominent communist members.[18] Nor was it possible to establish that Phạm Văn Huyến had been the movement's mastermind. In the weeks after the Tết holidays celebrating the Lunar New Year in 1965, Phạm Văn Huyến had joined at the last minute a group of friends meeting at a luncheon.[19] These intellectuals wanted to create something that might relieve the pain of their fellow compatriots. So they formed the Committee for the Defense of Peace to call for an end of the war. Many of those who served on the board were from sixty-five to eighty years old. They did not grow up surrounded by the RVN propaganda, nor were they young nationalists during the First Indochina War. Most were well-established professionals by the end of World War II. They had lived through colonization and Japanese occupation, and some had undergone the famine in the north in 1945.[20] Their diverse and long experience in the struggle for independence led them to one conclusion: too much suffering had occurred already.

The government sought to punish someone by example and exiled the three leaders of the committee to the DRV. "From the moment that Tôn Thất Dương Ky, Cao Minh Chiếm, and Phạm Văn Huyến cross the seventeenth parallel, they will no longer be citizens of this free south."[21] One officer joked about dropping them into North Vietnam by parachute.[22] In fact, the deportation became a public event to which foreign correspondents were invited. On March 19, 1965, a crowd gathered on both sides of the Hiền Lương Bridge, the main crossing point in the demilitarized zone between South and North Vietnam.[23] Soldiers escorted the three men to the bridge and prevented a dozen photographers and the crowd from approaching them. In the press, other evacuees called the committee's call for peace "communism in disguise." One newspaper even published the names of the 358 persons who signed their motion calling for peace.[24] This event revealed important fissures within southern Vietnam. Some prominent figures who had personified the opposition to partition now wanted to end the war.

New Global Christian Connections

Another major transformation that influenced the evacuees' worldview was in Christianity. The Second Vatican Council of the Roman Catholic Church, convened mostly to update the role of the Church in society, began in 1962 and concluded three years later. This included creating dialogue with other Christian denominations and adherents of other faiths. It also permitted the use of the vernacular in mass and abolition of the Index, which listed the names of books deemed heretical to the Catholic Church.[25] The Church could not remain isolated in the belief that it held the only acceptable truth. It had to open up to other views and become an active part of society, including in mission countries. The pace of change varied from one place to another. But it was decisive in Muslim and Buddhist countries, where the Church had been criticized by some independence movements.[26] The Church could not risk being expelled there as it had been from China. In newly independent countries, such as Algeria, the hierarchy put aside its proselytizing mission. Turning to social action, it decided to become a Church among Muslims.[27] This also had implications for Vietnam. Reading between the lines, Catholics had to refrain from mobilizing around their faith to oppose the government or Buddhist movements. Catholics who respected this new direction had to open up to others in Vietnam.

The same resignation applied to communism. Although Rome opposed atheism, it exercised pragmatism in its diplomatic relations.[28] On April 11, 1963, Pope John XXIII issued the encyclical *Pacem in Terris*, which suggested coexistence and collaboration with political regimes, even those at odds with their faith. His successor, Paul VI, pursued a policy of rapprochement. He supported the UN's mission to keep the peace and established relationships with socialist countries. The call to foster ecumenical dialogue allowed Catholics to reach out to those in other Christian denominations. They formed a joint forum, the World Council of Churches, along with many Protestants, Anglicans, and Eastern Orthodox. A series of conferences called Pacem in Terris discussed how Christians could promote peace on earth.[29] Some of them took a more active role early in the war. In 1965, two Quakers and a Catholic worker set themselves on fire in front of, respectively, UN headquarters in New York City and the Pentagon in Washington, DC, to protest US intervention in Vietnam. But the vast majority only contemplated what the pope's call for peace meant and reconsidered their position on the Cold War.

This emerging Christian peace movement merged with public advocacy for protecting human rights. The historian Samuel Moyn has shown that Christian support of human dignity paved the way for the interest in protecting human rights after World War II.[30] International law specialists attempted to prove that the US bombing of civilians in Vietnam constituted a genocide. These efforts did not succeed, mainly because the definition of genocide in the 1948 Convention for the Prevention and Punishment of the Crime of Genocide reduced its applicability to situations similar to the Holocaust.[31] But some still tried to make this case, and Christian networks supported their efforts. The Clergy and Laymen Concerned about Vietnam, formed in October 1965, supported the research of international law specialists in making the case for US war crimes in Vietnam. Three years later, Seymour Melman and Richard Falk published evidence that the US armed forces had committed crimes against humanity in their treatment of prisoners of war, civilian targets, and weapons use. Page after page, they produced news clippings and reports to support their case.[32] Christian networks that advocated for human rights had to denounce these atrocities.

Hanoi quickly seized this opportunity. The DRV supported the Russell Tribunal, a symbolic initiative launched by the British intellectual Bertrand Russell and other prominent personalities, such as the French philosopher Jean-Paul Sartre, to examine the legality of the US intervention.[33] As a symbolic tribunal, they had no jurisdiction but considered that everyone, in the name of humanity, had to address this question. Hồ Chí Minh had corresponded with Russell since 1963. Hanoi eventually committed the time, money, and investigating teams to collect evidence. This helped the DRV denounce "the war crimes of American imperialism" (điều tra tội ác chiến tranh của đế quốc Mỹ ở Việt Nam).[34] This symbolic trial amplified growing concern about atrocities around the world.

However, Hanoi's most important activities were directed at the Christian community. The networks connecting Catholics vertically to Rome and horizontally to their coreligionists overseas had damaged the DRV's reputation in 1954. But ten years later, they could be turned to Hanoi's advantage. In this context, the NLF's call for a temporary cease-fire on Christmas Eve 1965 comes as no surprise. The truce was respected, and Pope Paul VI urged the states involved in the armed conflict, especially Saigon, to "foresee serene and open negotiations."[35] The Vatican also called on Hanoi, Moscow, and Beijing, in private correspondence, to "spare no effort" to "encourage" a cease-fire, achieve "peace" and "protect the country's independence."[36] Hanoi ordered party cadres to respect the rights of Buddhists and Catholics by not using religious sites to store manure or open improvised maternity wards. In addition, they had to remember that everyone had contributed to the struggle for independence.[37] By the end of 1966, communists had revised their public relations strategy. The DRV invited Harrison Salisbury, the first Western reporter there who had no communist affiliation, to visit Hanoi.[38] His visit was timed to coincide with Christmas so that he could witness another truce, Catholics freely attending mass, and later the resumption of US bombing of the north. Hanoi had created a bridge between Western Catholics and Rome and ensured that nothing would compromise this new relationship.

This rapprochement deeply divided Catholics everywhere. Cardinal Spellman insisted that his interpretation of the Second Vatican Council remained valid.

> The Council Decree ... stated: "As long as the danger of war remains and there is no competent and sufficiently powerful authority at the International level, Governments cannot be denied the right to legitimate defense, once every means of peaceful settlement has been exhausted." ... It is in this light that I view our armed forces now struggling in Vietnam, and it is because of their defensive and peace-making role that I journey to them to bring whatever measure of consolation it is in my power to convey.[39]

A permanent peace meant the elimination of communism. This reasoning explained precisely why US troops were fighting. At a mass taped for broadcast on television in Saigon, Cardinal Spellman declared: "This war in Vietnam is, I believe, a war for civilization. Certainly, it is not a war of our seeking. It is a war thrust upon us and we cannot yield to tyranny."[40] Father Patrick O'Connor relayed the cardinal's interpretation of peace and highlighted his popularity with the troops.[41] Paul Yu Pin, the archbishop of Nanjing, who lived in exile in Taiwan, continued to extol the importance of regaining control over mainland China. The Chinese bishop, who in 1969 became one of the seven new cardinals from the developing world, believed that it was more important than ever. The Cultural Revolution, which began in 1966, was tearing China apart.

He believed that it was up to Christians to prepare for a resurrection in Chinese culture, including Confucianism, which had been repressed under the communist regime.[42] To them, peace meant total victory over communism.

Many Catholic evacuees in Vietnam agreed. *Xây dựng* commented on the pope's initiatives in its Christmas issue editorial.[43] The editorial did not oppose the idea of peace. But the issue and a supplement to it insisted that it could only mean liberation from communist rule.[44] The editor of *Bản thông tin công giáo hàng tuần* (*Vietnamese Catholic Information Weekly Bulletin*) gave a radio address to Catholics in the north on Christmas Eve. "Why, in all four solemn sessions of Vatican II, couldn't a single bishop in the north attend? . . . How much suffering for the last twenty years must compatriots in the south endure, and how many soldiers and people in the north must fall to uphold the spirit of patriotism and humanity and, instead, serve the inhumane ambitions of a handful of political leaders?"[45]

Communist rule was a threat to peace because it isolated Catholics in the north from the rest of the Church. An opinion piece declared, if American colonists could achieve independence from Britain, the Russians could withstand Napoleon's armies, and the Chinese could resist a Japanese invasion, then Vietnamese could defend themselves.[46] Vietnamese Catholics also reacted to the pope's address at St. Peter's Square. They could only speculate on Rome's actual contacts with Washington and Moscow.[47] Nevertheless, *Xây dựng* reassured readers again. According to the publication, these new developments only meant that the Vietnamese had to be ready in case the foreign powers tried to negotiate, as in Geneva in 1954.[48] As long as peace remained an abstract goal that did not involve the immediate cessation of hostilities, they respected Rome's call to end the armed conflict. They could even claim that the peace to which the pope referred was not a surrender but a reminder that communism threatened their country.

In contrast, a small but vocal minority demanded an end to the war. The Holy See's call had opened a new path. As the historian Claire Trần Thị Liên has shown, peace was no longer taboo.[49] On January 1, 1966, eleven priests published a statement calling on all people of goodwill on both sides of the seventeenth parallel and overseas to end a "fratricidal war" that had reached "a peak of cruelty." The devastating conditions and Pope Paul VI's calls for peace prompted them to stand up. "We cannot let the will to unite the country and the desire to build a better future serve as an excuse for continuing this fratricidal war."[50] Many of these priests continued their mobilization in a publication. *Sống đạo* (*Living the Faith*) denounced the suffering caused by the war. One article reported that the US Army had announced the burning of two villages where evacuees had resettled, placing blame for it on the communists. In retaliation, US planes bombed a Catholic village on the outskirts of Hanoi. "And, so, they are even," the weekly concluded.[51] Vietnamese on both sides were paying the price for an absurd war.

This publication also suggested that it was time to rethink whether Catholics had lived up to the teachings of Rome. The Church was changing, and its leadership had been renewed after Pope Paul VI asked for the resignation of all bishops who had attained the age of seventy-five.[52] Catholics needed to create a dialogue with other Christians, adherents of other religions, and atheists. It was also important to take a more pragmatic approach to communist countries. *Sống đạo* still warned about the Red Guard's attacks on religion in China and Vietnamese communists' pressure on the faithful in the DRV. But it also pointed out that Catholicism had not disappeared on the other side of the Iron Curtain.[53] The Polish population remained overwhelmingly Catholic, and Rome signed a treaty establishing a relationship with Yugoslavia.[54] Italian bishops also called for peace, and the pope even considered visiting Vietnam in person.[55] The Church had departed from a staunch opposition to communism.

Although *Sống đạo* failed to turn the most hawkishly anticommunist Catholics into doves, it shifted some of their views on Buddhism. Father Hoàng Quỳnh realized that perhaps his initiatives had gone too far, and so had those of the Buddhist movement. The Buddhist struggle seized control of central Vietnam in the spring of 1966, only to be crushed by the RVNAF. So, Father Hoàng Quỳnh contacted that movement's main leader, Thích Trí Quang. Together, they denounced the junta's interference in the process of drafting a new constitution, by appointing a chair of the Constituent Assembly with disproportionate power over the representatives.[56] "At a time when there is no National Assembly yet, who else can claim to represent the population apart from political and religious groups? Among all the religious groups, Buddhists are important. No single government can be respected and become victorious over the enemy without the support of a large religious group."[57] The elections eventually took place, with no modification in the chair's powers. But Father Hoàng Quỳnh had obviously softened his views about Buddhist activists. He even revived attempts to create interreligious solidarity. In August 1966, the short-lived Citizens' Front of Religions

(Mặt trận Công dân các tôn giáo) denounced the assassinations of well-known anticolonists by the communists.[58] This was not just an attempt to heal the sectarian divide; it also tried to unite the religious against communism.[59] The observance of the National Day of Shame in 1967 was a show of unity, with the participation of Archbishop Nguyễn Văn Bình and the Buddhist monk Thích Tâm Châu. But the absence of large crowds of monks and priests suggests that the divide had not ended.[60] The rapprochement still drew criticism from Xây dựng. Hoàng Quỳnh's open hand to the Buddhists could only benefit the communists.[61] But as pro-peace Catholics noted, the situation was unprecedented. For the first time since 1954, some Catholic evacuees had become critical of other Catholic evacuees.[62] The breach now extended all the way to their Catholic core.

The Threat of Another Geneva

The Tết Offensive was a watershed moment for the evacuees, but it did not create more unity among Vietnamese noncommunists. On January 30 and 31, communist troops from the north attacked most cities in South Vietnam, holding some of them for weeks. This event shook the world, especially the American public, which discovered that the US military did not have the situation under control. The wave of indignation prompted President Johnson to declare that he would neither run for reelection nor retaliate against the attacks. He stopped all bombing and invited Hanoi to negotiate an end to armed conflict. The two sides began to meet in the summer of 1968 in Paris, and talks ended five years later.[63] However, the offensive did not lead to the expected results in Vietnam. The NLF realized that the urban population did not welcome them as liberators. The attack prompted the US to upgrade RVNAF equipment and establish self-defense militias.[64] Likewise, anticommunist evacuees were concerned about the reactions to the attacks, which did not inspire the anticommunist surge they desired.

According to many evacuees, attacking on a holiday, when everyone was celebrating the Lunar New Year, confirmed the vile nature of the communists. But they worried most about Saigon's participation in the Paris talks.[65] The RVN had made the wrong choice in sending Bùi Diễm, an ambassador who had worked in Phan Huy Quát's cabinet, to Paris. Moreover, it refused to let the LLĐĐK broadcast anticommunist speeches over the radio or on television, which undermined the nationalist cause. Saigon needed to persuade the United States to leave Paris and to respect its newly adopted constitution. There could be no negotiations with the communists.[66] Those in power in Hanoi would remain enemies forever, in their view.

Their mobilization intensified in October 1968, when Washington and Hanoi almost reached an agreement. Catholic evacuees took part in two concurrent initiatives: the first consisted of reaching out to other religious groups, while the second was opposition to the prospect of a negotiated solution. The first effort, yet again, was initiated by Father Hoàng Quỳnh. A hundred and fifty representatives of all religious and political groups as well as labor unions met clandestinely on November 24, 1968, near the church in Tân Định. Only people with an invitation could enter the premises. The invitation mentioned the name of the religious group or political group, allowing them to send the representative of their choice. At a time when most public meetings were suspended, this resembled a representative assembly of noncommunists in South Vietnam. Hoàng Quỳnh underscored the gravity of the situation in a short address. He stated that although Europe had been able to enjoy some stability since the end of World War II, the situation in Asia had been radically different. Vietnam had not had "a minute of peace." Communism had taken over the north and now was trying to do the same in the south. But the nationalists now faced an impasse.

> For years, to achieve results in its struggle against communism, the people of the south have received the help of allies. Yet while we share the same aspirations, we are not in the same situation, nor do we have the same power. Hence, our positions regarding armed struggle are not the same; every country has rights and wants to protect them. Therefore, as you have noticed, Washington and Saigon have disagreed on their approach to negotiations.[67]

More than ever, Saigon had to determine how to "achieve real peace." It was time to discuss five questions:

- Should they pursue an immediate cease-fire or an armed struggle along with negotiations?
- Who would represent South Vietnam at the negotiations, who would it be negotiating against, and where should the talks take place?
- If the talks led to a referendum, would the solution of one person–one vote be appropriate for the north, the south, or both?

- How might the struggle against communism become political after the war?
- How could they unite to achieve peace in Vietnam?

As might be expected, the representatives disagreed with one another. Even if they tried to influence the Paris talks, no one knew what strategy to follow. A delegation sent to Paris could become a voice defending the interests of the South Vietnamese population; a boycott would also make a strong statement. Others ran short of ideas and mainly blamed Saigon's ineptitude in winning hearts and minds in international public opinion compared with Hanoi. There was an awkward sense of déjà vu. The fate of the country would be determined by a conference held outside it. Hence, Father Hoàng Quỳnh and many others were committed to achieving a different outcome than what had happened in Geneva in 1954. A consensus formed around three points. First, the attendees wanted to achieve an "honorable peace" (hòa bình trong danh dự). This echoed the words of Richard Nixon, the US presidential candidate, who sought to end the war while preventing Hanoi's total victory. Second, in order to express their views to their government, the DRV, and the rest of the world, they had to show unity. Last, in the face of the widespread violence, they demanded a cease-fire.[68] As they had done in forming the National Congress in late 1953, the Vietnamese improvised a democratic assembly. They could not remain trapped in the armed conflict and international geopolitics.

However, some did not want to consult others. The LLĐĐK planned a three-step strategy to oppose the government's efforts in the negotiations. First, they would organize a conference to denounce the proposal for once again dividing the country. If the government did not change its mind, then the mobilization of one hundred thousand people would show that Catholics were determined to reject such an agreement. Finally, the last course of action would be an armed rebellion, calling on all individual Catholics in society and in the army to overthrow the government.[69] The LLĐĐK would not let another conference decide their fate on its own. However, these anticommunist Catholics were blocked from taking even the first step. The government rejected their request to organize a conference, for security reasons. Instead, the LLĐĐK published a pamphlet stating its position.[70] The negotiations infringed on Vietnamese self-determination and territorial integrity. A cease-fire, the LLĐĐK stated, would be a ploy for supporting the communist strategy for world conquest. A neutral central Vietnam would become communist, which would increase the threat to southern Vietnam. Only one path led to peace: the withdrawal of all communist troops from the southern half of the country.[71] Ironically, this raised some hope of a truce similar to the Geneva cease-fire to which they had been opposed for so long. Dr. Hoàng Cơ Bình created the Bloc for National Restoration (Khối Phục hưng Quốc gia) on the National Day of Shame in 1968. He called for an end to armed conflict, the departure of all foreign troops, and normalized relations between the north and the south.[72] This would save the south and ultimately liberate the north because people and ideas would circulate northward. All Vietnamese would oppose Hanoi's "enslavement" to communism and voice their desire to "unite" and "restore" independence.[73] His brother, the lawyer Hoàng Cơ Thụy, made the same recommendation at an international meeting and published it in French and English.[74] This was one way, other than street protests, in which evacuees could influence the talks.

It is difficult to know what happened afterward, without access to LLĐĐK documents, but intelligence reports show that the Catholics lost momentum. Father Hoàng Quỳnh refused to protest the government and preferred positive action with other religious leaders.[75] He gave public lectures at a unique interreligious temple in Phú Lâm, which had an altar with four different faces, one for each faith. At the center was a globe and representations of them: a statue of Buddha, a replica of the basilica of Sacré Coeur, the red flag of the Hòa Hảo, and a blue eye for the Cao Đài. Every week, a different religious leader delivered a lecture before a diverse crowd.[76] The priest increasingly turned away from politics to remain anchored in spirituality. This helped heal the religious divide, but it also eroded the Catholics' solidarity.

At last the joint conference imagined by the LLĐĐK was held on November 30, 1969, but by then, several nationalists had dropped out.[77] The objectives and tone also conveyed a new message. Despite a long speech warning the Vietnamese not to fall for "middle positions in the world and in Vietnam" (Về thế đứng giữa trên thế giới và Việt Nam), the meeting focused on tax problems and electoral issues.[78] Most evacuees despaired about the failure to unite against communism. Even a strong shock, such as the Tết Offensive, did not lead to the mobilization that they desired. Instead, more people joined the calls for peace.

A Transnational Peace Movement

Because of shifting public opinion, the international movement to end the war intensified after the Tết Offensive. But the antiwar protests in the United States would remain a domestic movement if they did not include Vietnamese voices.[79] Overseas Vietnamese became instrumental in creating a transnational and more authentic peace movement. Father Trần Tam Tỉnh, a professor of ancient civilization at the Université de Laval in Québec, amplified the voices of the eleven Vietnamese priests who demanded peace. He republished their letter in January 1966 in a Québec newspaper, with a brief preface. "The position taken by my fellows—and me—is one of an SOS to the world, which has always considered Vietnam with self-interest and mostly in terms of its political and military aspects. The real problem is entirely different: it is a country of 30 million inhabitants, who have suffered because of the war for twenty-five years (1941–1966)."[80] Framing the call around human suffering, instead of a Cold War battlefront, gave the impression that Vietnamese, in both the north and south, were being held hostage and wanted to escape a situation for which they were not responsible.

The priest denied that he was following the lead of other antiwar Christians, such as Reverend Daniel Berrigan and Thomas Merton in the United States.[81] His personal journey from Vietnam to Québec explains this public position better. Born in Nam Định in the Red River delta in 1929, he entered a seminary at a young age and in 1954 was selected to study in Hong Kong. He then earned a doctorate in canon law at the Pontifical Lateran University in Rome.[82] From there, he left for the University of Fribourg in Switzerland and specialized in Egyptology. Like other evacuees, he could not return to the north. Unlike them, however, he had not experienced the evacuation. Most of his life was spent abroad, sheltered from the RVN propaganda and the Second Indochina War.

His research activities took him to Paris. He worked for the French Centre national de la recherche scientifique (National Center for Scientific Research), attended the École Pratique des Hautes Études, and volunteered in the Department of Greek and Roman Antics at the Musée du Louvre.[83] This solid experience landed him a position at the Université de Laval in 1964.

His time in France might also have exposed him to new influences. French Catholics did not fear that communism would create a schismatic church. Several members of the clergy and lay Catholics had remained politically active since 1945. They had fought together with the French Communist Party against the German occupation. After the war, many continued to hold common values and published their ideas in

Témoignage chrétien (*Christian Witness*), a left-wing newspaper. The French Catholic world in which Trần Tam Tỉnh had evolved did not see communism as an absolute evil.

He also witnessed the mobilization of academia against torture during the Algerian War. Of particular significance was the activism of a young Jewish scholar on ancient Greece, Pierre Vidal-Naquet, who lost his father in a Nazi concentration camp; he was suspended from his teaching duties because of his denunciation of torture in Algiers.[84] We have no evidence that Trần Tam Tỉnh identified with Vidal-Naquet, but he could not have been unaware of the shock in French academia. A colleague who was a specialist in a related field was dismissed by the Université de Caen. The Vietnamese researcher, in France, was surrounded by acts of civil disobedience.

Trần Tam Tỉnh was not Jewish, nor did he focus on torture. Nonetheless, calls by the pope, pleas by fellow priests, and misinformation spread by staunch anticommunists prompted him to take a stance against the war in Vietnam. In December 1966, Raymond de Jaegher, the missionary who had escaped from China and set his base in Saigon after 1955, had given a talk on the war at the Université de Laval in December 1966, and this was not his first visit to Canada. Since 1954, the missionary had gone there several times to deliver speeches with titles such as "Vietnam–Fact and Fiction" and "La situation du Vietnam d'aujourd'hui."[85] Those who heard his views had to believe them because of his firsthand experience with communism. Trần Tam Tỉnh reacted in a series of articles. According to him, Catholics in both the United States and Vietnam disagreed about what the pope's call for peace could mean. One portion of Christendom believed that the war in Vietnam had to continue as a crusade to save civilization, and the other wanted to end it.[86]

Although Trần Tam Tỉnh criticized the inaccuracy of anticommunist views on Vietnam, he did not yet embrace Hanoi's message. He rejected the views of pro-NLF students who claimed that Ngô Đình Diệm's regime had killed over four hundred thousand people and used a guillotine in public executions yet stated that neither American soldiers nor the NLF were to be trusted. The NLF's claim to represent the people was misleading. Nationalists, especially religious groups, might be eliminated after the war. What Catholics had endured in the DRV after 1954, despite having recognition in the constitution, was proof of this.[87]

The Tết Offensive reinvigorated both Christian communities and Québec's movement for independence, which naturally influenced Trần Tam

Tình and his followers. The 1967 Pacem in Terris conference in Geneva discussed the division of Germany and the war in Vietnam. The Reverend Dr. Martin Luther King Jr., who attended the meeting, condemned US intervention. After 1968, some Christian activists believed that this opposition should translate into action.[88] At a meeting of the World Council of Churches in Uppsala, Sweden, that year, ecumenical Protestants declared their commitment to the redistribution of wealth from north to south, which involved sending money to guerrilla organizations in Africa.[89] The assembly adopted a statement on Vietnam demanding an end to the war "at once," a political solution, and assistance in postwar reconstruction.[90] This part of Christendom was not just calling for peace; it was offering moral, logistical, and financial support to end the war.

Opposition to American imperialism also grew stronger in Québec, which had a large Vietnamese presence. After the United States, Belgium, and West Germany, Canada had the largest community of overseas Vietnamese outside the Indochinese peninsula or the former French colonies.[91] As of 1974, 1,100 of the 1,500 Vietnamese in Canada lived in Québec.[92] The Front de Libération du Québec (FLQ) radicalized the nationalist movement. In July 1967, Charles de Gaulle had fueled it, declaring: "Vive le Québec libre!" Eight hundred people protested in Québec and burned an effigy of US President Johnson under a sign that said "soldat du Christ" (soldier of Christ).[93] After the Tết Offensive, Montréal hosted the Hemispheric Conference to End the War in Vietnam, at which the Black Panthers, the Chilean socialist Salvador Allende, and the FLQ condemned US intervention in Vietnam (see fig. 5.1).[94] Canada was a haven for US draft dodgers and Québec had become a center for anti-imperialist movements. Transatlantic Christian activism and Québec's nationalist movements intersected precisely where Trần Tam Tình worked. He urged Canadians and people in Québec to "imagine, for example, what would happen if 500 million Catholics around the world launched an initiative" to end the war in Vietnam.[95] Because of its strong Catholic background and nationalist sentiment, Québec could present an example of solidarity.

His Vietnamese students absorbed these ideas and spread them in their own publications. At the Université of Laval, they published *Thế hệ* (*Generation*), which soon spread to the United States, France, Japan, and New Zealand.[96] The younger generation broke with their parents' views and took a stand of their own. They also broadcast the growing mobilization within South Vietnam. They wanted the world to know that Vietnamese students well beyond the Buddhist circles now took to

FIGURE 5.1. The Hemispheric Conference to End the War in Vietnam, 1968.
Source: Paul-Henri Talbot, Bibliothèque et Archives nationales du Québec.

the streets to demand the end of the war.[97] Overseas Vietnamese had to lobby their own governments to stop the war. They also spread New Left ideas through translating masterpieces by socialist intellectuals into Vietnamese: György Lukács, the Hungarian philosopher and editor in chief of *Kommunismus*; Joris Ivens, a politically active Dutch filmmaker who had made two movies on the war; and Albert Schweizer, the Alsatian scientist, theologian, and humanist.[98] This student awakening reflected transformations in the intellectual left around the world—making it less interested in class struggle and more involved in condemning imperialism. These students adopted new heroes, such as the late Che Guevara in Cuba, and believed in solidarity without borders.[99]

This New Left opposed all kinds of imperialism. Trần Tam Tỉnh compared the situations in South Vietnam and Czechoslovakia. In 1968 "two hundred thousand Soviet soldiers" had invaded the latter to put down an uprising in Prague that was defending reforms. He criticized what he viewed as infringement on Czech sovereignty by an imperial power (i.e., the Soviet Union) to protect its own interests. But instead of associating the DRV with that empire, the priest insisted that the imperial threat in South Vietnam came from the United States. Both countries had been invaded to "liberate" the local population, but they had become "strategic doors" to the creation of economic dependence on an informal center. He contended that the main difference between them was revealing: the Czech people rose up against imperialism, whereas South Vietnamese "girls . . . had welcomed" US soldiers as saviors with garlands of flowers.[100] Like many evacuees, Trần Tam Tỉnh thought that Vietnam had to free itself from an empire; unlike them, however, he saw Washington as Vietnam's main problem.

Father Trần Tam Tỉnh sought to have more Christians join in his opposition. His works were published in both French and English. *Pour la Paix au Vietnam, Témoignage d'un Vietnamien sur la guerre du Vietnam* (*Peace in Vietnam: A Roman Catholic Vietnamese Priest Looks at the War*) underscored his credibility as a Vietnamese and as a Catholic to debunk the myths that led to US intervention.[101] His perspective was that the existence of a separate nation-state and the idea of a northern invasion were both fictitious. Washington was the aggressor, and the more the US Air Force devastated the country, the stronger his enemy became. He said that, on January 1, 1968, all churches in Québec had united in prayer, responding to the pope's call for peace.[102] Everyone had to mobilize for peace in Vietnam.

The priest insisted that the Vietnamese Catholics perpetuated the antagonism fueling the war. This "majoritarian minority" comprised only 10 percent of the population in Vietnam, but they held key positions in the government or in the army and had thereby contributed to the escalation. He believed that the DRV had always protected religious freedom and considered Catholics its greatest allies. It was only because of tactless and uncontrollable local cadres that Catholics believed they had to move to the south in 1954. These Catholics had become radical anticommunists, muzzling all Buddhist voices, the priest declared. According to Trần Tam Tỉnh, it had been "twenty years of continuous and merciless struggle. Northern Catholics who sought refuge in the south look like the brave crusaders of the Middle Age. Their heroism and piety only equals their savagery and intolerance. . . . Like the combatants of all crusades, they serve, without knowing, the political and economic interests of others; the former, those of the spice trade merchants, the latter, those who sell uranium and firearms."[103]

Catholic evacuees could only abandon that warmongering mindset by taking a radical approach, which required no less than an updating similar to that of the Church or "self-criticism" sessions like those held by communist cadres.[104] The first of these two processes demanded sincerity, forgiveness, and acceptance of one another.[105] According to that antiwar movement, Catholics had enabled foreign intervention and polarized religious positions.[106] The onus was on them. Not only had the evacuees failed to find unanimity in the war effort against communism, but from the perspective of antiwar Christians elsewhere, they had also become the main obstacle to peace.

CHAPTER 6

Estranged from the War

In March 1971, Father Nguyễn Viết Khai stood in front of a crowd in the village of Hố Nai to offer a revelation. The priest had helped construct the village and led parishioners in Vinh diocese to resettle after they evacuated in 1955. For sixteen years, he fought communism as the editor in chief of *Luyện thép* (*Forging Steel*). He had also served as the chaplain of a youth group propagating the faith in central Vietnam to prevent communist expansion. But his views on Hanoi and the war had changed: he had made a mistake and urged fellow Catholics to see communists as their brothers.[1] Nine months later, under pressure from the government and Church hierarchy, he left his parish, though this did not change his position.[2] Despite fighting communism for decades, he was convinced that the war had to stop. What had caused many evacuees, including those who were the most opposed to communism, to call for peace?

Most books on the Second Indochina War state that, by early 1975, even right-wing political leaders and Catholics had turned against South Vietnam President Nguyễn Văn Thiệu. Corruption scandals involving high-ranking officials and members of the president's family caused this shift.[3] This chapter argues that behind this change was a more fundamental reason arising from the years prior to these scandals. Most anticommunist evacuees had become disillusioned. They no longer felt engaged in a global Cold War against communism, nor did they want Saigon to head the reunified nation-state. The historiography often highlights the importance of the Tết Offensive because of its impact on public opinion and the presidential election in the United States. But the main turning point of the war for the evacuees was the withdrawal of US troops. In July 1969, only six months after his election, President Richard Nixon declared in Guam that Asian countries threatened by communism should be responsible for defending themselves. Four months later, in a televised speech, he said that South Vietnam would have to rely on its own forces to defend its national security, thus announcing the departure of US soldiers.[4] The Vietnamization of the armed conflict meant South Vietnamese would have to rely on themselves to fight the NLF and the infiltration of the PAVN. Many evacuees, including the most anti-communist among them, understood that it was time to decouple from the United States. They believed they had been manipulated, dragged into the Cold War, and paid a price for it. Washington's national interests came first. Its ideological commitment to resist communism was secondary. The feeling that the evacuees could hope for a better future and the liberation of the north abruptly ended. They had to become pragmatic and rely on their own strength. Growing connections with the DRV also led some to question their previous views of Hanoi as an archenemy. But the failure of the RVN to become a credible alternative, combined with its repression and embezzlement scandals, led most evacuees to the same conclusion: none of the political authorities vying for power represented their search for independence and sovereignty.

Seeing the Dark Side of the Cold War

In 1968 Nixon campaigned on the promise that the United States could achieve a "victorious peace" in Vietnam. The best way to get results at the negotiating table was to take advantage of the growing rift between Moscow and Beijing. Washington sought a rapprochement with the PRC, which culminated with Nixon's presidential visit to China in 1972. The United States' growing closer to China would have an impact on the DRV. Hanoi would feel pressure from its northern neighbor, who supplied material and economic support, and become more open to US interests at the negotiation table. Meanwhile, the United States had to maintain as many soldiers as possible in South Vietnam and inflict damage on its opponent. So, the bombing, which had stopped for the negotiations, resumed with a vengeance in 1969, targeting the Hồ Chí Minh Trail passing through Cambodia to stop the flow of soldiers and weapons to the south. This escalation remained secret and extended the armed fighting to Cambodia and later Laos. It later backfired on Nixon when the public and members of the Congress discovered the president had secretly ordered the bombings.

The main justification for a slow withdrawal relied on the threat of a bloodbath. The possibility that a NLF victory would bring widespread violence caused a reconsideration of the 1954 evacuation in public opinion.[5] On November 3, 1969, President Nixon suggested in a televised speech that the DRV, after becoming sovereign over the northern half of Vietnam in 1954, had "murdered more than fifty thousand people and hundreds of thousands more died in slave labor camps."[6] He repeated these claims to justify a ground incursion of Cambodia in April 1970. According to the president, the communists could not be left unchecked because their coming to power would cause a massacre. He repeated communism was a threat because hundreds of thousands had fled communist rule in 1954. Thousands of others who had remained in the north had died because of the land reform, or so it seemed.[7]

This statement contrasted with revelations that were leaking at the same time. Beginning on June 15, 1971, the *New York Times* published passages of an internal report of the Department of Defense retracing the history of US involvement in Indochina, which later became famous as the *Pentagon Papers*. The disclosure of these internal discussions revealed the extent to which the United States, through four different administrations, had chosen further involvement and eventually a war in Vietnam. "Excerpts from Lansdale Team's Report on Covert Vietnam Mission in '54 and '55" revealed the role of Central Intelligence Agency operatives to encourage the population to leave the north.[8] According to this account, people had not voted with their feet but, rather, had been pushed by propaganda concocted by the US Secret Service. In the United States, the *Pentagon Papers* diminished the credibility of several presidential administrations, but its impact on perceptions of the situation in Vietnam was no less important. This first cardinal myth, of a nation that wanted to escape communism, was shattered.

Scholars who examined the land reform in the DRV in the early 1970s even claimed that the evacuees were liars. The study by Hoàng Văn Chí, *From Colonialism to Communism*, long remained a reference. Its author was in the Việt Minh, had experienced the DRV agrarian reforms, and then evacuated to the south.[9] The antiwar activist Gareth Porter, who had studied with George McTurnan Kahin at Cornell University, disagreed.

Relying on *Nhân dân* (*The People*), Hanoi's official newspaper, he wrote a dissertation and articles stating that no bloodbath had taken place.[10] Porter suggested that Hoàng Văn Chí's book could not be taken seriously. The man was a landlord and thus had good reason to fear the people's tribunal; he pretended to be a VWP member though he had never been one; he had worked for the Ministry of Information under Ngô Đình Diệm; his book was funded by the Congress for Cultural Freedom, which had received money from the CIA. In other words, it was pure propaganda. Moreover, Porter accused Hoàng Văn Chí of "linguistic deceit." A quotation of General Võ Nguyên Giáp acknowledging excesses during the land reform had been mistranslated.[11] According to Porter, evacuees like Hoàng Văn Chí had manipulated the public opinion for years.

The evacuees realized that the antiwar movement was depicting them as the worst impostors, who betrayed the West and Vietnam. They also reevaluated their alliance with Washington because of these shifts. Nu Anh Tran states that intellectuals voiced criticism of the US presence in Vietnam.[12] The evacuees, too, resented their patron and drew comparisons with the past. *Dân chủ mới* (*New Democracy*) ran a series of articles from May to August 1970 on war profiteering during the two Indochina wars.[13] The first articles covered the Affaire des piastres, a scandal that erupted in 1953, revealing the profit made by military and civil officers who took advantage of the difference in the francs-piastre fixed currency rate between France and Indochina.[14] The Second Indochina War also made a profit because the billions of dollars injected bought American goods. In both cases, Vietnamese were left with "nothing but their hard work."[15] The articles maintained that French and American imperialists had always exploited Vietnam.

Evacuee journalists also criticized what they felt was an American sense of superiority. On March 16, 1968, a US platoon had tortured, raped, and killed virtually all the inhabitants of Sơn Mỹ in Quảng Ngãi Province over the course of a single day, killing from 347 to 504 civilians depending on the estimate.[16] The *Washington Post*, the *New York Times,* and the *National Observer* all published articles on what became known as the Mỹ Lai massacre and *Dân chủ mới* translated them for the Vietnamese public. *Dân chủ mới* argued there was no reason to be surprised because this was only one in a long series of similar crimes: "American Indian massacres," "exploitation of Africans," the bombing of Tokyo, and the atomic bombs exploded over Hiroshima and Nagasaki were all evidence that American exceptionalism was manifested with ruthless violence.[17] Vietnamese, who had been at war for thirty years, saw that "those supposed to bring freedom take away freedom and children's lives."[18] According to *Dân chủ mới*, US newspapers expressing outrage at reports of Saigon imprisoning antiwar students and political dissidents in tiger cages were also misdirected.[19] The Vietnamese newspaper rejected the claim that it was only thanks to US pressure that this practice was eliminated. This affirmation, again, revealed an asymmetrical relationship. One journalist rhetorically asked: "Who do they think they are, to believe that their embassy alone can influence domestic policies?" and "Would Vietnamese people ever pretend to influence American politics?" Everyone knew the answer. According to *Dân chủ mới*, Americans would always know best and would never see their allies as equals.[20] Vietnamese public opinion changed their perception of the United States. A survey on Vietnamese attitudes toward the joint US and RVNAF intervention in Cambodia noted that popular support had declined. In May 1970, two months after that intervention had begun, 32 percent of the college-educated respondents believed that Washington was "not so dependable" and 16 percent said it was "not at all dependable."[21] Regarding the Paris conference, Father Hoàng Quỳnh commented: "Until now, the United States has behaved as if it had the upper hand in these negotiations, whereas the 'Vietnamization of the armed conflict' should also lead to the 'Vietnamization of the negotiations.'"[22] Many evacuees thought it was time for the RVN to leave the US orbit.

Many also denounced the disparity between Vietnamese and US soldiers in military operations. In the spring of 1972, Hanoi launched a massive operation, advancing with tanks to take territory along the demilitarized zone and the central highlands, which could give it an advantage in the negotiations in Paris (see fig. 6.1). This offensive did not hasten the talks as expected, but it caused massive disruption. The PAVN troops nearly advanced into Hue, and the RVNAF, despite its counteroffensive, eventually lost half of Quảng Trị Province. The inability to repel the PAVN incursion revealed a deep problem in coordination between the two armies. Two generals ordered evacuation, which led RVNAF soldiers from the Third Division to go rogue after they felt betrayed by officers who had abandoned them.[23] This chaotic situation harmed the morale and the military position of the RVNAF. As a result, President Thiệu dismissed the officers responsible for the orders. But the two generals had ordered the evacuation of Quảng Trị because of a misunderstanding. They thought, as all seventy-five American advisers had been airlifted from the city, they had to clear the area for an imminent bombing.[24] The South Vietnamese press and the parliament discussed the lack of communication between the two

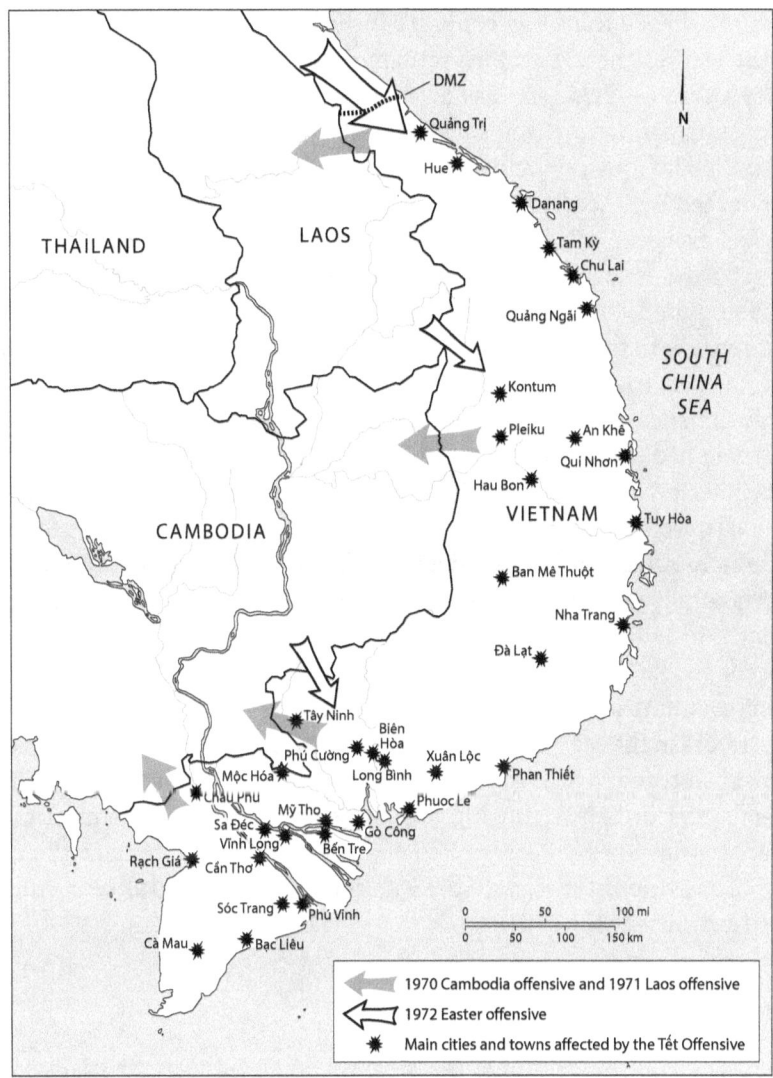

FIGURE 6.1. The Tết Offensive and intensification of the war.
Source: Map by Bill Nelson, adapted from the United States Military Academy, "Attack into Cambodia," "South Vietnam, 1971," "Lam Son," "The Enemy Situation Early 1964," "The Spring Offensive, 1972," West Point, accessed November 7, 2023, https://www.westpoint.edu/academics/academic-departments/history/digital-history-center/atlases/vietnam-war.

armies and the disparity that it revealed. Many Vietnamese officers evacuated over land, but American advisers reached safety by helicopter. This did not even account for the hundreds of civilians who got to Hue on foot or the hundred thousand displaced within the province.[25] Even those who were committed to fighting alongside US troops no longer believed that they could trust them. For the US troops, the end of the war was near, but, for Vietnamese soldiers, it was not in sight.

The greatest criticism was leveled when Washington turned to Beijing, culminating in Nixon's visit to China in 1972. This time, even the most diehard anticommunist newspaper, *Xây dựng*, the Catholic newspaper, lashed out. According to the paper, Nixon was a hypocrite and had tricked everyone with the promise of "peace with honor" to win reelection.[26] The newspaper reprinted a well-known photograph of Zhou Enlai grabbing food for the US president, with a caption that read: "Hitting the booze with friends."[27] So much for ideology—the worst enemies could become best friends if need be. *Xây dựng* also looked back on the history of the alliance. In *Việt Nam dưới thời đại Mỹ* (*Vietnam in the American Era*), Vietnam had evolved from French colonial rule to US guardianship. Yet this time, Indochina had had five million tons of bombs dropped on it, the equivalent of five atom bombs.[28] It also held the same contempt for US intentions. One article recalled a US officer who claimed that the troops had neutralized more than twenty-three thousand "Việt Cộng" over a few months in 1964. There were good reasons for wondering how many "innocent people" had lost their lives at the same time.[29] *Xây dựng*'s criticism went even further. One article claimed that the death of Buddhist demonstrators in the May 1963 crisis had been caused by an American agent, James Scott, and suggested the CIA might have been involved in Ngô Đình Diệm's overthrow.[30] A growing consensus emerged, from the most propeace to the most hardcore anticommunists. Their ideas became the pillars of a revisionist history of the war: the United States was responsible for the demise of the RVN.

A New Christianity against the War

These changing perceptions grew stronger when antiwar Christians connected with Vietnamese on both sides of the seventeenth parallel. Years after the first calls in *Sống đạo*, some of the most anticommunist Catholics voiced their desire to end the war. Together, they laid the foundations of a new Christianity, which would overcome past antagonism and stand together for peace. Many anticommunist Catholics opened up to the idea of making peace with communism. This shift probably emerged from the combined influence of overseas activists, domestic calls for peace, the destruction endured in the Tết Offensive, and the US withdrawal. Catholic evacuees considered it their duty, as Vietnamese and as Christians, to look at communism with a different mindset.

People from the Nghệ Tĩnh Bình region thought about the war in a new light. In 1970, several priests and laypeople who originated in the Vinh diocese created a self-help association and resumed their publishing activities in Saigon. A change in tone was signaled by the title of the publication *Quê mẹ* (*The Motherland*). Unlike *Luyện thép*, created after the 1956 uprising in the north, this publication insisted that the ties among Catholics transcended the seventeenth parallel. The two hundred thousand evacuees from the Nghệ Tĩnh Bình region were still brothers of the people who remained in the north, "regardless of their religion, social class, or nationalist political leaning."[31] Although this initiative "could have been launched fifteen years earlier," it had become more urgent than ever, Father Nguyễn Viết Khai believed, because "people seem to have lost trust in one another and in themselves."[32] But no one could remain indifferent to what was happening in Vinh. "All migrants have a responsibility to those who remain behind the Iron wall."[33] So, the purpose of the self-help association was to recreate a sense of brotherhood.

In contrast to the early years in southern Vietnam, when anything other than evacuee testimony fell into the category of communist propaganda, *Quê mẹ* published accounts of the war situation in the correspondence of priests and seminarians who remained in the north, as well as NLF and PAVN deserters. After having been cut off for years, they developed new ties to their homeland. The defectors (*hồi chánh viên*) highlighted the ambivalent nature of the armed conflict. American bombings targeted bridges, electrical plants, and water stations in Nghệ An and Hà Tĩnh.[34] Years of constant bombing had ravaged Vinh. The defectors criticized the DRV for luring them into the war effort or for using a church to store munitions. But local authorities helped Catholic communities to rebuild churches and infrastructure and offered shelter from the bombing. The line between victims and abusers had blurred, which the evacuees attached to their homeland were well placed to understand.

More evacuees changed their minds about communism. After *Sống đạo*, which had paved the way since November 1964, *Đối diện* (*Face to Face*), created by Father Chân Tín, a priest from the south, in 1969, continued in its path.[35] People often criticized the publication because no one on its editorial board had ever experienced communism. The March 1971 issue of *Đối diện* corrected that shortcoming and published the experiences of "Catholics of the interzone IV" who had endured DRV rule since 1945. Essays by a Catholic pastor from Hà Tĩnh studying in West Germany and a lieutenant colonel of the RVNAF from Quảng Bình reached the same conclusion: the war had to end.[36] From the most erudite to the most courageous evacuee, their many voices called for peace.

Therefore, it is not surprising that in March 1971 Father Nguyễn Viết Khai revealed to the villagers of Hố Nai that he had changed his mind about communism. His talk was the high point of a three-day conference on Catholicism and politics, which was then published in a special issue of Đối diện.[37] He reminded everyone of his staunch anticommunism. He had formed his own Catholic militia during the First Indochina War and was imprisoned for almost two years for doing so. Coming from Lưu Mỹ in Nghệ An, he resisted the PAVN and evacuated southward with the help of the ICC. But, he believed, the past should not blind Catholics to the current situation.

Why were Catholics fighting communists? he asked. Everyone had to reconsider the adage describing communists as the "three noes" (tam vô): no god, no nation, and no family. Although communists did not believe in God, they were loyal to their nation and to their family. According to him, it was the Vietnamese people south of the seventeenth parallel who proved to have no family, as the war and five hundred thousand foreign soldiers broke couples apart. Likewise, Saigon "sold" Danang and the coast to a foreign power. "We lost our country," the priest deplored. Catholics needed to open their minds. They had to stop dehumanizing communists, distinguishing between Christians and "creatures of Satan." Instead, they should listen to Rome's recommendation to love human beings because everyone is a child of God.[38] They would not remain true to their faith if they did not realize that their hatred of communism was wrong and had contributed to the armed conflict.

Father Nguyễn Viết Khai's call spread among Vietnamese Catholics and then elsewhere. Students overseas republished his essay together with other articles on Catholicism and communism.[39] John Spragens, the son of a Protestant pastor and a conscientious objector who went to Vietnam as a member of the International Voluntary Service, translated and published Father Khai's essay in English.[40] A letter explained the speech's significance. The priest had every reason to fight communism because of his personal history, yet, according to Spragens, he embodied two emerging trends. Not only were the most anticommunist Catholics calling for peace, but they advocated a "middle way" separate from Saigon and the NLF. The Journal of Contemporary Asia also published the document in its 1972 first issue, using a quotation by Khai, "Who has no family? Who has no Fatherland?" as the main title, and the Catholic News Service promoted it to American Catholics.[41] The transnational Christian mobilization against the war had come full circle. The transformation of Christianity within Vietnam and overseas supported each other. For an ever-growing number of Christians, including Vietnamese evacuees, being Catholic was not related to specific religious traditions. In a world concerned about the war, it meant being part of a transnational family striving for peace in Vietnam.

News of this epiphany in Vietnam reinvigorated Christian networks that had emerged earlier. French Christians had been outraged by Spellman's declaration made on Christmas Eve in 1966 that US troops were fighting in a war for civilization. The following year, fifty-two Catholic clergy members, eighteen Protestant pastors, and ten laypeople had sent a letter to their American counterparts to oppose the prelate's comments and show that Christians from various churches stood together across the Atlantic in this position.[42] Voices from Vietnam calling for peace after 1971 energized this existing connection. With the support of a Vietnamese priest in France, Father Nguyễn Đình Thi, a native of Vinh who had studied in France, they organized the First International Assembly of Christians in Solidarity with the Vietnamese, Laotians, and Cambodians, whose purpose was to encourage "American, Vietnamese, French, and English Christians to meet to discuss and create new projects promoting peace."[43] The meeting had little impact in France.[44] But across the Atlantic, American priests and laypeople returned from the assembly and shared how they had met with priests who had traveled from north of the seventeenth parallel.[45] Their openness to making contact with Catholics from the DRV encouraged a new mindset among American Catholics. Although not everyone called for the end of the war, many realized that Christians had not disappeared altogether in the north and accepted they had to shift from the intransigence of the previous generation. After Cardinal Spellman died in December 1967, the warnings of veteran journalists such as Father O'Connor began to sound anachronistic.[46] A new generation of Catholics had come and some activists wanted to achieve peace in Vietnam, even if it meant dealing with communists.

It did not take long for this transnational initiative to merge with the activism of Father Trần Tam Tỉnh and students in Québec.[47] The Second International Assembly of Christians in Solidarity with the Vietnamese, Laotians, and Cambodians took place in October 1972. Over three hundred people went to Québec.[48] Trần Tam Tỉnh's opposition to the war had hardened since 1971, after learning the revelations of the *Pentagon Papers* and details on CIA operatives trying to encourage Catholics to move south in 1954.⁴⁹ According to him, the Catholic Church in Vietnam was partly responsible for the war. A short history of the Vietnamese Church published in a Jesuit periodical included a grim account of the Church since 1954. Catholics had barely survived the departure of many priests to the south. Those who remained distrusted Hanoi, which reduced freedom of religion to the right to attend mass. Below the seventeenth parallel, evacuees dominated the Church. They also comprised 30 percent of the soldiers, 60 percent of the officers, and 50 percent of the members of parliament. But they were blinded by their anticommunism. According to Trần Tam Tỉnh, Catholics in the north remained isolated, whereas those in the south ignored the international calls for peace.⁵⁰ Writing for a Québécois newspaper, he urged all Catholics to oppose the war. Christians were "directly and indirectly responsible for the war," by financing the production of military arms, accepting collusion of the Church with "bellicose states," and perpetuating colonialism. Colonial and neocolonial empires were behind the ideal of a crusade, and it was time for Christians to disavow this notion.⁵¹ The United States could not claim to be fighting the war in God's name, and "clerics" who visited the troops, calling them "soldiers of God," were betraying the faith.⁵² The priest did not mince words when writing an article in a student newspaper. In a special issue of *Thế hệ* on South Vietnam, he wrote an article about "the role of Catholics in the neocolonial system" around the world.⁵³ Trần Tam Tỉnh indirectly accused his coreligionists of enabling neocolonialism in Vietnam.

This does not mean that Trần Tam Tỉnh's allegations went unchallenged. Redemptorist missionaries who had spent their lives in Vietnam insisted in a newspaper article that communism threatened freedom of religion. The professor pushed back, saying that Western missionaries had served the French empire and had taken advantage of their superiority to abuse Vietnamese members of the clergy and the population.⁵⁴ The Québécois missionaries acknowledged that they were foreigners when they arrived, but over time they had become Vietnamese by taking a vow of poverty and living side by side with the people in time of war. In contrast, Trần Tam Tỉnh, who had lived his entire adult life far from the armed conflict, earned a comfortable salary as a professor and "claimed to have a monopoly over all religious information on Vietnam." His "hatred of the white rather than his love for the yellow" resembled Hanoi's propaganda.⁵⁵ According to these missionaries, Trần Tam Tỉnh had abused his authority as a professor and as a Vietnamese to spread lies. But even this attack did not deter him; rather, it only pushed him to become even more involved in the battle over the representation of Vietnamese history and the role of Catholics.

This transnational network of Christians also succeeded in what Catholics in the south had deemed unthinkable since 1954. They reconnected with their coreligionists in the north. The First Assembly in Paris was unprecedented, as this was the first time that North Vietnamese priests had visited a Western country since 1954.[56] The three Catholics from the DRV, two priests and a layman, penned a letter to the pope, which was reprinted in Le Monde. Only two bishops from the ten dioceses had remained in the north after 1954, yet the church had continued to grow. It was now "persecuted," not by the government, as alleged by "propaganda," but by US bombings, which had destroyed over five hundred churches and claimed the lives of four priests.[57] Hence, they called the pope to help achieve an end to "American aggression." The following year, a delegation of Americans, including a priest and a laywoman, Marianne Hamilton, visited Hanoi.[58] In 1973, it was Trần Tam Tỉnh's turn to witness the destruction and describe it in another book.[59] A new Christianity, which was opposed to the war, emerged across political borders and now reconnected with those in communist areas.

At the same time, the two assemblies criticized Saigon for creating hindrances for its population. The official brochure announcing the Second Assembly disclosed the administrative barriers that they encountered. Whereas the North Vietnamese delegation could attend the first meeting, Saigon had refused to issue exit visas for South Vietnamese priests.[60] During the meeting in Québec, reports highlighted the situation in the north and the south. In the DRV, Catholics attended mass in trenches because of the bombing. The situation was just as bad in the RVN. Documents smuggled out of the country revealed that Saigon arrested and tortured Catholic students.[61] Nine chaplains of the Student Youth and Worker Association wrote a letter to American bishops, claiming that "over ten thousand people were imprisoned in the Chí Hòa prison" because of the police force and intelligence services funded by Washington.[62] The assembly's final declaration was clear. The participants refused to let their faith become the instrument of any oppressive force.[63] Saigon, not Hanoi, had become the greater source of persecution. Christians around the world joined in solidarity to denounce Saigon's authoritarianism.

Between Two States

The more the war dragged on into the 1970s, the more confused the evacuees became. Vietnamese communists realized that they would begin fighting a civil war as soon as the US troops left. On June 8, 1969, Hanoi avoided this by creating a new state, the Provisional Revolutionary Government of the Republic of South Vietnam (PRG). The rebellion against Saigon had evolved, from a movement led by the NLF into a state capable of ruling the population beyond its circle of supporters.[64] The VWP did just as the French had done in the creation of the ASVN in 1949. It challenged its enemy's sovereignty by creating an alternative state. This required looking at hostile groups, such as the 1954 evacuees, in a different light. These people were not just migrants (*di cư*) but, rather, "compatriots who had been forced to migrate" (*đồng bào bị cưỡng ép di cư*).[65] The nuance was revealing. Instead of being traitors, they had been victims of foreign manipulation.

The evacuees were unsure whether they could trust this new message. They knew too well that communists could hide under the veil of nationalism, but they could not avoid confronting the same question as before: Would the PRG consider interests of everyone in the population? Would the deep transnational commitment to peace in Vietnam guarantee that the communists would not take over? Many continued to hope that the situation had changed since the First Indochina War. *Đối diện* published Trần Tam Tỉnh's account of his visit to Hanoi in 1973. Unlike US reporters and Western Christians, he could give an authentic account of what had happened there. As a northern Catholic, he spoke the language, knew what the area had been like before DRV rule, and understood the true meaning of freedom of religion. In the course of eighty pages, Catholics in the south learned that US bombing was the greatest threat to the Church. Their coreligionists could hardly survive under these conditions.[66] Other influential people continued to urge their compatriots to reconsider the war. Trần Văn Tuyên, a nationalist who had represented the SVN at the Geneva Conference in 1954, said: "Before 1973, the RVN considered this was an invasion from northern Vietnam, and the NLF was a tool of northern Vietnam. The reality is not that simple. The nature of this war is complicated. It includes many elements and shows the dynamics of a special invasion, a civil war, a revolutionary war carried out by communists, an ideological dispute, etc."[67]

The war was not black and white, which southern Vietnamese and even some evacuees realized. The RVN had attempted several nation-building programs, but it was outpaced by the war and the security risks it entailed. The more that Saigon resorted to authoritarian measures, the stronger the evacuees' doubts became. In 1971 Nguyễn Văn Thiệu was reelected president in a one-man race. His opponents stopped campaigning and urged citizens to boycott the election after they discovered that he had ordered the arrest of several candidates in the election to the Lower House of the parliament.[68] When the PAVN launched the Spring Offensive in 1972 in the hope this would bring progress to the negotiations in Paris, the hundreds of thousands of people displaced posed a security threat. So, Saigon issued restrictions on public life but, this time, refused to lift them. Nguyễn Văn Thiệu's decision to impose martial law on May 10, 1972, only worsened this poor democratic record. Along with that came the decision to restrict freedom of the press. Decree 007 required newspapers to deposit large sums of money as proof that they could cover legal expenses if they were sued for defamation. This effectively closed down most of Saigon's newspapers. Transnational networks became logistical support in the Catholics' resistance to their government. Đối diện, the progressive newspaper run by Father Chân Tín, had to find new ways to survive after the police arrested him because of his political opposition. Its names and directors changed: it became Đồng dao (In Unison) and then Đứng dậy (Rise Up), with a head office at the Université de Laval, in Québec, under the leadership of Father Trần Tam Tỉnh, whereas the contact person was Father Nguyễn Viết Khai, the repentant priest, or Father Chân Tín, after he was released from prison.[69] Catholics could rely on their coreligionists overseas to challenge Saigon's restrictions.

Even the complete withdrawal of US troops, after the Paris Peace Accords were signed on January 27, 1973, failed to clarify the situation. While the talks were still ongoing, many Vietnamese tried to express their views. Father Nguyễn Ngọc Lan, Father Trương Bá Cẩn, and Father Nguyễn Viết Khai created the Catholic movement for peace contrary to the desires of their hierarchy.[70] Weeks later, the Ấn Quang pagoda, an influential institution in the mobilization of Buddhists since 1963, announced that the four most important religious groups—Buddhism, Catholicism, Hòa Hảo, and Cao Đài—were ready for another Geneva conference.[71] In fact, it seemed urgent to gather at a nationwide meeting to consult one another about their views on the war and the forthcoming peace. Although the RVN had its National Assembly since 1967, a larger congress, gathering all political and religious leaders, was required. The grave circumstances demanded a meeting similar to the Diên Hồng assembly convened in

1284 in Hanoi, which decided what to do in the face of the Mongol invasion.[72] Meetings failed to coalesce their views, but they continued to try.

Two weeks after the Paris Peace Accords were signed, everyone in the south realized that it was a toothless agreement.[73] Unlike in Geneva eighteen years earlier, both Saigon and Hanoi were party to this treaty, yet both violated the cease-fire immediately after it was signed. With no explanation of how the territory would be split, apart from requiring belligerents to drop their weapons where they stood, warring factions rushed to conquer as much land as possible. Many protested the resumption of armed conflict. On the day of the signing, the Citizens' Front for Peace and Self-Determination was created with the sole purpose of enforcing respect for the peace agreement.[74] Elected officials at all levels and representatives of political parties, religions, and eminent leaders would remain united.[75] The signatories included religious figures, such as Archbishop Nguyễn Văn Bình and Father Hoàng Quỳnh, as well as political leaders, such as Nguyễn Gia Hiến from the LLĐDK.[76] Together, they promoted peace and mobilized the population into "a political struggle against communism."[77] This new wording was key. These evacuees prepared for a political rather than military struggle. This signaled not only their willingness to respect the Paris Peace Accords but also their acceptance of ending the war against the communists.

In fact, most people felt trapped in an inescapable situation. On the ground, the population was taken hostage between the war front on one side and a hopeless economic crisis in the cities on the other. Saigon's devaluation of the piastre in 1970 and the intensification of the armed conflict after 1972 sent prices skyrocketing. It increased the gap between war profiteers, who made a fortune on the black market, and the population.[78] The revelation of corruption scandals involving the families of high-ranking officials provoked outrage.[79]

On June 18, 1974, over three hundred priests signed a letter denouncing corruption in southern Vietnam. They grounded their call in recent declarations of an Episcopal conference, which expressed concern over corruption and referred to the pope's message for the Day of Peace. There could be no peace under conditions of confusion and poverty.[80] The large number of signatories gave the impression that, despite the lack of official backing from the hierarchy, the Church as a whole called for an end to corruption. The list of signatories was not in alphabetical order, and their names did not reflect the years of antiwar activism. Instead, the very first signature was that of Father Hoàng Quỳnh, who for so long had personified the Catholic struggle against communism.[81] This symbolic gesture was revealing. Even to him, communism was no longer the number one enemy—it was corruption and the general state of chaos in southern Vietnam. The petition to the media was revealed at a press conference at Tân Sa Châu Church, on the outskirts of Saigon. Banners in the room set the mood for the meeting: "Down with the clique corrupting civil servants and selling out the country!" "Let's rise and get rid of corruption and selling out the country!" and "Corruption is the main risk of losing the country!"[82] Father Trần Hữu Thanh, born south of the seventeenth parallel but known for being a personalist advocate in the RVN, seized this opportunity. He denounced the police blockade in front of the building. This gesture and all other attempts to muzzle labor unions, religious groups, and the press confirmed that the government was abusing its authority.[83] The most pressing issue was neither the war nor the advance of the PAVN: nepotism would cause Saigon's demise.

The priests went on with the creation of the Association for the Protection and Reconstruction of the Nation (Hội Cứu trợ phòng vệ và tái thiết quốc gia). Father Hoàng Quỳnh had attempted to register this association formally with the Ministry of the Interior, to no avail. A police report commented on the reasons for this refusal: the association would effectively take on the functions of government.[84] Catholics were thus so disgruntled with Saigon that they believed they had to create a state within the state.

The idea of providing support in a total political vacuum is hardly surprising from a priest like Hoàng Quỳnh, who was mandated by Monsignor Lê Hữu Từ to provide relief to the population of Phát Diệm during the worst famine in a century. The petition signed by the three hundred priests only criticized the state of the economy, the distress among the population, the enrichment of war profiteers, and the state's complicity in spreading vices such as gambling, drug trafficking, and prostitution. It did not target a particular person, nor did it call for anything except a commitment by the faithful to stand against corruption. However, Father Trần Hữu Thanh was determined to take this mobilization further. In his opening address in the Church of Tân Sa Châu, the priest blamed President Nguyễn Văn Thiệu as the main culprit for this situation. "Who is selling, and who is making money? Who is making a profit when the president holds the right to nominate the provincial chiefs, the mayors, the division commanders, and the head of military zones?" The priest insisted that the population was trapped. "Stuck between communists and corruption, the people no longer have anywhere to live. How is it possible to even imagine a political struggle against communism or the right to self-determination?" American economic aid was the only thing keeping the RVN afloat. But it was a "house attacked from outside and sabotaged from the inside."[85] Two months later, the same priest reiterated its criticism. Instead of referring to corruption and social ills, his message denounced Saigon's attempt to censor public speech to conceal its own corruption.[86] He called on everyone to "save the nation and establish peace." It was necessary to create an alternative government.[87] For Father Thanh, the most pressing measure that could save the south was Nguyễn Văn Thiệu's resignation.

Đứng dậy published a cartoon contrasting the mobilization of religious groups with actions by political authorities (see fig. 6.2). On one side of the image, Catholic and Buddhist leaders, supported by a crowd of laypeople, hold a banner that says "People's Movement against Corruption" (*Phong trào Nhân dân Chống Tham nhũng*). At the same time, nameless government officials are seen on the television screen, their arms extended beyond the screen to hold a sign: "The Movement for Corruption against the People" (*Phong trào Tham nhũng Chống Nhân dân*).[88] The population demanded political change, but government authorities hid from them.

Đứng dậy also revealed secret government documents that requested photos of fifty-five prominent members of this anticorruption movement, as if they had become enemies of the state. The list included its most important organizers and spokespeople, such as the longtime peace activists Father Chân Tín and Father Lý Chánh Trung; advocates of a new coalition government demanding the inclusion of the NLF, such as Madame Ngô Bá Thành; as well as more recent critics of the state's corruption, such as Father Hoàng Quỳnh.[89] The state may have collected intelligence to investigate the risk of communist infiltration, but the information leaking to the public caused consternation. Once again, the government seemed busier fighting its own population than fighting communism. Nothing could preserve Saigon's sinking legitimacy.

This did not mean that people, especially Catholics, were completely unified. Neither the Vatican nor its hierarchy supported their efforts. The RVN ambassador did some heavy lifting in Rome to denounce the actions of the Vietnamese priests to their hierarchy. He reached out both to Rome's special attaché to Southeast Asia and to the Father Superior of the Redemptorists, Father Trần Hữu Thanh's congregation. Priests used churches for political action, called their faithful to rise up against the government, prevented the police from clamping down on illegal publications, and engaged in violent outbursts, smashing planters in front

Figure 6.2. A government disconnected from its constituents, 1974.
Source: Unknown author, "Đạo vào đời, Đời vào đạo, phụ chú của đđ," *Đứng dậy*, October 1974.

of the Legislative Assembly.[90] Rome, at the time, had already received criticism through internal channels, although accusing the Vietnamese Church this time, of being on the wrong side of history. Father Piero Gheddo, a member of the Pontifical Institute for Foreign Missions who had helped write *Ad Gentes* (the text recommending changes in missionary work in the wake of the Second Vatican Council), published a damning account of Vietnamese Catholics' mobilization against Buddhists.[91] In private correspondence, he also warned Rome's undersecretary of the council for the public affairs that Vietnamese Catholics did not adapt to the recommendations made since the Second Vatican Council and were too close to the government. This required immediate action by the Vatican to train new "progressive" priests, preparing seminarians to remain open to the rest of the world and to learn more about the Church's new political and social position.[92]

This diplomatic work probably influenced the pope's meeting with Henry Kissinger, who visited Rome. When asked what he thought about the Vietnamese priests' activism, "the Holy Father's response was prudent, but negative." He could not openly support members of the clergy who were openly opposing the government.[93] Hence, the Holy See and the episcopacy condemned Father Trần Hữu Thanh's frontal attack on the presidency.

Vietnamese Catholics also expressed their disagreement with Father Thanh's criticism of the presidency. Father Hoàng Quỳnh told the press that he had not asked the president to meet face to face with Father Thanh and demanded proof of any accusations before they were made public.[94] But he did not set the record straight. Most newspapers continued to distort his statements to support or denounce street protests.[95] Other Catholics thought that Father Thanh still drew too hard a line between Catholics and communists. The priest had been an anticommunist since 1945. His mobilization against the corrupt government was only a step toward challenging communism, Vietnam's number one enemy. Writing in *Đứng dậy*, someone named Hương Khê considered this reasoning dangerous. It perpetuated the misconception that communists and noncommunists could not live together, even though they were both Vietnamese. "The contradiction between communists and noncommunists is an illusion created and maintained by the colonialists and imperialists to cover up their invasion."[96] Father Thanh had resolutely opposed Saigon's legitimacy. This revealed that Vietnamese Catholics were no longer unified in their opposition to communism.

In January 1975, the advance of PAVN troops created so much disruption that Saigon decided to retreat from the central highlands to better protect the most populated areas in the south and along the coast. But the poor coordination between the military corps and the lack of aerial support in a country stretching over a relatively long distance made the defense of South Vietnam extremely difficult.[97] As the communist troops advanced, the front against corruption called for help from the International Red Cross.[98] Three months later, communist troops nearly encircled Saigon. Father Hoàng Quỳnh urged the UN and the twelve countries that signed the Paris Peace Accords to pressure Hanoi to oppose this "military invasion."[99] Despite all the attention that Vietnam had attracted among religious and human rights groups abroad, the communist conquest of the south inspired little reaction. On April 30, 1975, PAVN tanks entered Saigon, marking the end of the war. How the new authorities dealt with the population would determine whether the Vietnamese would finally enjoy peace.

CHAPTER 7

Lag Time

In her memoir in 1999, Dương Văn Mai Elliott captured a story that, for many other evacuees, was both unique and all too common. In the 1950s, she was one of the few female Vietnamese students to obtain a scholarship to study abroad, attending Georgetown University; she later married an American and both worked for the RAND Corporation, a think tank conducting research to advise the US military, during the Second Indochina War. However, like many others, her family was uprooted twice. In 1954, her father, an official who had held an important position in the ASVN government, left for the south. But two of Mai's sisters remained in the DRV, separating the family. Then, in April 1975, when Mai was in Ithaca, New York, as her husband was pursuing doctoral studies, she sponsored her family, who left Saigon on April 29, 1975, but without her brother who also stayed behind. He was later sent to reeducation camps and left for France in 1990, meeting her in California two years later. Mai also went back to Vietnam in 1993 to see her sisters who had remained in the north forty years earlier. These reunions brought closure, but after decades of war, most family members were scattered across the United States, Canada, France, Australia, and Vietnam.[1] Mai's family members were among the many northerners who left the country after 1975 and had the feeling, once more in their life, that there was no way back.² How did the experience of displacement in 1954 shape the evacuees' perception of exile in 1975?

Most history books end with the Vietnamese communist victory on April 30, 1975. But the departure of many 1954 evacuees after the Second Indochina War offers a unique opportunity to understand repeated displacement. Refugees left Vietnam after 1975 in three waves and channels: on airplanes and ships in the immediate aftermath of the fall of Saigon in April 1975; via land and maritime routes, from 1978 to 1979, after Hanoi introduced socialist reforms and engaged in a war against its neighbors, China and Cambodia; and on airplanes via the Orderly Departure Program, which enabled people to apply for asylum or for family reunion while still in Vietnam, beginning in 1979. Studies on these refugee flows have focused on the humanitarian crisis due to the departure of "boat people," power relations with host countries, and the changing physical, political, financial, and imagined connections with their homeland.³ Studying the evacuees who had previous experience with a forced departure offers a fresh outlook on these three dimensions.

Twice in their lifetime, they had left at a moment when their country was undergoing a major upheaval. Like in the 1954 partition, the end of the Second Indochina War gave the evacuees the impression their lives were shattered by a critical event. But a public interpretation of their departure as a metaphor for Vietnam's transformation emerged at different times. At the time of the evacuation in 1954, the mention of refugees fleeing communist expansion appeared before the cease-fire was even signed. Reports of the French withdrawal from the Red River delta had led to this narrative. What happened after 1975 was entirely different. Based on the publications and journeys of a few prominent evacuees, this chapter shows that they did not identify themselves as political exiles when they physically left Vietnam in 1975 but, rather, at the end of 1978. Although that delay could be explained by the need to address their basic needs and resettlement, other reasons were also in play. People resettled in countries where neither the government nor public opinion glorified them as heroes. They also joined an existing Vietnamese overseas community that was deeply divided by the war. After this period, at no time was the diaspora unified under the same political banner. But some began to advocate struggle against Hanoi and became prominent after two new developments. In 1976, Hanoi's decision to unify North and South Vietnam as the Socialist Republic of Vietnam (SRVN) became known to Vietnamese in exile. Then, in late 1978, Vietnam was criticized for its handling of the "boat people" crisis and its occupation of Cambodia, which marked a turning point. The international criticism against Hanoi and the possibility this could bring another military intervention offered a unique opportunity. Some activists among them, especially the evacuees, mobilized, first by claiming their departure reflected a political choice, and second, by trying to unite the diaspora in opposition to Hanoi. Displacement alone, even the most painful one, faraway into a foreign land after 1975, did not change how many evacuees saw themselves; but consensus on the political meaning of the massive departure of people away from Vietnam after 1978 led them to do so.

Facing Uncertainty

In the weeks before the arrival of PAVN troops in Saigon in 1975, many Vietnamese involved in the RVN war effort faced a choice between staying and leaving. Evacuees had experienced a similar choice twenty years earlier, but making that decision had not become easier. As in 1954, the United States did its best to enable as many people as possible to leave the country. At the same time, the situation was also very different. People were unsure about what would happen after communist troops completed the unification of the country, nor did they know what to do or where to go.

When the communist troops entered Saigon on April 30, many RVNAF members and civil servants left the country. The US Congress agreed to accept as many as two hundred thousand people who transited through Guam before reaching five camps across the United States.[4] But there was no correlation between a person's political orientation and their ability to leave the country. Many did not have the connections and information to get to the last airplanes and ships leaving the country. Others, such as Vietnamese Catholic priests and Western missionaries, remained wherever the NLF advanced. Even the bishops who were absent when the PAVN advanced and seized control of their region returned to their parishioners. Monsignor Nguyễn Văn Bình, the archbishop of Saigon, declared that this decision was not an order from the Vatican but, instead, "a consensus that emerged from an episcopal meeting in January."[5] Father Nguyễn Đình Thi in Paris proudly emphasized that, unlike in 1954, members of the clergy remained in their parishes.[6] Some thought they were too old to leave, and others hoped they could resist and continue to fight. Father Hoàng Quỳnh and the lawyer Trần Văn Tuyên could have left the country in April 1975 but opted to stay.[7] Others agreed to go to

Guam but later decided that they did not want to leave Vietnam. In his memoirs, Trần Đình Trụ reveals that a small delegation of people who had gone to Guam tried to obtain a ship so that they could return to Vietnam.[8] They did not fear the communist authorities, nor did they want to leave Vietnam for good.

The main reason for the lack of correlation between the decision to stay or go and the political perspective was Vietnam's uncertain future. Everyone knew that the DRV represented a communist regime, but in the spring of 1975, no one knew what would happen in the south. The PRG was officially in control, but a military administration was temporarily running the state. Would it keep the PRG's promise to create a coalition government? Would it organize free elections, allowing everyone to be represented? The military administration did not announce its plans for South Vietnam.

Many feared a bloodbath. In the United States, it was a subject of public debate. People in Vietnam were mentally preparing for that possibility. In response to questions by a Canadian reporter in early April, a Catholic evacuee declared the expectation that those who remained would be massacred. Another man stated that he was ready to emigrate and go anywhere, whereas a cigarette salesman, who had fought two wars, did not say a word. He only made a gesture of slitting his throat.[9] They expected bloodshed. Upon their arrival, PAVN soldiers paraded in the street. They discovered with curiosity a South Vietnam that they had been told to liberate from American imperialism. Despite the widespread assumption that soldiers of the ARVN deserted in numbers, some remained, to surrender or die by suicide before getting caught.[10] For their part, the urban residents of Saigon had to get to know the PAVN soldiers, whom they had only heard about for years.

The VWP introduced thought reform campaigns. The length of this political reeducation varied, depending on one's occupation before April 1975.[11] The new authorities also tried to ease overcrowding problems in Saigon by sending people to the New Economic Zones. On the evening of April 30, Saigon was renamed Ho Chi Minh City as part of its journey to a new future. Most of those steps seemed reasonable measures to restore balance after decades of war.[12]

This differed from what happened on the other side of the border with Cambodia, where another communist group had seized power on April 15, 1975. After taking over in Phnom Penh, the Khmer Rouge had emptied all major cities of the population, forcing everyone, including women, children, the elderly, and even the sick in hospitals, to go to the countryside. By the time Vietnamese communists entered Saigon two weeks later, virtually all Cambodians who had survived their exodus had forcibly become peasants. A similar radical transformation did not happen in Saigon in the spring of 1975.

In Vietnam, the reforms were gradual because the VWP was undecided about its course of action. The economic crisis was so serious that the communist party tried everything to attract foreign assistance, including normalization with the United States and even keeping Vietnam divided.[13] Two membership applications to the UN could increase the avenues for foreign assistance.[14] By the end of July, however, the party seemed to give up on applying for separate memberships and moved to unify the country. The coincidence in the dates is striking. The PRG filled out a formal application to become a member of the UN on July 17, followed by Hanoi two days later. On July 19, Hanoi gave up and sent resident observers.[15] The same day, PAVN tanks surrounded the PRG's headquarters, conducting what some called a silent coup.[16] Trương Như Tảng, a member of the NLF and former PRG minister of justice who later escaped Vietnam, claimed that the takeover intensified after the twenty-fourth plenum of the VWP's Central Committee in September. Representatives of the north and the south were summoned to accept a set plan for unification, rather than drafting one themselves.[17] Neither all interest groups of the south nor all members of the NLF could take part in these consultations. Loyal communist party members, rather than diverse portions of society, would play a role in this "democratic" process.

Unification

People soon understood what members of the NLF had already seen coming. Some never returned after they were sent for political reeducation. Many had to undergo further training, taking them to other labor camps in remote areas and sometimes above the seventeenth parallel, far from family and existing social networks. In his memoirs, Nguyễn Công Luận recalls going to three different camps in the south and three others in the north.[18] No one tried to escape, mostly because they knew that they would not last forty-eight hours without being spotted by the police.[19] Depending on the source, the number of people undergoing reeducation varied from forty thousand to four hundred thousand. Even Vietnamese officials acknowledged that it was important for some people to learn "to change their mentality."[20] The same realization was arrived at about the New Economic Zones. Not everyone was subject to resettlement in rural areas—mostly those viewed by the new regime as undesirables, such as civil servants or soldiers in the RVN. This measure did not entirely depopulate the city; it only made room for northerners who would take over positions in the local administration. An initiative first intended to reinvigorate the economy became a tool for "communizing" the largest cities in the south.

Catholics wondered whether this new regime would limit their freedom of religion. Some members of the clergy experienced the full force of the new authorities. Father Trần Hữu Thanh and Father Hoàng Quỳnh were imprisoned.[21] The first survived, while the other did not. The military command also arrested Nguyễn Văn Thuận, the recently nominated coadjutor bishop of Saigon, who was a nephew of Ngô Đình Diệm and eventually spent thirteen years in prison.[22] They also targeted Monsignor Henri Lemaître, the apostolic delegate, who was responsible for that appointment only weeks before the arrival of PAVN troops. To give the impression that Lemaître had abused his power and challenged Vietnam's sovereignty, the party orchestrated a demonstration on June 5, demanding his departure.[23] The apostolic delegate left the country, which prompted some Catholic evacuees to protest his expulsion.[24] Officially, the Church urged Catholics to remain peaceful, but in practice their relationship was tense.

The communist party did not attempt to impose a total clampdown on the Catholics, as it needed to maintain its image and receive international assistance. Monsignor Trịnh Như Khuê, the bishop of Hanoi, had received his first exit visa to attend the synod in Rome in September 1974. After the war, his nomination as cardinal resulted from rare cooperation. The Vatican had discussed this choice with Hanoi before calling the prelate about his nomination in Rome.[25] Hanoi wanted to maintain the impression that it would respect religious freedom.

Catholics enjoyed freedoms that most in the south could only dream of. First, unlike members of the former regime or armed forces, they were not required to register with the new authorities. From the perspective of the military command, they did not warrant special surveillance based on their religion.[26] Although most of the newspapers and journals had been shut down, Father Nguyễn Đình Thi from Paris came to Saigon and received authorization to publish *Công giáo và dân tộc* (*Catholics and the Nation*), the first private weekly unattached to the PRG or the VWP to get permission to circulate in the south.[27] Unsurprisingly, the journal extolled patriotism, highlighting the unity of the Church and Catholic resistance to French colonial rule as well as US intervention. It also pointed out the heavy Catholic participation in the DRV's thirtieth anniversary, celebrated in both Hanoi and Saigon on September 2, 1975.[28] According to this line of thought, any divisions among Vietnamese Catholics were due to foreign interference.[29]

This raised the question of whose interests the Church was truly serving. An article discussed the need to nominate a new apostolic delegate, claiming that only a Vietnamese could hold that position. This person would not represent the Holy See's ambassador but, rather, coordinate between the Vietnamese Church and the rest of the hierarchy.[30] This suggested that the apostolic delegate could represent Vietnamese interests in Rome, rather than the other way around. Father Nguyễn Đình Thi insisted that the priorities had to change. "In the past, we had Catholics who were also Vietnamese. Now what we ought to have is Vietnamese who are also Catholics," he confided to a journalist.[31] Professor Trần Tam Tỉnh made the same comment when he criticized Vietnamese bishops for their lack of cooperation with the DRV: "Are our bishops citizens of the Vatican or Vietnamese citizens?"[32] As in the French Revolution, the regime change and the radical overthrow of the former regime raised questions about the Church's ties to Rome. Under the new authorities, the Church had to show absolute loyalty to the country.

The newspaper also contacted the evacuees to seek their support. A travelogue by someone named Mai Thanh described his trip back to a diocese in the north, talking about the villages and the reunion with priests and parishioners. But the new regime left its imprint on this story, by imposing its own toponymy. Apart from the title, Mai Thanh took them back to Ninh Bình Province—not the diocese of Phát Diệm. The only legitimate jurisdiction that remained was that of the DRV. Moreover, every villager talking to Mai Thanh seemed to be transfixed on the mission of increasing economic production. "Moved by the memory of the compatriots who migrated to the south in 1954–1955, we worked with determination to increase the production. We understood that the faster we could contribute to the construction of a prosperous society, the faster the homeland would reunite, and the sooner our family members could meet again; from here, paradise has begun to exist."[33] This account not only reassured Catholic evacuees that their faith had survived in their homeland but also tried to persuade them that they could achieve another kind of salvation if they joined the socialist revolution.

Despite these attempts to mollify Vietnamese Catholics, tensions escalated. In August, priests needed to seek special authorization to gather with more than three people or to celebrate a wedding.[34] The following month, military authorities nationalized about a thousand primary and secondary Catholic schools in the south.[35] Around two hundred Catholic chaplains in the RVNAF underwent political reeducation, taking most of them all the way to the north.[36] In this tense context, it was not surprising that some Catholics had confrontations with local authorities.

In February 1976, a few RVNAF veterans barricaded themselves in the church in Vinh Sơn. During the fifteen-hour-long standoff and despite the attempts at mediation by a pro-NLF priest and a layman, the police broke into the church, and three people were killed in the shootout that followed.[37] The Committee of the NLF and the people's committee of Ho Chi Minh City announced that they had found a cache of weapons, counterfeit money, and radio equipment inside the church, at the same time reiterating that they respected freedom of religion.[38] Monsignor Nguyễn Văn Bình, the archbishop of Saigon, disavowed the rebels who had "believed they were serving the Church."[39] Most accounts blamed the priest, Father Nguyễn Quang Minh, an evacuee twenty years older than the other insurgents, for leading this rebellion. Contrary to newspaper accounts that claimed the priest had become a near gangster to sustain depraved habits, the Catholic newspaper *Công giáo và dân tộc* insisted that the reason for taking over the church was "the anticommunist spirit that the Church has crammed into the minds of this man and all other Vietnamese Catholics for decades."[40] It said that the Church had erred for too long, by encouraging priests such as Father Minh to believe that they were defending the faith through opposing communism.

Father Trần Tam Tỉnh voiced the same concern. While dining with a Western donor who had brought assistance to Hanoi, he insisted that the episcopal letter signed in 1951 still had tremendous consequences. Because of it, a large proportion of priests, especially those in the National Liaison Committee for Catholics, had been excommunicated.[41] The restoration of these priests was required for life in Vietnam to return to normal. This realization confirmed what many Catholics had feared from the outset: the party created a patriotic association of Catholics that had begun to control religious life. By June 1976, all foreign missionaries had been expelled, and priests had to attend political classes.[42] The Church, cut off from the rest of its hierarchy, lost its autonomy. It would be loyal to Vietnam first and to Rome a distant second.[43]

The hope that the new authorities would respect different interests in society was dashed when the party declared a new categorization of citizens. In 1975, the party ordered the organization of a census to assess the labor available for the economic recovery and to better "manage the population."⁴⁴ The following year, this project became key in organizing elections. Not everyone could vote. About 1.5 million people, encompassing members of the "puppet army" (ngụy quân), the "puppet government" (ngụy quyền), and "reactionary organizations and movements" would not be eligible.⁴⁵ When the January 1976 legislative elections were held, everyone understood that Hanoi would never create a coalition government. Those who had been part of the prior regime had been deemed undesirables, and all previous identification documents were superseded by the voter eligibility card, which established residency, working permits, or food rations until the state completed the system of household registration.⁴⁶ Even years after leaving reeducation camps, many people still had temporary permits or ended up homeless.⁴⁷ They had become noncitizens. This created an impossible situation for some members of the NLF with family members who had served in the RVNAF or the prior regime. In one case, a man who went to the north in 1954 returned to his family in the south, where his sons had served in the RVNAF. Constant harassment by the new authorities drove him to such a moral dilemma that he died by suicide.⁴⁸ Trương Như Tảng, the NLF member who captured these events in his memoirs, escaped the country and then resettled in France.

Finally, the political direction of the state became clear in the election. Although this was the first time since 1945 that the population in both the north and south voted together, the process was far from democratic. Only representatives of the Fatherland Front, created in 1955 in the north to replace the Liên Việt, and loyal members of the NLF in the south could be candidates for office. A new constitution, uniting the two halves of the country as the Socialist Republic of Vietnam, was adopted on July 2, 1976, and openly demonstrated a Marxist orientation. This completed the process that had started three months earlier. Vietnam had become a unified, one-party state.

Echoes Overseas

The reactions to this transformation outside the country were gradual. People who had left in 1975 arrived in unfamiliar countries and had few contacts on whom they could rely. In the United States, over a hundred thousand people had arrived at four military bases in Arkansas, California, Florida, and Pennsylvania and waited there until they could resettle. Journalists such as Tô Văn reached out to fellow contacts at news associations, and the former lieutenant colonel Phạm Văn Liễu, one of the first marines of the RVNAF, demanded that a US Army officer become his sponsor to resettle outside of the military base.⁴⁹ The more connections a refugee had to a Cold War community, such as the evacuees, the larger the network they had for assistance. However, they still had to become accustomed to their new lives, including a new language, road signs, drivers' license requirements, and rental leases.⁵⁰

They also experienced estrangement due to their mixed reception by the existing Vietnamese community. In Québec, where the Vietnamese had forcefully called for an end to the war, this gap was large. The first publication that emerged from the refugee community, *Chân trời mới* (*New Horizons*), appeared in Guam and then in Camp Pendleton in California. Sister publications were published later in the United States, Australia, and Canada, sometimes with the same name. The *Chân trời mới* that was published in Montréal was not run exclusively by evacuees.⁵¹ But discussions in it give us a glimpse of the conditions that faced newcomers to Canada. In April 1975, about ten Vietnamese associations operated in Montréal alone.⁵² Although some of these organizations supported Hanoi, others opposed it, and still others only called for peace. Many tried to put aside their political differences in order to help the hundreds of thousands of refugees.⁵³ But these efforts could not hide their divisions.

Hence, the Vietnamese community in Canada hardly seemed united. Much of the criticism targeted war profiteers or alleged war criminals in the RVN. In 1975, the arrival of Đặng Văn Quang, one of the most corrupt war profiteers who had sold exit visas for a fortune in April 1975 and lived in air-conditioned quarters in Guam, created a stir.⁵⁴ Concern about his resettlement was widespread in public opinion in Canada. A member of the parliament objected to the decision by the Immigration Service to grant him permission to resettle there, claiming that by doing so, Canada would become "a dumping ground for all of Saigon's undesirable elements."⁵⁵

This criticism extended to refugees in the United States. The Democratic representative for the state of New York sent a letter to the Immigration and Naturalization Service demanding an inquiry over former Vietnamese army officers who had escaped after April 1975 and come to the United States. The government had to make sure that no war criminal who should have been judged in Hanoi could hide among the refugees welcomed by the United States. Among those dubious officers, the letter insisted, were the former prime minister, Air Marshal Nguyễn Cao Kỳ, and the former Major General Nguyễn Ngọc Loan, who was known for his execution of a communist rebel at point-blank range after the Tết

Offensive, a gesture captured by the photographer Eddie Adams, who won the Pulitzer Prize for best photograph.⁵⁶ Americans and Canadians opened their doors to Vietnamese refugees, but they knew that not everyone was an innocent victim. Some were personae non grata.

Public opinion in the West also shifted. Initially, efforts were organized to help with postwar reconstruction. Father Nguyễn Đình Thi created Fraternité S.O.S. in the spring of 1975 to raise funds and send material support to the PRG. Political figures and journalists, such as Jean Lacouture, contributed to the campaigns.⁵⁷ This does not mean that the organization was a satellite of the communist government. It called on the PRG to allow people to circulate freely across zones, acknowledging that some Vietnamese were seeking shelter.⁵⁸ But it also raised funds to give postwar assistance to the PRG, through the network of international Christian assemblies. The International Assembly for Healing the Wounds of War and for the Reconstruction of Vietnam compiled evidence from multiple sources. Academic studies, newspapers, legal rulings, a US Senate subcommittee, and unofficial translations of *Nhân dân* (*The People*), the Vietnamese official newspaper, established the physical, human, and moral cost of the war.⁵⁹

However, these activists also started raising concerns. PRG did not live up to its promise of peace and a coalition government. In November 1975, twelve monks and nuns in Vietnam protested by setting themselves on fire. Their network smuggled out information about the self-immolations. People needed to know what the Vietnamese were enduring under the new regime. Months later, Richard Neuhaus, a senior editor of the Peace Corps' publication, and Jim Forest, a Catholic peace activist and a longtime friend of the Buddhist monk Thích Nhật Hạnh, called for an inquiry. The intellectual left, which was previously united, wondered whether the actual peace in Vietnam was the one they had sought.⁶⁰ Lacouture also became disenchanted with the regime after a visit to Hanoi. Now that the Vietnamese government was no longer a "resister," the "victor" looked very different. Lacouture concluded that "it is better for someone trying to preserve intact his admiration for a revolution not to know its victims."⁶¹ His reservations became total rejection of the new regimes in the former colonies of Indochina when he found out about the atrocities committed by the Khmer Rouge. News about mass graves and dead bodies lying on the street made him question his belief that socialism could save the decolonized world. Commenting on revelations about the executions by the Khmer Rouge, he declared that this "can be read only with shame by those of us who supported the Khmer Rouge cause."⁶² Lacouture's mea culpa referred to Cambodia, but it also raised doubt about the Vietnamese government's truthfulness to bring peace.

The constant flow of people escaping Vietnam reinforced suspicions about the PRG. Theodore Jacqueney, the editor of *Worldview* who had called for the end of the war before 1975, interviewed refugees, including members of the NLF and PRG who had escaped from their country. Although they did not endure the same torture as under the RVN, they were imprisoned. At its 1976 meeting, the World Conference on Religion and Peace in Singapore decided to help the refugees. The Boat People project, chaired by the monk Thích Nhật Hạnh, sent a ship to rescue refugees at sea.⁶³ Journalists, religious leaders, and antiwar activists increasingly turned against Hanoi.

Details that leaked through Christian channels were also alarming. Father André Gélinas, a French Canadian Jesuit, published a scathing report on life in South Vietnam published in *L'Express* in France and in the *New York Times Review of Books* in the United States. Gélinas claimed that over two hundred priests had been imprisoned, and those who were free remained silent out of fear of arrest. Moreover, he wrote that ordinary people had died by suicide to end the harassment by local authorities.⁶⁴ The French periodical *Informations catholiques internationales* had always been sympathetic to the Catholic left, but it also acknowledged the grave situation. Two years after the PRG's victory, one in every four priests in the south remained in a reeducation camp. Bishops could meet but had an agenda imposed on them, which they refused to discuss.⁶⁵ Political retribution targeted Vietnamese Christians.

Influential voices were raised to counter this narrative. Father Trần Tam Tỉnh refuted Gélinas's accusations.⁶⁶ The professor also published a book-length history of the Vietnamese Church, criticizing the excesses of the clergy against communist authorities and Buddhist movements. *Dieu et César* (*God and Caesar*) appeared first in Italian in 1975 and then was published in a more complete edition in French in 1978. It was eventually translated into Vietnamese by Sudest Asie, Father Nguyễn Đình Thi's publishing house in Paris. The title referred to the saying by Jesus that one must distinguish between what is the province of God and what is in the domain of the state. The Roman Catholic Church had failed to distinguish between the spiritual and the temporal.⁶⁷ By involving their religion in politics, Vietnamese Catholics had been in the wrong, and only now, when they were leaving political matters to the state, were they on the right path.

The dispute spread beyond the two priests. A woman named Nguyen Thi Minh Tam in Montréal warned readers not to fall for Hanoi's propaganda. Two Christians, Sister Françoise Vandermeersch and Trần Tam Tỉnh, only served as mouthpieces.[68] Neither of them had lived in Vietnam as long as Father Gélinas. Moreover, the writer found their rationale unacceptable: no one should refrain from denouncing repression of Vietnamese Catholics for fear that doing so would attract reprisal. Ignoring the violation of religious freedom could never be a solution.[69]

Overseas Vietnamese did not need the prompting from Western public opinion to be concerned about the situation. *Chân trời mới* documented restrictions on the press and arrests of people such as the bonze Thích Trí Quang and Father Trần Hữu Thanh, known for their opposition to Saigon before 1975.[70] But they became the most agitated after Hanoi took steps to unify the country without including a wide representation of the population.[71] On the first anniversary of the day that communist tanks entered Saigon, the journal called on overseas Vietnamese to unite against Hanoi. *Chân trời mới* maintained that it was not unpatriotic to do so because anticommunism was both new and old. It was novel in the sense that it could not be remotely associated with the "corrupt and rotten government" of Nguyễn Văn Thiệu, but in opposing authoritarian rule, it was old. "Our anticommunism is opposition not to Mr. [Nguyễn Hữu] Thọ, Mr. [Huỳnh Tấn] Phát, and Mme. [Nguyễn Thị] Bình but to the violent infringement on individual rights. We oppose communism to protect people's basic rights: freedom of speech, freedom of the press, freedom of religion, freedom of movement."[72] The symbolism for this new mobilization was not self-evident. The newspaper declared it still identified with the SVN's flag, a yellow background with three red stripes, and national anthem, which remained unchanged in the first and second republics in the south. However, it took pains to explain that this movement was not the same as "Nguyễn Văn Thiệu's anti-patriotic and corrupt regime," which fell in 1975. It identified with a thirty-year-long struggle and the values in the constitutions of past republics.[73] Once more, Vietnamese had to oppose communism, not out of nostalgia but because they rejected the regime's authoritarianism.[74]

Chân trời mới amplified news about local resistance to the PRG, compiling articles from the BBC, Reuters, Agence France-Presse, and Keesing's archives on the pockets of resistance in the highlands and in the countryside. A map showed "areas of operations by resistance fighters." RVNAF units that remained behind, the FULRO (the United Front for the Liberation of Oppressed Races, gathering several ethnic minorities of the central highlands), the Cao Đài, and Catholic forces all fought the new regime.[75] This gave the impression that these groups were rebelling at the same time and could hold their ground. That was highly unlikely in practice given the PRG's progress in holding a census, reeducation camps, and New Economic Zones. But this two-dimensional and highly optimistic view was necessary for mobilizing overseas Vietnamese.

This renewed anticommunism did not persuade everyone. The observances on April 30 were not called a "National Day of Shame" (*Ngày quốc hận*) or "Black April" (*Tháng tư đen*), as it is sometimes referred to nowadays. Back then, Black April was a group of marines and paratroopers, formed in Guam. They aimed "to eradicate corrupt officials in the Saigon government" and settle accounts with the people responsible for the fall of Saigon.[76] Therefore, it was a group of veterans determined to reckon with RVN's bad leadership, not the communists in Hanoi. Overseas Vietnamese also held separate ceremonies. In Ottawa, one event celebrated the victory and liberation of Vietnam, while another marked "one year away from the homeland."[77] In Washington, DC, the largest celebration avoided any commentary on what had happened a year earlier. Vietnamese there commemorated the mythical Hùng kings in a ceremony that displayed neither the yellow five-point star nor the yellow flag with three red stripes.[78] Overseas Vietnamese did not unite, and most did not know what position to take regarding Hanoi's control over the PRG.

Phạm Duy's memoir and songs also portray the massive confusion after the departure from Vietnam. He was stunned by the end of the armed conflict: "Because I had lost my country, my four children, I had lost the desire to live." He composed a musical piece so filled with sadness and despair that even his children who remained in Vietnam feared that he was dying. But after being contacted by two Vietnamese newspapers, he wrote some new songs, including *Nguyên vẹn hình hài* (*An Unscathed Body*), published in a California newspaper in 1977, which recalled the smell, sounds, and sights of Vietnam. The lyrics, in the first person, spoke of visitors to the singer's grave in a country where the "snow has been falling for a thousand years." The visitor would open the coffin and see his body, shaped like a "portrait of Vietnam": the south as the belly, the center as the heart, and the north as the head. This suggests that he had come to terms with living in exile. In contrast, another song, *Ta chống cộng hay ta trốn cộng* (*Are We Opposing Communism or Are We Hiding from Communism?*), whose lyrics were published under a pseudonym in a French newspaper, called on overseas Vietnamese to become proactive again. Their departure did not mean defeat but, rather, "success" and a strong "rejection of communism." The Vietnamese maintained the desire to return to their homeland and restore "the civil rights of our people." Phạm Duy reflected on this transition in his memoirs: "I had to return to Vietnam. To put it clearly, when refugees are scattered like this, I had to return to a place with many Vietnamese people. I had to go to California."[79] The composer shifted from nostalgia to the claim, similar to the one after the evacuation, that people did not leave out of fear. They did so because of their political convictions. Unlike in 1954, however, there was a delay in the transition from apathy to a call for action. This new mobilization had lagged but then gained momentum with a new war and another refugee crisis.

Awakening

Two crises put Hanoi on the hot seat again. People leaving Vietnam under horrible conditions affected neighboring countries and was poorly received in Western public opinion. In addition, Vietnam's occupation of Cambodia beginning in December of 1978 revived the potential for an escalating war in the region. Combined, these two events elicited a reaction by Hanoi's adversaries, mainly China and the United States, who reacted diplomatically and militarily to show that the SRVN was a threat to peace in the region. The Cold War entered a new stage. This drove many evacuees to mobilize again and call for war against Hanoi.

Soon after 1975, tensions emerged between Beijing and Hanoi.[80] Vietnamese communists resented their Chinese counterparts for fraternizing with the United States in 1972, whereas the People's Republic of China (PRC) was angered by Vietnamese communists' lack of loyalty. In Beijing's view, Hanoi was supposed to choose a winner in the confrontation between the Soviet Union and the PRC. The two communist states had competed against each other to lead the world revolution ever since the de-Stalinization of 1956.[81] In 1969, last-minute diplomatic exchanges at Hồ Chí Minh's funeral in Hanoi averted a full-scale border conflict between them. The Cold War still mattered, but for Beijing the number one enemy was no longer Washington—it was the other communist giant, which had nuclear weapons, relied on a large conscription army, and shared a 2,500-mile-long land border with China. From Beijing's perspective, Hanoi's neutrality was intolerable.

Moreover, the SRVN seemed to engage in hostile measures against Chinese interests. In 1978, Hanoi imposed tighter control over the economy, beginning with the seizure of private property. It also introduced reforms that targeted small-scale capitalism, which disproportionately affected ethnic Chinese. In the north, conditions for the ethnic Chinese community deteriorated as well. They no longer enjoyed a status as "privileged outsiders" and were repatriated to China.[82] Vietnam saw these people, especially the ethnic Chinese involved in business in the south, as "migrants" who were leaving because they refused to endure the hardships of a postwar economy.[83] However, China had not accepted their assimilation in the RVN, considering them Chinese citizens who required protection.[84] Any hostile gesture toward them would be considered an affront to Beijing itself, regardless of Hanoi's desire to implement a socialist revolution and demote people it saw as capitalists. Again, people, moving or not, could have grounds for a dispute.

The number of boat departures from Vietnam ballooned due to the hurried departure of ethnic Chinese. From July 1975 to October 1978, countries in the region had received almost 350,000 Vietnamese who had arrived over land and more than 72,000 by boat. Only 32 to 46 percent of them resettled in a third country, such as France or the United States. Most remained in the region, waiting for their resettlement. What made the situation particularly concerning was the marked increase in boat arrivals, evolving from 2,257 arrivals in March to 12,524—a more than fivefold increase—only six months later in October 1978.[85] Mounting evidence suggested that smugglers and Vietnamese authorities profited from this traffic.[86] Traffickers used a trick to force countries to accept people without documents. Boat captains pretended that their vessel was in distress in order to gain permission for refugees to disembark in countries near their position at sea. Soon, however, this deception stopped working. Although Indonesia and Malaysia had accepted refugees in the past, they kept a boat, the *Hải Hồng*, at sea, provided repairs on board, and then escorted the ship back to international waters in November 1978 (see fig. 7.1). This situation challenged maritime customs that require states to shelter ships in distress. This meant that Southeast Asian states could push boats back and people could remain at sea indefinitely.

Other than the United Kingdom in Hong Kong, the countries in the region were not signatories to the 1951 convention on refugee status. So, the United Nations High Commissioner for Refugees (UNHCR) took a firm position and asserted that all passengers qualified as refugees, regardless of the reason for their departure or the channel by which they fled.[87] It convened a consultative meeting in Geneva in December 1978, attended by countries of first asylum and any country "indicating an interest . . . in resettlement or potential resettlement."[88] Hanoi rejected

152   CHAPTER 7

FIGURE 7.1.   Passengers of the *Hải Hồng*, November 1978.
Source: Alain Dejean, UNHCR/Sygma, RF141628.

"any responsibility for, and accusation relating to, the 'boat people affair.'"[89] But it could not avoid being cast as the main culprit in the situation.[90] The UNHCR issued a press release calling on states to accept more refugees and asked Vietnam to try to halt illegal departures. This paved the way for the Orderly Departure Program, established in May 1979. The UNHCR could screen Vietnamese for resettlement overseas while still within the country.[91] The population movement had escalated from a dispute with China to an international problem requiring the UNHCR's intervention.

Vietnam's armed intervention in Cambodia attracted more opprobrium. Hanoi had failed to normalize its relationship with the United States, so the SRVN turned to the Soviet Union for political, military, and economic support. In November 1978, Hanoi and Moscow signed a treaty of mutual friendship, guaranteeing assistance in the event of an attack by a foreign power.[92] China felt surrounded by the Soviet Union now that Vietnam had become Moscow's ally. This fear became a panic. In response to violent incursions into Vietnamese territory, Hanoi attacked the Khmer Rouge; the PAVN invaded Cambodia in December 1978 and installed a new government, the People's Republic of Kampuchea, prompting the Khmer Rouge to hide along the Cambodian-Thai border.[93]

The Vietnamese attack on the Khmer Rouge, whom Beijing considered to be disciples of Maoism, materialized China's worst fears. After ensuring that Washington would not interpret a punitive expedition as a threat, Beijing launched a military operation into the northern highlands of Vietnam on February 17, 1979 (see fig. 7.2). However, the invasion did not produce the desired results. China had promised Washington and Southeast Asian countries a short intervention that would not escalate further. Instead, the Chinese army failed to progress against a well-trained and armed PAVN. After twenty-seven days, Beijing announced its withdrawal, having made only a disappointing dent in the highlands. Nothing had changed. Hanoi did not end its treaty with Moscow, nor did it withdraw its troops from Cambodia. The Third Indochina War reflected the open rift in the communist world.[94] Although it did not settle the competition between Moscow and Beijing, it shed new light on the SRVN. The courageous country fighting for its independence now looked like a conqueror, ready to subjugate Cambodia.

As in past armed conflicts in the Cold War, a stalemate or de-escalation only meant that the struggle could continue by other means. As the number of Vietnamese people stuck at sea rose and became a cause for public concern, a conference to deal with the refugee crisis was held in Geneva on July 21, 1979. The date chosen was significant, as it was exactly twenty-five years after a prior conference held on the same shores had decided Vietnam's fate. China, the United States, and the United Kingdom seized this opportunity to present Hanoi as the only wrongdoer in the refugee crisis and a threat to peace. The combined effect of the humanitarian mobilization to rescue refugees and the diplomatic offensive launched by Hanoi's enemies bore fruit. By the end of the conference, several countries had pledged money and resettlement quotas. Their large numbers reassured Southeast Asian countries. This meant people reaching processing centers set up by the UNHCR could resettle into a third country (see fig. 7.2). This solution created a new consensus: people did not need to prove they were victims of persecution in order to resettle elsewhere. Hanoi was so dangerous that anyone who reached these centers would be considered a "de facto" refugee.[95]

For many evacuees who had resettled elsewhere, the mention in news reports that Hanoi was menacing world peace was electrifying. Vietnam was plunged yet again into the Cold War. Communists were no longer fighting noncommunists. This time, a coalition of states led by the United States and China was opposing Vietnam and the Soviet Union, which opened up new avenues and created more leverage for bringing about

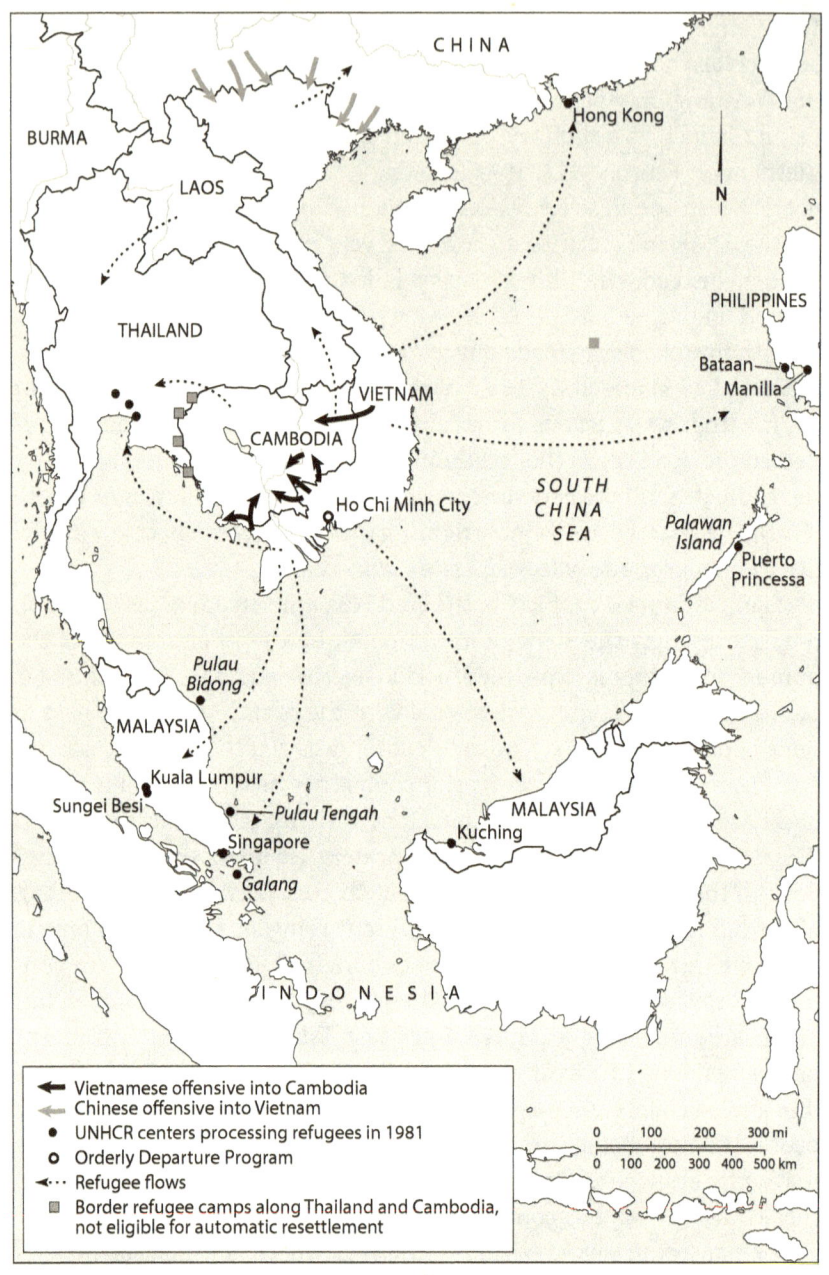

FIGURE 7.2. Vietnam at the epicenter of an armed conflict and humanitarian crisis, 1979.
Source: Map by Bill Nelson, adapted from *The State of the World's Refugees 2000: Fifty Years of Humanitarian Action* (Geneva: UNHCR, 2000); Report to the United Nations General Assembly, Thirty-Sixth Session, Supplement No. 12 (a/36/12), August 28, 1981.

political change. Hence, many overseas Vietnamese reinterpreted their past, rethought the present, and imagined new prospects for themselves and their compatriots. Overseas Vietnamese organized demonstrations across the West to raise awareness about the refugee crisis. They gathered in associations, discussing how to support their compatriots and condemn Hanoi's persecution.

The newspaper *Thức tỉnh* (*Awakening*), published in California, exemplifies this new mobilization. Tô Văn, its manager, resumed his work as a journalist. His rushed departure from Saigon this time was just as traumatic as it had been in 1954.[96] He left with his wife, children, and grandchildren, but his eldest son remained, for which Tô Văn felt responsible. He had advised him to join his military unit and assured him that he would take care of his children. "This is perhaps the biggest regret in my life," he recalled. Because of this grief, he never dared to write letters home to Vietnam, nor did he open mail that he received. "Why would I write that I miss my homeland? Why would I write that I can feed and clothe myself here? Why would I open letters to read bitter comments, the pain of loved ones who endure the oppression of the Lê Duẩn clique?"[97] The pain was too sharp for him to keep in touch.

However, Tô Văn did not entirely give up on Vietnam. *Thức tỉnh* called on overseas Vietnamese after the first months and years of disruption and resettlement. Gathering scattered refugees into a community, this journal of the Greater Vietnamese Overseas Alliance for the Restoration of Vietnam based in Santa Ana, California, appeared twice a month from 1978 to 1984. *Thức tỉnh*'s first issue came out on April 30, 1978, three years after the fall of Saigon. The publication acknowledged that Vietnamese had been divided. Photographs of protests illustrated articles condemning Nguyễn Văn Thiệu and his consorts as "people who had sold out the nation."[98] But overseas Vietnamese had to remember that they had let the armed conflict end because of their fatigue—not acceptance of the new regime. Communists could not be trusted: "Since Vietnamese communists conquered southern Vietnam, the entire population in the north and in the south have seen the true face of the communist clique. . . . Southern Vietnamese have now woken up and have no reservations about what northern migrants reported when they came to the south in 1954."[99] The evacuees, who had urged their compatriots never to let their guard down, had been right all along.

The newspaper interpreted the two Indochina wars as one continuous civil war. Specific events, exemplifying Hanoi's moral failure, punctuated that narrative. The communists, the paper argued, had sacrificed the nation twice: in the 1946 modus vivendi, allowing the French to return, and at the Geneva Conference in 1954. They had slaughtered the population countless times: Ôn Như Hầu in Hanoi, Ba Tơ, Quảng Ngãi, Quỳnh Lưu, Ba Lang, Trà Lý, Nghệ Anh, the Tết attack on cities in 1968, and the 1972 Spring Offensive.[100] This list of events ignored the context of each of these confrontations, but that did not matter. It would persuade everyone that the communists had betrayed the nation.

Therefore, *Thức tỉnh* urged its readers to consider April 30 not as a sad day but as one of national recovery (*ngày phục quốc*). It was time to take Vietnam back from the communists. "Leaving in countless ways, the Vietnamese have called on the world to wake up and see the atrocities of the communists, who spread nothing but suffering for humanity."[101] Vietnam had a long history of resistance, and, in 1970, no one could tell whether the United States would abandon Vietnam, nor who would win the war.[102] Back then, everything seemed possible, and so it seemed again now that the international community was berating Hanoi. Quoting a ninth-century poem, "Bạc tần hoài," an article claimed that only prostitutes could find comfort away from home and that real patriots would never see anywhere other than Vietnam as a homeland.[103] The reason they had to act was simple: the war was inevitable. If they wanted to overthrow communism, readers had to "unite, show resolute solidarity, overcome any difference in party orientations or religious membership, and support a genuine revolution."[104] According to *Thức tỉnh*, this could overthrow communism.

Its editorial board reacted to Hanoi's invasion of Cambodia with an opinion piece in January 1979, criticizing the inaction by the international community. The United States and China were "bowing down" to Vietnam and the Soviet Union.[105] China, the true "master" of the Khmer Rouge, did not retaliate for the invasion. Washington's passivity regarding Cambodia mirrored its inaction when communists invaded Angola, South Vietnam, and Ethiopia. Had the United States given up on containing communism? *Thức tỉnh* was outraged that no one had punished Hanoi for the invasion of its neighbor. The group wrote a letter to the secretary general of the United Nations insisting the situation could not be resolved through negotiation. In the 1973 Paris Peace Accords, the communists showed that they would not respect international treaties. It was "time to force the communist aggressors to withdraw from Cambodia."[106] According to *Thức tỉnh*, the world had to retaliate.

Other organizations, including those for RVNAF veterans, also considered that the time was ripe. Lieutenant Colonel Phạm Văn Liễu, an evacuee who had opposed Ngô Đình Diệm and become the chief of police in 1964, recalled the difficulty of mobilizing overseas Vietnamese. "Every refugee brings with them a cultural, political, and economic heritage that is specific to them; hard to command and coordinate."[107] They struggled to find the right path, independent of the former regime in Saigon, that would still unite them against communism. Another evacuee, Hoàng Cơ Minh, joined him to activate the overseas Vietnamese. The Vietnamese Armed Forces Overseas (Lực lượng Quân nhân Việt Nam Hải ngoại), created on April 30, 1977, also identified itself with the former flag and anthem of the RVN, despite the stigma attached to it. Its second general assembly, held on May 24, 1980, gathered over two hundred representatives and four hundred observers. But Phạm Văn Liễu believed that a real struggle against Hanoi would have to involve everyone.

The opportunity came in July with the assembly of Friends of Overseas Vietnamese. Working with Hoàng Cơ Minh, Phạm Văn Liễu created a movement that was "more open, wider, larger, and more prestigious" than the veteran's organization and had mobilized overseas Vietnamese and sought support from the international community. The National Unified Front for the Liberation of Vietnam (Mặt trận Quốc gia Thống nhất Giải phóng Việt Nam) was brought to life, with a name that showed its ambitions. This organization had to be large, not just a group of veterans who were already divided into western, eastern, and northern branches within North America. To demonstrate its opposition to communism, it was nationalist and was unified "to underscore the spirit of coordination of different organizations which share the same fighting objectives, policy, and position." Its ultimate aim "in essence, [was] the struggle to eliminate communists, and liberate entirely the north and the south of the Vietnamese homeland."[108] According to the front, all Vietnamese forces had to unite against communism.

Many overseas Vietnamese emerged from a state of confusion. Like Phạm Duy, they had tried to return to Vietnam, but it was not a community in California. The prospect that foreign powers might attack Hanoi made them believe that they could affect their homeland in Southeast Asia. Overseas Vietnamese remained divided. However, the outbreak of the Third Indochina War led some evacuees to think it was possible to return to their country.

CHAPTER 8

Breaking Free of the War

Nearly twenty years after Vietnam's reunification, the country was at peace, and yet a woman in Ho Chi Minh City filled out an application to leave what she called hell on earth. As the widow of a soldier, she qualified for the Orderly Departure Program (ODP), helping members and their families of the former RVN resettle in the United States. Candidates had to prove their service in the defunct government or US services in order to qualify for the program. Sometimes, their applications also included letters. The woman wrote a long description of her husband's origins in the north, as if this demonstrated a lifelong opposition to communism. She then detailed his career in the RVNAF.[1] She was not the only one. Nearly half the applications sent to the Families of Vietnamese Political Prisoners Association (FVPPA), a nongovernmental organization helping people apply for asylum, mentioned that they or their families had fled the north in 1954.[2] Leaving Vietnam was not merely an administrative matter. Many saw it as an opportunity to express their resentment. Since the Đổi mới (Renovation) reforms initiated in 1986, Vietnam had abandoned plans to collectivize farms and opened up a market economy. But that woman and many others believed they could find peace only by leaving the country. How and when did the Cold War end for these evacuees?

Between 1975 and 1997, over 1.6 million Vietnamese left their country, not counting the estimated 10 percent of people who died on the journey.³ If we combine the departures by land, boat, and through the ODP, 2 to 3 percent of Vietnam's population departed.⁴ The reasons for leaving, the conditions of departure, and their resettlement are well covered in the literature.⁵ Critical refugee studies highlight the fraught relationship between refugees, who were expected to be grateful for being rescued, and host countries, such as the United States, which used refugee protection to whitewash their responsibility for the crisis.⁶ Scholars of the Vietnamese diaspora show that bellicose talk reappeared after 1980 as the administration of Ronald Reagan restored the military role of the United States in the world.⁷ To the sociologist Y Thien Nguyen, however, political tensions in Southeast Asia were key in the reemergence of anticommunism. It perpetuated the social and political hierarchy that had prevailed before 1975.⁸ Recent contributions also highlight transnational initiatives for reconnecting Vietnamese across borders.⁹

This chapter examines several publications on the diaspora, focusing specifically on the evacuees, based on the notion that anticommunism is highly contextual and shifts depending on the audience and venue. The revival of anticommunism highlighted important contradictions, which activists failed to resolve. International conditions had changed a lot since the 1950s. The new Cold War blurred the lines between communists and anticommunists, so they were not merely two ideological blocs in opposition to each other. The evacuees disagreed about the struggle they should lead, their true enemy, their allies, and the methods they should use. These endless debates led many to the same conclusion: because of the Cold War, which had led them to believe for the past thirty years that they could overthrow Vietnamese communists, they had been out of touch with reality. They understood that they could not liberate Vietnam from communism. Sooner or later, they would have to leave the war behind and make peace.

Lost in a New Cold War

In the 1980s, Hanoi was once again on the fault line of a cold war. Hanoi faced attacks on two fronts for ten years. In the northern highlands, it confronted limited Chinese military interventions. The resettlement of Vietnamese abroad implied that the SRVN was dangerous for its own population. Moreover, the United States, most other Western countries, and China refused to recognize the new Khmer state. Instead, they insisted the Khmer Rouge was the legitimate state of Cambodia and hence defended its representation at the UN. Vietnam's occupation of Cambodia echoed the Soviet Union's invasion of Afghanistan, which had started in December 1979. Ten years later, when Moscow pulled its troops out of Afghanistan, Hanoi also withdrew the PAVN from Cambodia.[10] This paved the way for normalization of relations between Hanoi and its Southeast Asian neighbors, completing a process that had started in 1988.[11] The UN organized a conference in 1989 to introduce a comprehensive plan of action and end the de facto refugee status granted at processing centers.[12] The political conflict in Cambodia took longer to settle. Talks in August 1989 failed to achieve a consensus. Hanoi wondered whether Beijing, which had showed a commitment to communism by repressing the Tiananmen Square protests in June that year, would become more open to its perspective.[13] It also briefly explored the possibility of siding with the Khmer Rouge to exclude non-communists from the coalition government.[14] Eventually, the dissolution of the Soviet Union in 1991 forced the SRVN to take a more conciliatory approach. A month after the UN General Assembly accepted Estonia, Latvia, and Lithuania as members, Vietnam signed the Paris Peace Agreement, ending the war in Cambodia.

This new Cold War lasted for ten years. Refugee protection and talks on Cambodia expressed at the diplomatic level the violence of a military confrontation on the ground. But the opposing camps looked entirely different from combatants in the Cold War of the 1950s. Gone were the days when two antagonistic blocs opposed each other based on ideology. Moscow and Hanoi faced a large and eclectic coalition globally. The United States and its Western allies stood alongside communists, such as the PRC and the Khmer Rouge, in containing the Soviet Bloc's growing influence.[15] Although the modus operandi of international pressure combined with limited military confrontation remained the same, the core task was checking the opponent's expansionism, rather than defending a different conception of freedom and democracy.

This shift away from ideology spurred an identity crisis in the West. The left was first divided about the competition between Beijing and Moscow. Disbelief grew stronger as revelations from Soviet defectors, missionaries escaping the Khmer Rouge, and refugees leaving Vietnam gave a less romantic picture of socialist regimes. People were unsure what their commitment to socialist values and decolonization movements meant in this context.[16] This unprecedented situation equally unsettled the evacuees, because they did not know what kind of cold war they should fight. How they should think about the Chinese attack on Hanoi remained confusing. For example, when China launched its punitive expedition in February 1979, *Thức tỉnh* almost declared victory: "Today, the war between Vietnamese and Cambodians and the armed conflict between Vietnamese and Chinese reveals that international communism has shattered into pieces. Materialism has been replaced by geopolitics and nationalism. Because of this, the overthrow of Vietnamese communists is only a matter of time."[17]

From the perspective of *Thức tỉnh*, Beijing had won. The attack not only contradicted the Vietnamese "legendary success" but also showed that Moscow had left its ally on its own.[18] In August 1979, *Thức tỉnh* added: "For 35 years, during the most dangerous and convoluted moments in 1945–1946, Hanoi's communists have never been as embarrassed, have never failed as tragically, and have never fallen as deeply into a sinking hole as they have today." The communists were surrounded, and the only possible step forward was "neutralization of Indochina as a whole, including Vietnam."[19] Hanoi was stuck and would soon crumble under the pressure. This window of opportunity was compounded by growing criticism over Vietnam's handling of the refugee crisis. These evacuees believed that they could finally eliminate Vietnamese communists.

China's invasion of Vietnam presented anticommunists with an unprecedented choice. They needed to reevaluate the meaning of communism in this new Cold War. *Thức tỉnh* argued it was important to take advantage of the communist world's implosion. When Trương Như Tảng, the NLF leader, fled Vietnam, he resettled in France. From there, he called on everyone to join him in denouncing Hanoi's one-sided reunification of the country. *Thức tỉnh* reported with enthusiasm on the defector's attempt to challenge the SRVN.[20]

This initiative raised a difficult question. Were communists, after all, the enemy? Who was responsible for the country's demise? Was it the ideology or people hiding beneath the veil of Marxism? *Thức tỉnh* had no firm answer to that question. Communism was no longer a monolithic enemy. Hoàng Văn Hoan, the former ambassador of the DRV in Beijing who had sought refuge in China, urged the Vietnamese to overthrow the "Lê Duẩn clique."[21] A response to this call came in the last issue of *Thức tỉnh*. It reprinted an article from *Tin Việt Nam* (*News of Vietnam*), published in Beijing: "Are we opposing communism or are we opposing the Lê Duẩn clique?"[22] Marxism, intellectuals who embraced these ideas, and individuals who had taken advantage of them to seize power could not be lumped together. A look at the past suggests that both nationalists and communists had fought for their country. But Lê Duẩn, who assumed leadership of the VWP in 1963 and remained the party's general secretary until 1986, was not representative of communism, according to the article. Since 1975, he had allowed the Soviet Union to take over the country. He did not care about the well-being of the population and used secret police to eliminate any opponents, the article stated. Vietnamese patriots had to distinguish between communism and Lê Duẩn. That a former Việt Minh such as Tô Văn, who served as *Thức tỉnh*'s manager and penned many of its articles, could remain open to the idea of siding with the communists is not surprising. Until Vietnamese communists took over the DRV starting in 1950, he and many other nationalists had worked side by side with communists. The circumstances required the largest possible front. To him, this meant reaching across any past divide, even an ideological one. The Cold War had always been a game of alliances, deterrence, and proxy wars. Strategy mattered more than ideology.

These new circumstances also raised the question of new alliances. Should nationalist Vietnamese follow the example of Richard Nixon in 1972 and become closer to Beijing? Some evacuees believed that they could not trust China or any other communists. Lieutenant Colonel Phạm Văn Liễu did not share Tô Văn's pragmatism. The Chinese attack represented dangerous interference in Vietnamese affairs. Anyone who was enthusiastic about it, the former officer declared, instilled confusion within the community. In his view, it was impossible to consider China anything other than a threat to Vietnam. "The Chinese have always wanted to conquer Vietnam, from the time of its creation until today, to turn it into a Chinese province.... Countless times, the [Chinese] Han, Tang, Song, and Ming [dynasties] brought hundreds of thousands to conquer our country and failed as the Vietnamese people sent them back to China." This past military prowess had not saved Vietnam multiple times since the tenth century only to let China "divide the country" once again.[23] To some evacuees such as Phạm Văn Liễu, the ideological opposition to communism went hand in hand with nationalist opposition to China. Untangling ideology from this nationalist paradigm might undermine any patriotic movements.

Some opposed the idea of such an alliance so forcefully that they were ready to punish any overseas Vietnamese who leaned in that direction. Hoàng Cơ Minh, a fellow evacuee then based in the United States, sent his henchmen to scare some Vietnamese on the East Coast. They could not welcome Trương Như Tảng during his American tour. Eventually, the former NLF member had to stay with American hosts.[24] Vietnamese patriots could not bridge the ideological divide, rally with NLF defectors, and imagine an alliance with Beijing. The new circumstances revealed important problems with their mobilization. The evacuees had become increasingly confused. On the one hand, the situation demanded pragmatism. But on the other, this down-to-earth approach could compromise a cardinal rule of Vietnamese nationalism. The configuration of this new Cold War meant that these nationalists had no easy choices.

Divergent Strategies

Contrasting understandings of anticommunism called for different strategies. They also revealed different interpretations of the two prior decades of war and what had proven decisive in its outcome. The armed conflict was fought with weapons in the fields, proposals at the negotiating table, and stories in newspapers. But the evacuees who wanted to end communist rule in Hanoi after 1979 disagreed on the impact of these various strategies.

The National United Front for the Liberation of Vietnam opted for armed resistance in Southeast Asia. In late 1981, Hoàng Cơ Minh left the United States with six other volunteers to create a resistance force based in the jungle in Laos, with the help of a Thai general in charge of a bordering province.[25] This recalled what Hoàng Cơ Minh's older brother had attempted to do in 1954. A committee for self-defense had proposed leaving units behind to challenge the DRV's authority above the seventeenth parallel. Twenty-six years later, Hoàng Cơ Minh wanted to do the same because he believed only an armed rebellion could overthrow Hanoi. To truly bring political change, overseas Vietnamese needed to support armed rebellion against Hanoi.[26]

For Tô Văn and others, this battle was on multiple fronts. History showed that the communists had won the war because they used public opinion and diplomacy as leverage. An editorial recalled that the war in 1975 had not been lost on the battleground. Hanoi won in Paris, Washington, and Beijing, "places where communists carried out a political struggle on the diplomatic front."[27] Overseas Vietnamese could apply the same strategy, except, this time, they would turn it against Hanoi. From other countries, they could launch a "revolution" in public opinion. They could oppose Vietnamese communists and speak out about their human rights abuses.[28]

They needed to realize that their voice could influence a changing geopolitical situation. Not only did Reagan's election in 1980 initiate remilitarization in the United States, but demonstrations in Poland led by Lech Wałęsa, a trade union activist, also suggested that communism was imploding. "The world's chessboard is being redrawn," *Thức tỉnh* declared.[29] This was why the option of turning to China became interesting. Although such a move would betray other Asian anticommunists such as the Chinese in the Asian People's Anti-Communist League, who demanded the creation of a strong bloc in the Association of Southeast Asian Nations (ASEAN) to resist communism, *Thức tỉnh* argued that the PRC was ready to "teach Hanoi another lesson" in the early 1980s.[30] Overseas Vietnamese could use this situation to overthrow their enemy. The newspaper followed the initiatives of Trương Như Tảng, the NLF defector who had left France and toured the United States and Asia.[31] On his return from Beijing, the defector stated that China was ready to attack Vietnam again and yet respect the country's sovereignty afterward.[32] This tentative rapprochement by former officers of the RVNAF, such as Nguyễn Cao Kỳ, was more surprising. *Thức tỉnh* claimed that the former prime minister had also gone to China and served as a military adviser in southern China in 1980.[33] The following year, the newspaper revealed that Professor Nguyễn Ngọc Huy, a Đại Việt, had also reached out to Beijing.[34] Although the editors of *Thức tỉnh* remained curious and even hopeful that China would attack Hanoi, they were not entirely sure that this would be the best solution

The best chance to bring political change in Vietnam was a negotiated solution, similar to what was being discussed regarding Cambodia. Extensive diplomatic work strove to reduce international tensions, de-escalate the violence, and find a satisfactory alternative to the government that Hanoi had installed in Cambodia. The same could happen in Vietnam, according to various articles in *Thức tỉnh*. They documented Norodom Sihanouk's trips and public declarations. Articles in the newspaper analyzed his movements and meetings with US representatives, but this obsession was not innocent.[35] It described how he had disavowed the Khmer Rouge and claimed that he would create a coalition government. The editors of *Thức tỉnh* hoped that someone could play the same role in Vietnam.[36] The same newspaper even changed its depiction of Khieu Samphan, the Khmer Rouge leader. Although initially *Thức tỉnh* stated that he had caused millions of deaths in Cambodia, it did not hesitate to declare, two years later, that the same person could serve in a new coalition government.[37] A *Thức tỉnh* correspondent attended meetings involving overseas Vietnamese in the United States and France in March 1979 to create a government in exile. Yet the journalist warned that the situations in Vietnam and Cambodia were different. Anyone who was dreaming about a "Vietnamese Sihanouk" had to remember that political leaders often serve their own interests, rather than those of their country.[38] Despite these reservations, on November 6, 1979, overseas Vietnamese in Brussels and, clandestinely, in Saigon created a "movement for peace, neutrality, and democratic freedom in Vietnam."[39] An article in the September 1979 issue of *Le Monde diplomatique* by a writer in Paris named Nguyễn Xuân Thọ called for Vietnam to become a neutral country.

Imagining that the diplomatic momentum in Cambodia could extend to Vietnam, however, came with its own caveats. Coverage in *Thức tỉnh* about dreams of neutrality warned against falling into the classic trap of negotiating with communists. *Thức tỉnh* distinguished between longtime anticommunists, such as the members of the Greater Association for the Restoration of Vietnam and "post 30-4-1975 anti-communists." The former knew that a third force that would be capable of bringing all sides together was a fantasy. Only "an armed overthrow" could guarantee "the neutrality of Vietnam and peace in Southeast Asia." Then, a new coalition government could take over.[40] Not every Vietnamese abroad had experienced communism. "Not all refugees know communism. Overseas Vietnamese still carry past hopes and believe the lies resulting from decades of being tricked."[41] They had to recall that negotiations without an armed rebellion would stand no chance. Plans for a "free zone" allowing communists and noncommunists to coexist was pure fiction.[42] The Cold War had changed, and so had the methods needed to fight it. But many evacuees still believed they had to lead the effort.

Facing Failure

Over time, none of the strategies proposed had results. Only a handful of fighters joined the National Unified Front for the Liberation of Vietnam's resistance in the jungle, which had at most a few hundred members. Hoàng Cơ Minh, its leader, spent more time in Japan, meeting with other anticommunists, than in Laos. All attempts to merge the front with other forces, including armed resistance, utterly failed.[43] In 1984, Phạm Văn Liễu split with the front due to a dispute over management of outreach activities within the diaspora. However, one cannot help but wonder whether he left for another reason. As a former marine with long wartime experience, Phạm Văn Liễu may have felt embarrassed. The front had performed poorly and made almost no military progress.

Hoàng Cơ Minh's fighters had not inflicted any serious harm on Hanoi. Nor did the front recruit more fighters or even adjust its strategy. Perhaps Phạm Văn Liễu decided to jump ship before it sank because of the front's terrible results.

In contrast, the front's overseas support and media attention exceeded its performance on the ground. Phạm Văn Liễu recalled that the fundraising cultural events, featuring performances by South Vietnam's greatest stars, were sold out weeks in advance.[44] At these venues, banners were emblazoned with slogans such as "The resistance will win," "Eliminate communism," and "Free Vietnam," as if they would achieve the objectives regardless of the front's progress. Projections of a certain victory, no matter the circumstances, recalled the tales of liberation told by some evacuees under Ngô Đình Diệm. The disconnect became even more evident when a CBS News reporter, Morley Safer, traveled all the way through Thailand to reach the front's base to interview Hoàng Cơ Minh.[45] The three-minute segment on US television was perhaps the front's most important moment of glory, as if a portion of the diaspora needed validation more than effective progress on the ground. Cold War enthusiasts, obsessed with the excitement of real-life heroes fighting for a lost cause in the jungle, might have contributed to the front's visibility. Stan Atkinson, a seasoned filmmaker who had captured in the 1950s the story of the "fighting" priest, Father Nguyễn Lạc Hóa, in a movie, was ready to tell again the story of unsung heroes resisting communism. But he traveled to Thailand in 1983 and, despite a personal introduction from Phạm Văn Liễu, could not find Hoàng Cơ Minh.[46] The front existed more in the media than in reality.

The lack of coordination between a diplomatic strategy and armed resistance raises questions about the ultimate objectives. Did these various nationalist leaders try to bring about a state project? Or were these initiatives more the reflection of a personal vision or a small group's objectives? Both partisans and observers of the front wondered whether the maquis was merely a vanity project for Hoàng Cơ Minh. As a navy veteran, he had little experience in combat on land. He also changed his appearance to resemble Hồ Chí Minh, a choice that many found questionable. When Phạm Văn Liễu flew to Bangkok and traveled to see the resistance fighters in February 1982, he was surprised to see Hoàng Cơ Minh sporting a mustache and a beard, "making us all think he looked like the Hồ Chí Minh we saw in magazines." He also claimed to have created a path into Vietnam, which led front members to say that he was creating another HCM trail: the Hoàng Cơ Minh trail. The use of these references was not to everyone's taste. The former RVN prime minister said: "I did not like to see Minh wearing the black outfit, a scarf around the neck, a green bucket hat, rubber sandals, and facial hair exactly like Hồ Chí Minh, the communist leader. One Hồ Chí Minh is already one too many for our people. With a second Hồ Chí Minh, will our country fall into a miserable situation again?"[47] The resemblance was striking and almost ironic. Not only had the front borrowed the Việt Minh's cult of personality, but its leader had tried to look exactly like the father of Vietnamese communism.

The front's attempt to rewrite history for the umpteenth time once again showed that resistance existed mostly in theory, rather than reality. Fighters in the jungle took lessons on politics and history, recounting the exploits of nationalist fighters. These stories were compiled in a book, *Anh hùng nước tôi* (*The Heroes of My Country*). Basing their study on a classic, Trần Trọng Kim's *Việt Nam sử lược* (*A Brief History of Vietnam*), the authors of *Anh hùng nước tôi* examined each historical character who had led Vietnam against foreign invasions.[48] Front members contributing to the book added personal commentary on each of these heroes. The result was revealing. The first edition was published in 1986 in the jungle, using basic supplies and a mimeograph. Back in 1946, when all lines of distribution had been destroyed by the Pacific War, the Việt Minh had no other choice but to use this method. However, that forty years later people went to the dense Laotian forest and used the same techniques is jarring. At a time of computers and fax machines, the front seemed to operate in a parallel dimension. We do not know what the first edition looked like. But the third edition, which appeared in California in 1988, may have tried to lift the spirits of members who learned that Hoàng Cơ Minh had died in battle. Among the historical figures, only twenty-three included notes by people in the jungle, whereas forty-five others had a commentary from overseas members (*đoàn viên hải ngoại*). Again, the small number of actual soldiers in Laos suggests that this tale of resistance existed mostly in the minds of some overseas veterans, rather than in a Southeast Asian jungle.[49]

The dream of achieving a diplomatic revolution was not realized either. First, anyone who had hoped that an international conference would replace Hanoi's authorities completely misread the situation. In Cambodia, talks could work because it was at a military impasse, with competing groups that each received international backing. None of them had fought and won not one, but two wars over the prior decades, as the DRV had done. Replacing the SRVN through a diplomatic consensus had always been out of the question. Even Tô Văn realized that if a negotiated solution were attempted, it would come at a cost. The more overseas Vietnamese internationalized their struggle, the more vulnerable they became to the demands and priorities of others. They could end up, yet again, in an unequal relationship. *Thức tỉnh* recounted that a recent gathering to unify overseas Vietnamese in the United States had been chaired by an American, Don Bailey. Newspapers called that event the "Don Bailey" meeting.[50] Those who attended the event could not even speak Vietnamese because the discussions were all held in English. The article about the meeting raised an important question: Could Vietnamese opposition groups make their own decisions if they allied with the United States again?

Despite the initial momentum toward mobilization in 1979, the failure to unite overseas Vietnamese led the editors of *Thức tỉnh* to draw a sad conclusion. Overseas Vietnamese did not achieve the mobilization called for by the historical circumstances. The Tết issue in 1984 recognized reality. Resistance in Southeast Asia was mostly a fiction. Chinese attacks had failed, and international pressure had not worked. After nine long years, the SRVN remained, and Lê Duẩn was still in power. But the mobilization of overseas Vietnamese had not achieved anything substantial (see fig. 8.1). People in Vietnam had to serve in the military and fight a war in Cambodia or in the northern highlands, work in fields, and endure reeducation camps. At the same time, "400,000 overseas Vietnamese" were publishing more newspapers and magazines "than used to be published in Saigon, where there were 25 million inhabitants." Even this journalistic frenzy could not achieve unity. Vietnamese accused one another of dishonoring the refugee community or becoming "communist puppets."[51] The editors of *Thức tỉnh* tired of this endless bickering and ceased publication.

Tô Văn, as *Thức tỉnh*'s director, wrote a letter addressed to "all patriots within the country and abroad." At age seventy-two, he had met and known almost all the journalists in the community. But he realized that many had embarked on this journey for personal glory, rather than to contribute to history. He, too, was appalled by the lack of results, announced that the publication would end, and invited journalists to "ask for forgiveness from his compatriots and his nation."[52] Anticommunism failed to adjust to the new stage in the Cold War. Nationalist projects intended to lead to a different nation-state, whether through diplomatic or violent means, did not survive either.

FIGURE 8.1. Tô Văn (*second from the right, in a dark suit and holding a small piece of paper in his hand*) and Saigon's political elite outside of the Independence Palace on April 28, 1975.
Source: Photograph by Jens Nauntofte, as reproduced in Tiziano Terzani, *Giai Phong! The Fall and Liberation of Saigon* (New York: St Martin's Press, 1976). Printed with the authorization of Maria Stenz.

New Forms of Protest

Because of the transformation of the Cold War, liberating Vietnam from communism had become only a distant dream, but this did not mean that everyone abandoned anticommunism. Some opposition remained, sometimes on a long-term basis. The main difference is that it no longer aimed to overthrow the regime, and ideology and physical location no longer mattered. Regardless of its ideological orientation, a state had to respect individual freedom. All Vietnamese in the country or elsewhere could join a movement like this. In the 1970s, the "language of human rights" had become central.[53] In the Vietnamese context, it had also been used during the war. But by the end of that decade, this language also allowed a smooth transition from denunciation of Nguyễn Văn Thiệu's regime to criticism of the SRVN. Individual freedoms worked in both an ideological era and a post–Cold War world.

The newspaper *Dân quyền* (*Civic Rights*) in Montréal documented human rights abuses in Vietnam. Bác Phong, one of the main contributors to it, was an evacuee who became famous for his poems and reporting.[54] An editorial in the first issue reminisced about Vietnamese rebellion against French colonial rule. It claimed that the situation was complicated by communism because it created divisions in the population. "Communist authorities became overconfident. They believed that Marxism was an absolute ideal and imposed it at all costs. This caused a tragic reality (prisons, reeducation camps, misery, lack of freedom, patriots risking their lives to escape, citizens losing faith in the administration and hope for the future . . .) and make the people's destiny uncertain."[55] Readers of *Dân quyền* had to oppose Hanoi, but not because of its materialism and atheism. And they should not mobilize because it had "stolen" the struggle for independence from the population, nor was it solely responsible for the deaths or damages from the war. Rather, its poor human rights record alone should prompt Vietnamese to raise their voices. The newspaper documented demonstrations that focused on human rights advocacy. In bringing attention to Hanoi's abuses, it publicized the nonpartisan work of Amnesty International.[56] The newspaper's desire to transcend past divisions was also reflected by showing the victims among both anticommunists and members of the NLF.[57] Vietnamese faced violations of their basic rights regardless of which side of the ideological divide they were on.

Past divides were transcended by the joint consideration of all victims of human rights violations. Both nationalists and communist defectors condemned the regime's abuse. Associations such as PEN International reflected this new solidarity to protect freedom of expression. In 1978, a Vietnamese author, Trần Tam Tiệp, reached out to join the association, as Vietnamese authors detained in Vietnam needed external support.[58] To this day, PEN International is the only organization that recognizes South Vietnam as a representative of the country.[59] Trần Thanh Hiệp, a young law student who called on others to oppose the cease-fire in 1954 and claimed that the evacuees would return like a "suicide squad" to Hanoi, even rose to the organization's highest position. Under his presidency, PEN International pressured the SRVN to release journalists. Eventually, the lawyer continued to call for democratic change in Vietnam, by reflecting on human rights, past constitutions, and the rule of law.[60] At a time when communism and anticommunism no longer meant much, the language of human rights could still call into question the actions of a party-state.

In fact, people wondered whether several Vietnams could coexist. For some, it became increasingly clear that there were multiple Vietnams that existed across political borders and interacted with one another. This was obvious in how people used remittances over the years. Although the process of sending money back to Vietnam initially had the potential for acting as a sign of resistance to the communist authorities, it increasingly evolved into a gesture, just as political, but not necessarily related to a desire to destabilize the regime. In 1982, the editors of *Thức tỉnh* were still convinced that diplomatic pressure could force Hanoi to back down. At the same time, the population within the country refused to meet economic targets and some could even try to join the armed resistance. Overseas Vietnamese had to contribute to this two-pronged attack, according to the newspaper, by denouncing communist atrocities abroad and sending remittances back to people in their homeland.[61] This flow of money gave people some relief from the pressure by local authorities—a strategy that the newspaper reported was successful. Then, starting in April 1983, Hanoi announced that Vietnamese citizens would be forbidden to receive gifts and money from overseas.[62] In reality, the SRVN introduced legislation that limited the amount of money that each household could receive within a predetermined period.[63] The Vietnamese government and members of the diaspora both had their fingers on the pulse of the war. The more external money came from unofficial channels, the stronger the resistance could become.

However, over time, the purpose of the remittances changed. The SRVN's transition to an open economy was a long process that had started before 1986, when the Đổi mới reforms were announced.[64] It led the state to redefine what made it revolutionary, in view of its abandonment of the Marxist ideals that had animated it for decades.[65] For members of the diaspora, this transformation also raised new questions, which oral histories, recorded by several projects, help us uncover.[66] It is impossible to determine whether the selection of the people interviewed was subject to any bias, though many respondents were evacuees and Catholics. Virtually all of those interviewed said they sent money back to Vietnam, mostly to family members. Hanoi's introduction of reforms to enable a market economy paved the way for business opportunities. Vietnamese authorities and governments in the West both encouraged overseas Vietnamese to return to create business relations.[67] Even restrictions, such as the US trade embargo, which remained until 1994, did not deter some from traveling back to Vietnam with briefcases full of dollars.[68] Others considered it their duty to channel the money to where it was most needed, creating charities.⁶⁹ The Vietnamese community continued to be diverse: it had become transnational, connecting people overseas to their compatriots in the country. Remittances transferred not only money to the country but also cultural preferences, new trends, and practices.⁷⁰ The circulation of goods, ideas, and people transitioned from the Cold War era to a globalized and market-oriented world.

One Vietnam across Borders

With the opening of borders after the Đổi mới reforms, the Vietnamese increasingly saw themselves as a diverse community existing across political borders, rather than a united population striving to exist under the same nation-state. People from various life experiences—whether from a communist state in the north, a fallen anticommunist south, or outside of the country—began to engage with one another.⁷¹ Even the most anticommunist evacuees, regardless of their location, softened their views, reconsidering their antagonism and opening up to the prospect of renewed exchanges.

Catholics experienced this transition from an antagonistic relationship to a new, post–Cold War reconnection with their fellow Vietnamese. Many priests of the same congregations or lay associations resettled together once abroad.⁷² Their interpretation of the Vietnamese Church's history exemplified this changing mindset. Bùi Đức Sinh, a Dominican priest born in the north before 1954 who later studied abroad, wrote one of the most important written historical accounts, the three-volume *History of the Catholic Church*, which was published in Calgary in 1998.⁷³ Volume 3 went up to 1975, and a supplement was planned to cover the period up to 2000. This volume, which discussed every single diocese in Vietnam, could not be considered a history, but added a "chapter on current affairs."⁷⁴ Despite its focus on the development of a church under the RVN, its tone in comparison with previous Catholic narratives had changed. The author did not ignore the 1951 episcopal letter condemning communism or periods of conflict. But he stressed propagation of the faith, the creation of new churches, and other accomplishments, highlighting the Church's resilience during periods of political and military chaos. Unlike earlier stories published by many Catholic evacuees, this Church's history did not present a narrative of resistance and opposition.⁷⁵ Perhaps because of the absence of ideological rigidity, to this day the opus has remained a reference for historians and for many members of the clergy, even in Vietnam.

Even Catholics of the Bùi Chu diocese who were most famous for their political opposition to communism seemed to calm down. Members who had resettled in the United States formed the Association of the Bùi Chu Family, which is reminiscent of the organizations that developed in the south after 1954. The association was obviously Catholic, but its official name referred to people from the same place of origin. They observed not only Catholic occasions but also local ones, such as the hundredth day of mourning after the death of Father Trần Đức Huân, a Confucian tradition maintained by members of the family. As Joseph Nguyen suggests, being a member of the diocese of Bùi Chu meant more than respecting Catholic traditions—it meant being part of a family.[76]

In their history of the Church, the members of the association blamed communism for their exile, but at the same time, they highlighted the existence of several Bùi Chus. A chronological account of the diocese's history, using headings such as "Early Days," "Maturity with the Rise of Local Clergy," and "Bùi Chu Migrating and Seeking Refuge in 1954," revealed that there were three Bùi Chus: the original diocese in the north, the diocese in exile in the south under the RVN, and the diocese of refuge after 1975. News that the communist authorities had nationalized many assets from Bùi Chu, including the Nguyễn Bá Tòng High School in Ho Chi Minh City in 1977, renaming it the Bùi Thị Xuân High School, meant that parishioners from Bùi Chu who had remained in southern Vietnam had lost important sources of funding and gathering places. Therefore, members of the diocese overseas had to raise money for those in the other Bùi Chus, in northern and southern Vietnam, eventually collecting $12,691 (the equivalent of more than $35,000 today). Later, they doubled the amount solicited from across the United States and France. The history featured photographs of the feast of the Immaculate Conception, held in both Orange County, California, and Bùi Chu, in the Red River delta. Regardless of where they lived, these representations insisted members of the diocese remained in communion with one another.[77]

Three years later, the association published another history, so that the younger generation, born during the war, would know about the original Bùi Chu diocese. The list of names, places, and events of the diocese was compiled again for another reason. The end of the Cold War in 1989 enabled a larger number of overseas Vietnamese, including young people, to return to Vietnam for a visit. The later publication no longer described separate Bùi Chus; rather, everyone and everywhere were part of the same diocese. Photographs showed the new archbishop of Bùi Chu visiting coreligionists in Ho Chi Minh City, alternating with news about members in Minnesota and California. Although it had stories about soldiers, which recalled the wounds of war, new ideas were also represented. After decades of separation, the community was healing, and the diocese was, at last, reunited.[78]

Not everyone was ready to travel across borders and experience this psychological reunification. Oral interviews with overseas Vietnamese and evacuees among them suggest that many were happy to return to visit their family. However, others felt uncomfortable with the local authorities or would never consider staying in Vietnam for good. Some were more at ease, after seeing the Communist Party grant people more economic freedom, which enabled the country to emerge slowly from poverty.[79] But others concluded that "this was no longer the country of [their] youth. It turned into something to which [they] had no attachment."[80] The gap between the Vietnam in their imagination and the one that existed in reality was obvious. Returning to the north was unthinkable. Many had lost contact with people they had known, and some were so young when they evacuated that the north was a foreign land.[81] Their *Heimat* no longer existed.

Sometimes, those who lived in Vietnam still sought to find peace. In 1997, a man named Trần Quý Phúc, born in Ninh Bình Province in the Red River delta in 1950, sent to the FVPPA a copy of a letter he had sent to the Vietnamese government about a property that had been confiscated. He lamented that the armed conflict had caused more suffering in Vietnam than anywhere else affected by the Cold War:

> I believe that our brains are those of human beings and not one that evolved from animals. What makes it human is its personality. Is the war between the north and the south in 1954–1974 twenty years of sorrow and mistakes that we should accept?!! Korea was divided in 1952, and Germany in 1945, and those two partitions predate the one in Vietnam, but were the German and Korean people affected by adversity, destruction, and Agent Orange?

The man went through reeducation from 1975 to 1977. He tried to leave the country twice and failed, ending up in prison or remaining free but as a citizen of the lowest rank, with limited job or housing opportunities. When he left prison the second time, he realized that people from different Vietnamese communities were coming together.

> In July 1997, upon my release, I saw many Việt kiều [overseas Vietnamese] from overseas visiting their homeland (both people who

left legally and those who escaped by boat) participate in activities freely. Where I live, there is a Việt kiều association, a branch of the Fatherland front [an organization responsible for mass mobilization in the SRVN]. I read that government authorities organize meetings with the Việt kiều, who are eager to do business in Vietnam. Meanwhile, the government is urging Việt kiều overseas to invest in Vietnam's economic development. This makes me think that I will no longer try to leave. Some people, such as my extended family, escaped—left illegally. But the only difference between them and others is that they succeeded. They did not drown in the middle of the ocean. Their body has not been lost somewhere in the jungle along the border between Vietnam, Cambodia, Laos, and Thailand. They arrived at a destination and resettled in a third country, whereas I was thrown into prison and lost my property.[82]

Vietnam's Cold War transition enabled the reconnection of different parts of its community. Nationals within the country and abroad exchanged ideas, location, and money. Neither Hanoi's legitimacy nor one-party rule is what brought Vietnamese together; the forces of a global and intertwined world enabled them to reunite across political borders. But even under these new, transnational conditions, some remained at the bottom of the social hierarchy. Those who had succeeded overseas brought enough business opportunities for local authorities to overlook their past "blemishes." But others continued to pay for the consequences of the wars. Their success or failure was often determined by chance, yet circumstances often determined the long-lasting impact. In 1954, from the perspective of the competing states, the evacuation meant that people had voted with their feet. Their choice as to whether they migrated elsewhere or remained in the country still made a difference forty years later. It distinguished desirable business partners from less profitable elements of society.

Conclusion

Today, many people from the first, second, and third generations in the Vietnamese diaspora still hold celebrations, waving a yellow flag with three red stripes and singing the RVN's national anthem. Political activists among them condemn human rights abuses and criticize the absence of individual freedoms in the SRVN. They also call for contributions to the production of historical sources and analyses.[1] But they rarely include plans to overthrow the authorities in Hanoi. Nevertheless, expressions of anticommunism vary from one place to another. In the United States, declaiming communism remains a cultural praxis, making the Vietnamese distinctive from other ethnic groups and perpetuating the social hierarchy that existed before 1975.[2] Overseas Vietnamese elsewhere also manifest their opposition to the SRVN on a regular basis. In general, though, the trend is toward a reduction in the importance of anticommunism.

This also reflects the changing composition of Vietnamese overseas. Other waves of Vietnamese have moved to a different country on a temporary or permanent basis for countless reasons. Vietnamese from the DRV, back when it was north of the seventeenth parallel, engaged in student, technical, and cultural exchanges with the rest of the socialist world, taking them to the Soviet Union or Eastern Europe. Since Germany's unification in 1990, they, too, circulated in new spaces and

CONCLUSION

reconnected with other parts of the Vietnamese community. Today, Vietnamese travel, study, and work overseas. Most do not share the political outlook of some veterans, civil servants, and intellectuals of the RVN who departed from Vietnam after 1975.[3] Many feel uncomfortable with the idea that overseas Vietnamese might prefer one political authority or ideology over another. In other words, among overseas Vietnamese, anticommunism remains, but its influence and meaning have changed since the end of the Cold War.

It seems almost self-evident that most evacuees became anticommunists after being forced to leave the north in 1954. But reaching that conclusion based on this experience alone tends to simplify a history that is a lot more complex. This book explains why people who evacuated from the north in 1954 became the most anticommunist group in the RVN. Their debates and changing positions show that none of them intended to be anticommunist and remain so forever. Even the most outspoken activists among them changed their mind and displayed various levels of public advocacy. Changing political, military, and cultural circumstances were key to the reemergence and fading of this self-awareness.

Looking at their history also elucidates the nature and role of anticommunism. Were all evacuees anticommunists? Did anticommunism emerge from the evacuation? What is anticommunism after all? Likewise, an ideology or political orientation alone still requires the right window of opportunity to be turned into concrete action. Anticommunism remained a sincere belief and long-standing value. Many leaders among the evacuees saw it as a lifelong commitment that is manifested in fighting and rising in the RVNAF or becoming active in a nationalist party. Yet ideology did not guide all their decisions. Spiritual values, pragmatism, international pressure, and historical contingencies compelled the evacuees to reevaluate the role of ideology in their decisions. In other words, anticommunism was not a foregone conclusion.

Approaching the First Indochina War both as a struggle for decolonization and a civil war shows that anticommunism existed before the evacuation. Nationalist party members, such as the newspaper director Nghiêm Xuân Thiện or the lawyer Trần Văn Tuyên, have opposed communism since the 1930s, whereas others, such as Tô Văn, adopted these views after leaving the DRV in 1951. These varying experiences meant that one could also soften from an unshakeable anticommunism. The bacteriologist Phạm Văn Huyến, Father Nguyễn Việt Khái, and to a different extent, the Québec professor Trần Tam Tỉnh, transitioned from opposition to the DRV to an open-mindedness or an outright support.

CONCLUSION

Neither the timing for anticommunism nor the personal trajectory was the same for all the evacuees.

Displacement was neither a necessary nor a sufficient condition for the emergence of an anticommunist position. People did not need to have the same lived experience with evacuation to share the same outlook on the war. Younger generations, overseas Vietnamese, and people with a different personal history in the war could hold the same collective memory of the partition and political representation of exile. Displacement did not suffice either. The lag time between departure and the emergence of a new political consciousness after 1975 shows the crucial role of validation and political representations of displacement for this to happen.

The evacuees adamantly reminded their compatriots that only those who had experienced and escaped communist rule could comprehend the DRV or the NLF. But this was not the manifestation of northern superiority over their southern compatriots.[4] Other people in interzone V who did not cross the seventeenth parallel but, nonetheless, "left" communist rule because the DRV had regrouped in the north also joined the movement. Likewise, northern evacuees opposed anyone, including "old Tonkinese" or other evacuees who wanted to negotiate a settlement with Hanoi. Catholics believed that this was also a spiritual war, with reinforcement of horizontal connections to other national churches, such as those in China and the United States, and vertical links to Rome. But none of these institutions were monolithic during the Cold War. Their influence did not entirely permeate Vietnam. Moreover, it amplified local and global voices calling for war at times and calling for peace at others. These networks became new forms of leverage for the choices, ideas, and initiatives of Vietnamese Catholics, but they worked both ways. There was no primordial trait determining whether one would become an anticommunist and even the communities to which people belonged could reinforce or soften their views.

In fact, while most considered only those who had lived under DRV rule and left it could understand why it was crucial to oppose communism, the evacuees' experience of the wars was different from one person to another. For some, the departure from the north was perhaps the single most important moment in their lives and in the war. For others, however, the land reform or the 1951 episcopal letter urging Catholics not to contribute to any organization facilitating the rise of communism was their turning point. In fact, people fought in different struggles, for independence, the victory of a political party, or the protection of the Church, all of which converged when many of these fighters, especially

CONCLUSION 179

Church and political leaders, left for the south in 1954. The partition and the evacuation of the north formed a focal point helping those intertwined struggles to converge.

The evacuees studied here are not representative of all of Vietnamese society. Nor is their tendency to latch on to every event supposed to mean that the cause of South Vietnam was in vain or that everyone was living in a fantasy land. But their relentless penchant for imagining alternative spaces and projecting themselves into the future is striking. The Cold War introduced a new historical condition for the evacuees by altering their perception of time, space, and reality. Every escalation in Vietnam opened up a new set of contingencies.

Since there is no single factor common to all the evacuees, one could wonder what brought them to remobilize again and again over the years. Anniversaries and celebrations brought the evacuees to commemorate the partition and their departure from the north. These were obvious moments in time that led them to recall or reflect on their experience. But a bird's-eye view over three decades of their history shows that the most important parameter in sparking a renewed mobilization came from the Cold War and how it intensified, stalled, or weakened the political struggle in Vietnam. The Cold War brought high stakes, and with it, from the perspective of the evacuees, came the potential of high rewards. In fact, many believed they embodied a new historical condition in which the restrictions and limitations they faced could easily be overcome in the future thanks to the support they received by Western states and public opinion. This was why they mobilized when they felt international tensions could bring political change in Vietnam. Hence, their hopes rose in 1956, when they believed insurrections in socialist states announced a possible collapse of the communist world.

These evacuees also understood their fate depended not only on foreign states but also on international public opinion. Because the support they got from the West came from elected governments, they knew public perception remained central to the possibility they received support. This was why many were persuaded there could be political change in 1978 and 1979, when public outrage at the refugee crisis coincided with diplomatic pressure and military operations on the ground. Yet it was also because they felt public opinion went against their views in 1968 and 1972, when it demanded an immediate cease-fire, that they began to rethink their perception of communism.

To be sure, the evacuees alone did not provoke the war. Nor did they have the power of heads of states or bishops. But their voice, while not changing the entire course of the war, still mattered. Their opposition to Ngô Đình Diệm helped to reduce his legitimacy. Their determination to take to the streets, call for a march to the north, and never stop the fight illustrated that a small but vocal section of the society rejected a halt in the armed conflict. The war had become so deeply embedded with their sense of self that, despite their profound disappointment over Nixon's rapprochement with China in 1972, they did not entirely give up. Scattered overseas, they imagined new alliances and opportunities for opposing Hanoi when the Cold War resumed in 1979. Their commitment also influenced the prospects for peace. Whenever the armed conflict seemed to pause or end, the evacuees vehemently protested.

Their elastic perception of what was possible might also explain why factionalism always plagued the nationalists during the wars. The Cold War often imposed a choice among all the possible paths. A single international conference too often determined the fate of an entire country; foreign interference encouraged a coup; or a fateful meeting decided which leader among several contenders could take charge. The evacuees in particular and nationalists in general received international support from various sources early on. France, the United States, the Catholic Church, and, to some extent, anticommunist Chinese in exile were ready to adopt their mobilization as their own. Perhaps this is because the nationalists were persuaded that this support and some luck made everything possible, so they did not focus enough on building their own strength. This contrasts with the early years in isolation by the DRV. Hồ Chí Minh was snubbed by Stalin for being too nationalist and suspected by India for being a communist, so he had no choice but to rely on the self-sufficiency of the Việt Minh.[5] Therefore, one might consider whether the evacuees' relentless projection into possible futures might have worked against them, because they neglected the work of prioritizing self-reliance and unity.

The history of the evacuees also matters because it gives us an entirely new perspective on displaced people. The Vietnam wars are well known for the millions of displaced and the hundreds of thousands who sought asylum in other countries. But their experience shows that they were not merely "victims" or "survivors."[6] A clear-eyed view of their mental journey reveals that they were not so innocent after all. By portraying the evacuees as refugees or victims of persecution, states employed international mobilization as an opportunity for denouncing their political enemy. Refugee protection, therefore, entailed much more than a humanitarian response. It became a potent tool in the state's diplomatic arsenal.[7] For nationalists on the ground, this specific representation of population movement also became a platform for reaching out to other countries and advancing a political agenda. This does not mean that the people who sought asylum did not deserve protection. Rather, it calls into question the notion that only one-dimensional victims should be granted protection. An in-depth understanding of refugee flows in the context of contested nation-states must take into account the politics of mobility and its long-lasting consequences.

Understanding the Vietnam wars through the evacuees involves the representation of population movements. This complicates the number of stakeholders in the war, as it comprises humanitarian groups, international organizations, and religious networks. The circulation of people and ideas across borders shows that the war had more participants than was suggested by the official number of belligerents negotiating at peace talks. Some members of the Catholic Church in East Asia wanted to prevent the emergence of a schismatic church. At the end of the Cold War, Christians of all denominations mobilized to protect human dignity on all sides and eventually denounced new forms of imperialism. Civil society also shifted its focus, from the protection of emergent nation-states from communist expansion to the condemnation of human rights abuses. Therefore, the Cold War was not only a confrontation between two blocs or local conflicts among competing political authorities. It was also a moment for soul searching about the place and role of faith and changing perceptions of democracy and collective action.

Taking these dimensions into consideration, the Cold War appears as a highly subjective experience that we mostly knew to date through the perspective of states. For many historians, the conflict was a global war embedded in regional wars. Although for most of the world this was a "long peace," people on the front line faced immeasurable destruction at the local level.[8] For anthropologists and cultural historians, however, the Cold War reveals local practices and alternative chronologies. At the family level, the Cold War did not end when the Berlin Wall came down or the Soviet Union disintegrated. It ended only when a mother could commemorate the deaths of both of her sons, who fought on opposite sides in the war.[9] The evacuees show that ordinary Vietnamese, individuals, families, and communities were connected to regional and global dynamics.[10] Their projection into possible futures not only explains the evacuees' relentless mobilization but also shows why the armed conflict escalated and intensified beyond its original scale because there were people on the ground who hoped for a resumption in the war. The Cold

War created for them a new time dimension, heightened expectations, and, therefore, enabled violence at a new scale.

Catholics, whose influence on war and peace was reinforced and weakened by their connections with transnational networks, relied on their coreligionists elsewhere as leverage, but it exposed them to transformations within the Church that affected their mobilization. This was also evident as the Vietnamese spread across the seventeenth parallel and, later, overseas. Population movements can either reinforce or undermine the formation of nation-states. After all, a country is defined by its people more than its borders. The evacuation did not shatter but, rather, reinforced the way in which nationalists imagined their country. This ideal of a Vietnamese nation faded but survived, and then reappeared, depending on the circumstances. The end of the Cold War ultimately led many evacuees to acknowledge that the Vietnam of their imagination would never exist within the borders they envisioned. Vietnam would continue to exist across continents.

Notes

Introduction

1. For a translation of the song with commentary, see Tuấn Hoàng, "Song of Refugees #2: 1954 cha bỏ quê, 1975 con bỏ nước [Father Left Home in 1954, Son Left Country in 1975]" (2016), https://tuannyriver.com/2016/06/06/song-of-refugees-2-1954-cha-bo-que-1975-con-bo-nuoc-father-left-home-in-1954-son-left-country-in-1975/.

2. Phạm Duy, *Một đời nhìn lại*, 4 vols. (Midway City, CA: PDC Musical Production, 1989).

3. The partition prioritized the sovereignty of a religious majority by creating nation-states over the protection of individuals in maintaining heterogeneous states. See Aishwary Kumar, *Radical Equality: Ambedkar, Gandhi, and the Risk of Democracy* (Redwood City, CA: Stanford University Press, 2015); Dirk Moses, "Partitions and the Sisyphean Making of Peoples," *Refugee Watch* 46 (2015): 36–50; Moses, "Partitions, Hostages, Transfer: Retributive Violence and National Security," in *Partitions: A Transnational History of Twentieth-Century Territorial Separatism*, ed. Arie M. Dubnov and Laura Robson (Redwood City, CA: Stanford University Press, 2019).

4. Vazira Fazila Yacoobali-Zamindar, *The Long Partition and the Making of Modern South Asia* (New York: Columbia University Press, 2007); Veena Das, *Critical Events: An Anthropological Perspective on Contemporary India* (Delhi: Oxford University Press, 1995); Dipesh Chakrabarty, "Remembered Villages: Representation of Hindu-Bengali Memories in the Aftermath of the Partition," *Economic & Political Weekly* 31, no. 32 (1996): 2143–45, 2147–51.

5. Dominic Meng-Hsuan Yang, *The Great Exodus from China: Trauma, Memory, and Identity in Modern Taiwan* (Cambridge: Cambridge University Press, 2021).

6. Taomo Zhou, *Migration in the Time of Revolution: China, Indonesia, and the Cold War* (Ithaca, NY: Cornell University Press, 2019); Shelly Chan, *Diaspora's Homeland: Modern China in the Age of Global Migration* (Durham, NC: Duke University Press, 2018).

7. Monica Kim, *The Interrogation Rooms of the Korean War: The Untold History* (Princeton, NJ: Princeton University Press, 2019); Yumi Moon, "Northern Refugees and the Rise of Cold War Nationalism in South Korea, 1945–1950" (forthcoming).

8. For example, an analysis of the elections under the Second Republic of Vietnam suggests that being from the north or being a Catholic meant supporting war against communism. Allan E. Goodman, *Politics in War: The Bases of Political Community in South Vietnam* (Cambridge, MA: Harvard University Press, 1973).

9. *Pháp luật trừng trị bọn cưỡng ép dụ dỗ người đi Nam* (Hanoi, 1955).

10. Commemorations on the fiftieth anniversary emphasized the story of a continuous struggle against communism. Vương Kỳ Sơn, *Di cư 54, Triệu người muốn sống* (New Orleans: Lĩnh Nam, 2009).

11. Claire Trần Thị Liên, "The Catholic Question in North Vietnam: From Polish Sources, 1954–1956," *Cold War History* 5, no. 4 (2005): 427–49; Robert B. Frankum, *Operation Passage to Freedom: The United States Navy in Vietnam, 1954–1955* (Lubbock: Texas Tech University Press, 2007); Philip Catton, "The Royal Navy's Vietnam War: H.M.S. Warrior and the Evacuation from North Vietnam, September 1954," *Historical Research* 83, no. 220 (2010): 358–77; Bernard Broussole and Lucien Provençal, "L'évacuation des catholiques du Tonkin en 1954–1955," *Bulletin de l'Association amicale Santé navale et d'Outre-mer* 125 (2013): 24–30.

12. For recent accounts reinforcing a classic criticism of American nation-building programs, see Seth Jacobs, *America's Miracle Man in Vietnam: Ngo Dinh Diem, Religion, Race and U.S. Intervention in Southeast Asia, 1950–1957* (Durham, NC: Duke University Press, 2005); Jacobs, *Cold War Mandarin: Ngo Dinh Diem and the Origins of the America's War in Vietnam* (Lanham, MD: Rowman and Littlefield, 2006); James M. Carter, *Inventing Vietnam: The United States and State Building, 1954–1968* (Cambridge: Cambridge University Press, 2008).

13. On a new understanding of the republic in the south, see Philip Catton, *Diem's Final Failure: Prelude to America's War in Vietnam* (Lawrence: University Press of Kansas, 2002); Edward Miller, *Misalliance: Ngo Dinh Diem, the United States and the Fate of South Vietnam* (Cambridge, MA: Harvard University Press, 2013); Jessica Chapman, *Cauldron of Resistance: Ngo Dinh Diem, the United States, and 1950s Southern Vietnam* (Ithaca, NY: Cornell University Press, 2013). On the Catholic evacuees, see Peter Hansen, "The Virgin Heads South: Northern Catholic Refugees in South Vietnam, 1954–1964" (PhD diss., Melbourne College of Divinity, 2008); Hansen, "Bắc Di Cư: Catholic Refugees from the North of Vietnam, and Their Role in the Southern Republic, 1954–1959," *Journal of Vietnamese Studies* 4, no. 3 (2009): 173–211; Phi-Vân Nguyen, "Fighting the First Indochina War Again? Catholic Refugees in South Vietnam, 1954–1959," *Sojourn* 31, no. 1 (2016): 207–46.

14. Vân Nguyen-Marshall, "Tools of Empire? Vietnamese Catholics in South Vietnam," *Revue de la société historique du Canada* 20, no. 2 (2009): 138–59; Phi-Vân Nguyen, "Les résidus de la guerre, La mobilisation des réfugiés du nord pour un Vietnam non-communiste, 1954–1965" (PhD diss., Université du Québec à Montréal, 2015); Jason A. Picard, "'Renegades': The Story of South Vietnam's First National Opposition Newspaper, 1955–1958," *Journal of Vietnamese Studies* 10, no. 4 (2015): 1–29; Picard, "'Fertile Lands Await': The Promise and Pitfalls of Directed Resettlement, 1954–1959," *Journal of Vietnamese Studies* 11, nos. 3–4 (2016): 58–102.

15. On their role in politics, see Nu-Anh Tran, "South Vietnamese Identity, American Intervention, and the Newspaper Chính Luận Political Discussion, 1965–1969," *Journal of Vietnamese Studies* 1, nos. 1–2 (2006): 169–209; Nu-Anh Tran, "Contested Identities: Nationalism in the Republic of Vietnam

(1954–1963)" (PhD diss., University of California at Berkeley, 2013); Nu-Anh Tran, *Disunion: Anticommunist Nationalism and the Making of the Republic of Vietnam* (Honolulu: University of Hawai'i Press, 2022); Sean Fear, "The Ambiguous Legacy of Ngô Đình Diệm in South Vietnam's Second Republic (1967–1975)," *Journal of Vietnamese Studies* 11, no. 1 (2016): 1–75. On their role in culture, see Hoàng Phong Tuấn and Nguyễn Thị Minh, "Striving for the Quintessence," in *Building a Republican Nation in Vietnam, 1920–1963*, ed. Nu-Anh Tran and Tuong Vu (Honolulu: University of Hawai'i Press, 2023); on their anticommunist stance, see Tuấn Hoàng, "The Early South Vietnamese Critique of Communism," in *Dynamics of the Cold War in Asia*, ed. Tường Vũ and Wasana Wongsurawat (New York: Palgrave Macmillan, 2009).

16. Joseph Nguyễn, "Bắc di cư in the Diaspora: Mapping a Vietnamese Catholic Refugee Identity" (master's thesis, Columbia University, 2022); Nguyễn, "Bắc di cư in the Diaspora: Mapping a Vietnamese Catholic Refugee Identity" (paper presented at a webinar on Global Vietnamese Catholicism, ISAC, Initiative for the Study of Asian Catholics, Singapore, 2023).

17. Three publications have underscored the repetition of displacement and their implications on political orientations: Lien-Hang T. Nguyen, "The Double Diaspora of Vietnam's Catholics," *Orbis* 39, no. 4 (1995): 491–501; Andrew Hardy, "Internal Transnationalism and the Formation of the Vietnamese Diaspora," in *State/Nation/Transnation: Perspectives on Transnationalism in the Asia-Pacific*, ed. Brenda S. A. Yeoh and Katie Willis (London: Routledge, 2004), 218–37; and the most elaborate synthesis, mentioning defections in the early 1950s and debates on possible bloodbaths related to population movements in the 1970s, Martin Grossheim, "'1954 verlor der Vater seine Heimat, 1975 verlor der Sohn sein Vaterland,' Teilung, Flucht und Wiedervereinigung in Vietnam," in *Die geteilte Nation: Nationale Verluste und Identitäten im 20. Jahrhundert*, ed. Andreas Hilger and Oliver von Wrochem (München, Germany: Oldenbourg Verlag, 2013), 97–115. Recent works have not dealt with the evacuees exclusively, but discussed democratic ideas in the south. See Tuong Vu and Sean Fear, eds., *The Republic of Vietnam, 1955–1975: Vietnamese Perspectives on Nation Building* (Ithaca, NY: Cornell University Press, 2019); Linda Ho Peché, Alex Thai Vo, and Tuong Vu, eds., *Toward a Framework for Vietnamese American Studies* (Philadelphia: Temple University Press, 2023); Nu-Anh Tran and Tuong Vu, eds., *Building a Republican Nation in Vietnam, 1920–1963* (Honolulu: University of Hawai'i Press, 2023). On anticommunism, see Tuan Hoang, "The August Revolution, the Fall of Saigon, and Postwar Reeducation Camps: Understanding Vietnamese Diasporic Anticommunism," in Peché, Vo, and Vu, *Toward a Framework*, 76–95; Y Thien Nguyen, "When State Propaganda Becomes Social Knowledge," in Tran and Vu, *Building a Republican Nation in Vietnam*, 202–30.

18. For a rebuttal of the idea of an unchanging anticommunism, see Nguyen, "When State Propaganda Becomes Social Knowledge."

19. In fact, a large proportion of northern evacuees were elderly, women, and children, because men were then conscripted. See Mission de liaison armée de la CIC (Commission internationale de contrôle), April 29, 1955, Service Historique de l'armée de Terre, SHAT/10H/5784.

20. "Convention Relating to the Status of Refugees," July 28, 1951, United Nations Treaty Series 189: 152, https://www.unhcr.org/3b66c2aa10/.

21. Guy Goodwin-Gill, "The Politics of Refugee Protection," *Refugee Survey Quarterly* 27, no. 1 (2008): 8–23. I give a very brief overview of the politics of refugee protection during the Vietnam wars in Phi-Vân Nguyen, "Refugees in Violent Decolonizations," in *The Oxford Handbook of Late Colonial Insurgencies and Counterinsurgencies*, eds. Martin Thomas and Gareth Curless (Oxford: Oxford University Press, 2023), 565–79.

1. Alternative Vietnams

1. The official RVN figures estimate that 80 percent—that is, 640,000—of the evacuees were Catholic. Bùi Văn Lương, "The Role of Friendly Nations," in *Vietnam: The First Five Years: An International Symposium*, ed. Richard W. Lindholm (East Lansing: Michigan State University Press, 1959), 48–54. But these figures are subject to some reservations. Phi-Vân Nguyen, "Réfugiés, religion et politique: La signification du regroupement de 1954," in *Travail, migrations et culture au Viêt-Nam, du début du 19e s. à nos jours*, ed. Éric Guérassimoff, Thi Phuong Ngoc Nguyen, and Emmanuel Poisson (Paris: Maisonneuve Larose, 2020), 185–201. One evacuee claimed that the figure is exaggerated. Đặng Phương Nghi, "Về số người công giáo di cư từ Bắc vào Nam sau Hiệp định Genève," 2002, accessed September 15, 2009, http://vantuyen.net/index.php?view=story&subjectid=20311/ (site discontinued). Another estimate puts them around 543,500. Trần Tam Tỉnh, *Dieu et César: Les Catholiques dans l'histoire du Vietnam* (Paris: Sud-Est Asie, 1978). On the new proportion of Catholics in the south, see Phạm Ngọc Chi Committee of Aid for Resettlement of the Refugees from North Vietnam, *Refugees of North Vietnam: The Refugees Fled for the Sake of Their Faith* (Saigon: n.p., 1955), 1.

2. La compagnie des Jésuites, "Georges Naïdenoff (1910–1998), Journaliste et directeur de revue," accessed September 15, 2009, http://www.jesuites.com/histoire/20eme/naidenoff.htm.

3. George Naïdenoff, "Vainqueurs aux mains nues, les réfugiés viêt-namiens demandent justice à l'opinion," *Missi* 5 (1955): 161.

4. "Excerpts from Lansdale Team's Report on Covert Vietnam Mission in '54 and '55: Lansdale Report Gives Details of Assistance to Diem, Dewey Appeals for Refugees," *New York Times*, July 5, 1971; "Chỉ thị của Ban bí thư, về việc đối phó với âm mưu của địch lừa phỉnh và áp bức Công giáo di cư vào Nam, 6-11-1954," in *Văn kiện Đảng*, ed. Đảng Cộng sản Việt Nam (Hanoi: NXB Chính trị quốc gia, 2001), 15: 361–69.

5. Chester Cooper, *The Lost Crusade: America in Vietnam* (New York: Dodd, Mead, 1970); Edward G. Lansdale, *In the Midst of Wars: An American Mission to Southeast Asia* (New York: Harper & Row, 1972). For a more recent claim along these lines, see Jacobs, *America's Miracle Man*.

6. Laurent Césari, *L'Indochine en guerres, 1945-1993* (Paris: Belin, 1995), 43.

7. Jérémy Jammes, *Les Oracles du Cao Dai: Étude d'un mouvement religieux vietnamien et de ses réseaux* (Paris: Indes savantes, 2014); Jammes, "Caodaism

in Times of War: Spirits of Struggle and Struggle of Spirits," *Sojourn* 31, no. 1 (2017): 247-94. On the Hòa Hảo's Socialist Democratic Party, see Pascal Bourdeaux, *Bouddhisme Hòa Hảo, d'un royaume à l'autre: Religion et Révolution au Sud Việt Nam (1935-1955)* (Paris: Les Indes savantes, 2022): 221-22; Tran, *Disunion*, 28-30.

8. Đoàn Độc Thư and Xuân Huy, *Giám mục Lê Hữu Từ & Phát Diệm* (Saigon: Kim Studio, 1973), 38.

9. On Phan Bội Châu's changing views, see Mark W. McLeod, "Nationalism and Religion in Vietnam: Phan Boi Chau and the Catholic Question," *International History Review* 14, no. 4 (1992): 661-80.

10. Étude n. 1300, June 8, 1951, Service historique de l'armée de Terre (hereafter cited as SHAT)/Archives du Service de documentation extérieure et de contre-espionage (hereafter cited as GR10R)/95, 5.

11. Forces terrestres du nord Việt Nam (FTNV) Zone Sud Bureau de liaison pour la pacification, Notice concernant les évêchés de Phat Diem & Bui Chu, 1951, SHAT/GR10R/95, 1. On the relationship with the DRV, see Trần Thị Liên, "Les catholiques vietnamiens pendant la guerre d'indépendance (1945-1954) entre la reconquête coloniale et la résistance communiste" (PhD diss., Institut d'études politiques, 1996); David Marr, *Vietnam, State, War, Revolution 1945-1946* (Berkeley: University of California Press, 2013), 428-41.

12. Étude n. 1300, 6-7; Trần Thị Liên, "Les catholiques vietnamiens," 45.

13. On this "fracture," see François Guillemot, *Viêt-Nam, fractures d'une nation: Une histoire contemporaine de 1858 à nos jours* (Paris: La Découverte, 2018); on the November 1945 ultimatum, see Guillemot, "Au coeur de la fracture vietnamienne: l'élimination de l'opposition nationaliste et anticolonialiste dans le Nord du Vietnam (1945-1946)," in *Naissance d'un État-Parti: Le Viet Nam depuis 1945*, ed. Christopher E. Goscha and Benoît de Tréglodé (Paris: Les Indes savantes, 2004), 175-216; Guillemot, "Autopsy of a Massacre, on a Political Purge in the Early Days of the Indochina War (Nam Bo 1947)," *European Journal of East Asian Studies* 9, no. 2 (2010): 225-65; Christopher E. Goscha, "Le premier échec contre-révolutionnaire au Vietnam: La destruction des partis nationalistes non-communistes devant le Viet Minh et la France en 1946" (Dipl. d'études approfondies, Paris VII, Histoire, 1994).

14. Viễn, "Việt Minh với tôn giáo," *Dân mới Nghệ Tĩnh Bình*, May 15, 1946.

15. Trần Thị Liên, "Les catholiques vietnamiens," 46. In May 1946, Indochinese bishops stated that any layperson or member of the clergy who claimed authority over a Catholic organization without the authorization of the hierarchy would be censored and even risk excommunication. Les catholiques du Vietnam après 1946, June 8, 1951, SHAT/GR10R/95, 3-4.

16. Marine au Tonkin, Rapport n. 191 sur l'évolution de la situation politico-religieuse à Phat Diem, February 18, 1951, SHAT/Archives de l'Indochine (hereafter cited as 10H)/1039.

17. Brett Reilly, "The Sovereign States of Vietnam, 1945-1955," *Journal of Vietnamese Studies* 11, nos. 3-4 (2016). On the Republic of Cochinchina, see Reilly, "The Origins of the Vietnamese Civil War and the State of Vietnam" (PhD diss., University of Wisconsin-Madison, 2018), chap. 2.

18. La question Nung, 1955, SHAT/10H/1040; Shawn McHale, *The First Vietnam War: Violence, Sovereignty, and the Fracture of the South, 1945-1956* (Cambridge: Cambridge University Press, 2021): 115-16; Bourdeaux, *Bouddhisme Hòa Hảo*, 240-48.

19. Christopher E. Goscha, *Vietnam: Un état né de la guerre, 1945-1954* (Paris: Armand Colin, 2011); Mark Philip Bradley, *Imagining Vietnam and America: The Making of Postcolonial Vietnam, 1919-1950* (Chapel Hill: University of North Carolina Press, 2000).

20. Xuân Thao Ninh, "L'État du Viêt-Nam dans ses rapports avec la France (1949-1955)" (PhD diss., Université de Bordeaux, 2019).

21. A Soviet veto blocked the ASVN's admission to the UN in 1952, but France succeeded in establishing working relationships with technical agencies. The Socialist Republic of Vietnam became a member of the UN in 1977. Joëlle Nguyen Duy Tân, "La représentation du Viet-Nam dans les institutions spécialisées," *Annuaire français de droit international* 22 (1976): 405-14; "The Associated States of Indo-China," *Civilisations* 3, no. 1 (1953): 111-20; Marie-Thérèse Blanchet, *La naissance de l'état associé du Viêt-Nam* (Paris: Éditions M. Th. Génin, 1954), 152.

22. Christopher E. Goscha, *The Road to Dien Bien Phu: A History of the First War for Vietnam* (Princeton, NJ: Princeton University Press, 2022), 294-99.

23. Michel Goya, "Quand l'autorité plie les événements: de Lattre en Indochine," *Inflexions* 24, no. 3 (2013): 27-35.

24. Goscha, *Vietnam*, 63-66; Goscha, *The Road to Dien Bien Phu*, 36-47.

25. On associating mass mobilization policies with propaganda exhorting the population to oppose foreign intervention, see Alec G. Holcombe, *Mass Mobilization in the Democratic Republic of Vietnam, 1945-1960* (Honolulu: University of Hawai'i Press, 2020). On the political rather than the economic objectives of the land reform, see Alex Thai Vo, "From Anticolonialism to Mobilizing Socialist Transformation in the Democratic Republic of Vietnam, 1945-1960" (PhD diss., Cornell University, 2019). On the elimination of bourgeois elements from the Việt Minh, see Alex Thai Vo, "Nguyễn Thị Năm and the Land Reform in North Vietnam, 1953," *Journal of Vietnamese Studies* 10, no. 1 (2015): 1-62.

26. Vietnam Presse, "Le Dr. Pham Van Huyen," Commissaire général aux réfugiés, December 5, 1954, Comité international de la Croix-Rouge (hereafter cited as CICR)/Réfugiés-requérants d'asile/234-223-002.

27. "Bác sĩ Phạm Văn Huyền, Giám đốc vi trùng Viện ở Thanh Hóa ra khỏi khu vực Việt Minh," *Gió Việt* 17 (1951): 27-29.

28. Royal Institute of International Affairs, "Chronology, 18 December 1950-3 January 1951," *Chronology of International Events and Documents* 1 (1950): 1-30.

29. "Le syndicalisme chrétien au Viet-Nam," *La Croix*, March 31, 1954.

30. Đặng Phúc Việt, "Cuộc phỏng vấn ba đại biểu đồng bào hồi cư ở Quảng Bình mới đến Huế," *Gió Việt* 11 (1950): 12.

31. "Số dân hồi cư trong tháng 6/1950," *Gió Việt* 10 (1950): 20; "Số dân hồi cư trong tháng 7/1950," *Gió Việt* 10 (1950): 15; "Số dân trở về với chính phủ quốc gia tại Nam Việt từ khi Đức Quốc trưởng Bảo Đại hồi loan," *Gió Việt* 10 (1950): 21; "Số dân hồi cư trong tháng 10/1950," *Gió Việt* 17 (1951): 32; "Số dân hồi cư trong tháng 12/1950," *Gió Việt* 19 (1951): 34.

32. FTNV, Rapport d'activité de propagande 15 avril–15 mai, May 27, 1954, SHAT/10H/2559, app. 5.

33. Parts of the following section have been explored further in Phi-Vân Nguyen, "Fighting the First Indochina War Again?"; Phi-Vân Nguyen, "Victims of Atheist Persecution: Transnational Catholic Solidarity and Refugee Protection in Cold War Asia," in *Refugees and Religion: Ethnographic Studies of Global Trajectories*, ed. Birgit Meyer and Peter van der Veer (London: Bloomsbury Publishing, 2021), 51–67. A more global outlook at the different path for the decolonization of the Catholic Church in Vietnam can be found in Phi-Vân Nguyen, "Vietnamese Catholics' Search for Independence, 1941–1963," in *Decolonization and the Remaking of Christianity*, ed. Elizabeth Foster and Udi Greenberg (Philadelphia: University of Pennsylvania Press, 2023), 51–66.

34. Albert Wu, *From Christ to Confucius: German Missionaries, Chinese Christians, and the Globalization of Christianity, 1860–1950* (New Haven, CT: Yale University Press, 2016), 56–57.

35. For a translation of an article exposing the PRC's treatment of Christians, see "Le point de vue communiste sur l'église en Chine," *Église vivante* 3 (1951): 53–58. See also Tch'ang Djen Tsuain, "Fidélité de l'église de Chine," *Église vivante* 3 (1951): 299.

36. Pius XII, "L'Église et la Chine, Lettre apostolique Cupimus Imprimis du 18 janvier 1952," *Église vivante* 4 (1952): 5–11; Pius XII, "Ad Apostolorum Principis, 29 June 1958," accessed May 25, 2021, https://www.vatican.va/content/pius-xii/en/encyclicals/documents/hf_p-xii_enc_29061958_ad-apostolorum-principis.html; Pius XII, "Ad Apostolorum Principis, 29 June 1958," *Église vivante* 10 (1958): 331–44, published with a commentary from *Église vivante*; Pius XII, "Thông điệp Ad Apostolorum Principis," *Sacerdos Linh mục* 24, no. 30 (1964): 445–56. On Indochinese bishops warning against a schism, see Các Đức giám mục Việt Nam, "Thư chung, 1952," in *Hàng giáo phẩm công giáo Việt Nam (1960–1995)*, ed. Trần Anh Dũng (Paris: Mission catholique vietnamienne, 1996), 101; Các Đức giám mục Việt Nam, "Thư, 1953," in Trần Anh Dũng, *Hàng giáo phẩm công giáo Việt Nam*, 117.

37. G. L. B., "Acta Diurna, Viêt Nam: questione internazionale," *Osservatore Romano*, February 5, 1949.

38. "Phái đoàn Việt Nam dự lễ phong thánh các vị tử đạo Việt Nam ở Tòa thánh La Mã," *Gió Việt* 23 (1951): 6–8.

39. "Vers l'établissement de relations diplomatiques entre le Saint-Siège et le Vietnam," *Le Monde*, May 15, 1950.

40. Pierre Darcourt, *De Lattre au Viet-Nam, Une année de victoires* (Paris: La Table ronde, 1965), 256–57.

41. Các Đức giám mục Việt Nam, "Thư chung các giám mục Đông Dương, 1951," in Trần Anh Dũng, *Hàng giáo phẩm công giáo Việt Nam*, 93–95. For the handwritten version, see "Thư luân lưu của các vị giám mục gửi anh chị em công giáo Việt Nam, 9/11/1951," *Gió Việt* 39 (1952): supplement.

42. T. B. C., "Các Đức giám mục Việt Nam hôm nay với thư chung của các Đức giám mục Đông Dương năm 1951," *Công giáo và dân tộc* 40–41 (1976): 40–41.

43. Trần Thị Liên, "Quelle loyauté et déloyauté? Le cas des catholiques vietnamiens pendant la période coloniale et post-coloniale" (paper presented at the

Atelier 37: Entre loyauté et déloyauté: la complexité du choix en contexte colonial en Indochine, Congrès Réseau Asie, 2003). A short book published in Phát Diệm in 1946 prepared people for an ideological battle against communism by urging readers to see the flaws of idealism and materialism. Tá Chung, *Duy vật với duy thực* (Bui Chu: Sao Biển, 1946).

44. On the scorched-earth tactics, see Goscha, *The Road to Dien Bien Phu*, 139; in the south, Bourdeaux, *Bouddhisme Hòa Hảo*, 232.

45. Đoàn Độc Thư and Xuân Huy, *Giám mục Lê Hữu Từ*, 158–66. On temples and pagodas, see Trương Bích Thủy and Vương Hân, "Đốt đình làng để tiêu thổ kháng chiến," Quân đội nhân dân Online (2006), accessed August 17, 2022, https://www.qdnd.vn/quoc-phong-an-ninh/xay-dung-quan-doi/dot-dinh-lang-de-tieu-tho-khang-chien-425718/. For a memoir describing these scorched-earth tactics in Vinh, published in the wake of Saigon's campaign to denounce the communists, see Thanh Sang, *Địa ngục nhân gian, Hồi Ký* (Saigon: n.p., 1955).

46. Fides, "Il Vietmin è un partito comunista?" *Osservatore Romano*, April 27, 1949.

47. Fides, "I Viet-Minh continuano ad accumulare rovine," *Osservatore Romano*, October 11, 1949.

48. Fides, "Esodo di popolazioni nel Vietnam," *Osservatore Romano*, December 24, 1950. *Osservatore Romano* may have used press releases from the French embassy to the Vatican, listing the priests and seminarians who were detained or executed. Ambassade de France près le Saint-Siège, Annexe à la dépèche, La chrétienté en Indochine (situation en septembre 1953), December 30, 1953, SHAT/GR10R/95. On persecutions, see Fides, "Difficoltà per le Missioni nel Vietnam settentrionale," *Osservatore Romano*, February 21, 1952.

49. Trần Thị Liên, "Les catholiques vietnamiens," 551. On the ASVN's propaganda using these arrests, see "Tình trạng đồng bào công giáo ở ngoài bưng," *Gió Việt* 39 (1952): 15–16; "Cộng sản quấy rối các giáo khu," *Gió Việt* 41 (1952): 14–15.

50. "Thay lời tựa," in *Kính chúa yêu nước, Đoàn kết giáo lương*, ed. Phạm Bá Trực (Hanoi: Ủy ban Liên Việt toàn quốc, 1954), 8.

51. Phạm Bá Trực, "Lời kêu gọi đồng bào và ngụy binh công giáo, 1/6/1951," in Phạm Bá Trực, *Kính chúa yêu nước*, 18–21.

52. Phạm Bá Trực, "Thư gửi đồng bào công giáo sau khi đi thăm Trung Quốc và Triều Tiên," in Phạm Bá Trực, *Kính chúa yêu nước*, 22–25.

53. "Về vấn đề Bùi Chu và Phát Diệm trở về lĩnh thổ Việt Nam," *Gió Việt* 19 (1951): 30–32. Two lay Catholics, Châu Xuân Phan and Đinh Van Nam, were nominated to be head and vice-head of Bùi Chu when it became a province. "Bùi Chu trở thành tỉnh," *Gió Việt* 24 (1951): 23.

54. FTNV Zone Sud Bureau de liaison pour la pacification, SHAT/GR10R/95, 2–3.

55. FTNV Zone Sud Bureau de liaison pour la pacification, SHAT/GR10R/95, 5.

56. "Tình hình công giáo Trung Hoa," *Đạo binh Đức Mẹ*, March 1, 1952.

57. Trịnh Trấn Nguyên, "Giáo hội với quốc gia," *Đạo binh Đức Mẹ*, July 31, 1952, 5. Thượng Chí, a Chinese refugee, wrote two articles under a pseudonym: "Họ thất thểu trên đường ly hương," *Đạo binh Đức Mẹ*, April 10, 1954; and "Toàn thể

nhân loại vui mừng," *Đạo binh Đức Mẹ*, April 15, 1954. The pseudonym, which is the Vietnamese name for Harbin in northeast China, might indicate the refugee's place of origin.

58. The Legion of Mary was created in Ireland and gathered lay Catholics around the adoration of Mary. The association in China became the target of communist repression. See David E. Mungello, *The Catholic Invasion of China: Remaking Chinese Christianity* (Lanham, MD: Rowman & Littlefield, 2015), 58; Paul Mariani, *Church Militant: Bishop Kung and Catholic Resistance in Communist Shanghai* (Cambridge, MA: Harvard University Press, 2011), 47–52. On squads in Vietnam, see "Muốn lập đạo binh Đức bà phải làm gì?" *Đạo binh Đức Mẹ*, March 1, 1952.

59. "Tình hình công giáo Trung Hoa"; Trịnh Trấn Nguyên, "Giáo hội với quốc gia," 5; "Thế nào chúng tà cùng phải đấu tranh với cộng sản," *Đạo binh Đức Mẹ*, July 1, 1954, 17. On Korea, see "Tình hình giáo hội Cao Ly," *Đạo binh Đức Mẹ*, May 31, 1952; "Hội Thanh niên công giáo Triều Tiên," *Đạo binh Đức Mẹ*, August 15, 1952.

60. C. Pierre Bodin, "Choses vues à Hong Kong: Fête religieuse, événement politique: le sacre du 10ème évêque vietnamien," *Journal d'Extrême-Orient*, March 23, 1953.

61. C. Pierre Bodin, "Le Discours de M. Nguyen Huy Lai au sacre de Mgr. Dai," *Journal d'Extrême-Orient*, March 23, 1953.

62. Marr, *Vietnam*, 405.

63. "Người 'quốc gia' Việt Nam có chủ nghĩa chi không?" *Tinh thần*, August 19, 1949; see also Tinh Thần, "Thống nhứt và độc lập, là bánh vẽ, nếu . . .," *Tinh thần*, August 12, 1949.

64. For the original text, see Ngô Đình Diệm, "Lời tuyên bố ông Ngô Đình Diệm," *Tinh thần*, June 16, 1949. The official translation is in *Major Policy Speeches by President Ngo Dinh Diem* (Saigon: Press Office, Presidency of the Republic of Viet Nam, 1956), 41–42. For an analysis, see Miller, *Misalliance*, 35–36; Duy Lap Nguyen, *The Unimagined Community: Imperialism and Culture in South Vietnam* (Manchester, UK: Manchester University Press, 2020), chap. 2. For a brief overview of his ascension to power, see Phi-Vân Nguyen, "Ngô Đình Diệm and the Republic of Vietnam," in *The Cambridge History of the Vietnam War*, Vol. 1, *Origins*, ed. Edward Miller and Lien-Hang Nguyen (New York: Cambridge University Press, 2024), 302–25.

65. On the government that he tried to form with the Japanese, see Trần Mỹ Vân, *A Vietnamese Royal Exile in Japan, Prince Cường Để (1882-1951)* (London: Routledge, 2005).

66. Miller, *Misalliance*, 37.

67. Sol Sanders, "Beautiful Saigon Crowded with Viet Nam Refugees," *Christian Science Monitor*, November 14, 1950; "French Repatriate 29,000 in Indo-China to Formosa," *New York Times*, July 3, 1953. The weekly radio program "Yale Interprets the News" reported on Asian events. Harry Rudin claimed that communism was winning the war of ideas, in "Asia Reds Winning Idea Battle?" *Christian Science Monitor*, January 11, 1954.

68. Edmund Wehrle, "'Awakening the Conscience of the Masses': The Vietnamese Confederation of Labour, 1947–1975," in *Labour in Vietnam*, ed. Anita Chan (Singapore: ISEAS, 2011), 18.

69. Tâm Ngọc, "Đạo Cao Đài," *Đạo binh Đức Mẹ*, March 1954.
70. "Thái độ công giáo với đảng phái," *Đạo binh Đức Mẹ*, April 3, 1954.
71. "Ce qu'un adhérent du parti Dai Viet doit savoir," trans. Capitaine Boisson, SHAT/10H/643.
72. "Thái độ công giáo với đảng phái"; "Thường thuật hội nghị báo chí công giáo Việt Nam," *Đạo binh Đức Mẹ*, April 10, 1954.
73. On gradual autonomy, see McHale, *The First Vietnam War*.
74. "Un congrès des nationalistes va se tenir à Saigon," *Le Monde*, September 5, 1953; Tran, *Disunion*, 40–42.
75. "Le Congrès national de Saigon rejette la participation du Vietnam à l'Union française," *Le Monde*, October 17, 1953; "L'Union française et le choix vietnamien," *Le Monde*, October 19, 1953. Paris failed to reform the French Union and the entire project became obsolete in 1956 because most states had established bilateral relationships and abandoned the idea of a commonwealth of nations. See Pierre Grosser, "Une 'création continue'? L'Indochine, le Maghreb et l'Union française," *Monde(s)* 12, no. 2 (2017): 71–94.
76. "Tại sao Việt Nam lại muốn 2 hiệp ước riêng biệt?," *Gió Việt*, April 1, 1954. One of the most important transfers of authority over the economy, customs, and a common currency took place only in December 1954. Roger Pinto, "La France et les États d'Indochine devant les accords de Genève," *Revue française de science politique* 5, no. 1 (1955): 84. For a retrospective account, see Vũ Quốc Thúc, "The Birth of Central Banking, 1955–1956," in Vu and Fear, *The Republic of Vietnam*, 25–34.
77. Hugues Tertrais, *La Piastre et le fusil: Le Coût de la guerre d'Indochine, 1945–1954* (Paris: Institut de la gestion publique et du développement économique, 2002); Grosser, "Une 'création continue'?"
78. On the concept of an archipelago state, see Goscha, *Vietnam*, 63–66. On the comparison to a leopard skin, see Ramesh Thakur, *Peacekeeping in Vietnam: Canada, India, Poland, and the International Commission* (Edmonton: University of Alberta Press, 1984), 104.
79. The idea of a territorial division was both old and new. The idea of France's holding on to the southern part of Vietnam had emerged in 1946 and again in 1951 after the narrowest part of Vietnam was suggested as a natural hindrance to communist expansion. See Denise Artaud, "La menace américaine et le règlement indochinois à la conférence de Genève," *Histoire, économie et société* 13, no. 1 (1994): 48; Paul Ély, *Mémoires: L'Indochine dans la tourmente* (Paris: Plon, 1964), 1:100. Moscow and Beijing also declared that they would be satisfied with partition at the sixteenth parallel; see Mari Olsen, *Soviet-Vietnam Relations and the Role of China: Changing Alliances* (London: Routledge, 2006), 38. On the state of Vietnam's proposal, see Robert F. Randle, *The Settlement of the Indochinese War* (Princeton, NJ: Princeton University Press, 1969), 211.
80. "Vietnam: Traité d'indépendance du 4 juin 1954," Dijithèque MJP, accessed January 11, 2021, https://mjp.univ-perp.fr/constit/vn1954.htm. The treaty stipulated France was responsible for negotiating the SVN's international agreements. See Pinto, "La France et les États d'Indochine," 83.
81. Internal correspondence insisted that appending a French signature on provisions engaging the SVN would be sensitive. Randle, *The Settlement of the Indochinese War*, 243–44.

82. Motion du "Mouvement pour la grande union et pour la paix" au sujet des négociations entre la France et les communistes, May 1, 1954, SHAT/10H/4202.

83. Directives de propagande et documentation n. 854, Annexe 2, Message de sa Majesté Bao Dai au peuple vietnamien, July 15, 1954, SHAT/10H/2559.

84. Pierre Asselin, "The Democratic Republic of Vietnam and the 1954 Geneva Conference: A Revisionist Critique," *Cold War History* 11, no. 2 (2010): 168–69.

85. Randle, *The Settlement of the Indochinese War*, 235.

86. Commandement en chef des forces terrestres navales et aériennes en Indochine, Directive n. 1, June 12, 1954, SHAT/10H/2545; Ély, *Mémoires*, 166–67, 181–83.

87. Chef de Bataillon Legrand, Plans de destruction, June 23, 1954, SHAT/10H/2545.

88. Max Clos, "En dépit des mises au point, Hanoi ne repousse plus l'hypothèse d'un abandon du delta," *Le Monde*, June 30, 1954.

89. Max Clos, "Imposée par l'évolution militaire au Tonkin, l'évacuation du sud du delta a de profondes répercussions sur la situation intérieure du Vietnam," *Le Monde*, July 3, 1954.

90. "Le périmètre défensif se resserre autour de Hanoï, Les forces franco-vietnamiennes évacuent le sud du delta tonkinois," *Le Monde*, July 2, 1954.

91. Trần Văn Tuyên, *Hội nghị Genève 1954, Hồi ký* (Saigon: Chim đàn, 1964), 104.

92. On Zhou Enlai's pressure, see Chen Jian, "China and the Indochina Settlement at the Geneva Conference of 1954," in *The First Vietnam War: Colonial Conflict and Cold War Crisis*, ed. Mark Lawrence and Frederik Logevall (Cambridge, MA: Harvard University Press, 2007), 240–62; Goscha, *Vietnam*, 413–14. On trusting Soviet and Chinese advice, see Tuong Vu, *Vietnam's Communist Revolution: The Power and Limits of Ideology* (Cambridge: Cambridge University Press, 2017), 131. On the DRV's interests, see Asselin, "The Democratic Republic of Vietnam," 174.

93. Max Clos, "Imposée par l'évolution militaire au Tonkin."

94. "Scende su Hanoi il 'sipario di bambù,'" *Osservatore Romano*, August 10, 1954; "Le operazioni sul fronte indocinese, Il nuovo schieramento franco-vietnamita nella regione del Delta del Fiume Rosso," *Osservatore Romano*, July 3, 1954; "La situazione in Indocina, Il Primo Ministro Diem riafferma l'ostilità del Vietnam a qualsiasi divisione," *Osservatore Romano*, July 8, 1954; "L'esodo dei cattolici dai Vietnam del Nord," *Osservatore Romano*, August 15, 1954; "Nel Vietnam 118 sacerdoti sono stati fatti prigioneri," *Osservatore Romano*, August 21, 1954; "Un sacerdote ucciso nel Vietnam mentre impartiva gli ultimi Sacramenti a soldati morenti," *Osservatore Romano*, September 11, 1954; Fides, "Situazione nei Vicariati Apostolici del Vietnam settentrionale," *Osservatore Romano*, December 4, 1954; Fides, "Il dramma delle popolazioni nel Vietnam del Nord," *Osservatore Romano*, February 17, 1955; Fides, "Le persecuzioni anticattoliche nel Vietnam del Nord," *Osservatore Romano*, March 10, 1955; Fides, "Continua l'esodo nel Vietnam," *Osservatore Romano*, February 6, 1955; F. A., "Panorama vietnamita," *Osservatore Romano*, August 13, 1955.

95. United Press International, "French Abandon Province South of Hanoi to Vietminh," *New York Times*, June 30, 1954.

96. "Indochina Going," *New York Times*, July 4, 1954.

97. On the French withdrawal, see United Press International, "French Abandon Province South of Hanoi to Vietminh." On the Vietnamese reaction, see Reuters, "Tonkin Lines Shortened; Southern Area Evacuated," *Christian Science Monitor*, July 7, 1954; "Evacuation Rush Strikes Nam Dinh: Red River Defense Keystone in State of Confusion as French Troops Leave," *New York Times*, July 3, 1954; Henry R. Lieberman, "Vietnam Premier Protests French Pull-Back in Delta," *New York Times*, July 3, 1954; Henry R. Lieberman, "French Give Up South Zone of Vietnam's Delta to Reds," *New York Times*, July 2, 1954.

98. Lieberman, "French Give Up South Zone."

99. Philip Catton, "'It Would Be a Terrible Thing If We Handed These People over to the Communists': The Eisenhower Administration, Article 14(d), and the Origins of the Refugee Exodus from North Vietnam," *Diplomatic History* 39, no. 2 (2015): 331–58.

100. On the legal status of the temporary zones, see Nguyen Duy Tân, "L'évolution du statut juridique," 73; Pinto, "La France et les États d'Indochine," 86.

101. On assembly areas and cutoff dates, see Anita Lauve Nutt, "Regroupment, Withdrawals, and Transfers—Vietnam: 1954–1955 Part I," Rand Memorandum RM-6163-ARPA (Santa Monica, CA: RAND, 1969).

2. "Refugees" on a Mission

1. See, for example, "Nghị định số 299 NĐ/BTT ngày mùng 3 tháng chạp năm 1954 cho phép Ô. Bằng Bá Lân xuất bản tại Sài Gòn tờ tuần báo Việt ngữ nhân đề 'Di cư,'" *Công báo Việt Nam*, December 18, 1954. This includes publications produced by the evacuees. A periodical published by Catholic evacuees, *Đường sống, Tuần báo của đồng bào di cư* [*The Living Path, The Weekly of Migrant Compatriots*], presented itself as *The Living Path: A Weekly for Refugees* when it sought funding from USOM. *Đường sống* [*The Living Path*], November 1, 1954, National Archives and Records Administration (hereafter cited as NARA)/US Foreign Assistance Agencies (hereafter cited as RG469)/1452; Duong Song Refugee Newspaper, 1955, NARA/RG469/1450.

2. The French referred to "civilian refugees" in their French-language propaganda documents in August 1954 while the Vietnamese-language version called them "evacuees" (*tản cư*). Vài điều chỉ dẫn cho đồng bào tản cư, tract n. 168, tirage 20.000, August 1954, SHAT/10H/430.

3. Cùng đồng bào Bắc Việt, tract no. 176, tirage 50.000, August 1954, SHAT/10H/430. Except for the *Official Gazette* translating "refugee" into its Vietnamese equivalent, *tỵ nạn* and *di dân* (population movement), which appeared early in the evacuation, the use of *di cư* was omnipresent.

4. Việt Nam Cộng Hòa, "Diễn từ đọc trong buổi lễ đón người di cư thứ 10 vạn do tàu Mỹ chuyên chở tới Saigon, 22/12/1954," in *Con đường chính nghĩa độc lập, dân chủ, Hiệu triệu và diễn văn quan trọng của Tổng thống Ngô Đình Diệm, quyển I, từ 16-6-1954 đến 7-7-1955* (Saigon: Sở báo chí thông tin Phủ Tổng thống, 1956), 170–71. About the ceremony, see Vietnam Presse, "Sous

le patronage du Président Ngo Dinh Diem, une cérémonie solennelle a été organisée en l'honneur du 100.000ème réfugié, évacué par la flotte américaine," September 24, 1954, Archives nationales d'outre-mer (hereafter cited as ANOM)/Haut Commissariat à l'Indochine (hereafter cited as HCI)/Service de protection du Corps expéditionnaire français en Indochine (hereafter cited as SPCE)/74.

5. Le Commissariat général des réfugiés est touché par les mortiers, 1955, Établissement de communication et de production audiovisuelle de la Défense (hereafter cited as ECPAD)/Fonds Indochine/SC 55-94.

6. COMIGAL reflected the French administrative practice of abbreviating complex names. *Haut commissaire* became *haussaire* and *président du conseil* became *présiconseil*.

7. Việt Nam Cộng Hòa, "Kêu gọi thế giới giúp đỡ dân chúng di cư vào Nam, 10/8/1954," in *Con đường chính nghĩa độc lập, dân chủ*, 166–67.

8. Forces terrestres nord-Việt Nam (FTNV) Secteur Grand Haiphong, "Evacuation des civils" Étude du Groupement des unités de points sensibles relative aux Opérations "à chaud," January 29, 1955, SHAT/10H/1039. The British and Polish navies also contributed to the transportation.

9. Plan d'action du projet pour le Vietnam signé entre l'administrateur général de l'Aide économique américaine et le Commissaire général aux réfugiés, October 12, 1954, NARA/RG469/1431.

10. Special Report on the Resettlement and Rehabilitation of Refugees from North Vietnam, October 12, 1956, NARA/RG469/1431.

11. On claims that the cost was $89 per refugee, above the average annual income of $85, see Bernard B. Fall, "Commentary: Bernard B. Fall on Bùi Văn Lương," in *Vietnam: The First Five Years, An International Symposium*, ed. Richard W. Lindholm (East Lansing: Michigan State University Press, 1959), 56; Piero Gheddo, *The Cross and the Bo-Tree, Catholics & Buddhist in Vietnam* (New York: Sheed and Ward, 1970), 70; Jacobs, *America's Miracle Man*, 133. In fact, excluding expenses for the US Navy, US aid per refugee was around $69 per refugee, of which $25 was for the purchase of goods paid in USD, and the remaining $45 was converted into piastres in Vietnam. Adjusted to the market rate, this was the equivalent of $47 per refugee. D. C. Lavergne, Memorandum for the Record, February 27, 1956, NARA/RG469/1431.

12. On the UNHCR in Asia, see Meredith Oyen, *The Diplomacy of Migration: Transnational Lives and the Making of U.S.-Chinese Relations in the Cold War* (Ithaca, NY: Cornell University Press, 2016); Glen Peterson, "The Uneven Development of the International Refugee Regime in Postwar Asia: Evidence from China, Hong Kong and Indonesia," *Journal of Refugee Studies* 25, no. 3 (2012): 326–43. On the ICRC in Indochina, see Véronique Harouel-Bureloup, "L'action du CICR en Indochine," *Grotius* (2010): 1–4. On NGO support, see Jessica Elkind, *Aid under Fire: Nation Building and the Vietnam War* (Lexington: University Press of Kentucky, 2016); Delia T. Pergande, "Private Voluntary Aid in Vietnam: The Humanitarian Politics of Catholic Relief Services and CARE, 1954–1965" (PhD diss., University of Kentucky, 1999); Christopher J. Kauffman, "Politics, Programs, and Protests: Catholic Relief Services in Vietnam, 1954–1975," *Catholic Historical Review* 91,

no. 2 (2005): 223-50. The Cooperative for American Remittances to Europe (CARE) signed an agreement with the SVN on August 9, 1954.

13. For example, see Official Report of the Meeting, December 6, 1954, NARA/RG469/1431.

14. On Michigan State University's Vietnam Project, see John Ernst, *Forging a Fateful Alliance: Michigan State University and the Vietnam War* (East Lansing: Michigan State University Press, 1998); Carter, *Inventing Vietnam*, chap. 1; Elkind, *Aid under Fire*.

15. President of the Government, State of Vietnam to Cardinal Spellman, July 25, 1954, translation, Cardinal Spellman Funds/S/C-49/To Card, Spellman Vietnam/folder 2. I have developed the idea of a Catholic arc of resistance against communism in Phi-Vân Nguyen, "Victims of Atheist Persecution: Transnational Catholic Solidarity and Refugee Protection in Cold War Asia," in *Refugees and Religions: Ethnographic Studies of Global Trajectories*, ed. Birgit Meyer and Peter van der Veer, 51-67 (London: Bloomsbury, 2021).

16. Vietnam Presse, "Soldats du Christ," January 8, 1955, Trung tâm Lưu trữ quốc gia 2 (hereafter cited as TTLT2)/Phủ Tổng thống Đệ nhất Cộng Hòa (hereafter cited as PTTĐICH)/29.790. On his support of China, see Cardinal Spellman to an undisclosed recipient based in New York, June 10, 1948, Cardinal Spellman Funds/S/B-10/To Card, Spellman, Pacific Visits/folder 11; John T. Mao, Praefectura apostolica Taipeihensis, to Cardinal Spellman, January 19, 1952, Cardinal Spellman Funds/S/B-10/To Card, Spellman Korea/folder 8. On Korea, see "The Korean Dead," *Korean Information Bulletin* 2, no. 5 (1951): 1-2; John T. Mao, Praefectura apostolica Taipeihensis, to Cardinal Spellman, and Cardinal Spellman to Monsignor Tardini, February 11, 1952, Cardinal Spellman Funds/S/C-15/From Card, Spellman China.

17. Raymond de Jaegher, *The Enemy Within: An Eyewitness Account of the Communist Conquest of China* (New York: Doubleday, 1952). On the Free Pacific Association, see de Jaegher, *The Growth of the Free Pacific Association in Vietnam* (Saigon: Free Pacific Association, 1962). His articles in *Free Front* covered India, Burma, Latin America, and China. On Saigon's connections to the APACL, see Mitchell Tan, "Spiritual Fraternities: The Transnational Networks of Ngô Đình Diệm's Personalist Revolution and South Vietnam's First Republic, 1955-1963," *Journal of Vietnamese Studies* 14, no. 2 (2019): 1-67.

18. Fides, "Stampa et radio cattoliche in Cina," *Osservatore Romano*, July 17, 1947; Columban Fathers, *Those Who Journeyed with Us, 1918-2016* (St. Columbans, NE: Missionary Society of St. Columban, 2017), 107.

19. Fides, Lettre à Mgr. Phạm Ngọc Chi, December 4, 1954, TTLT2/Phủ Thủ tướng (hereafter cited as PThT)/An Ninh/14.748.

20. For example, see "Refugees in Vietnam," *New York Times*, August 7, 1954.

21. Henry R. Lieberman, "Battle for Allegiance Goes on in Indochina," *New York Times*, August 8, 1954; Lieberman, "'Go South' Slogans on Buildings Spur Mass Exodus from Hanoi," *New York Times*, August 21, 1954.

22. Thomas A. Dooley, *Deliver Us from Evil* (New York: Farrar, Straus, and Cudahy, 1956).

23. Bùi Văn Lương, "The Role of Friendly Nations," 49.

24. Fall, "Commentary."

25. Nguyen, "Réfugiés, religion et politique."
26. Bùi Văn Lương, "The Role of Friendly Nations," 50.
27. Memorandum on Vietnam's Population in 1955, 1955, NARA/RG469/1435.
28. Directives de Propagande et Documentation n.656, Annexe XII, Bilan des manifestations contre le partage du Vietnam, May 25, 1954, SHAT/10H/2559.
29. Bulletin de renseignement (hereafter cited as BR) Activités politiques vietnamiennes a/s Conférence de Genève, June 1, 1954, ANOM/HCI/SPCE/4.
30. BR au sujet du séjour de Ngo Dinh Diem à Hanoi, July 5, 1954, ANOM/HCI/SPCE/4.
31. BR, Manifestation populaire organisée le 18 juillet à Saigon-Cholon pour protester contre un partage éventuel du Viêt-Nam, July 18, 1954, ANOM/HCI/SPCE/4.
32. Thủ tướng chính phủ, Lời tuyên bố, July 22, 1954, TTLT2/PThT/An Ninh/14.626.
33. FTNV, Rapport d'activités de propagande 15 juillet–15 août 1954, July 19, 1954, SHAT/10H/4304, appendix.
34. For example, see Toàn thể đồng bào trung châu Bắc Việt!, tract no. 142, tirage 300,000, July 1954, SHAT/10H/430.
35. For example, see Anh em đi lính cho Pháp và bù nhìn. Anh em công chức ngụy quyền, tract p.y. n. 151, tirage 500,000, July 1954, SHAT/10H/430.
36. Đây sự thực tại Nam Định—Bùi Chu và Phủ Lý hiện nay, tract no. 163, tirage 100,000, July 1954, SHAT/10H/430.
37. Số phận của các thiếu nữ vùng Việt-Minh kiểm soát, tract no. 167, tirage 100,000, August 1954, SHAT/10H/430.
38. HCI, Note no. 52, Traduction d'un document Viet Minh, Comité exécutif du parti, Interzone du nord, no. 34, Instructions du Bureau permanent du comité central du parti concernant les Chinois émigrés au Vietnam, March 26, 1952, SHAT/10H/3239.
39. For example, see Việt Minh dâng nước ta cho cộng sản Tàu, tract no. 155, tirage 100,000, July 1954, SHAT/10H/430.
40. Độc lập kiểu . . ., tract no. 180, tirage 20,000, August 1954, SHAT/10H/430.
41. Commandement en chef des forces terrestres navales et aériennes en Indochine, Directive no. 1, no. 161; FTNV état major 2ème bureau, Fiche no. 2540/FTNV/2, 1954, SHAT/10H/2545.
42. Cùng toàn thể đồng bào những vùng bị tản cư, tract no. 137, tirage 50,000, July 1954, SHAT/10H/430, Chiến lược "quả đấm" đã mang lại cho liên quân Việt Pháp nhiều thành tích vẻ vang, tract no. 145, tirage 400,000, July 1954, SHAT/10H/430.
43. Nắm tay cho chặt để đấm cho mạnh, tract no. 135, tirage 500,000, July 1954, SHAT/10H/430.
44. Dân chúng Bình Lục tỉnh Hà Nam biểu tình đả đảo Việt Minh, Trung Cộng, tract no. 170, tirage 50,000, August 1954, SHAT/10H/430.
45. Nhiệm vụ hiện tại của chúng ta, tract no. 178, tirage 20,000, August 1954, SHAT/10H/430. It was then translated into French as "returning to the north."
46. Vào Nam quyết hẹn ngày về, tract no. 172, tirage 40,000, August 1954, SHAT/10H/430.
47. On the VWP's perception, see Holcombe, *Mass Mobilization*, 225–27.

48. On Hồ Chí Minh's message, see Hồ Chủ tịch gửi đồng bào công giáo đã đi vào Nam, April 29, 1955, TTLT2/PThT/An Ninh/14.748; on the party's instructions, see, for example, "Thông tư của Ban bí thư số 19-TT/TW về việc tổ chức lễ Phúc sinh cho đồng bào công giáo và đề phòng địch lời dụng dịp này để dụ dỗ cưỡng ép đồng bào di cư, 24-3-1955," in *Văn kiện Đảng*, 16: 234-36. On French and US soldiers using a drawing of the Virgin Mary to wipe up puddles in a camp, see Sao Mai, *Trại di cư Pa Gốt Hải Phòng, Phóng sự điều tra* (Hanoi: NXB Văn nghệ, 1955), 8, 12-13.

49. In the north, a pro-DRV priest urged Catholics to refuse any work on the plantations. Forces terrestres du sud-Viêt Nam (FTSV), Note 8261, Utilisation des réfugiés comme coolies, 1954, SHAT/10H/5224. Evacuees in the south also reported hearing those claims. Général de division Forces terrestres du centre-Viêt Nam (FTCV), Réclamation d'habitants du xa de Duc-Ninh, transmise pour suite à donner auprès de la CIC, March 23, 1955, SHAT/10H/5811, 3.

50. Sao Mai, *Trại di cư Pa Gốt*, 20-21. Photographs show that the banner existed and included diacritics to prevent this confusion. We do not know whether they were there originally or if they were added afterwards. Visite officielle du général Lawton Collins à Haïphong, January 13, 1955, ECPAD/Fonds Indochine/NVN 55-3 R5.

51. On this early anti-American propaganda, see Vu, *Vietnam's Communist Revolution*, 127-31.

52. Hoàng Linh, *Tội ác của đế quốc Mỹ, Trong việc bắt ép đồng bào di cư vào Nam* (Hanoi: NXB Sự thật, 1955), 24-25.

53. "Thông tư của Ban bí thư số 19-TT/TW"; "Chỉ thị của Ban bí thư số 16-CT/TW Tăng cường chỉ đạo tích cực đấu tránh phá âm mưu địch cưỡng ép và dụ dỗ giáo dân di cư, 21-4-1955," in *Văn kiện Đảng* 16: 268-76.

54. One meeting in Thái Nguyên urged two thousand faithful to identify "those who sought discord and disunity." Nguyễn Văn Thời and Trịnh Thị Mai, "Đồng bào công giáo tỉnh Thái Nguyên phát huy tấm gương sống 'tốt đẹp đạo' của Linh mục Phạm Bá Trực trong công guộc xây dựng và bảo vệ tổ quốc," in *Linh mục Phạm Bá Trực và đường hướng Công giáo đồng hành cùng với dân tộc trong thời kỳ kháng chiến chống thực dân Pháp (1946-1954)*, ed. Nguyễn Hồng Dương (NXB Từ điển bách khoa, 2011), 84. A pro-DRV priest denounced foreign propaganda and the lies of priests. "Lột trân âm mưu di dân vào Nam," *Dân mới*, October 17, 1954.

55. *Pháp luật trừng trị bọn cưỡng ép dụ dỗ người đi Nam*, 8-9.

56. Graham Greene, "Last Drama of Indochina II: Refugees and Victors," *Sunday Times*, May 1, 1955; see also Greene, "Drama of Indochina: The Dilemma of the South," *Sunday Times*, April 24, 1955; Greene, "Last Drama of Indochina III: The Man as Pure as Lucifer," *Sunday Times*, May 8, 1955. I have analyzed this criticism of the changing role of the Church in Phi-Vân Nguyen, "Victims of Atheist Persecution."

57. Attitude des autorités ecclésiastiques du Nord à l'égard de l'évacuation des populations civiles, August 25, 1954, SHAT/GR10R/95; Gheddo, *The Cross and the Bo-Tree*, 70; Hansen, "The Virgin Heads South," 123.

58. BR, September 23, 1954, SHAT/10H/4195.

59. FTNV, Note no. 1761, Cérémonies militaires au départ d'Hanoi, September 16, 1954, SHAT/10H/2550.

60. Hansen, "The Virgin Heads South," 119, shows figures that include all members of the clergy. George Naïdenoff, "Les restes de la chrétienté du nord," *Missi* 2 (1956), 40 only refers to the secular clergy because of their responsibility for administering the faith. Over three-quarters of the secular clergy, from five dioceses, left: Haiphong (87%), Bắc Ninh (81%), Phát Diệm (78%), Thái Bình (77%), and Bùi Chu (76%). Over half also left from three other dioceses: Lặng Sơn (64%), Hanoi (56%), and Thanh Hóa (58%). The fewest left from the dioceses of Hưng Hoa (39%) and Vinh (24%).

61. Naïdenoff, "Vainqueurs aux mains nues."

62. Broussole and Provençal, "L'évacuation des catholiques."

63. Article 29 mentions the creation of an international commission for the supervision and control of the cease-fire agreements, which is why some archives use the acronym ICSC, instead of ICC. "Geneva Agreements on the Cessation of Hostilities in Vietnam, Cambodia, and Laos 20–21 July 1954; Final Declaration of the Geneva Conference on the Problem of Restoring Peace in Indo-China, 21 July 1954," accessed July 9, 2018, https://peacemaker.un.org/sites/peacemaker.un.org/files/KH-LA-VN_540720_GenevaAgreements.pdf.

64. Phi-Vân Nguyen, "Vietnam's 1954 Partition and Displacement in Perspective," in *Cold War Refugees: Violence, Ideologies, and Space in Postcolonial Asia*, ed. Yumi Moon (forthcoming).

65. Thakur, *Peacekeeping in Vietnam*, 132.

66. Affaire Ba Lang, Nom des personnes et des chrétientés qui avaient déjà fait leur demande aux autorités locales V.N. et n'avaient pas encore la réponse lorsque nous avons quitté Vinh, December 20, 1954, SHAT/10H/967.

67. Enquête de la Commission internationale à Ba Lang, February 6, 1955, SHAT/10H/5783.

68. Général de Brigade Brebisson, Lettre no. 3483 au Général d'armée, Commissaire général de France et Commandant en chef de l'Indochine, Enquête de la Commission internationale à Luu My, March 16, 1955, SHAT/10H/5783.

69. D. R. Sardesai, *Indian Foreign Policy in Cambodia, Laos, and Vietnam, 1947–1964* (Berkeley: University of California Press, 1968), 89, 92; Jarema Slowiak, "The Role of the International Commission for Supervision and Control in Vietnam in the Population Exchange between Vietnamese States during the Years 1954–1955," *Prace Historyczne* 146, no. 3 (2019): 621–35.

70. Lại Nguyên Ân, "Thử tìm dấu vết người bút Vũ Bằng ở hai tờ báo 'Trung Việt tân văn' (Hanoi, 1946) và 'Lửa sống' (Hải Phòng, 1954–1955)," 2013, accessed March 24, 2015, http://www.viet-studies.info/LaiNguyenAn_TimDauVetVuBang.htm. On the Procession of the Land, see "Hoặt động của đoàn ký giả tiền tuyến," *Thời luận*, April 30, 1955.

71. National Day celebrated both the French vote to let Cochinchina join the ASVN and the day Emperor Gia Long unified the country. H. G., "Lễ trộn đất, Một ngày đầy ý nghĩa," *Hồ Gươm*, June 7, 1951; "Ngày hội Việt Nam thống nhất," *Gió Việt* 25 (1951): back cover; "Tin chính trị, tại thủ đô hơn 120,000 người dự ngày lễ Việt Nam thống nhất," *Gió Việt* 25 (1951): 26.

72. Cérémonie d'adieux au monument aux morts du cimetière de Haïphong, en présence des autorités civiles et militaires, May 11, 1955, ECPAD/Fonds Indochine/NVN 55-64.

73. "Hoặt động của đoàn ký giả tiền tuyến."

74. *Thời luận* claimed that around twenty thousand people attended. "Đất thiêng miền Bắc sẽ đến thủ đô Sài Gòn," *Thời luận*, May 18, 1955; "Đất thiêng miền Bắc đã vô Nam trong một cuộc rước long trọng tưng bừng và muôn vạn cảm động," *Thời luận*, May 21, 1955. However, French intelligence estimated a crowd of six thousand. BR Réception de la terre du Nord, May 22, 1955, SHAT/10H/4195.

75. "Đất thiêng miền Bắc đã vô Nam trong một cuộc rước long trọng tưng bừng và muôn vạn cảm động"; Châu Sinh, "Kỹ nghệ lừa bịp," *Dân nguyện*, September 1, 1955.

76. BR SP 50.295 Réception de la terre du Nord, May 22, 1955, SHAT/10H/4195.

77. On denouncing the Geneva cease-fire in the anticommunist rhetoric, see Nguyen, "When State Propaganda Becomes Social Knowledge," 216–18.

78. Nghiêm Xuân Thiện, "Góp phần xây dựng miền Nam: Ước vọng và trách nhiệm của chúng ta," *Thời luận*, February 22, 1955. On *Thời luận* and Nghiêm Xuân Thiện, see Phạm Trần, "Life and Work of a Journalist," in Vu and Fear, *The Republic of Vietnam*, 118; Picard, "'Renegades.'"

79. "Thân Hòa bình," *Quan điểm*, August 20, 1955; "Văn nghệ sĩ, anh là ai?," *Văn nghệ tự do*, July 6, 1955.

80. "Hà Nội: Thượng Toạ Vĩnh Tường uống thuốc độc tự tử," *Quan điểm*, September 10, 1955.

81. "Phòng hộ tịch," *Văn nghệ tự do*, October 29, 1955.

82. C. L. Dau, "Hiện tại, tại Bắc Việt," *Văn nghệ tự do*, October 8, 1955.

83. C. L. Dau, "Mặt trận Tổ quốc," *Văn nghệ tự do*, November 12, 1955.

84. C. L. Dau, "Đường lối 'Đảng,'" *Văn nghệ tự do*, January 3, 1956.

85. "Bắc Việt trong đêm tối," *Văn nghệ tự do*, August 13, 1955.

86. Chakrabarty, "Remembered Villages."

87. On scholars in the DRV, see Patricia Pelley, *Postcolonial Vietnam: New Histories of the National Past* (Durham, NC: Duke University Press, 2002); Christoph Giebel, *Imagined Ancestries of Vietnamese Communism: Ton Duc Thang and the Politics of History and Memory* (Seattle: University of Washington Press, 2011).

88. "Hoặt động của đoàn ký giả tiền tuyến." On the August Revolution as a recurrent theme, see Hoang, "The August Revolution."

89. "Việt Cộng đã phủ nhận tinh thần cách mạng toàn dân trong cuộc Tổng khởi nghĩa 19/8/1945," *Dân nguyện*, August 19, 1955.

90. "Việt Cộng đã phủ nhận tinh thần cách mạng," 4.

91. Narratives distinguished between the Việt Minh, the nationalist front, and the Việt Cộng in identifying the communist takeover. On this derogatory term, see Brett Reilly, "The True Origin of the Term 'Viet Cong,'" *The Diplomat*, January 13, 2018, https://thediplomat.com/2018/01/the-true-origin-of-the-term-viet-cong/. On claims that the population was lured by communists, see "Nhớ xứ Nghệ, Bút ký của Thanh Hoan," *Luyện thép*, January 24, 1958. For a narrative that ignores any past alliances, see Nguyễn Viết Khai, "Bức thư của cha Nguyễn Viết Khai," *Luyện thép*, June 1, 1957.

92. On the Việt Minh in the August Revolution, see David Marr, *Vietnam, 1945: The Quest for Power* (Berkeley: University of California Press, 1997).

93. Mai Thảo, *Đêm giã từ Hà Nội* (Saigon: Người Việt, 1955).
94. André Malraux, *La Condition humaine* (Paris: Gallimard, 1933). Novels in French also conveyed the idea of a battle between East and West and recalled Malraux's *condition humaine*. See Nguyễn Hữu Châu, *Les Reflets de nos jours* (Paris: René Julliard, 1955), as analyzed by Nathalie Huynh Chau Nguyen, *Vietnamese Voices: Gender and Cultural Identity in the Vietnamese Francophone Novel* (DeKalb, IL: Southeast Asia Publications, Northern Illinois University Press, 2003), 132–37.
95. In fact, civilians were not the last to depart through official channels. Their movements were limited, as authorities imposed curfews and restrictions on civilians. FTNV, Note 6367 sur l'application de l'état d'alerte au Nord-Vietnam, June 30, 1954, SHAT/10H/2544.
96. Mai Thảo, *Đêm giã từ Hà Nội*, 29.
97. Mai Thảo, *Đêm giã từ Hà Nội*, 30.
98. Mai Thảo, *Đêm giã từ Hà Nội*, 35.
99. Nguyễn Công Luận, *Nationalist in the Viet Nam Wars: Memoirs of a Victim Turned Soldier* (Bloomington: Indiana University Press, 2012), 136, 141.
100. Minh Đạo, "Người Việt tranh dấu viết một trang sử mới," *Người Việt*, August 27, 1955.
101. Trần Thanh Hiệp, "Hướng về Miền Nam," *Người Việt*, August 27, 1955; "Hướng về tương lai," *Tự do*, Spring, 1955.
102. Vietnam Presse, "Le Dr. Pham Van Huyen," Commissaire général aux réfugiés, December 5, 1954, CICR/Réfugiés-requérants d'asile/234-223-002.
103. On his message to the evacuees, see M. Pham Van Huyen lance un appel aux compatriotes réfugiés du nord, 1954, TTLT2/PThT/Tổ chức/4.140. On entertaining foreign delegations, see, for example, Le docteur Pham Van Huyen s'entretenant avec Mme Ely (vue de dos), 1954, ECPAD/Fonds Indochine/SC 55-126-8.
104. Nha Tổng giám đốc Cảnh sát quốc gia, Thư gửi ông Thủ tướng Bộ Nội vụ, December 13, 1954, TTLT2/PThT/An Ninh/14.748.
105. Trần Thanh Hiệp, "Hướng về Miền Nam."
106. T. V. S., "Bình luận, Những vấn đề của chúng ta, Vấn đề di cư," *Đại chúng*, February 16, 1955.
107. Vietnam Presse, "La journée de l'Unité nationale organisée par les étudiants du Nord-Vietnam commencera ce soir à 21 heures, salle Norodom, 1954," ANOM/HCI/Service du Conseiller diplomatique (hereafter cited as Consdiplo)/161. Students also demanded the release of soldiers imprisoned in the DRV. "Cuộc biểu tình của các sinh viên và học sinh đòi phóng thích 100 sĩ quan trong quân đội quốc gia bị Việt Cộng giam giữ," *Lửa sống*, July 15, 1955.
108. Lam Giang, *Nói với quần chúng, Thực nghiệm biện chứng pháp* (Saigon: Ấn quang Nguyễn Văn Cửa, 1956).
109. Copie du résumé de l'entretien entre le Lt-Colonel Gouzes et Monsieur le Recteur Lassus, April 13, 1955, SHAT/10H/4195.
110. Commandement en chef des forces terrestres, aériennes et navales en Indochine, BR no. 3129/2, May 17, 1955, SHAT/10H/4195.
111. Article du journal Tự quyết dans la revue hebdomadaire de la presse sud vietnamienne, December 5, 1954, ANOM/HCI/SPCE/65.

112. "Sinh viên S.O.S.," *Lửa sống*, July 13, 1955.

113. "Tán thành tuyên ngôn của Thủ tướng năm vạn người biểu tình hoan hô Ngô Thủ tướng," *Dân Việt*, July 21, 1955.

114. 2ème Division d'Infanterie en Extrême Orient, BR valeur C/3 sur la création d'un mouvement "nouveaux Tonkinois contre anciens Tonkinois," July 21, 1955, SHAT/10H/4203.

115. On the Bình Xuyên, see Kevin Li, "Partisan to Sovereign: The Making of the Bình Xuyên in Southern Vietnam, 1945–1948," *Journal of Vietnamese Studies* 11, nos. 3–4 (2016): 140–87; Commandement en chef des forces terrestres aériennes et navales en Indochine, Fiche no. 4100/2 au sujet de documents en provenance du Comité directeur du Dai doan ket va Hoa Binh, May 1, 1954, SHAT/10H/4202; BR, Manifestation populaire organisée le 18 juillet à Saigon-Cholon pour protester contre un partage éventuel du Viêt-Nam; SPCE, Note au sujet des activités gouvernementales et nationalistes, August 5, 1954, ANOM/HCI/SPCE/4, 8.

116. Tran, *Disunion*, chap. 2. On the insurrections by nationalist parties in central Vietnam, see François Guillemot, *Dai Viêt, indépendance et révolution au Viêt-Nam: L'échec de la troisième voie (1938-1955)* (Paris: Les Indes savantes, 2012), 574–77, although Ngô Đình Diệm knew that the French would never back them.

117. Note sur les activités du Professeur Buu Hoi, Traduction des passages principaux des lettres des étudiants de Hanoi, August 28, 1954, ANOM/HCI/SPCE/65.

118. SPCE, Note de renseignement, November 12, 1954, ANOM/HCI/SPCE/9. On Jacques Servant-Schreiber's lobbying for Bửu Hội's appointment, see Pierre Grosser, "La France et l'Indochine (1953–1956): Une 'carte de visite' en 'peau de chagrin'" (PhD diss., Institut d'études politiques, 2002), 1289–96.

119. For a generous estimate, see Vietnam Presse, "Des réfugiés manifestent et lancent un appel en faveur du gouvernement Ngo Dinh Diem," September 21, 1954, ANOM/HCI/Consdiplo/161. On French conservative figures, see SPCE, Note sur la manifestation des réfugiés du 21 septembre, September 22, 1954, ANOM/HCI/SPCE/74, Commandement des forces terrestres du Sud Vietnam, Message au sujet des manifestations de réfugiés dans Saigon-Cholon, porté, secret, très urgent, September 21, 1954, SHAT/10H/4195.

120. SPCE, Note sur la manifestation des réfugiés du 21 septembre; SPCE, Note, Mécontentement chez les troupes vietnamiennes évacuées du Nord-V.N., September 29, 1954, ANOM/HCI/SPCE/74.

121. Trần Tam Tỉnh, *Dieu et César*, 109.

122. Commandement des FTSV, Message au sujet des manifestations de réfugiés dans Saigon-Cholon, porté, secret, très urgent, September 21, 1954, SHAT/10H/4195. They clashed again in November 1954 (FTSV, BR no. 10217, December 3, 1954, SHAT/10H/4214) and in August 1955 (Danh sách đồng bào di cư bị đạn chết hồi 13 giờ 50 trên chuyến tàu Nam Việt từ Tourane tới bến Charner Saigon hồi 11 giờ kể sau, August 31, 1955, TTLT2/PThT/An Ninh/14.750).

123. Bureau militaire de liaison auprès du Commissariat général aux réfugiés, Fiche no. 585, May 14, 1955, SHAT/10H/4195.

124. Jessica Chapman, "Staging Democracy: South Vietnam's 1955 Referendum to Depose Bao Dai," *Diplomatic History* 30, no. 4 (2006); Chapman, *Cauldron of*

Resistance. On the democratic debates, see Tran, *Disunion*; for a shorter version, see Nu-Anh Tran, "How Democratic Should Vietnam Be? The Constitutional Transition of 1955-1956 and the Debate on Democracy," in Tran and Vu, *Building a Republican Nation in Vietnam*, 100-119.

125. For an account of the DRV's return to Hanoi, see Nguyễn Bắc, *Au coeur de la ville captive*, trans. Philippe Papin (Paris: Arléa, 2004), 131; PhaoLô Lê Đắc Trọng, *Chứng từ của một giám mục: Những câu chuyện về một thời* (San Diego, CA: Nguyệt san Diễn đàn giáo dân, 2009), 353-54, 373-434.

126. On the Việt Minh's failure to win over the south, see McHale, *The First Vietnam War*.

127. SPCE, Note sur le Mouvement de Défense pour la Paix, January 14, 1955, ANOM/HCI/SPCE/83. See also Heather Marie Stur, *Saigon at War: South Vietnam and the Global Sixties* (Cambridge: Cambridge University Press, 2020), 57.

128. SPCE, BR no. 922 au sujet du Mouvement pour la Défense de la Paix, February 11, 1955, ANOM/HCI/SPCE/83.

129. SPCE, BR no. 968 au sujet du Mouvement pour la Défense de la Paix, February 16, 1965, ANOM/HCI/SPCE/83; RDVN Instructions a/s des mesures de défense contre les manœuvres de l'ennemi qui projette à organiser une manifestation en vue de protester contre nos combattants de la paix arrêtés dans le Sud Vietnam et transférés à Haiphong, February 15, 1955, SHAT/10H/5787.

130. Requête adressée par les affiliés du "Mouvement pour la défense de la paix" en résidence obligatoire à Haiphong au Président du Conseil du gouvernement national du Vietnam à Saigon, February 28, 1955, ANOM/HCI/SPCE/83; BR no. 108 au sujet du Mouvement pour la Défense de la Paix, February 7, 1955, ANOM/HCI/SPCE/83; BR no. 149 au sujet de la Manifestation des élèves de l'école Nam Viet, sise 5 rue Lucien Lacouture, February 19, 1955, ANOM/HCI/SPCE/83.

131. Correspondance expédiée au Haut Commissaire de France en Indochine, pétitions et motions, 1955, ANOM/HCI/Série générale/487. The folder contains hundreds of petitions.

132. Des réfugiés catholiques fuient le nouveau régime du Nord Viêt-Nam, visite de la Commission internationale de contrôle, 1955, ECPAD/Fonds Indochine/SVN 55-13.

133. Commentaires de la partie UF sur les recommandations de la CIC no. ICSC/FB/55/2/5138 concernant la liberté de mouvement entre les deux zones du Vietnam, October 22, 1955, SHAT/10H/5785.

134. Chef de bataillon de la Ménardière chargé des réfugiés du nord Viet Nam pour la province de Bien Hoa, Rapport, March 19, 1955, SHAT/10H/967, 2.

135. Biên bản Đại hội nghị các trại định cư thuộc các tỉnh miền đông Nam-Việt (Biên Hòa, Thủ Dầu Một, Tây Ninh, Gia Định, Baria, Vũng Tàu, Saigon, Cholon), July 8, 1955, TTLT2/PThT/An Ninh/14.747.

136. Đại hội các trại định cư các tỉnh miền Đông Nam Việt, Kiến nghị, July 8, 1955, TTLT2/PThT/An Ninh/14.747.

137. Biên bản Đại hội nghị các trại định cư thuộc các tỉnh miền đông Nam-Việt.

138. Les étudiants manifestent devant l'hôtel Majestic où sont logés de nombreux représentants de la CIC, July 13, 1955, ECPAD/Fonds Indochine/SC 55-177.
139. Miller, *Misalliance*, 141.
140. Phủ Tổng ủy Di cư Ty nạn, Tập báo cáo hoạt động về tình hình di cư định cư.
141. Das, *Critical Events*.
142. Heonik Kwon, *The Other Cold War* (New York: Columbia University Press, 2010); Hajimu Masuda, *Cold War Crucible: The Korean Conflict and the Postwar World* (Cambridge, MA: Harvard University Press, 2014).

3. Keeping Hope Alive

1. Manifestation devant le palais de l'indépendance. Les étudiants demandent audience au président, 1955, ECPAD/Fonds Indochine/SC 55-113.
2. "Đất thiêng miền Bắc đã vô Nam trong một cuộc rước long trọng tưng bừng và muôn vạn cảm động," *Thời luận*, May 21, 1955.
3. BR SP 50.295 Réception de la terre du nord; Dans la soirée, deux milliers de manifestants ont descendu le bvd Norodom vers le palais de l'indépendance, May 18, 1955, ECPAD/Fonds Indochine/SVN 55-128.
4. Picard, "'Fertile Lands Await'"; Picard, "'Renegades'"; Tran, *Disunion*, chap. 4.
5. Gouvernement de Bruxelles, Lettre à l'attention du Haut commissaire du Vietnam à Paris au sujet de l'exposition universelle de Bruxelles, 1958, TTLT2/PTTĐICH/Nội An/5.511; Phiếu trình ông Bộ trưởng tại Phủ Tổng thống v/v quay phim về di cư, định cư và dinh điền để dự hội chợ Bruxelles, 1958, TTLT2/PTTĐICH/Nội An/5.511; Phủ Tổng ủy Di cư Ty nạn, Xin ngân khoản cho cuộc triển lãm "Di cư 1954" tại Bruxelles, February 4, 1958, TTLT2/PTTĐICH/Nội An/5.511.
6. World Refugee Year Secretariat, *World Refugee Year: The Refugee Problem in the Republic of Viet-Nam* (Geneva, Switzerland: United Nations, 1959). The following year, the Committee for World Refugee Year in Vietnam raised money to support Tibetan refugees. Press Release No. REF/692, "World Refugee Year Committee in Vietnam sends $30,482 to High Commissioner's Office," November 27, 1961, United Nations High Commissioner for Refugees (hereafter cited as UNHCR)/F106/10c/PRE-1961/61.
7. Phạm Văn Huyến, Thư gửi Thủ tướng chánh phủ, November 16, 1954, TTLT2/PThT/Tổ chức/4.140.
8. A dossier compiled by Phạm Văn Liễu, an evacuee who became chief of police in March 1965, claimed that the director took money from the COMIGAL to bring it to communists in Paris, shortly after his resignation. Picard, "'Fertile Lands Await,'" 68–69. However, the sources backing this claim were produced a year later, when the COMIGAL had to conclude the resettlement, or ten years later, in March 1965, when Phạm Văn Huyến was expelled from South Vietnam. This line of thought implies that he had been a communist from the outset. Apart from this rumor, another police report in 1957 claimed that he handed the money to the Bình Xuyên. Thiếu tướng Nguyễn Văn Là, Thư gửi Bộ trưởng

Phủ Tổng thống, July 7, 1958, TTLT2/PTTĐICH/Nội An/7.218. To date, it remains impossible to determine whether this money went to the DRV, the Bình Xuyên, or someone's pocket. On the real reasons for his resignation, see Bureau militaire de liaison auprès du Commissariat général aux réfugiés, Fiche concernant une conversation entre M. Pham Van Huyen et le capitaine Sarcelet, May 13, 1955, SHAT/10H/4195; Fiche au sujet de la suppression de la cérémonie organisée par le Commissariat aux réfugiés, May 18, 1955, SHAT/10H/4195.

9. Miller, *Misalliance*, 94; BR 394 sur le conflit entre les ministres du groupe "Tinh Thanh" et le Président Ngo Dinh Diem, November 17, 1954, ANOM/HCI/SPCE, 24.

10. Fernand Parrel, "Syndicalisme au Vietnam," *Revue des missions étrangères de Paris* 149 (1967): 38–43.

11. Interview with Le Dinh Cu, Confédération des Syndicats des Travailleurs du Vietnam "C.S.T.V." Hôtel Majestic, October 29, 1963, United Nations Archives and Records Management Section (hereafter cited as UNARMS)/United Nations Fact-Finding Mission to South Vietnam/S-0709/0004/8; Wehrle, "'Awakening the Conscience of the Masses,'" 21. See also Van Nguyen-Marshall, *Between War and the State: Civil Society in South Vietnam, 1954-1975* (Ithaca, NY: Cornell University Press, 2023), chap. 2.

12. La question Nung, 1955, SHAT/10H/1040. Decree 768 of September 4, 1956, demobilized the colonel. Hồ sơ v/v Đại tá Vòng A Sáng xin sử dụng một chiến tàu thủy và đăng bộ 11 chiếc xe (tài sản công xã Nùng), 1957, TTLT2/PTTĐICH/Nội An/5.857. The Bảo chính đoàn had decreased from seventeen thousand men in 1953–1954 in the Red River delta to roughly thirteen thousand men by the time of the cease-fire. Guillemot, *Dai Viet*, 556; Fiche n. 594, B.5 Évacuation des paramilitaires et de leurs familles, July 30, 1954, SHAT/10H/2549. The argument on the centralization of powers also appeared in Nguyen, "Ngô Đình Diệm and the Republic of Vietnam."

13. Giám đốc Nha Trước bạ và Công sản, Thư gởi đồng lý văn phòng Bộ trưởng tại Phủ Tổng thống, September 2, 1957, TTLT2/PTTĐICH/Nội An/5.857.

14. Nguyễn Đình Thuận, Thư gửi đến Bộ trưởng Nội vụ về tài sản của công xã Nùng, July 9, 1958; Tỉnh trưởng tỉnh Bình Thuận, Thư gửi ông Bộ trưởng tại Phủ Tổng thống, June 19, 1958, 4; Vòng Á Sang, Thư gửi Tỉnh trưởng Bình Thuận, December 15, 1958; Bộ trưởng Bộ Nội vụ, Thư gửi Tỉnh trưởng Bình Thuận, January 19, 1959; Trích báo Tự do số 594, Năm 1959 sẽ chuyển giao công xã Nùng cho quân địa phương, December 22, 1958; all in TTLT2/PTTĐICH/Nội An/5.857.

15. On the convention on the control of immigration, see Cabinet militaire aux délégués du commissaire au Centre Vietnam, Lettre no. 1144 Étrangers bénéficiant d'un statut privilégié et asiatiques étrangers, December 30, 1950, SHAT/10H/3239.

16. Khanh Tran, *The Ethnic Chinese and Economic Development in Vietnam* (Singapore: ISEAS, 1993), 28–29.

17. Memorandum of a conversation, Blair House, Washington, Subject: Chinese Minority Problem, May 9, 1957, FRUS 1955–1957 Vietnam Volume I; Cheng-Kang Ku to Cardinal Spellman, May 10, 1957, Cardinal Spellman Funds/S/C-15/To Card, Spellman China; Ku to Cardinal Spellman; Conseil général p.i. de la

République de Chine à Saigon, March 9, 1955, TTLT2/PThT/An Ninh/14.765; Président de la chambre de commerce chinoise au Sud Vietnam et Président du comité de secours aux réfugiés chinois du NVN, March 8, 1955, TTLT2/PThT/An Ninh/14.765. This contrasts with the relative freedom in the DRV. Xiaorong Han, "Spoiled Guests or Dedicated Patriots? The Chinese in North Vietnam, 1954–1978," *International Journal of Asian Studies* 6 (2009): 1–36.

18. David Andrew Biggs and Edward Miller, "Landscape, Counterinsurgency, and the Strange Saga of Binh Hung Village" (paper presented at the Waterlands & Wonderlands: Critiques of Development in Southeast Asia, 2013); Edward Lansdale, Binh Hung: A Counter-Guerrilla Case-Study, February 1, 1961, CARE)/471; Stan Atkinson, *The Village That Refuses to Die* (1962), film, 56 min.

19. Commandement du groupement des réserves générales, Fiche au sujet du R.P. Khue, May 20, 1955, SHAT/10H/4195; Commandement du groupement des réserves générales, Fiche n. 3910/2 au sujet des raisons du désaccord Ngô Đình Nhu-Trần Trung Dung, June 29, 1955, SHAT/10H/4195.

20. David Andrew Biggs, "Canals in the Mekong Delta from 200 C.E. to the Present," in *Water Encyclopedia*, ed. J. H. Lehr and J. Keeley, 2005, https://doi.org/10.1002/047147844X.wh18; Miller, *Misalliance*, chap. 5; Carter, *Inventing Vietnam*, chap. 3.

21. Picard, "'Fertile Lands Await,'" 75; Jason Picard, "'They Eat the Flesh of Children': Migration, Resettlement, and Sectionalism in South Vietnam, 1954–1957," in Tran and Vu, *Building a Republican Nation in Vietnam*, 155–59; Elkind, *Aid under Fire*, 49–53.

22. Tổng thống, Diễn văn trong cuộc lễ khánh thành làng di cư thứ nhất trở thành làng địa phương, Gia Kiệm, October 11, 1956, TTLT2/PTTĐICH/Nội An/4.442.

23. Phúc trình công văn của các tỉnh v/v địa phương hóa các trại định cư, 1957, TTLT2/PTTĐICH/Kinh tế/10.850.

24. Tổng ủy trưởng gửi đại diện định cư tỉnh Nam phần và Trung phần, June 3, 1957, TTLT2/PTTĐICH/Kinh tế/10.849.

25. Nghị định số 5737-UB/ND, Hanoi, September 7, 1954, TTLT2/PThT/Tổ chức/5.359.

26. Đổng lý văn phòng Bộ Nội vụ, Thư gửi đổng lý văn phòng các bộ, July 22, 1955, TTLT2/PThT/Tổ chức/5.359.

27. Phủ Chủ tịch Ủy ban hành pháp trung ương, Phiếu trình Thiếu tướng Chủ tịch Ủy ban hành pháp trung ương, October 1965, TTLT2/PThT/Tổ chức/5.359. It was only in 1960 that Saigon made plans for sending commandos in the north. Sedgwick Tourison, *Secret Army, Secret War: Washington's Tragic Spy Operation in North Vietnam* (Annapolis, MD: Naval Institute Press, 1995).

28. Phan Thị Xuân Yến, *Ban thống nhất trung ương trong cuộc kháng chiến chống Mỹ cứu nước (1954–1975)* (Ho Chi Minh City: NXB Tổng hợp T.P. Hồ Chí Minh, 2011).

29. Hoàng, "Early South Vietnamese Critique."

30. Hồ sơ về trao đổi bưu thiếp giữa hai miền Nam Bắc, 1954, TTLT2/PThT/Kinh tế/21.458. Saigon accepted that users could add a picture in 1960. Hồ sơ v/v liên lạc bưu chính Bắc Nam, 1959, TTLT2/PTTĐICH/Kinh tế/13.372. The

preformatted content disappeared in 1962. Hồ sơ v/v trao đổi bưu tiếp gia đình giữa hai vùng Nam Bắc, 1962, TTLT2/PTTĐICH/Kinh tế/15.099.

31. The section "Finding People" (Tìm người) was in the newspapers *Thời luận, Tự do, Dân đen, Dân nguyện,* and *Lửa sống* and the periodicals *Đường sống, Thời báo, Dân Việt, Hà Nội,* and *Tin Bắc.*

32. The Association of Northern Vietnam (Hội tương tế Bắc Việt) gathered several smaller associations, some religious, such as the Association of the Nghệ Tĩnh Bình (Hội tương tế Nghệ Tĩnh Bình), regrouping people from the diocese of Vinh, and some purely regional, on a scale as small as a village, such as Đông Ngạc, located on the outskirts of Hanoi.

33. Marie-Eve Blanc, *Tương tế hội, La pratique associative vietnamienne, Tradition et modernité* (Aix-en-Provence: Université de Provence, 1994); Nguyễn Văn Vĩnh, *Savings and Mutual Lending Societies (Ho): A Translation of an Article from a Series by Nguyen Van Vinh on Vietnamese Customs and Institutions* (New Haven, CT: Yale University Southeast Asia Studies, 1949). On the mutual aid associations in the RVN, see Nguyen-Marshall, *Between War and the State,* chap. 2.

34. Nguyễn Viết Khai, "Diễn văn khai mạc Đại hội tương trợ Nghệ Tĩnh Bình khóa thứ hai," *Luyện thép,* July 16, 1957.

35. "Lễ khánh thành Đông Ngạc nghĩa trang (2/10/1960)," *Đông Ngạc tương tế hội, Đặc san Tập II, 1961* (January 1961): 5–15.

36. For example, see Phạm Như Kim, "Nhớ quê hương (Đông Ngạc)," *Đông Ngạc tương tế hội, Đặc san Tập II, 1960* (January 1959): 24–25.

37. Celia Applegate, *A Nation of Provincials: The German Idea of Heimat* (Berkeley: University of California Press, 1990); Peter Blickle, *Heimat: A Critical Theory of the German Idea of Homeland* (Rochester, NY: Camden House, 2002).

38. "Hoạt động của đoàn ký giả tiền tuyến," *Thời Luận,* April 13, 1955; "Hoạt động của đoàn ký giả tiền tuyến," *Thời Luận,* April 30, 1955; "Đất thiêng miền Bắc đã vô Nam trong một cuộc rước long trọng tưng bừng và muôn vạn cảm động."

39. "Tán thành tuyên ngôn của Thủ tướng năm vạn người biểu tình hoan hô Ngô Thủ tướng."

40. A survey conducted in 1958 suggested that 15.7 percent of the population in Saigon came from the north, totaling 24 percent in some areas, such as Gia Định, and 22 percent or 15 percent in other cities, such as Nha Trang and Đà Lạt. République du Viet-Nam: Secrétariat d'État à l'économie nationale, *Enquêtes démographiques au Vietnam en 1958* (Saigon: Institut national de la statistique, 1958). One notable exception was Cần Thơ, where only 0.2 percent of the people surveyed declared that they had come from the north.

41. R. W. Safford, Special Report on Press of South Vietnam, April 10, 1956, NARA/RG469/1450. This proliferation of new publications slowed in 1955. The communist historians declare that readers did not buy the newspaper because it was anticommunist. Tầm Nguyên, "Báo chí Sài Gòn trong 30 năm kháng chiến," in *Địa chí văn hoá Thành phố Hồ Chí Minh, tập II,* ed. Trần Văn Giàu, Trần Bạch Đằng, and Nguyễn Công Bình (Ho Chi Minh City: NXB T.P. Hồ Chí Minh, 1988). But the increased cost of paper and censorship led 60 percent of the print press to close down. Safford, Special Report on Press of South Vietnam. On censorship and production costs, see Nguyễn Xuân Tuấn,

"Báo chí Việt Nam nhìn dưới khía cạnh kinh tế" (PhD diss., Học Viên Quốc Gia Hành Chánh Sài Gòn, 1971), 18, 36.

42. On the CIA implications, see Nhân Hưng, "Hoa hậu là nhà báo và điệp báo," *Công an nhân dân*, June 28, 2009; Kiều Chinh, "The Cinema Industry," in Vu and Fear, *The Republic of Vietnam*, 168.

43. Vĩnh Noãn wrote the scenario based on the 1954 migration in Vietnam. He codirected the movie with Manuel Conde. "Chúng tôi muốn sống" in Vietnamese and "Krus Na Kawayan" in Tagalog both mean "Let Us Live."

44. For example, Joseph Mankiewicz's adaptation of Graham Greene's novel, *The Quiet American*, which was shot in Saigon in 1957.

45. Hoàng Khởi Phong, "Phim 'Chúng tôi muốn sống', sử liệu về một giai đoạn tang thương của đất nước," Radio Free Asia, May 21, 2006, https://www.rfa.org/vietnamese/in_depth/InterviewExActressMaiTram_HKPhong-20060521.html.

46. Bernard B. Fall, *Le Viêt Minh, La République démocratique du Viêt-Nam, 1945-1960* (Paris: Armand Colin, 1960), 169.

47. Ủy ban Liên lạc công giáo toàn quốc, *Báo cáo kỷ niệm 5 năm ngày thành lập Ủy ban Liên lạc công giáo yêu tổ quốc, yêu hòa bình toàn quốc* (Hanoi: Đồng Tiến, 1960).

48. Nguyễn Quang Hưng, *Katholizismus in Vietnam von 1954 bis 1975* (Berlin: Logos, 2003), 200.

49. Bernard B. Fall, *The Two Vietnams* (New York: Praeger, 1963), 154.

50. Général de Brigade Brebisson, Lettre no. 2098 à la Commission mixte centrale pour le Vietnam, à Monsieur le Général, Chef de la délégation de l'Armée Populaire vietnamienne, December 26, 1954, SHAT/10H/5783.

51. Nguyễn Quang Hưng, *Katholizismus in Vietnam*, 201–2.

52. Mission vietnamienne chargée des relations avec la Commission de contrôle, Lettre, November 29, 1956, TTLT2/PTTĐICH/Nội An/4.898.

53. Fall, *Le Viêt Minh*, 169; Nguyễn Quang Hưng, *Katholizismus in Vietnam*, 205.

54. See the editorial "Quan Điểm," *Tin Bắc: Tuần san trào phúng—văn hóa—xã hội*, May 18, 1957.

55. *Đây hiện tình Bắc Việt: Tiết lộ của Nguyễn Mạnh Tường tại đại hội trung ương Mặt trận Liên Việt* (n.p., 1957), 12–13.

56. Thiên San, "Ngày Bắc tiến," *Văn nghệ tự do*, January 10, 1956.

57. James Lawton Collins, *The Development and Training of the South Vietnamese Army, 1950-1972* (Washington, DC: Department of the Army, US Government Printing Office, 1975), app. D.

58. Until 1968, the overwhelming majority of RVNAF units used World War II weapons, heavy equipment, vehicles, ships, and airplanes; and, unlike the DRV, they had not developed a military industry and thus relied on imported weapons and ammunition. Martin Loicano, "Military and Political Roles of Weapons Systems in the Republic of Viet Nam Armed Forces, 1966–1972" (PhD diss., Cornell University, 2008), 50–52, 94–95.

59. "Dân Việt duyên mùa Bắc tiến," *Dân Việt*, July 7, 1956.

60. "Biểu tình tại trại Bạch Đằng mừng ngày lễ song thất Ngô Tổng thống," *Dân Việt*, July 7, 1956.

61. The last resettlement villages became part of the local administration in 1957. "Sự sinh hoạt của đồng bào định cư thuộc tỉnh Tây Nguyên," *Dân Việt*, July 4, 1957. Even Monsignor Phạm Ngọc Chi, in the Catholic auxiliary committee's final report, declared that the evacuees would continue to make significant efforts, "waiting for the day they could return to the north." Uỷ ban Hỗ trợ định cư, *Ban thống kê tình hình các trại định cư tháng 8/1956* (Saigon: Nhà in Nguyễn Văn Của, 1956), ii.

62. Tô Văn, "Chúng tôi thỉnh cầu quốc hội chuẩn y ngay dự án luật đá cộng sản ra ngoài vòng pháp luật," *Tin Bắc: Tuần san trào phúng—văn hóa—xã hội*, October 28, 1957; "Tin Bắc phê bình chính quyền," *Tin Bắc: Tuần san trào phúng—văn hóa—xã hội*, January 20, 1958.

63. Vũ Bằng, *Bốn mươi năm nói láo* (Saigon: Phạm Quang Khải, 1969).

64. Tô Văn's excesses might be explained in part by his addiction. He smoked opium for more than thirty-seven years and suddenly gave it up in 1969. Tô Văn, "Nghiệp viết văn viết báo, hội ký," *Thức tỉnh* 79 (1981): 54–56.

65. Tô Văn, "Nghiệp viết văn viết báo, hội ký," *Thức tỉnh* 106 (1983): 76–78; Tô Văn, "Nghiệp viết văn viết báo, hội ký," *Thức tỉnh* 107-8 (1984): 75–77.

66. Tô Văn, "Chúng tôi đề nghị với chinh phủ xét lại những vụ án phản gián kiểu Việt Cộng như trên," *Tin Bắc: Cơ quan đấu tranh diệt Cộng để thống nhất lãnh thổ*, August 9, 1958. He represented the newspaper *Ngôn luận* (Debate) in the Procession of the Sacred Land and was part of the organizing committee. "Hoạt động của đoàn ký giả tiền tuyến."

67. "Cạc! Cạc! Cuộc thi thường trực của tuần báo Hà Nội," *Hà Nội*, July 5, 1958.

68. Directives de Propagande et Documentation n.656, Đây sự thật vùng cộng sản, May 25, 1954, SHAT/10H/2559.

69. Peter Zinoman, "Reading Revolutionary Prison Memoirs," in *The Country of Memory: Remaking the Past in Late Socialist Vietnam*, ed. Hue-Tam Ho Tai (Berkeley: University of California Press, 2001), 21–45.

70. "Vấn đề thống nhất Việt Nam," *Hà Nội*, July 18, 1958.

71. Phi-Vân Nguyen, "A Secular State for a Religious Nation: The Republic of Vietnam and Religious Nationalism, 1946–1963," *Journal of Asian Studies* 77, no. 3 (2018): 741–71.

72. A high school, named in honor of the first Vietnamese bishop, Nguyễn Bá Tòng, was funded with donations from the newspaper *Le Figaro*, UNESCO, and the National Catholic Welfare Council (NCWC). On Catholic involvement in education, see Marie Le Thi Hoa, "L'Enseignement catholique aux prises avec les mutations de la société et de l'Église au Vietnam de 1930 à 1990" (PhD diss., Paris Diderot, 2018). On projects before 1954, see Extrait du n. 68, January 6, 1954, SHAT/GR10R/95; Amaury de Saint Martin, "La contribution de la SAM (Société Auxiliaire des Missions) auprès du monde catholique vietnamien entre 1945 et 1975," in *Vincent Lebbe et son héritage*, ed. Arnaud Join-Lambert et al. (Louvain-la-Neuve: Presses Universitaires de Louvain, 2017), 160; Claire Trân Thi Lien, "The Role of Education Mobilities and Transnational Networks in the Building of a Modern Vietnamese Catholic Elite (1920s–1950s)," *Sojourn* 35, no. 2 (2020): 259. On the inauguration of the university, including Cardinal Spellman's visit, see Ngô Đình Diệm to Cardinal Spellman, November 30, 1957, Cardinal Spellman

Funds/S/B-10/To Card, Spellman Korea/folder 8; "Vie des missions: Dalat," *Bulletin des missions étrangères de Paris* (1961): 501.

73. I have studied the mobilization of Catholic evacuees to commemorate the forced migration and continue the fight in Phi-Vân Nguyen, "Fighting the First Indochina War Again?"

74. An Châu Lộc, "Giới thiệu nhân vật: Phrêrô Nguyễn Viết Khai," *Bình Giả quê hương yêu dấu*, accessed September 14, 2009, http://binhgia.net/PrintArticle. php?mName=Tin%20T%E1%/.

75. Nguyễn Viết Khai, "Bức thư của cha Nguyễn Viết Khai," *Luyện thép*, June 1, 1957.

76. "Nhớ xứ Nghệ, Bút ký của Thanh Hoan," *Luyện thép*, March 16, 1958; "Lập trường: Tại sao cộng sản thất bại?," *Luyện thép*, May 16, 1957. On his relationship with Ngô Đình Diệm, see Phúc trình về buổi học tập do Hội tương trợ Nghệ Tĩnh Bình, 1958, TTLT2/PTTĐICH/22.432; Linh mục Nguyễn Viết Khai, Thư gửi ông Tổng thống, 1961, TTLT2/PTTĐICH/22.432.

77. "Lập trường: Hiệp định Genève có giá trị gì?" *Luyện thép*, August 1, 1957.

78. "Lập trường: Nhân dịp kỷ niệm cuộc khởi nghĩa Hưng Yên," *Luyện thép*, April 16, 1957, 3; "Lập trường: nhân ngày kỷ niệm cuộc khởi nghĩa Quỳnh Lưu," *Luyện thép*, November 16, 1957, 3; "Nhân ngày kỷ niệm Lưu Mỹ đẫm máu, 17/1/1955," *Luyện thép*, January 16, 1958, 20–21; "Nhớ xứ Nghệ, Bút ký của Thanh Hoan," *Luyện thép*, March 16, 1958, 24–25.

79. "Chỉ đạo tổ cộng," *Đường sống*, July 14, 1956.

80. N. V., "Di cư và truyền giáo," *Luyện thép*, October 30, 1958.

81. "Tin các trại định cư," *Luyện thép*, March 1, 1957; "Tin các trại định cư," *Luyện thép*, May 16, 1957; "Tổng kết thành tích hoạt động của đoàn tuyên huấn lưu động," *Luyện thép*, June 16, 1958; "Đi theo tổ tuyên huấn lưu động di cư Nghệ Tĩnh Bình tại Cao Nguyên," *Luyện thép*, September 15, 1957.

82. Geoffrey Stewart, *Vietnam's Lost Revolution: Ngô Đình Diệm's Failure to Build an Independent Nation, 1955-1963* (New York: Cambridge University Press, 2017).

83. Linh mục đại diện địa phận Vinh, Thư gửi Đặc ủy trưởng Phủ Đặc ủy Công dân vụ, August 23, 1957, TTLT2/PTTĐICH/22.432; Linh mục Nguyễn Viết Khai, Thư gửi Trung tá Huỳnh Công Tình, Giám đốc Xã hội Cao Nguyên Trung phần tại Đà Lạt, September 16, 1957, TTLT2/PTTĐICH/22.432.

84. Fides, "Necessità di procedere alla conversione nel Sud Vietnam," *Osservatore Romano*, September 11, 1957.

85. Lien-Hang T. Nguyen, *Hanoi's War: An International History of the War for Peace in Vietnam* (Chapel Hill: University of North Carolina Press, 2012), 31–47; Vu, *Vietnam's Communist Revolution*, 156–58; Pierre Asselin, *Vietnam's American War* (Cambridge: Cambridge University Press, 2018), 99–103.

86. Các Đức giám mục Việt Nam, "Thư chung về vấn đề cộng sản vô thần của các Đức giám mục miền Nam, mùa chay, 02/03/1960," in Trần Anh Dũng, *Hàng giáo phẩm công giáo Việt Nam*, 130; Các Đức giám mục miền Nam, "Thư chung về vấn đề cộng sản vô thần của các Đức giám mục miền Nam, mùa chay 1960," *Sacerdos Linh mục* 24, no. 30 (1964): 461–72.

87. Các Đức giám mục Việt Nam, "Thư chung về vấn đề cộng sản vô thần của các Đức giám mục miền Nam, mùa chay, 02/03/1960," 131.

88. F. A., "Una Lettera del Santo Padre per il Congresso Mariano del Vietnam, XXV Ianuarii MCMLIX," *Osservatore Romano*, January 31, 1959; "Il Papa per il Vietnam," *Osservatore Romano*, February 1, 1959.

89. A. S., "Missioni nel Nord-Vietnam," *Osservatore Romano*, April 14, 1960.

90. Eduardo Pecoraio, "Con l'instituzione della Gerarchia Episcopale nel Vietnam sono premiati tre secoli de fatiche apostoliche," *Osservatore Romano*, December 8, 1960. In an interview with Pierro Gheddo in 1962, Monsignor Nguyễn Văn Bình insisted that Catholics had resisted the DRV authorities whenever they came to arrest a priest. Pierro Gheddo, "La voce dei padri conciliari, La Chiesa nel Vietnam: persecuzione al Nord, fioritura christiana al Sud," *Osservatore Romano*, December 10–11, 1962.

91. "L'anima vietnamese ed il cristianesimo," *Osservatore Romano*, February 18, 1961.

92. Giáo hoàng Gioan XXIII, "Thông điệp Đức giáo hoàng Gioan XXIII gửi hàng giáo phẩm Việt Nam, 14/1/1961," in Trần Anh Dũng, *Hàng giáo phẩm công giáo Việt Nam*, 147; "Vie des missions: Huê," *Bulletin des Missions étrangères de Paris* (1961): 495–500.

93. "Du 17 au 22 août 1961, Une semaine glorieuse à La-Vang pour les catholiques du Viêt-Nam et pour la chrétienté toute entière, La consécration de la Basilique, le congrès marial, le pèlerinage national et la consécration du Viêt-Nam à la Vierge Marie," *Extrême Asie* 104 (1961): 1–7.

94. Ngô Đình Thục, "Mấy lời phi lộ," *Đức Mẹ Lavang* 1, no. 1 (1961): 3–4.

95. J. M. T., "Lavang và Đức Mẹ Lavang," *Đức Mẹ Lavang* 1, no. 1 (1961): 5.

96. Catton, *Diem's Final Failure*; Miller, *Misalliance*; Stewart, *Vietnam's Lost Revolution*.

97. On the success of *Tự do*, see a/s de la grève de la faim des membres du "Mouvement pour la défense de la Paix," suite à la note ci-jointe n.81 C/SP-I du 8.1.55 de DirProtec, January 14, 1955, ANOM/HCI/SPCE/83. On the Cần Lao infiltration of the newspaper, see Vũ Đình Trắc, *Công giáo Việt Nam trong truyền thống văn hóa dân tộc* (Orange, CA: Thời điển công giáo, 1996), 460–61; Phạm Trần, "Life and Work of a Journalist."

98. "Cover," *Tự do*, January 25, 1960; "Bí mật của bức tranh Tết khiến Ngô Đình Diệm lồng lộn," accessed March 10, 2015, http://reds.vn/index.php/nghe-thuat/my-thuat/3536-buc-tranh-tet-khien-ngo-dinh-diem-long-lon/.

99. Picard, "'Renegades'"; Tran, *Disunion*, chap. 5.

100. On their relationship with the government and USOM, see, for example, "Nhân dịp đại hội văn hóa toàn quốc kiểm điểm những hoạt động văn hóa của đồng bào di cư," *Dân Việt*, January 3, 1957; Duong Song Refugee Newspaper, 1955, NARA/RG469/1450; Báo cáo thường nguyệt về tháng 6 năm 1956, July 18, 1956, TTLT2/PTTĐICH/Nội An/4.401. On their political positions, see Vũ Đình Trắc, *Công giáo Việt Nam*, 574. On their criticism of resettlement, see Nhị Hồ, *Điệp viên giữa sa mạc lửa* (Hanoi: NXB Công an nhân dân, 2002), chap. 14. On their criticism of embezzlement, see Phủ Tổng ủy Di cư Tỵ nạn, Thư gửi Giám đốc Nha Cảnh sát và công an Nam Việt v/v bài báo Đường sống "vấn đề đấu thầu," July 18, 1956, TTLT2/PTTĐICH/Nội An/4.440. On Father Vũ Đình Trắc's sentence, see Nguyễn Ngọc Lan, "Chúa đang sắp vác chiến ra tòa," *Đối diện* 13 (1970): 35; Vũ Đình Trắc, *Công giáo Việt Nam*, 174.

101. Nu-Anh Tran, trans., "Will the Real Caravelle Manifesto Please Stand Up? A Critique and a New Translation," *Journal of Vietnamese Studies* 18, no. 3 (2023): 1–55.

102. BR du SDECE sur l'organisation des milices catholiques, September 13, 1961, SHAT/Archives du 2ème bureau (hereafter cited as 10T)/969; Rapport de l'Ambassade de France n. 1034 sur la situation politique au Vietnam en novembre 1961, November 30, 1961, SHAT/10T/964.

103. BR secret, valeur A/3, source à protéger tout particulièrement sur la mésentente entre les V.C. et les forces du R.P. Hoang Quynh, February 4, 1963, SHAT/10T/974.

104. Vương Văn Đông, *Binh biến 11/11/1960* (Westminster, CA: Văn Nghệ, 2002).

105. Stanley Karnow, *Vietnam: A History, the First Complete Account of Vietnam at War* (New York: Viking Press, 1983), 280–81.

106. Ambassade de France à Saigon, Rapport n. 182 sur la situation politique au Vietnam, March 31, 1962, SHAT/10T/965.

107. I am grateful to Ed Miller for this information. Miller, *Misalliance*, 251; Information Report, Indication of Planning for the Reoccupation of North Vietnam, November 20, 1962, CIA/0000242371, https://www.cia.gov/readingroom/document/0000242371/.

108. File memorandum, February 19, 1963, Michigan State University, Wesley Fishel Papers/MSU/1191.

109. Ellen J. Hammer, *A Death in November: America in Vietnam, 1963* (New York: E.P. Dutton, 1987), 250.

4. Counterrevolution

1. Sao Biển, "Đây, khúc phim đẫm máu ngày 22 8 1964 tại Đà Nẵng," *Thời luận*, September 2, 1964; "Đà Nẵng, những ngày khói lửa," *Tự do*, October 9, 1964.

2. "Thiên điều tra đổ máu và nước mắt vì Thanh Bồ Đức Lợi," *Thời luận*, September 3, 1964.

3. "Danang Rioters Hit U.S.-Run Hospital," *New York Times*, August 27, 1964.

4. For a reference to a holy war, see "Town Burned in Buddhist Rioting: 50 Houses Standing, Nothing More to Eat," *Washington Post*, August 27, 1964. See also Hansen, "The Virgin Heads South," 290; Robert J. Topmiller, *The Lotus Unleashed: The Buddhist Peace Movement in South Vietnam, 1964-1966* (Lexington: University Press of Kentucky, 2006), 19.

5. On the May 1963 revolution and Buddhist nationalism, see Edward Miller, "Buddhist Revival and the Politics of Nation Building: Reinterpreting the 1963 'Buddhist Crisis' in South Vietnam," *Modern Asian Studies* 49, no. 6 (2015): 1903–62; Nguyễn Thế Anh, "Le bouddhisme dans la pensée politique du Việt-Nam traditionnel," *Bulletin de l'École française d'Extrême-Orient* 89 (2002): 127–43; Elise Anne DeVido, "'Buddhism for This World': The Buddhist Revival in Vietnam, 1920 to 1951, and Its Legacy," in *Modernity and Re-enchantment: Religion in Post-revolutionary Vietnam*, ed. Philip Taylor (Singapore: ISEAS, 2007), 250–96.

6. Fredrik Logevall, *Choosing War: The Lost Chance for Peace and the Escalation of War in Vietnam* (Berkeley: University of California Press, 1999); Mark Moyar,

Triumph Forsaken: The Vietnam War 1954-1965 (Cambridge: Cambridge University Press, 2006); Robert Shaplen, *The Lost Revolution, The U.S. in Vietnam, 1946-1966*, rev. ed. (New York: Harper & Row, 1966); Topmiller, *The Lotus Unleashed*; James McAllister, "'Only Religions Count in Vietnam': Thich Tri Quang and the Vietnam War," *Modern Asian Studies* 42, no. 4 (2008): 751–82; Gheddo, *The Cross and the Bo-Tree*. An account on the main political events appears in Vinh-The Lam, *The History of South Vietnam: The Quest for Legitimacy and Stability, 1963-1967* (London: Routledge, 2021).

7. "Xây dựng chế độ dân chủ: chế độ cũ, công ít, tội nhiều, chế độ mới: thực thi dân chủ," *Tự do*, February 10, 1964; "Chọn chế độ tương lai," *Tự do*, September 11, 1964. On political exiles, see Ambassade de France à Saigon, Rapport sur la situation politique au Vietnam, December 12, 1963, SHAT/10T/966. On political parties, see Bản sao CV số 1028 VP M của Tổng trưởng Ngoại giao gởi Tổng trưởng Bộ An ninh về các ông Hoàng Cơ Thụy, Phạm Huy Cơ, Trần Văn Tủng và đại tá Vương Văn Đông có xin được cấp giấy trở về VN, November 8, 1963, TTLT2/PThT/An Ninh/15.090; Cao Văn Tánh, Thư gửi về hồi hương quân nhân Việt Nam tỵ nạn tại Cao Miên, November 11, 1963, TTLT2/PThT/An Ninh/15.090.

8. "Ý kiến bạn đọc: Quân đội cải tổ," *Thời luận*, February 19, 1964.

9. Activités du gouvernement provisoire à travers les activités des différents départements ministériels, November 1963, SHAT/10T/968.

10. François Furet, *Penser la Révolution française* (Paris: Gallimard, 1978); François Furet and Mona Ozouf, *Dictionnaire critique de la révolution française* (Paris: Flammarion, 1988); Arno Mayer, *The Furies: Violence and Terror in the French and Russian Revolutions* (Princeton, NJ: Princeton University Press, 2000); Jean-Clément Martin, *La Terreur, vérités et légendes* (Paris: Perrin, 2017); Simon Schama, *Citizens: A Chronicle of the French Revolution* (New York: Knopf, 1989).

11. Meeting with Ngô Đình Nhu, the political adviser to the president of the Republic of Vietnam, October 25, 1963, United Nations Archives and Records Management Section/United Nations Fact-Finding Mission to South Vietnam/S-0709/0004/6.

12. On Thích Tâm Châu's views, see Memorandum of conversation between Father Vu Duc Trinh, Vietnamese-English translator, and Charles Flower and Marvin Levine, Embassy Officers, June 15, 1964, United States State Department Files 1963–1969/reel 39.

13. Về hoạt động của công giáo tại Sài Gòn và các tỉnh, 1964, TTLT2/PThT/Văn Hóa/29.380b; Nghiêm Xuân Thiện, "'Tách rời chính trị và tôn giáo,'" *Thời luận*, November 5, 1964.

14. Joseph Harnett to Rev. Edward E. Swanstrom, Catholic Relief Services—NCWC, November 15, 1963, Cardinal Spellman Funds/S/C-72/To Card, Spellman/Vietnam/folder 2, 1.

15. Joseph Harnett to Rev. Edward E. Swanstrom, Catholic Relief Services—NCWC, November 7, 1963, Cardinal Spellman Funds/S/C-72/To Card, Spellman/Vietnam/folder 2, 2.

16. Joseph Harnett to Rev. Edward E. Swanstrom, Catholic Relief Services—NCWC, November 21, 1963, Cardinal Spellman Funds/S/C-72/To Card, Spellman/Vietnam/folder 2, 2.

17. Activités du gouvernement provisoire à travers les activités des différents départements ministériels, SHAT/10T/968, 26.

18. Ambassade de France à Saigon, Rapport sur la situation politique au Vietnam, February 29, 1964, SHAT/10T/967.

19. Ambassade de France à Saigon, Rapport sur la situation politique au Vietnam; "Triển lãm tội ác Diệm Nhu ở phòng thông tin đường Tự do," Thời luận, March 24, 1964.

20. Consulate at Hue, 292. Telegram to the Department of State, November 4, 1963, Foreign Relations of the United States (hereafter cited as FRUS), 1961–1963, Volume IV: Vietnam August–December 1963, https://history.state.gov/historicaldocuments/frus1961-63v04/d292/.

21. Harnett to Swanstrom, November 7, 1963.

22. Harnett to Swanstrom, November 7, 1963.

23. Ambassade de France à Saigon, Rapport sur la situation politique au Vietnam, April 30, 1964, SHAT/10T/967.

24. BR sur la situation politique intérieure du Vietnam national au 1er août 1956, September 24, 1956, SHAT/10T/968, 7.

25. The apostolic delegation in the United States to Cardinal Spellman, May 8, 1963, Cardinal Spellman Funds/S/C-72/To Card, Spellman/Vietnam/folder 7; Cardinal Spellman to Archbishop Vagnozzi, May 9, 1964, Cardinal Spellman Funds/S/C-72/To Card, Spellman/Vietnam/folder 7; US Embassy in Vietnam, 123; Telegram to the Department of State, April 22, 1964, FRUS; Memorandum of conversation between Nguyen Khac Tan, attorney, and John R. Burke, political officer, June 12, 1964, United States State Department Files 1963–1969/reel 39.

26. Views confirming Major Đặng Sỹ's culpability cite the report of German doctors on the bodies. Others, claiming his innocence, insist grenades used by the RVNAF could not cause such damage. Hammer, *A Death in November*, 114–15; Arthur J. Dommen, *The Indochinese Experience of the French and the Americans: Nationalism and Communism in Cambodia, Laos, and Vietnam* (Bloomington: Indiana University Press, 2002), 510–13.

27. "Hai giới phật giáo và công giáo đều xin khoan hồng cho Đặng Sỹ," *Tự do*, May 14, 1964.

28. "Đây, bản cáo trạng Đăng Sỹ," *Tự do*, June 3, 1964; "Đây, bản cáo trạng Đăng Sỹ," *Tự do*, June 4, 1964.

29. Memorandum of conversation between Nguyen Khac Tan, attorney, and John R. Burke, political officer, June 12, 1964, United States State Department Files 1963–1969/reel 39.

30. Harry Haas, *Vietnam: The Other Conflict* (London: Sheed and Ward, 1971), 87–88.

31. Patrick O'Connor to Cardinal Spellman, December 6, 1966, Cardinal Spellman Funds/S/C-88/To Card, Spellman/Vietnam/folder 20, annex. Rumors had it that Lodge had promised US$3 million in exchange for the confession. Lược trình của B3, triệu tập phiên họp khẩn cấp để học tập và phổ biến bản kiến nghị của 350 linh mục thuộc địa phận Sài Gòn gửi Tướng Nguyễn Khánh, June 19, 1964, TTLT2/PThT/Văn Hóa/29.537b.

32. The sentence was commuted to lifetime imprisonment and forced labor. A few weeks after the sentence, Father Hoàng Quỳnh had been promised

that Major Đặng Sỹ would be "pardoned as soon as [a] suitable interval passes," Memorandum of conversation between Father Hoang Quynh and Melvin Manfull, Counselor for Political Affairs, July 17, 1964, United States State Department Files 1963-1969/reel 36; Nguyen-Marshall, "Tools of Empire?," 154.

33. Trung tướng tư lệnh quân đoàn II và vùng 2 chiến thuật kiêm Đại biểu chính phủ, Thư gửi ông Tỉnh trưởng thuộc vùng 2 chiến thuật v.v. giải quyết tình trạng các công chức phạm lỗi, March 30, 1964, TTLT2/PThT/An Ninh/15.099.

34. Thư về các thân nhân đưa đi Côn Đảo, November 5, 1964, TTLT2/PThT/An Ninh/15.099; Phiếu trình Thủ tướng v/v giải quyết trường hợp những người có liên quan đến chế độ cũ bị đày ra Côn Đảo ngày 1/10/1964 và được Ủy ban đề nghị trả tự do, November 1964, TTLT2/PThT/An Ninh/15.099.

35. 54 công dân thuộc đủ thành phần công chức, tư chức, thương gia, trí thức, Thư gửi Thủ tướng chính phủ, August 31, 1964, TTLT2/PThT/An Ninh/15.099.

36. O'Connor to Spellman, December 6, 1966. One important former official detained without trial and released three years later was Ngô Trọng Hiếu, the former minister for civic action.

37. Các Đức giám mục Việt Nam, "Thông cáo hội nghị giám mục Việt Nam, 20–22/1/1964," in Trần Anh Dũng, *Hàng giáo phẩm công giáo Việt Nam*, 159–62.

38. Các Đức giám mục Việt Nam, "Thư luân lưu của các giám mục Việt Nam, 22/1/1964," 164–65.

39. Các Đức giám mục Việt Nam, "Thông cáo hội nghị giám mục Việt Nam, 20–22/1/1964," 173.

40. From Saigon to Secstate 2204, May 14, 1965, United States State Department Files 1963–1969/reel 39.

41. Về hoạt động của công giáo tại Sài Gòn và các tỉnh, 1964, TTLT2/PThT/Văn Hóa/29.380b. On this Catholic mobilization, see Chi-Thien Bui, "The Way of the Fortress: Catholics and Political Engagement in the Republic of Vietnam, 1964–1967" (paper presented in a webinar on global Vietnamese Catholicism, sponsored by the Initiative for the Study of Asian Catholics, February 21, 2023).

42. Về cuộc mít tinh biểu tình phản đối chính phủ của đồng bào công giáo tại Sài Gòn và các tỉnh vùng I chiến thuật, June 14, 1964, TTLT2/PThT/Văn Hóa/29.380a.

43. Phiếu trình v.v. hoạt động của Khối công giáo tại Hố Nai (Biên Hòa), July 1964, TTLT2/PThT/Văn Hóa/29.537b.

44. Lâm Thanh Duy, "Trong vụ 'Đàn áp Phật Giáo' tại sao chỉ có Thiếu tá Đặng Sỹ mới bị đem ra xử? Còn những ai có trách nhiệm trong vụ này?" *Xây dựng*, June 4, 1964.

45. Harnett to Swanstrom, November 7, 1963.

46. For example, see Trường Giang, "Tuỳ Bút, Quảng Bình quê tôi ơi," *Tự do*, September 11, 1964, or Nhất Thanh, "Nhớ Xuân Bắc," *Tự do*, February 3, 1964.

47. "Tòa Tổng giám mục gửi đồng bào miền Bắc," *Tự do*, December 25, 1964; "Lập trường: Lại gửi đồng bào miền Bắc," *Tự do*, July 29, 1964; Nghiêm Xuân Thiện, "Xã Luận: Một vấn đề giả tạo, vấn đề Nam Bắc," *Thời luận*, March 7, 1965.

48. "Nhân ngày Quốc hận 20/7/1964, 10 năm trôi qua hận chia cắt vẫn còn …!" *Xây dựng*, July 14, 1964.

49. Nam Định, "Genève, Hà Nội, Saigon: 19/7/1954," *Xây dựng*, July 19, 1964.

50. "Thức trắng một đêm với sinh viên, 2 giờ đêm hát quốc ca và mặc niệm giữa đường phố để kỷ niệm giờ bán nước," *Tự do*, July 22, 1964. Parts in this section have been reproduced from a previous article. Phi-Vân Nguyen, "Le saccage de l'ambassade de France à Saigon en juillet 1964, Une réaction des réfugiés du Nord face à la double menace de neutralisation," *Revue historique des armées* 276 (2014): 57–68.

51. Lê Hữu Bội later enrolled in the RVNAF. Lê Đình Điêu, the external affairs attaché of the association, later headed the National News Service and the Ministry for Propaganda and Amnesty (Bộ Dân vận—Chiêu hồi); and Nguyễn Trọng Nho, chief of the Action Committee, became a representative in the National Assembly from 1967 to 1975. "Nhà báo Lê Đình Điêu từ trần," Việt báo, May 26, 1999, https://vietbao.com/a29726/nha-bao-le-dinh-dieu-tu-tran; Frank Mickadeit, "O.C.'s First Vietnamese Judge Retires," *Orange County Register*, September 25, 2013; Lê Bảo Hoàng, *Tác giả Việt Nam* (Miami: Songvan Magazine xuất bản, 2005).

52. "Trong một cuộc họp báo sôi nổi, Tổng hội Sinh viên nhìn nhận có đập phá công trường chiến sĩ Pháp và 1 lần nữa phủ nhận việc ở Toà Đại sứ, đòi đoạn giao tịch thu tài sản Pháp," *Dân chủ mới*, July 24, 1964.

53. "Thông cáo của Tổng hội Sinh viên Saigon về cuộc tuần hành trong đêm không ngủ," *Tự do*, July 22, 1964.

54. Đỗ Mậu, *Việt Nam máu lửa quê hương tôi* (Westminster, CA: NXB Văn nghệ, 1993), 706, 710.

55. On the mythical kings, see Keith Taylor, *The Birth of Vietnam* (Berkeley: University of California Press, 1983); Liam Kelley, "The Biography of the Hồng Bàng Clan as a Medieval Vietnamese Invented Tradition," *Journal of Vietnamese Studies* 7, no. 2 (2012): 87–130.

56. On Confucian studies in southern Vietnam, see Nguyễn Tuấn Cường, "The Promotion of Confucianism in South Vietnam (1955–1975) and the Role of Nguyễn Đăng Thục as a New Confucian Scholar," *Journal of Vietnamese Studies* 10, no. 4 (2016): 30–81. It was a national holiday in 1949 and remained an official celebration in 1955. The anniversary was abandoned the following year until the association asked to reintroduce it in 1959. Văn phòng ông Bộ trưởng tại P.T.T., III, Hội Khổng học Việt Nam và Hội Bắc Việt tương tế xin công nhận ngày kỷ niệm lễ giỗ Tổ Hùng Vương (10/3 âm lịch) là ngày quốc lễ, 1964, TTLT2/PThT/ Văn Hóa/29.277.

57. Đỗ Mậu, *Việt Nam máu lửa*, 711; Văn phòng ông Bộ trưởng tại P.T.T., III, Hội Khổng học Việt Nam và Hội Bắc Việt tương tế xin công nhận ngày kỷ niệm lễ giỗ Tổ Hùng Vương (10/3 âm lịch) là ngày quốc lễ.

58. Đỗ Mậu, Thư gửi Trung tướng Thủ tướng, April 24, 1964, TTLT2/PThT/ Văn Hóa/29.277.

59. Diễn văn đọc ngày giỗ Tổ Hùng Vương, năm Giáp Thìn, 1964, TTLT2/ PThT/Văn Hóa/29.277.

60. Edwin Moïse, *Tonkin Gulf and the Escalation of the Vietnam War* (Chapel Hill: University of North Carolina Press, 1996), 38; Moyar, *Triumph Forsaken*, 308. The celebration the following year mixed earth again. Phiếu trình Thủ tướng về tổ chức lễ giỗ Tổ Hùng Vương tại Sài Gòn, March 20, 1965, TTLT2/PThT/Văn Hóa/29.398.

61. "Cuộc mít tinh vĩ đại nhân ngày Quốc hận, Một triệu người gồm đủ giới đã tham gia," *Dân chủ mới*, July 21, 1964; "Cả triệu người tham dự mít tinh gồm đủ các mọi tôn giáo đoàn thể đảng phái," *Thời luận*, July 21, 1964.

62. Ủy viên Tâm lý chiến Chủ tịch Ủy ban liên bộ tổ chức Ngày toàn dân đoàn kết chuẩn bị giải phóng miền Bắc, Thư gửi ông Phụ tá Hành chánh chánh phủ Chủ tịch Ủy ban pháp trung ương, July 17, 1965, TTLT2/PThT/Văn Hóa/29.400.

63. Bùi Chí Thanh, "Công giáo (hoạt động chính trị sau cách mạng 1.11.1963)" (PhD diss., ĐH Sài Gòn, 1971), 89.

64. "Biển người tràn ngập công trường Lam Sơn hét vang khẩu hiệu chống cộng trung lập," *Thời luận*, July 21, 1964.

65. "Đoạn giao với Pháp," *Tự do*, July 22, 1964.

66. B. H. Lê Chân, Lập trường: vấn đề liên hiệp quốc dân chống cộng và thành lập nội các chiến tranh, 1964, TTLT2/PThT/Văn Hóa/29.387; Vài trò của đảng Cần lao dưới chánh thể Cộng Hòa hiện nay, September 16, 1964, TTLT2/PThT/Văn Hóa/29.387; Phong trào thanh trừng cán bộ Cần lao của Cộng sản, September 26, 1964, TTLT2/PThT/Văn Hóa/29.387; Chủ trương của khối liên hiệp quốc gia chống cộng, 1964, TTLT2/PThT/Văn Hóa/29.387.

67. Bùi Văn Mâu, Thư gửi Quốc trưởng Việt Nam Cộng Hòa tại Sài Gòn, February 9, 1965, TTLT2/PThT/An Ninh/15.165; Lương Trọng Hạp, Thư gửi Thủ tướng v.v tình nguyện tòng quân diệt cộng nếu chính phủ Việt Nam Cộng Hòa và hiệp chung quốc Hòa Kỳ cương quyết tấn công ra Bắc Việt, February 9, 1965, TTLT2/PThT/An Ninh/15.165.

68. Trình Thủ tướng, Thỉnh nguyện của đồng bào thiểu số Bắc Việt, December 11, 1964, TTLT2/PThT/Văn Hóa/29.389; Đồng bào thiểu số Bắc Việt di cư, Bức thư ngỏ kính gởi quý ông cựu Đại tá Vòng Á Sáng, cựu Tỉnh trưởng Đinh Ngọc Phụng, cựu Tỉnh trưởng Chương Văn Vĩnh, cựu Khu trưởng Se Cô Tin, December 1964, TTLT2/PThT/Văn Hóa/29.389.

69. Thượng du Bắc Việt tương tế hội, Nội quy, August 10, 1964, TTLT2/PThT/Văn Hóa/29.389.

70. Phiếu trình Thủ tướng v/v/ hoạt động của Khối công giáo, August 1964, TTLT2/PThT/Văn Hóa/29.380b; Tổng Nha Cảnh sát quốc gia, Phiếu trình về buổi tiếp tận ra mắt của Lực lượng Đại đoàn kết, April 22, 1965, TTLT2/PThT/Văn Hóa/30.856.

71. Bảng đúc kết nghiên cứu về hoạt động của Lực lượng Đại đoàn kết, May 5, 1966, TTLT2/Ủy ban Lãnh đạo Quốc gia (hereafter cited as UBLĐQG)/569.

72. Christopher E. Goscha and Karine Laplante, eds., *L'échec de la paix en Indochine, 1954–1962* (Paris: Les Indes savantes, 2010).

73. Hammer, *A Death in November*; Jacobs, *Cold War Mandarin*; Moyar, *Triumph Forsaken*; Miller, "Buddhist Revival"; Harnett to Swanstrom, November 7, 1963, 6; Memorandum of conversation between Father Vu Duc Trinh, Vietnamese-English translator, and Charles Flower and Marvin Levine, embassy officers, June 15, 1964, United States State Department Files 1963–1969/reel 39; "Tôi bị ép khai cho Đức tổng giám mục Ngô Đình Thục," *Xây dựng*, June 4, 1964; Lược trình của B3, triệu tập phiên họp khẩn cấp để học tập và phổ biến bản kiến nghị của 350 linh mục thuộc địa phận Sài Gòn gửi tướng Nguyễn Khánh, June 19, 1964, TTLT2/PThT/Văn Hóa/29.537b.

74. "Viet Paper Suspended," *Catholic Advocate*, July 2, 1964.

75. Đại tá Nguyễn Văn Phước, Phiếu trình gửi Trung tướng, Tổng trưởng Quốc phòng (Bí thư) về cuộc biểu tình của đồng bào công giáo khu Sài Gòn, Gia Định, Biên Hòa, Vũng Tàu, June 7, 1964, TTLT2/PThT/Văn Hóa/29.380a. For video footage of the inauguration, see Reuters, "South Vietnam: Saigon: Vietnamese Square Named After President Kennedy, 3/6/1964," accessed June 8, 2021, https://www.britishpathe.com/video/VLVA5NK6I2M7JK622ODQLF6M57LI8-SOUTH-VIETNAM-SAIGON-VIETNAMESE-SQUARE-NAMED-AFTER-PRESIDENT.

76. "Saigon Guards JFK Memorial," *Washington Post*, June 15, 1964; "1964: Saigon Moves U.S. Monument," *New York Herald Tribune*, August 20, 1964.

77. Lorenz Lüthi, *Cold Wars: Asia, the Middle East, Europe* (Cambridge: Cambridge University Press, 2020). On the mobilization of the diaspora, see Zhou, *Migration in the Time of Revolution*.

78. Bernard Firestone, "The U Thant-Stevenson Peace Initiatives in Vietnam, 1964-1965," *Diplomatic History* 1, no. 3 (1977): 285-95; Logevall, *Choosing War*; Bernard Firestone, "Failed Mediation: U Thant, the Johnson Administration, and the Vietnam War," *Diplomatic History* 37, no. 5 (2013): 1060-89.

79. "Mỹ: Không cần hội nghị Genève về Việt Nam như ông Thant Tổng thơ ký LHQ vừa đề nghị," *Dân chủ mới*, July 10, 1964; "Ngoại trưởng VN tuyên bố không tán thành đề nghị của ông Tổng thơ ký LHQ họp hội nghị Genève về Việt Nam," *Dân chủ mới*, July 11, 1964; "Thế cuộc trong tuần: Đề nghị của U Thant," *Dân chủ mới*, July 12, 1964; "Nhân dịp kỷ niệm 10 năm phân ly: 3 hình thức xâm nhập của VC vào miền Nam," *Dân chủ mới*, July 15, 1964; "Nhân dịp kỷ niệm 10 năm phân ly: Võ khí Nga-TC đã được bí mật tải vào Nam," *Dân chủ mới*, July 16, 1964; "Nhân dịp kỷ niệm 10 năm phân ly: VC âm mưu trung lập hóa miền Nam Việt Nam. Chính Ủy hội quốc tế xác nhận Việt Cộng xâm lăng miền Nam," *Dân chủ mới*, July 18, 1964.

80. Frédéric Turpin, *De Gaulle, les gaullistes et l'Indochine* (Paris: Les Indes savantes, 2005).

81. Fredrik Logevall, "De Gaulle, Neutralization, and American Involvement in Vietnam, 1963-1964," *Pacific Historical Review* 61, no. 1 (1992): 69-102; Turpin, *De Gaulle*; Maurice Vaïsse, "De Gaulle and the Vietnam War," in *The Search for Peace in Vietnam, 1964-1968*, ed. Lloyd C. Gardner and Tet Gittinger (College Station: Texas A&M Press, 2004); Pierre Journoud, *De Gaulle et le Vietnam* (Paris: Tallandier, 2011); Irwin M. Wall, *France, the United States and the Algerian War* (Berkeley: University of California Press, 2001).

82. Not everyone agreed with de Gaulle's reading of the circumstances. See Journoud, *De Gaulle et le Vietnam*; Bernard Krouck, *De Gaulle et la Chine: La politique française à l'égard de la République populaire de Chine, 1958-1959* (Paris: Les Indes savantes, 2012); Martin Garret, "Playing the China Card? Revisiting France's Recognition of Communist China, 1963-1964," *Journal of Cold War Studies* 10, no. 1 (2008): 52-80; Lorenz Lüthi, "Rearranging International Relations? How Mao's China and de Gaulle's France Recognized Each Other in 1963-1964," *Journal of Cold War Studies* 16, no. 1 (2014): 111-45.

83. Conference of Heads of State of Government of Non-Aligned Countries, "Programme for Peace and International Co-Operation, Declaration as Adopted by the Conference, 10 October 1964," accessed March 27, 2015, http://cns.miis.

edu/nam/documents/Official_Document/2nd_Summit_FD_Cairo_Declaration_1964.pdf. Sihanouk convened a meeting gathering representatives of Laos, Cambodia, and northern Vietnam and offered to host talks between the belligerents. See Lorenz Lüthi, "The Non-Aligned Movement and the Cold War, 1961–1973," *Journal of Cold War Studies* 18, no. 4 (2016): 98–147.

84. Ambassade de France à Saigon, Rapport sur la situation politique au Vietnam, January 31, 1964, SHAT/10T/967.

85. "Tổng hội Sinh viên và Học sinh đã đạp phá công trường chiến sĩ vào lúc nửa đêm 19-7," *Thời luận*, July 21, 1964.

86. On the GSA's opposition to de Gaulle, see also Stur, *Saigon at War*, 86.

87. "Đoạn giao với Pháp"; "Tổng hội Sinh viên lên tiếng," *Thời luận*, July 24, 1964.

88. On the relationships in the following years, see Laurent Césari, "Business as (Almost) Usual: The French Consulate General in Saigon during the Break of Diplomatic Relations between France and the Republic of Vietnam, 1965–1973," in *Consuls in the Cold War*, ed. Sue Onslow and Lori Maguire (Leiden, The Netherlands: Brill, 2023).

89. Picard, "'Renegades.'"

90. Sophie Quinn-Judge, *The Third Force in the Vietnam War: The Elusive Search for Peace, 1954–1975* (London: I.B. Tauris, 2017); Sophie Quinn-Judge, "Giving Peace a Chance: National Reconciliation and Neutral South Vietnam, 1954–1964," *Peace and Change* 38, no. 4 (2013): 385–410; Yen Vu, "Trần Văn Tùng's Vietnam of a New Nationalism for a New Vietnam," in Tran and Vu, *Building a Republican Nation in Vietnam*, 81–99; BR secret, valeur A/1, Initiatives viet-minh pour constituer un gouvernement nationaliste, October 20, 1961, SHAT/10T/974; Note sur la République du Vietnam: Partis politiques, January 14, 1960, SHAT/10T/968; M. l'Attaché des Forces armées près de l'Ambassade de France à Saigon, "La situation au Sud Vietnam," December 7, 1960, SHAT/10T/970.

91. Topmiller, *The Lotus Unleashed*, 46.

92. William Conrad Gibbons, *The US Government and the Vietnam War: Executive and Legislative Roles and Relationships, Part III* (Princeton, NJ: Princeton University Press, 1984), 103.

93. Service de protection du Corps expéditionnaire français en Indochine, BR sur les menaces de sécession du Centre-Vietnam, May 16, 1966, SHAT/10T/973.

94. "Tóm tắt lý lịch, Nguyễn Phúc Liên," accessed March 20, 2015, http://viettudan.net/36984/index.html (site discontinued).

95. "Tổng hội Sinh viên lên tiếng."

96. "Quá trình tránh đấu của Tổng liên đoàn Sinh viên Học sinh Tự dân," *Đại đoàn kết*, January 1964; "Tóm tắt lý lịch, Nguyễn Phúc Liên."

97. Võ phòng, Tài liệu về tình hình an ninh tại khu vực đồng bào công giáo tại Biên Hoà và Gia Định, tài liệu hạn chế, 1964, TTLT2/PThT/An Ninh/15.166.

98. Goodman, *Politics in War*.

99. On how they overcame the Buddhist uprising, see Topmiller, *The Lotus Unleashed*; on regionalism, see George J. Veith, *Drawn Swords in a Distant Land: South Vietnam's Shattered Dreams* (New York: Encounter Books, 2021), 183–84.

100. Christopher E. Goscha, *Historical Dictionary of the Indochina War (1945–1954): An International and Interdisciplinary Approach* (Copenhagen: NIAS Press, 2011), 377.

101. Bùi Diễm, *Gọng kìm lịch sử, Hồi Ký* (Paris: SudAsie, 2000), 229.
102. Trần Văn Tuyên, *Hội nghị Genève 1954*.
103. Trần Thị Đam Phương, "In Memoriam: Tran Van Tuyen," *Worldview* 7–8 (1978): 7–8.
104. Tô Văn, "Trần Văn Tuyên, Một chính trị gia cô đơn trong vòng vây của đế quốc tư bản và cộng sản," *Thức tỉnh* 7 (1978): 45–46.
105. Mesures envisagées par le Président Phat Huy Quat, May 28, 1965, SHAT/10T/973.
106. Bùi Diễm, *Gọng kìm lịch sử*, 221–23.
107. Trung ương công giáo Đại đoàn kết, Biên bản phiên họp bất thường thứ ba, mật, February 12, 1965, TTLT2/PThT/An Ninh/15.166.
108. Trung ương công giáo Đại đoàn kết, Biên bản phiên họp bất thường, mật, January 27, 1965, TTLT2/PThT/An Ninh/15.166.
109. Phiếu trình quốc trưởng Việt Nam Cộng Hòa v.v. lập trường người công giáo trước thời cuộc, March 2, 1965, TTLT2/PThT/Văn Hóa/29.536.
110. Bandung was also a follow-up to the 1947 Asian Relations Conference, which tried to unite Asian countries into a bloc. See Vineet Thakur, "An Asian Drama: The Asian Relations Conference, 1947," *International History Review* 3 (2018): 673–95; Olivier Campeau, "La perception française de l'Inde durant la guerre d'Indochine, 1947–1954: une étude de cas du mouvement anticolonialiste sur la scène internationale avant Bandung" (master's thesis, Université du Québec à Montréal, 2014); Lüthi, *Cold Wars*.
111. Bruce D. Larkin, *China and Africa, 1949-1970: The Foreign Policy of the People's Republic of China* (Berkeley: University of California Press, 1971); Eric Gettig, "'Trouble Ahead in Afro-Asia': The United States, the Second Bandung Conference, and the Struggle for the Third World, 1964–1965," *Diplomatic History* 39, no. 1 (2015): 126–56.
112. Phiếu trình v.v. biên pháp đối với các loại truyền đơn, báo "lậu" xuất xứ từ các trại định cư công giáo, May 20, 1965, TTLT2/PThT/Văn Hóa/29.536.
113. Renée Bridel, *Neutralité: Une voie pour le tiers monde?* (Paris: L'Âge d'Homme, 1968), 44.
114. Khối Công cán Ủy viên, Phiếu trình gửi Trung tướng Chủ tịch Ủy ban Lãnh đạo Quốc gia, June 16, 1965, TTLT2/UBLĐQG/569.
115. Lực lượng Đại đoàn kết, Quyết nghị trong đại hội bất thường, May 9, 1965, TTLT2/PThT/An Ninh/15.166.
116. ĐĐK và Phan Huy Quát, May 26, 1965, TTLT2/PThT/Văn Hóa/30.230.
117. Tô Văn, "Trần Văn Tuyên, Một chính trị gia cô đơn trong vòng vây của đế quốc tư bản và cộng sản," *Thức tỉnh* 8 (1978): 49–50.
118. Tỉnh trưởng Biên Hòa, Phiếu trình gửi tổng trưởng Bộ Nội vụ, v.v. tổng kết tình hình hoạt động của LLĐĐK Hố Nai từ 1–12/6/1965, June 18, 1965, TTLT2/PThT/Văn Hóa/29.387b.
119. Tỉnh trưởng Biên Hòa, Phiếu trình, June 8, 1965, TTLT2/PThT/Văn Hóa/30.230.
120. Phiếu trình Trung ương công giáo Đại đoàn kết tổ chức lễ kỷ niệm Đệ nhất chu niên ngày thành lập khối tranh đấu công giáo, June 7, 1965, TTLT2/PThT/Văn Hóa/29.536.
121. Logevall, *Choosing War*.

5. Peace in Vietnam

1. Victor Zorza, "Seen as Propaganda Move, 12-Hour Yule Truce Offered by Vietcong," *Washington Post*, December 8, 1965; "Christmas Eve Truce Announced by Vietcong," *New York Times*, December 8, 1965.

2. Quoted in "Pope Urges Truce in Vietnam," *Globe and Mail*, December 20, 1965.

3. Archdiocese of New York, Christmas Message of His Eminence, Francis Cardinal Spellman, news release, December 25, 1965, Cardinal Spellman Funds/S/A-14/Addresses, Remarks, Speeches and Statements/folder 10.

4. Lê Thượng Hòa, "Ngày trọng đại thiên chúa giáng sinh với nền hòa bình ở VN," *Xây dựng*, December 25, 1965.

5. "Prêtres vietnamiens devant les problèmes de la paix au Vietnam," *L'Action, quotidien catholique*, January 31, 1966.

6. Goodman, *Politics in War*; Fear, "The Ambiguous Legacy of Ngô Đình Diệm"; Sean Fear, "Saigon Goes Global: South Vietnam's Quest for International Legitimacy in the Age of Détente," *Diplomatic History* 42, no. 3 (2018): 428–55; Veith, *Drawn Swords in a Distant Land*; Simon Toner, "Imagining Taiwan: The Nixon Administration, the Developmental States, and South Vietnam's Search for Economic Viability, 1969–1975," *Diplomatic History* 41, no. 4 (2017): 772–98; Toner, "'The Paradise of the Latrine': American Toilet-Building and the Continuities of Colonial and Post-Colonial Development," *Modern American History* 2 (2019): 299–320.

7. Tran, *Disunion*; Stur, *Saigon at War*; Van Nguyen-Marshall, "Student Activism in Time of War: Youth in the Republic of Vietnam, 1960s–1970s," *Journal of Vietnamese Studies* 10, no. 2 (2015): 43–81; Nguyen-Marshall, *Between War and the State*; Vu and Fear, *The Republic of Vietnam*.

8. 88th Congress of the United States, "Tonkin Gulf Resolution (1964)," August 7, 1964, https://www.archives.gov/milestone-documents/tonkin-gulf-resolution. On the veracity of the attacks, see Moïse, *Tonkin Gulf*; Pat Paterson, "The Truth about Tonkin," *Naval History* 22, no. 1 (2008), https://www.usni.org/magazines/naval-history-magazine/2008/february/truth-about-tonkin.

9. US Department of State, *Aggression from the North: The Record of North Viet-Nam's Campaign to Conquer South Viet-Nam* (Washington, DC: US Government Printing Office, 1965).

10. Australia, New Zealand, South Korea, Thailand, and the Philippines joined the war effort, dispatching contingents on the ground from 1964 to 1973.

11. Christina Schwenkel, *Building Socialism: The Afterlife of East German Architecture in Urban Vietnam* (Durham, NC: Duke University Press, 2020).

12. Croix-Rouge française au CICR, December 18, 1964, CICR/Matériel/280; Fernand Parrel Caritas Vietnam, Lettre à SOS Services Urgences, November 28, 1964, CICR/Matériel/280.

13. Fernand Parrel, "De l'emploi des armes spirituelles ou 43 ans de vie missionnaire au Viet-Nam," (unpublished manuscript, 1974), 162.

14. Fernand Parrel, On réclame une trêve pour les affamés, November 24, 1964, CICR/Matériel/280.

15. Three men headed the committee: Tôn Thất Dương Ky, a professor; Cao Minh Chiếm, a journalist; and Phạm Văn Huyến. Trương Như Tảng, *Mémoires*

d'un Vietcong (Paris: Flammarion, 1985), 114–15. Thích Quảng Liên, a Buddhist monk, had joined the committee on a personal basis. Phạm Văn Liễu, *Trả ta sông núi, Tập 2* (Houston: Văn Hóa, 2003), 256.

16. Stur, *Saigon at War*, 52; Picard, "'Fertile Lands Await,'" 69. On other members, see Veith, *Drawn Swords in a Distant Land*, 148.

17. See the archives quoted in Stur, *Saigon at War*, and "Theo cuộc điều tra của chính quyền, Đây bộ mặt thật của bọn vận động hòa bình," *Xây dựng*, March 21–22, 1965.

18. Trương Như Tảng, *Mémoires*, 116–17.

19. Bien bản hỏi cung Phạm Văn Huyến, February 24, 1965, TTLT2/PThT/Văn Hóa/30.226; Phạm Văn Huyến, tường thuật và giải thích các điểm, March 15, 1965, TTLT2/PThT/Văn Hóa/30.226. Tôn Thất Dương Kỵ was a VWP member and confessed during his interrogation that Phạm Văn Huyến was contacted in February 1965, weeks after the creation of the movement for self-determination in December 1964. Bien bản hỏi cung Dương Kỵ, March 1, 1965, TTLT2/PThT/Văn Hóa/30.226.

20. Bien bản hỏi cung Phạm Văn Huyến, February 27, 1965, TTLT2/PThT/Văn Hóa/30.226.

21. "Đã tống xuất 3 ông 'Hòa bình' sang bên kia cầu Hiền Lương," *Xây dựng*, March 21–22, 1965.

22. "Hoãn việc cho nhảy dù xuống Bắc Việt 3 nhân vật Ủy ban Hòa bình mà sẽ đưa ra cầu Hiền Lương," *Dân chủ mới*, March 18, 1965; US embassy in Vietnam to the Department of State, telegram, March 17, 1965, FRUS 1964–1969, Volume II, Vietnam January–June 1965.

23. Hoàng Chí Hiếu, *Đôi bờ giới tuyến (1954-1967)* (Ho Chi Minh City: NXB Tổng hợp T.P. Hồ Chí Minh, 2014), 194.

24. On March 11, the petition of Thích Quảng Liên and the Committee for the Defense of Peace obtained 358 signatures from students, workers, professors, and lawyers. Đỗ Mậu, *Việt Nam máu lửa*, 694; "Qua bản quyết nghị ngày 25/2/1965 chủ trương của Ủy ban Vận động Hòa bình chỉ là một tổ chức bán nước," *Xây dựng*, March 3, 1965; "Sinh viên Saigon tố cáo 2 tổ chức C.S. trá hình 'Ủy ban Vận động Hòa bình và Phong trào Dân tộc Tự quyết,'" *Xây dựng*, March 3, 1965; "Thượng tọa Thích Quảng Liên nói về phong trào hòa bình," *Xây dựng*, March 6, 1965; "Thượng tọa Quảng Liên đã từ chức chủ tịch Phong trào Bảo vệ HBHPDT?" *Xây dựng*, March 12, 1965; "Theo cuộc thăm dò của 1 thông tín viên, ý kiến của các tôn giáo về Phong trào Bảo vệ HBHPDT," *Xây dựng*, March 13, 1965; "Thượng tọa Thích Quảng Liên sẵn sàng từ chức ở VHĐ không từ chức chủ tịch PTBVHB," *Xây dựng*, March 14–15, 1965; "Chính phủ đã công bố đầy đủ danh tính 358 người ký tên vào bản kiến nghị của 'UBVĐHB' khuynh Cộng," *Xây dựng*, March 13, 1965; "Chính phủ đã công bố đầy đủ danh tính 358 người ký tên vào bản kiến nghị của 'UBVĐHB' khuynh Cộng," *Xây dựng*, March 14–15, 1965; "Chính phủ đã công bố đầy đủ danh tính 358 người ký tên vào bản kiến nghị của 'UBVĐHB' khuynh Cộng," *Xây dựng*, March 16, 1965.

25. Giuseppe Alberigo and Joseph A. Komonchak, eds., *History of Vatican II* (Leuven, Belgium: Peeters, 1995).

26. Fides, Rome's news agency, reported concerns in South Sudan and in Ceylon (now Sri Lanka). Fides, "Scores Buddhists, Moslem Action against Missions," January 18, 1965.

27. Darcie Fontaine, *Decolonizing Christianity: Religion and the End of Empire in France and Algeria, 1940-1965* (Cambridge: Cambridge University Press, 2016); Fontaine, "At the Crossroads of East and West: Christianity and the Legacy of Colonialism in North Africa," in *Decolonization and the Remaking of Christianity*, ed. Elizabeth Ann Foster and Udi Greenberg (Philadelphia: University of Pennsylvania Press, 2023).

28. Lüthi, *Cold Wars*, chap. 19.

29. Marie Le Thi Hoa, "Le rôle des papes Jean XXIII et Paul VI dans la recherche de la paix au Việt Nam de 1963 à 1969," *Moussons* 32 (2018): 133-51.

30. Samuel Moyn, *Christian Human Rights* (Philadelphia: University of Pennsylvania Press, 2015).

31. Dirk Moses, *The Problems of Genocide* (Cambridge: Cambridge University Press, 2021).

32. Seymour Melman, Melvyn Baron, and Dodge Ely, *In the Name of America: The Conduct of the War in Vietnam by the Armed Forces of the United States as Shown by Published Reports, Compared with the Laws of War Binding on the United States Government and on Its Citizens* ([New York]: Clergy and Laymen Concerned about Vietnam, 1968), 343-64. See also Stefan Andersson, ed., *Revisiting the Vietnam War and International Law: Views and Interpretation of Richard Falk* (Cambridge: Cambridge University Press, 2018).

33. Harish C. Mehta, "North Vietnam's Informal Diplomacy with Bertrand Russell: Peace Activism and the International War Crimes Tribunal," *Peace and Change* 37, no. 1 (2012): 64-94; Harish C. Mehta, *People's Diplomacy of Vietnam: Soft Power in the Resistance War, 1965-1972* (Newcastle upon Tyne, UK: Cambridge Scholar Publishing, 2019), chap. 5. On French intellectuals' implication, see Pierre Journoud, "Des Savants français contre la guerre du Vietnam: De l'anti-impérialisme à la construction d'une paix positive," *Bulletin de l'Institut Pierre Renouveau* 44, no. 2 (2016): 87-102.

34. On Hanoi's initial reluctance to use humanitarian law as a lever, see Boyd Van Dijk, "Internationalizing Colonial War: On the Unintended Consequences of the Interventions of the International Committee of the Red Cross in South-East Asia, 1945-1949," *Past and Present* 250, no. 1 (2021): 243-83; "Chỉ thị của ban bí thư số 128-CT/TW về việc tăng cường công tác tuyên truyền đối ngoại, 6 tháng 6 1966," in *Văn kiện Đảng*, 27: 197-203; "Thông Tri của ban bí thư số 183-TT/TW về tổ chức điều tra tội ác chiến tranh của đế quốc Mỹ ở Việt Nam, 28 tháng 6 1966," in *Văn kiện Đảng*, 27: 252-55. On raising awareness, see "Text of Ho Chi Minh's Note to the Pope," *New York Times*, December 30, 1965; "Guerre d'extermination," *Le Courrier du Vietnam*, November 18, 1965; "Thư của chủ tịch Hồ Chí Minh trả lời Tổng thống Mỹ Giônxơn, 2 tháng 7 1967," in *Văn Kiên Đảng, Tập*, 28: 180-83. For a synthesis of Hanoi's public diplomacy, see Mark Philip Bradley and Viet Thanh Nguyen, "Vietnam: American and Vietnamese Public Diplomacy," in *Isolate or Engage: Adversarial States, US Foreign Policy, and Public Diplomacy*, ed. Geoffrey Wiseman (Redwood City, CA: Stanford University Press, 2015).

35. Le Thi Hoa, "Le rôle des papes," para. 30.

36. Paul VI, "Message to His Excellency Lyndon B. Johnson, President of the United States of America, 30 December 1965," *Acta Apostolicae Sedis*, 58 (1966): 161-62; Paul VI, "Message au Général Nguyen Van Thieu, Président du Comité de Direction Nationale, Saigon, 31 décembre 1965," *Acta Apostolicae Sedis*, 58 (1966): 162;

Paul VI, "Message à Son Excellence Ho Chi Minh, Président de la République démocratique du Vietnam du Nord, 31 décembre 1965," *Acta Apostolicae Sedis*, 58 (1966): 163; Paul VI, "Message à Son Excellence Podgorny, Président du Praesidium du Soviet Suprême, Moscou, 31 décembre 1965," *Acta Apostolicae Sedis*, 58 (1966): 163; Paul VI, "Message à Son Excellence le Président Mao Tse Tung, Secrétaire du Comité Central du P.C. de la République Populaire de Chine, Pékin, 31 décembre 1965," *Acta Apostolicae Sedis*, 58 (1966): 164.

37. "Thông tri của ban bí thư số 180-TT/TW về việc chấp hành chính sách tôn giáo đối với đạo Phật, 16 tháng 5 1966," in *Văn kiện Đảng*, 27: 157–60; "Thông tri của ban bí thư số 181-TT/TW về việc tăng cường công tác vận động đồng bào theo đạo Thiên chúa trước tình hình mới, 16 tháng 5 1966," in *Văn kiện Đảng*, 27: 161–66.

38. "Correspondent Reached Hanoi on an I.C.C. Plane," *New York Times*, December 25, 1966; Harry [Harrison] E. Salisbury, "A Visitor to Hanoi Inspects Damage Laid to US Raids," *New York Times*, December 25, 1966; Salisbury, "US Raids Batter 2 Towns, Supply Route Is Little Hurt," *New York Times*, December 27, 1966; Salisbury, "Hanoi Propaganda Stresses Tradition: War against Odds," *New York Times*, December 30, 1966. Several American, French, and Canadian dailies used Salisbury's reports. Seeing this wide impact, Hanoi announced it would allow other Western journalists to visit. "Hanoi Seen Exploiting Its Civilian Casualties," *Washington Post*, December 28, 1966. Salisbury's reports drew Washington's ire. See Mark Atwood Lawrence, "Mission Intolerable: Harrison Salisbury's Trip to Hanoi and the Limits of Dissent against the Vietnam War," *Pacific Historical Review* 75, no. 3 (2006): 429–60. On Hanoi's carefully crafted itineraries for foreign visitors, see Pierre Asselin, "National Liberation by Other Means: US Visitor Diplomacy in the Vietnam War," *Past and Present* (2024): advance access, https://doi.org/10.1093/pastj/gtad021.

39. Archdiocese of New York, Christmas Message, December 25, 1965.

40. John Cogley, "The Spellman Dispute: Cardinal's Words Are Found out of Key with Church's Continuing Peace Drive," *New York Times*, December 29, 1966.

41. Patrick O'Connor, "Cardinal Spellman with Troops Day and Night," NCWC News Service (Foreign), December 23, 1965.

42. "Communisme: En Asie, Il faut récupérer la Chine continentale, affirme le cardinal Yu-Pin," *Informations catholiques internationales* (1969), 20.

43. "Tại công trường Thánh Phêrô, Đức Phaolô tuyên bố ngài cầu mong việc tạm ngừng bắn dịp lễ giáng sinh sẽ là bước đầu dẫn tới thương thuyết và hòa bình ở Việt Nam," *Xây dựng*, December 25, 1965; "Thông điệp giáng sinh của Đức giáo hoàng," *Xây dựng*, December 25, 1965.

44. Lê Thượng Hòa, "Ngày trọng đại thiên chúa giáng sinh với nền hòa bình ở VN."

45. Nguyễn Duy Vi, "Lời chào giáng sinh của thông tin công giáo VN gửi anh em công giáo miền Bắc," *Xây dựng*, December 25, 1965.

46. Nguyên Tử Năng, "Để được hòa bình và sống cho đáng sống dân tộc VN phải chiến với chiến tranh," *Xây dựng*, December 25, 1965.

47. "Nội dung thông điệp của Đ. giáo hoàng gửi 5 nước Mỹ, Nga, TC, Bắc Việt, VNCH là đưa ra giải pháp điều giải để chấm dứt chiến cuộc Việt Nam," *Xây dựng*,

January 4, 1966; "Khẩn điệp của Đức giáo hoàng gửi TT Johnson đừng bỏ qua một cơ hội bào dù nhỏ, để vãn hồi hòa bình VN," *Xây dựng*, January 6, 1966; "Thông điệp của ĐGH gửi TT Johnson đã được công bố, Đức giáo hoàng vẫn kiên nhẫn vận động thực hiện hòa bình tại VN," *Xây dựng*, January 7, 1966; "Đ.G. hoàng tiếp ngoại trưởng Nga," *Xây dựng*, January 13, 1966.

48. Lê Thượng Hoa, "Thời cuộc, Cả thế giới đang vận động hòa bình, chúng ta cần chuẩn bị sẵn sàng là vừa," *Xây dựng*, January 4, 1966.

49. Claire Trần Thị Liên, "The Challenge for Peace within South Vietnam's Catholic Community: A History of Peace Activism," *Peace and Change* 38, no. 4 (2013): 456–57.

50. For a reproduction of the letter, see Trần Tam Tỉnh, "L'Opinion du lecteur: Une lettre du Vietnam," *Le Soleil*, January 31, 1966. The article was published on January 27 in *Témoignage chrétien*, according to Sabine Rousseau, "Des chrétiens français face à la guerre du Vietnam," *Vingtième siècle, Revue d'histoire* 47 (1995): 176–90. It appeared four days later in Québec as "Prêtres vietnamiens devant les problèmes de la paix au Vietnam." Trần Tam Tỉnh, "L'Opinion du lecteur: Une lettre du Vietnam." And again, in the January issue of an important French-language Catholic missionary periodical, which appeared on February 1. "Onze prêtres vietnamiens: Une seule victoire, celle de l'homme," *Informations catholiques internationales* 255 (1966): 28.

51. "2 làng CG bị đốt," *Sống đạo*, August 21, 1966.

52. "Biến cố, Đức Phao-Lô VI vừa ký thêm một tự sắc xin các giám mục 75 về hưu," *Sống đạo*, September 3, 1966.

53. Trần Vươn Thạch, "Cách mạng văn hóa hay tôn giáo mới," *Sống đạo*, September 3, 1966; "Tại giáo hội thầm lặng miền Bắc VN, Giáo dân phải "kể tội" các cha," *Sống đạo*, September 18, 1966.

54. "Liên xô còn tôn giáo không?" *Sống đạo*, August 21, 1966; "Trong nước Ba Lan cộng sản, 90 phần 100 dân vẫn theo công giáo," *Sống đạo*, August 28, 1966; "Thỏa ước giữa Nam tư và Vatican . . .," *Sống đạo*, August 14, 1966.

55. "Lại kêu gọi hòa bình cho Việt Nam," *Sống đạo*, August 28, 1966; "Vatican và chiến tranh Việt Nam," *Sống đạo*, September 3, 1966.

56. "Thực chất của Mặt trận Công dân các tôn giáo," *Xây dựng*, August 7–8, 1966; Khối Công dân các tôn giáo và toàn thể chính trị, Nhận định về hai sắc luật số 21 và 22 ấn định tổ chức và thể thức bầu cử quốc hội lập hiến, June 19, 1966, TTLT2/PThT/Văn Hóa/29.689; Mặt trận Công tác các tôn giáo và các đoàn thể chính trị, Thông cáo, August 18, 1966, TTLT2/PThT/Văn Hóa/29.689.

57. Mặt trân Công dân các tôn giáo, Tuyên cáo quốc dân, August 27, 1966, TTLT2/PThT/Văn Hóa/29.689. Around two hundred people, including foreign correspondents, attended the press conference. Phiếu trình Trung tướng v.v. học báo của Mặt trận Công dân các tôn giáo, July 7, 1966, TTLT2/UBLĐQG/527. Saigon's intelligence service was convinced that the LLĐĐK's internal divisions had inspired Hoàng Quỳnh's rapprochement with other religious groups. Tổng bộ An ninh, Dư luận, July 15, 1966, TTLT2/UBLĐQG/556.

58. The press conference prepared a statement in both Vietnamese and English, denouncing the assassination of the Trotskyists Tạ Thu Thâu and Phan Văn Hùm, the Freemason Dương Văn Giáo, and the founder of the Hòa Hảo Buddhist

reformist branch, Huỳnh Phú Sổ. The Citizens' Front of Religions, Official Statement, August 27, 1966, TTLT2/PThT/Văn Hóa/29.689.

59. Father Hoàng Quỳnh and two other priests signed on behalf of Catholics. Thích Pháp Trí represented the United Buddhist Association, along with Cao Đài, Hòa Hảo, and Protestants signatories. Mặt trân Công dân các tôn giáo, Tuyên cáo quốc dân, 5, August 27, 1966, TTLT2/PThT/Văn Hóa/29.689.

60. Catholic Citizens Bloc and the General Student Association took part in the protest. Hình ảnh ngày Bắc tiến, TTLT2/Sưu tập liệu ảnh/4830 0012; Hình ảnh ngày Bắc tiến, TTLT2/Sưu tập liệu ảnh/4830 0013; Hình ảnh ngày Bắc tiến, TTLT2/Sưu tập liệu ảnh/4830 0015; Hình ảnh ngày Bắc tiến, TTLT2/Sưu tập liệu ảnh/4830 0008.

61. "Thực chất của Mặt trận Công dân các tôn giáo," *Xây dựng*, August 9, 1966; "Thực chất của Mặt trận Công dân các tôn giáo," *Xây dựng*, August 11, 1966; "Phải chăng Mặt trận CDCTG của linh mục Hoàng Quỳnh đã hợp pháp hóa vụ nổi loạn miền Trung của Thượng tọa Thích Trí Quang?" *Xây dựng*, August 12, 1966.

62. "Công giáo . . . đả công giáo," *Sống đạo*, August 21, 1966.

63. Pierre Asselin, *A Bitter Peace: Washington, Hanoi, and the Making of the Paris Agreement* (Chapel Hill: University of North Carolina Press, 2002); Nguyen, *Hanoi's War*; Ang Cheng Guan, *Ending the Vietnam War: The Vietnamese Communists' Perspective* (London: Routledge, 2003); and Pierre Journoud and Cécile Ménétrey-Monchau, eds., *Vietnam, 1968-1976: La sortie de guerre* (Bruxelles: Peter Lang, 2011).

64. Loicano, "Military and Political Roles," 138–43, 160–61; Veith, *Drawn Swords in a Distant Land*, 302.

65. Chủ tịch Lực lượng Đại đoàn kết, Lời kêu gọi, February 1, 1968, TTLT2/Phủ Tổng thống Đệ nhị Cộng Hòa (hereafter cited as PTTĐIICH)/Đoàn thể/4.490.

66. Tổng Nha Cảnh sát quốc gia, Phiếu trình gửi Tổng trưởng Nội vụ, July 6, 1968, TTLT2/PThT/Văn Hóa/31.513; Lực lượng Đại đoàn kết, Quyết nghị sau cuộc hội thảo tại Sài Gòn, June 23, 1968, TTLT2/PTTĐIICH/Đoàn thể/4.490; Nha Cảnh sát quốc gia Saigon gửi Bộ Nội vụ, July 20, 1968, TTLT2/PThT/Văn Hóa/31.513.

67. Hoàng Quỳnh, Diễn văn đọc trong buổi họp mặt, November 24, 1968, TTLT2/PTTĐIICH/4.115.

68. Phủ Tổng thống tòa tổng thơ ký văn phòng, Phiếu trình về cuộc họp sơ bộ các đoàn thể, tôn giáo, chính trị, nghiệp đoàn và các hiệp hội, November 25, 1968, TTLT2/PTTĐIICH/4.115; Hoàng Quỳnh, Đại cương đề nghị với các đoàn thể tôn giáo chính trị nghiệp đoàn và hiệp hội, November 24, 1968, TTLT2/PTTĐIICH/4.115.

69. Quân lực Việt Nam Cộng Hòa quân đoàn III văn phòng tư lệnh, Phiếu trình gửi Thủ tướng chinh phủ, October 10, 1968, TTLT2/PThT/Văn Hóa/31.513; Quân đoàn III văn phòng tư lệnh, Phiếu trình v.v. kế hoạch hoạt động tranh đấu của Khối công giáo, 1968, TTLT2/PTTĐIICH/Đoàn thể/4.490.

70. Phiếu trình v/v hoạt động của Lực lượng Đại đoàn kết, October 29, 1968, TTLT2/PThT/Văn Hóa/31.856.

71. Nhận định về đường lối thương thuyết hòa bình vơi cộng sản Hà Nội, 1968, TTLT2/PThT/Văn Hóa/30.856; Nhận định về đường lối thương thuyết hòa bình với cộng sản Hà Nội, 1968, TTLT2/PTTĐIICH/Đoàn thể/4.490.

72. Phiếu trình v.v. Khối Phục hưng quốc gia mới thành lập, July 20, 1968, TTLT2/PTTĐIICH/Đoàn thể/4.297; Chính cương và chương trình hoạt động của Khối Phục hưng quốc gia (tắt Khối Hưng Quốc), September 8, 1968, TTLT2/PTTĐIICH/Đoàn thể/4.297.

73. Khối Phục hưng quốc gia, Lời hiệu triệu, July 20, 1968, TTLT2/PTTĐIICH/Đoàn thể/4.297; Tìm một giải pháp chấm dứt chiến trành Việt Nam, thuyết trình của ông Hoàng Cơ Thụy dự đọc trong cuộc hội thảo chính trị tại toà đô chính, Saigon, August 21, 1968, TTLT2/PTTĐIICH/An Ninh/843; Bài nghiên cứu về vấn đề đình chiến, Thuyết trình viên Nguyễn Triệu Đan, September 28, 1968, TTLT2/PTTĐIICH/An Ninh/843.

74. Various Avenues Offered by Public International Law to End the Vietnam War by Peaceful Means, July 14, 1968, Vietnam Archive/Douglas Pike Collection/Units 11–Monograph/B03F12, https://vva.vietnam.ttu.edu/repositories/2/digital_objects/54488/.

75. Tổng Giám đốc Cảnh sát, Phiếu trình, November 8, 1968, TTLT2/PThT/Văn Hóa/31.513. Other religious leaders participated in the National Day of Shame. Tổng Nha Cảnh sát quốc gia, Phiếu trình gửi Tổng trưởng Nội vụ, July 6, 1968, TTLT2/PThT/Văn Hóa/31.513. They stood together again in September 1968, to denounce the NLF. Nha Tổng Giám đọc Cảnh sát quốc gia, Phiếu trình v.v. báo Hòa bình, September 28, 1966, TTLT2/PThT/Văn Hóa/31.513; Nha Tổng giám đốc Cảnh sát quốc gia, Ban tin tức, October 12, 1968, TTLT2/PThT/Văn Hóa/31.518.

76. Jean-Pierre Reneau, "Leader du 'front uni des religions,' à Saigon, Le père Hoang Quynh nous parle," *Informations catholiques internationales* (1969): 21–23.

77. Phiếu trình, December 11, 1969, TTLT2/PThT/Văn Hóa/31.856; Khối Phục hưng quốc gia, Nhận định về thông điệp của Tổng thống Việt Nam Cộng Hòa, July 11, 1969, TTLT2/PTTĐIICH/Đoàn thể/4.297.

78. Về thế đứng giữa trên thế giới và ở Việt Nam, November 30, 1969, TTLT2/PThT/Văn Hóa/31.856; Đề tài hội thảo, November 30, 1969, TTLT2/PThT/Văn Hóa/31.856.

79. Kenneth J. Heineman, *Campus Wars: The Peace Movement at American State Universities in the Vietnam Era* (New York: New York University Press, 1992). This did not mean that American Christians unanimously supported the end of the war. Gene Zubovich, epilogue to *Before the Religious Right: Liberal Protestants, Human Rights, and the Polarization of the United States* (Philadelphia: University of Pennsylvania Press, 2022).

80. Trần Tam Tinh, "L'Opinion du lecteur: Une lettre du Vietnam."

81. "Nói chuyện với linh mục Trần Tam Tỉnh, Người công giáo và hòa bình Việt Nam," *Thế hệ* 15 (1970): 25–31.

82. Vũ Đình Trắc, *Công giáo Việt Nam*, 401.

83. Marie-Odile Jentel and Gisèle Deschênes-Wagner, eds., *Tranquilitas, Mélanges en l'honneur de Tran Tam Tinh* (Québec: Hier pour aujourd'hui, 1994), xiv.

84. The French academic world mobilized after a young mathematician at the University of Algiers was arrested and tortured for his opposition to the war. His wife and former colleagues called for an inquiry into the circumstances of his death in jail. Vidal-Naquet became the most prominent critic of the use of torture after the publication of a book. Pierre Vidal-Naquet, *L'Affaire Audin*

(Paris: Éditions de Minuit, 1958). See also Vidal-Naquet, "L'O.A.S. et la torture," *Esprit* 306 (1962): 825–39; and Vidal-Naquet, "Opération Catharsis," *Esprit* 312 (1962): 996–98, which appeared when Trần Tam Tỉnh lived in Paris.

85. "Vietnam Subject of Talk at Brescia College," *University of Western Ontario News* 1, no. 11 (1965): 3; "Convocations," *Le Soleil*, February 9, 1955.

86. Trần Tam Tỉnh, "Au fond des choses, avec ou sans arrière-pensée, Le catholicisme et la guerre du Vietnam," *Le Soleil*, November 27, 1967; Trần Tam Tỉnh, "Au fond des choses, avec ou sans arrière-pensée, Le catholique américain et le conflit vietnamien," *Le Soleil*, November 28, 1967; Trần Tam Tỉnh, "Au fond des choses," *Le Soleil*, November 29, 1967.

87. Trần Tam Tỉnh, "L'Opinion du lecteur: Le Vietnam et la Paix," *Le Soleil*, October 16, 1966.

88. Jill K. Gill, *Embattled Ecumenism: The National Council of Churches, the Vietnam War, and the Trials of the Protestant Left* (DeKalb: Northern Illinois University Press, 2011).

89. Udi Greenberg, "The Rise of the Global South and the Protestant Peace with Socialism," *Contemporary European History* 29 (2020): 202–19.

90. World Council of Churches, *The Uppsala Report 1968: Official Report of the Fourth Assembly of the World Council of Churches, Uppsala, July 4th–20th 1968* (Sweden: World Council of Churches, 1968).

91. In 1971, the presence of Vietnamese in Cambodia, Laos, and Thailand averaged 280,000; in France or former territories, less than 20,000; in the United States, 2,009; in Belgium, 858; in West Germany, 831; in Canada, 519, while nationals in Japan, Italy, and Switzerland averaged less than 150 each. Statistics of the Ministry of Foreign Affairs of the RVN, quoted in Joseph Pouvatchy, "Les Vietnamiens au Cambodge, étude d'une minorité étrangère" (PhD diss., Paris VII, 1975), 8.

92. Louis-Jacques Dorais, "Vietnamese Communities in Canada, France, and Denmark," *Journal of Refugee Studies* 11, no. 2 (1998): 107–25.

93. Michel Samson, "Manifestation pacifiste dans les rues de Québec contre la guerre au Vietnam," *Le Soleil*, November 18, 1967.

94. "La conférence hémisphérique pour mettre fin à la guerre au Viêt Nam," *Thế hệ*, special issue (February 1969): 30–32.

95. Monique Duval, "Un livre de l'abbé Tran Tam Tinh, 'Pour la paix au Vietnam,' une étude à caractère moral," *Le Soleil*, March 19, 1968. Students from Montréal, Sherbrooke, and Québec founded the publishing house and produced a periodical whose circulation averaged two hundred. Nguyen Van Nha, "Un organisme privé," *Le Soleil*, April 1, 1968.

96. "Lá thư tòa soạn," *Thế hệ* 6 (1968): 3–4.

97. On March 1, 1968, Vietnamese students, headed by Ngô Vĩnh Long, who went on with an academic career, held a press conference in Washington, DC, demanding the end of the war. "Étudiants vietnamiens en Amérique du Nord face à la guerre," *Thế hệ*, special issue (February 1969): 45.

98. "Cuộc tranh đấu sinh viên Sài Gòn," *Thế hệ* 8 (1968): 4–10; "Tin tức Québec," *Thế hệ* 6 (1968): 61. Special issues in April and May 1970 covered student protests in Saigon. On works requiring translation, see Phu Tuy, "Nhân vật thời đại," *Thế hệ* 6 (1968): 31–39. Other personalities presented to the readers included

the Yugoslav leader Josip Broz Tito, the French journalist and communist René Andrieu, and the German philosopher Herbert Marcuse. Phu Tuy, "Nhân vật thời đại," *Thế hệ* 12 (1969): 35–50.

99. Quang Việt and Nguyễn Thạch, "Che Guevara, Chiến sĩ cách mạng Châu Mỹ La tinh (1928–1967)," *Thế hệ* 8 (1968): 22–26.

100. Trần Tam Tỉnh, "Từ Tiệp Khắc đến Việt Nam," *Thế hệ* 8 (1968): 11–14.

101. Trần Tam Tỉnh, *Pour la paix au Vietnam* (Québec: Thế hệ, 1968); Trần Tam Tỉnh, *Peace in Vietnam: A Roman Catholic Vietnamese Priest Looks at the War*, trans. Peter Weldon (Québec: Thế hệ, 1968).

102. Trần Tam Tỉnh, *Pour la paix*, 45.

103. Trần Tam Tỉnh, "Catholiques et communistes au sud Viet Nam," *Thế hệ*, special issue (February 1969): 16.

104. Trần Tam Tỉnh, "Catholiques et communistes au sud Viet Nam," 22.

105. Thế hệ, "Nói chuyện với linh mục Trần Tam Tỉnh, Người công giáo và hòa bình Việt Nam."

106. Thất Sơn, "Influence de la guerre sur les religions du Viet Nam," *Thế hệ*, special issue (February 1969): 22–29.

6. Estranged from the War

1. Nguyễn Viết Khai, "Người công giáo và cộng sản hôm nay," *Đối diện* 21 (1971): 8.

2. Trần Tam Tỉnh, *Dieu et César*, 146.

3. For example, see Nguyen-Marshall, "Tools of Empire?"

4. On Vietnamization, see Miller Center, "Vietnamization," accessed May 30, 2022, https://millercenter.org/the-presidency/educational-resources/vietnamization/. For a discussion of the irony of Vietnamizing the war and its cultural impact, see Long T. Bui, *Returns of War: South Vietnam and the Price of Refugee Memory* (New York: New York University Press, 2018). For a key study of the 1973 Paris Peace Accord as a turning point in the war from the perspective of South Vietnam, see George J. Veith, *Black April: The Fall of South Vietnam, 1973-1975* (New York: Encounter Books, 2012).

5. For an excellent discussion of the "bloodbath theory" in the historiography of the land reform, see Vo, "From Anticolonialism to Mobilizing Socialist Transformation," 15–22.

6. Richard Nixon, "Address to the Nation on the War in Vietnam, November 3, 1969," Miller Center, accessed February 17, 2022, https://millercenter.org/the-presidency/presidential-speeches/november-3-1969-address-nation-war-vietnam/.

7. Richard Nixon, "Address to the Nation on the Situation in Southeast Asia, April 30, 1970," Miller Center, accessed February 17, 2022, https://millercenter.org/the-presidency/presidential-speeches/april-30-1970-address-nation-situation-southeast-asia/; Richard Nixon, "The President's News Conference," May 8, 1970, The American Presidency Project, accessed February 17, 2022, https://www.presidency.ucsb.edu/documents/the-presidents-news-conference-144/.

8. "Excerpts from Lansdale Team's Report on Covert Vietnam Mission in '54 and '55: Lansdale Report Gives Details of Assistance to Diem," The Pentagon

Papers, *New York Times*, July 5, 1971. The story also appeared in the first book-length publication of the Pentagon Papers in 1971. Neil Sheehan et al., *The Pentagon Papers: The Secret History of the Vietnam War; The Complete and Unabridged Series as Published by the New York Times* (New York: Bantam Books, 1971), 16–17.

9. The book appeared in New York, London, and New Delhi in 1964 and was translated into several languages. The cover mentioned Hoàng Văn Chí was a member of the Việt Minh. Hoàng Văn Chí, *From Colonialism to Communism* (New York: Praeger, 1964). Hoàng Văn Chí was already an authority in South Vietnam. In 1955, he gave televised interviews on his experience with land reform and elections in Thanh Hóa. Hoàng Văn Chí, *The Fate of the Last Viets* (Saigon: Hoa Mai, 1956), 30.

10. Gareth Porter, "The Myth of the Bloodbath: North Vietnam's Land Reform Reconsidered," *Bulletin of Concerned Asian Scholars* 5, no. 2 (1973): 2–15. In newspapers, see George Wilson, "Cornell Author Disputes N. Vietnamese Bloodbath," *Washington Post*, September 12, 1972; Gareth Porter, "By D. Gareth Porter," *New York Times*, October 24, 1972. Extracts from an interview of Hoàng Văn Chí criticized the latter's method of extrapolating and cast doubt on its accuracy. George Wilson, "Figure on N. Vietnam's Killings 'Just a Guess,' Author Says," *Washington Post*, September 13, 1972. For a rebuttal, see John S. Carroll, "After We Get Out, Will There Be a Bloodbath in South Vietnam? The Past Warns That a Great Many Innocent People Will Be Executed," *New York Times*, October 15, 1972. The debate continued. Gareth Porter and John S. Carroll, "Bloodbaths, or Allegations? Letters Disputed Body Count," *New York Times*, November 26, 1972. For another essay debating Porter's argument, see Robert F. Turner, "Gareth Porter Refuted, Expert Punctures 'No Bloodbath' Myth," *Human Events*, November 11, 1972. Dương Văn Mai Elliott, an evacuee who studied at Georgetown in Washington, DC, and then followed her husband to Cornell University, felt conflicted about the war situation. After realizing there was no bloodbath in the DRV after 1955, she joined the antiwar protests on the campus. Duong Van Mai Elliott, *The Sacred Willow: Four Generations in the Life of a Vietnamese Family* (Oxford: Oxford University Press, 1999), 334.

11. Porter, "The Myth of the Bloodbath."

12. Tran, "South Vietnamese Identity."

13. The series starts in May. Minh Ngọc, "Từ vụ buôn lậu đồng bạc Đông Dương (1945–1954) đến những vụ tải bạc Việt Nam hiện nay ra nước ngoài," *Dân chủ mới*, May 11, 1970. It continues with a different title to the end of the series in August. Minh Ngọc, "Những bước thăng trầm của đồng bạc Việt Nam," *Dân chủ mới*, August 23, 1970.

14. Tertrais, *La Piastre et le fusil*.

15. "Những bước thăng trầm của đồng bạc Việt Nam," *Dân chủ mới*, August 21, 1970; "Những bước thăng trầm của đồng bạc Việt Nam," *Dân chủ mới*, August 22–23, 1970.

16. On Mỹ Lai, see David Anderson, *Facing My Lai: Moving beyond the Massacre* (Lawrence: University Press of Kansas, 1998); on the claim that this was calculated, see Nick Turse, *Kill Anything That Moves: The Real American War in Vietnam* (New York: Metropolitan Books, 2013); on indiscriminate and premeditated

killings on all sides, see William S. Turley, *The Second Indochina War: A Concise Political and Military History*, 2nd ed. (Lanham, MD: Rowman & Littlefield, 2009), chap. 7, n. 26.

17. "Mỹ Lai: nơi chấm dứt 1 kiếp luân hồi những thân hình giả tạm của 1 số phụ lão hài nhi VN vô tội, hay là nơi đào sâu chôn chặt cái tinh thần bất diệt của những George Washington, Thomas Jefferson, Abraham Lincoln?" *Dân chủ mới*, November 24, 1970.

18. "Calley! Calley!" *Dân chủ mới*, April 4, 1971.

19. On student movements, see Nguyen-Marshall, *Between War and the State*, chap. 5, 7; Stur, *Saigon at War*; issue 19 of *Đối diện* (January 1971); Lý Chánh Trung, "Người công giáo và chính trị ở VN," *Đối diện* 19 (1971): 8.

20. Nguyễn Bắc Giang, "Dân chủ mới: Nỗi đau lòng về 'chuồng cọp,'" *Dân chủ mới*, July 16, 1970.

21. JUSPAO, Saigon Public Attitudes as Expressed in Sample Survey Conducted May 3–10, 1970, research report, NARA/Records of the US Forces in Southeast Asia, 1950–1972 (hereafter cited as RG472)/462, 3.

22. Nguyễn Bắc Giang, "Linh mục Hoàng Quỳnh: đã có dấu hiệu hòa bình đến gần hơn qua các biến chuyển chính trị mới," *Dân chủ mới*, July 8, 1970.

23. Sydney Schanberg, "'It's Everyone for Himself' as Troops Rampage in Hue: Deserters Loot Hue as 150,000 Flee the City," *New York Times*, May 4, 1972.

24. "Giờ chót, Xắc nhận Quốc gia. Trị di tản ... để cho B-52 oanh tạc," *Dân chủ mới*, May 3, 1972; "Các viên tư lịnh VN và cố vấn Mỹ di tản khỏi thị xã để tiếp tục chỉ huy chiến đấu," *Dân chủ mới*, May 3, 1972.

25. "Sau cuộc di tản Quảng Trị, TT Thiệu vội vàng bay ra Huế, Tướng Giai sẽ ra trước tòa án QS," *Dân chủ mới*, May 7, 1972.

26. "Hàng trăm triệu dân Hoa nghe tên Nixon lần đầu, đài Hà Nội bưng bít thật kỹ dân BV không biết Nixon đi TC," *Xây dựng*, February 27, 1972.

27. "Nhậu nhẹt thân hữu," *Xây dựng*, February 29, 1972; "Ứng cử viên Đảng Dân Chủ đo ván là cái chắc, Nga và TC đều 'bỏ phiếu' cho Nixon tháng 11 tới đây," *Xây dựng*, March 10, 1972; Cao Thế Dung, "Miền Nam VN dưới thời đại Mỹ," *Xây dựng*, April 26, 1972.

28. Cao Thế Dung, "Miền Nam VN dưới thời đại Mỹ," *Xây dựng*, February 23, 1972.

29. Cao Thế Dung, "Miền Nam VN dưới thời đại Mỹ," *Xây dựng*, March 21, 1972. On the disproportionate use of force, see Bernard B. Fall, "This Isn't Munich, It's Spain," *Ramparts* 4, no. 8 (December 1965): 23–29.

30. This thesis was first elaborated in 1970. Lương Khải Minh, *Làm thế nào để giết một Tổng thống? Bút ký lịch sử* (Saigon: Định Minh Ngọc, 1970).

31. "Tâm thư gửi Hội viên ái hữu," *Quê mẹ. Hội ái hữu địa phận Vinh. Nội san* 1 (1970): 4–5. On the estimate of two hundred thousand, see "Hộp thư," *Quê mẹ. Hội ái hữu địa phận Vinh. Nội san* 1 (1970): 32.

32. Cao Hữu Bầu, "Cảm nghĩ về đại hội ái hữu địa phận Vinh tại Lái Thiêu," *Quê mẹ. Hội ái hữu địa phận Vinh. Nội san* 1 (1970): 7–8.

33. "Tâm thư gửi Hội viên ái hữu."

34. "Nghệ Tĩnh sau các cuộc đánh bom Mỹ," *Quê mẹ. Hội ái hữu địa phận Vinh. Nội san* 1 (1970): 12–14.

35. Tô Huy Rúa, ed. *Thư tịch báo chí Việt Nam* (Hanoi: NXB Chính trị quốc gia, 1998), 51.

36. Lưu Hồng Khanh, "Ki-tô giáo và Mác-xít chủ nghĩa," *Đối diện* 21 (1971): 34–51; Nguyễn Văn Châu, "Thư ngỏ gởi các chiến hữu," *Đối diện* 21 (1971): 52–64.

37. Nguyễn Viết Khai, "Ngừoi công giáo và cộng sản hôm nay," 8.

38. *Đối diện* later insisted that the call was echoed by *La Vang*, a nonpolitical periodical for Catholics around Hue. See also Nguyễn Bình, "Người công giáo và cộng sản hôm nay," *Đối diện* 30 (1971): 51.

39. "Vài vấn đề về người cộng sản Việt Nam và công giáo," *Thế hệ* 31–32 (1973).

40. Nguyen Viet Khai and John Spragens, *Catholics and Communists Today: Old Voices, New Sounds in South Viet Nam* (Kawasaki-shi: John Spragens, Jr., 1971). On John Spragens Jr., see "Obituary of John Brewer Spragens," 2013, accessed October 12, 2021, https://www.legacy.com/us/obituaries/registerguard/name/john-spragens-obituary?pid=163224628/; Archives West, "John Spragens Collection, Biographical Note," 2012, accessed October 12, 2021, http://archiveswest.orbiscascade.org/ark:/80444/xv43237/. I thank Liang Shuang at the ISEAS Yusof Ishak Institute library, who helped me identify him as the translator.

41. Doi Zien, "Who Has No Family? Who Has No Fatherland?" *Journal of Contemporary Asia* 1 (1972): 125–24; NC News Service, "Bishop Interdicts Parish for Supporting Former Pastor," Catholic News Service, June 27, 1972.

42. Sabine Rousseau, *La Colombe et le napalm: Des Chrétiens français contre les guerres d'Indochine et du Vietnam, 1945-1975* (Paris: CNRS, 2002), 172–79, 347–50.

43. Opening remarks by Bernard Schreier, as quoted in Rousseau, *La Colombe et le napalm*, 219. For a shorter analysis, see Sabine Rousseau, "Christianisme français et engagement politique à travers les guerres d'Indochine et du Vietnam (1945-1975)," *Chrétiens et sociétés* 7 (2003): 75–98. On Father Nguyễn Đình Thi's birthdate, see Ủy ban Đoàn kết Công giáo Việt Nam, "Cáo Phó, Linh mục Gioan Baotixia Nguyễn Đình Thi," 2010, accessed May 25, 2022, http://ubdkcgvn.org.vn/vi/tin-tuc-hoat-dong/cao-pho-081E20248.html. The priest created the movement Công giáo và dân tộc to support the Vietnamese students arrested by the RVN. Phong trào Công giáo và dân tộc, "Quyết nghị của Phong trào Công giáo và dân tộc," *Công giáo và dân tộc*, April 4, 1970. The movement published a periodical urging Catholics to demand the end of the war. Ủy ban Đoàn kết Công giáo Việt Nam, "Cáo Phó, Linh mục Gioan Baotixia Nguyễn Đình Thi"; Trần Thị Liên, "The Challenge for Peace," 473n70. The priest then created an association, Europasie, for priests, Catholics, and Buddhist students to raise funds for war victims. Rousseau, *La Colombe et le napalm*, 218–19.

44. Tổng trưởng Ngoại giao, Thư gửi Thủ tướng chinh phủ Việt Nam Cộng Hòa v/v Đại hội quốc tế công giáo đoàn kết với các dân tộc Việt Kampuchia Lào họp tại Paris từ 21/5 đến 23/5/1971, June 17, 1971, TTLT2/PTTĐIICH/4.115.

45. Richard B. Griffin, "Priests of Vietnam," *New York Times*, July 2, 1971.

46. Republic of Vietnam, citation, December 12, 1967, TTLT2/PTTĐIICH/1.561; John T. Donovan, "The American Catholic Press and the Cold War in Asia: The Case of Father Patrick O'Connor, S.S.C. (1899-1987)," *American Catholic Studies* 115, no. 3 (2004): 23–49.

47. Father Trần Tam Tỉnh was a member of the editorial board of *Công giáo và dân tộc*. Trần Tam Tỉnh, "Tự do tôn giáo giả tạo," *Công giáo và dân tộc*, December 1971; "Miền Bắc và Đại hội," *Công giáo và dân tộc*, Spring 1974.

48. Phan Toán, "Đại hội kitô giáo quốc tế lần thứ II đoàn kết với các dân tộc Việt Nam–Lào–Cam-pu-chia," *Thế hệ* 27–28 (1972): 15–23; "Đại hội kitô giáo quốc tế, từ đại hội thứ nhất đến dại hội thứ hai," *Công giáo và dân tộc*, November 1972.

49. Trần Tam Tỉnh, "L'Opinion du lecteur: Pour une force de paix conscientisée et impartiale," *Le Soleil*, December 5, 1972.

50. Trần Tam Tỉnh, "L'Église du Vietnam face à la guerre de libération," *Relations* 375 (1972): 270–73.

51. Trần Tam Tỉnh, "L'opinion du lecteur: Pourquoi la guerre au Vietnam concerne les chrétiens," *Le Soleil*, October 2, 1972.

52. Trần Tam Tỉnh, "Người công giáo và hòa bình," *Đối diện* 13 (1970): 17.

53. Trần Tam Tỉnh, "Thập giá và lưỡi gươm, Tìm hiểu vai trò kitô giáo trong chế độ thực dân mới," *Thế hệ* 27–28 (1972): 27–28.

54. Trần Tam Tỉnh, "L'opinion du lecteur: Réponse aux pères X et Y, missionnaires au Vietnam," *Le Soleil*, January 20, 1973.

55. R. B., "Deux missionnaires voudraient faire une sérieuse mise au point à une diatribe mensongère d'un lecteur vietnamien," *Le Soleil*, January 31, 1973; Gérard Trempe, "L'opinion du lecteur: Si un rat visitait Paris," *Le Soleil*, February 2, 1973.

56. For a photograph, see "Các linh mục miền Bắc đi dự Đại hội thiên chúa giáo quốc tế," *Công giáo và dân tộc*, December 1971.

57. "Trois catholiques nord-vietnamiens s'adressent au pape," *Le Monde*, June 9, 1971.

58. Mary Hershberger, *Traveling to Vietnam: American Peace Activists and the War* (Syracuse: Syracuse University Press, 1998), 216. They returned with a letter from Vietnamese priests addressed to American Christians. "70 linh mục miền Bắc gửi người thiên chúa giáo Hoa Kỳ," *Công giáo và dân tộc*, November 1972.

59. "What Happened in North Vietnam," by Rev. Tran Tam Tinh, published in *Dong dao* (February 1974), Vietnam Archive/Douglas Pike Collection/Units 06–Democratic Republic of Vietnam, https://vva.vietnam.ttu.edu/repositories/2/digital_objects/54488/. On his return to Hanoi, see Trần Tam Tỉnh, *Tôi về Hà Nội* (Paris: Cộng đồng Việt Nam, 1975).

60. "2nd International Assembly of Christians in Solidarity with the Vietnamese, Laotians and Cambodian Peoples brochure," 1972, accessed May 11, 2013, http://ufdc.ufl.edu/UF00089486/00001.

61. Shepherd Bliss, "East-West Peace Bonds Strengthened at Christian Antiwar Parley in Quebec," *Christian Century*, November 15, 1972.

62. "Des croyants sud-vietnamiens envoient leurs témoignages," *Le Monde*, October 9, 1972. Letters from imprisoned priests and Catholic students were read aloud during the assembly. Phan Toán, "Đại hội kitô giáo quốc tế lần thứ II đoàn kết với các dân tộc Việt Nam–Lào–Cam-pu-chia," 18.

63. Đại hội kitô giáo quốc tế lần thứ II đoàn kết với các dân tộc Việt Nam–Lào–Cam-pu-chia, "Tuyên bố chung của Đại hội," *Thế hệ* 27–28 (1972): 24–25.

64. "Nghị quyết của Thường vụ trung ương cục số 12–NQNT về tổ chức bộ máy chinh phủ cách mạng lâm thời, 5 tháng 10 1969," in *Văn kiện Đảng*, 30: appendix.

65. "Nghị quyết hội nghị lần thứ 12 của Trung ương cục, tháng 12 1973," in *Văn kiện Đảng*, 34: appendix.

66. Trần Tam Tỉnh, *Miền Bắc có gì lạ?* (1974).

67. Trần Văn Tuyên, "'Thành phần thứ ba là một thực tế . . .,'" *Đồng dao* 58 (1974): 30.

68. "Legislative Unit in Saigon Accuses Thieu of Rigging," *New York Times*, August 28, 1971.

69. There was no attempt to hide the lineage of these publications. *Đối diện* published fifty-four issues. *Đồng dao* continued with issues 55 to 60, and *Đứng dậy* continued with issue 61 in September 1974 and closed down in 1978.

70. "Thư của Ủy ban Vận động Phong trào Công giáo Xây dựng Hòa bình, Saigon, 25–11–1970," *Đối diện* 19 (1970): 18–21; "Về đề nghị triệu tập quốc dân đại hội của phật giáo, công giáo không hỗ trợ nhưng tán thành các cuộc vận động hòa bình, Để tùy giáo dân tham dự," *Dân chủ mới*, July 3, 1970.

71. "TT Thích Pháp Diệu cho hay: 4 tôn giáo lớn Phật giáo, Cao Đài, Hòa Hảo, Công giáo đồng ý mở hội nghị Genève mới," *Dân chủ mới*, July 20, 1970.

72. "TT Th. Thiện Hoa tin tưởng sẽ phải có 1 'hội nghị Diên Hồng' để người Việt tự giải quyết hòa bình vấn đề Việt Nam," *Dân chủ mới*, June 19, 1970. However, Father Hoàng Quỳnh, on a visit to Châu Đốc for the Huỳnh Phú Sổ's thirty-second birthday, thought a conference like Diên Hồng would be too large. "Linh mục Hoàng Quỳnh không tán thành đề nghị của PG về một hội nghị Diên Hồng và cũng không định tổ chức một 'Đại hội quốc dân,'" *Dân chủ mới*, June 24, 1970.

73. Some chaos happened in the days immediately preceding and following the signature but Hanoi's official decision to resume the war came in June 1973. Veith, *Black April*, 18, 45.

74. Phiếu trình Tổng thống Việt Nam Cộng Hòa v.v. Mặt trận Nhân dân Bảo vệ Hòa bình và Thực thi Quyền Dân tộc Tự quyết, February 15, 1973, TTLT2/PTTĐIICH/Đoàn thể/4.608.

75. Phúc trình về buổi họp, February 19, 1973, TTLT2/PTTĐIICH/Đoàn thể/4.608.

76. Hồ sơ phiên họp của Mặt trận Nhân dân Tranh thủ Hòa bình và Thực thi Quyền Dân tộc Tự quyết tại Dinh Độc lập, February 17, 1973, TTLT2/PTTĐIICH/Đoàn thể/4.611.

77. Phiếu trình Tổng thống Việt Nam Cộng Hòa v.v. Mặt trận Nhân dân Bảo vệ hòa bình và Thực thi quyền dân tộc tự quyết.

78. Douglas Dacy, *Foreign Aid, War and Economic Development: South Vietnam, 1955-1975* (Cambridge: Cambridge University Press, 1986); Đặng Phong, *Kinh tế miền Nam Việt Nam thời kỳ 1955-1975* (Hanoi: NXB Khoa học xã hội, 2004).

79. On the anticorruption movement, see Nguyen-Marshall, *Between War and the State*, chap. 7; Stur, *Saigon at War*, 235–36.

80. Bản tuyên ngôn chống tham nhũng, bất công và tệ đoan xã hội, June 18, 1974, TTLT2/PTTĐIICH/4.649.

81. Bác sĩ Trần Cao Đễ, *Tuyên ngôn chống tham nhũng, bất công và tệ đoan xã hội của hàng linh mục miền Nam V.N., Lời tuyên bố trong cuộc họp báo tại Tân Sa Châu 18-6-1974* (Vũng Tàu: n.p., 1974), 10.

82. Trưởng cơ sở Dân vận và Chiêu hồi tỉnh Gia Định, Tờ trình gửi ông Tổng trưởng Bộ Dân vận và Chiêu hồi Saigon, mật, June 18, 1974, TTLT2/PTTĐIICH/4.649.

83. Trần Hữu Thanh, "Thư ngỏ của L.M. Trần Hữu Thanh, 18/6/1974," *Đứng dậy* 61 (1974): 63–70.

84. Trưởng cơ sở Dân vận và Chiêu hồi tỉnh Gia Định, Tờ trình gửi ông Tổng trưởng Bộ Dân vận và Chiêu hồi Saigon, mật.

85. Tuyên ngôn trong cuộc họp báo, June 18, 1974, TTLT2/PTTĐIICH/4.649.

86. Trần Hữu Thanh, "Lời tuyên bố ngày 18/8/1974 của linh mục Trần Hữu Thanh Chủ tịch lam thời Phong trào Nhân dân Chống Tham nhũng," *Đứng dậy* 61 (1974): 80–84.

87. "Tuyên cáo ngày 18/8/1974 của Phong trào Nhân dân Chống Tham nhũng để cứu nước và kiên tạo hòa bình," *Đứng dậy* 61 (1974): 85–89.

88. "Đạo vào đời, đời vào đạo," *Đứng dậy* 62 (1974): 33.

89. "55 người, mỗi ngừơi 200 ảnh," *Đứng dậy* 62 (1974): 114–17.

90. Cao Văn Chiếu, Thư gửi Tổng thống, November 21, 1974, TTLT2/PTTĐIICH/4.649.

91. Gheddo, *The Cross and the Bo-Tree*.

92. "Hai tài liệu tường trình, Thư của Piero Gheddo gửi Achille Silvestrini 29 tháng 12 1973," *Công giáo và dân tộc*, December 1974.

93. Coupures de presse, "Le Saint-Père n'approuve pas les agissements du P. Thanh," *Tiền tuyến*, November 21, 1974, TTLT2/PTTĐIICH/4.649.

94. Hoàng Quỳnh, Thư gửi chủ nhiệm nhật báo Hòa bình, Điện tín, Đại dân tộc, Công luận, Sống thần, September 18, 1974, TTLT2/PTTĐIICH/4.649.

95. Extraits de journaux illustrant les activités du Père Tran Huu Thanh pendant les deux dernières semaines, November 21, 1974, TTLT2/PTTĐIICH/4.649.

96. Hương Khê, "Thế đứng của LM Trần Hữu Thanh," *Đứng dậy* 65 (1974): 51.

97. Veith, *Black April*, chap. 8.

98. Mặt trận Bài trừ Tệ đoan xã hội và Kiến tạo Hòa bình, Quyết nghị, January 3, 1975, TTLT2/PTTĐIICH/Đoàn thế/4.744.

99. Mặt trận Bài trừ Tệ đoan xã hội và Kiến tạo Hòa bình, tuyên ngôn về cuộc xâm lăng của cộng sản Bắc Việt, April 1, 1975, TTLT2/PTTĐIICH/Đoàn thế/4.744.

7. Lag Time

1. Elliott, *The Sacred Willow*.

2. The historian Nathalie Huynh Chau Nguyen writes that her father lost his country twice, in 1954 and in 1975. Nathalie Huynh Chau Nguyen, *South Vietnamese Soldiers: Memories of the Vietnam War and After* (Santa Barbara, CA: Praeger, 2016), 3.

3. On the refugee crisis, see Courtland Robinson, *Terms of Refuge: The Indochinese Exodus and International Response* (New York: Zed Books, 1998). On its

political overtones, see Charles Keely, "The International Refugee Regime(s): The End of the Cold War Matters," *International Migration Review* 35, no. 1 (2001): 303–14; Karen Akoka, "Crise des réfugiés, ou des politiques d'asile?" *La Vie des Idées*, May 31, 2016, accessed August 20, 2020, https://laviedesidees.fr/Crise-des-refugies-ou-des-politiques-d-asile.html; Phi-Vân Nguyen, "The Politics of the Southeast Asian Refugee Crisis, 1978–1979," *Journal of Cold War Studies* (forthcoming). On relationships with the homeland through oral interviews or archives, see Kieu-Linh Caroline Valverde, *Transnationalizing Viet Nam: Community, Culture, and Politics in the Diaspora* (Philadelphia: Temple University Press, 2012); and Phuong Tran Nguyen, *Becoming Refugee American: The Politics of Rescue in Little Saigon* (Champaign: University of Illinois Press, 2017). For those highlighting continuities before and after 1975, see Y Thien Nguyen, "(Re)making the South Vietnamese Past in America," *Journal of Asian American Studies* 21, no. 1 (2018): 65–103; Nguyen, "When State Propaganda Becomes Social Knowledge"; Bui, *Returns of War*; Peché, Vo, and Vu, *Toward a Framework*.

4. Carl Bon Tempo, *Americans at the Gate: The United States and Refugees during the Cold War* (Princeton, NJ: Princeton University Press, 2009), 146. See also Amanda Demmer, *After Saigon's Fall: Refugees and US-Vietnamese Relations, 1975-2000* (New York: Cambridge University Press, 2021), 34.

5. Jean Vogel, "Vietnam: Les évêques n'ont pas demandé aux catholiques de quitter leurs villes et leurs villages," *Informations catholiques internationales* 5 (1975): 6–7.

6. "Un Appel en faveur des populations du Sud," *Le Monde*, April 4, 1975.

7. Vũ Ngọc Ánh, "'Thà mất nước chứ không mất đạo' Nhân nói chuyện về một câu nói được gán cho linh mục Hoàng Quỳnh," *Hồn Việt UK*, 2012, https://hon-viet.co.uk/VuNgocAnh_ThaMatNuocChuKhongMatDaoNhanNoiChuyenVeMotCauNoiDuocGanChoLinhMucHoangQuynh.htm; Nguyễn Phúc Liên, "Xin đừng làm hoen ố tinh thần l.m. Hoàng Quỳnh," *Hồn Việt UK*, October 17, 2012, https://hon-viet.co.uk/VuNgocAnh_ThaMatNuocChuKhongMatDaoNhanNoiChuyenVeMotCauNoiDuocGanChoLinhMucHoangQuynh.htm.

8. Jana K. Lipman, "'Give Us a Ship': The Vietnamese Repatriate Movement on Guam, 1975," *American Quarterly* 64, no. 1 (2012): 1–31; Heather Marie Stur, "'Hiding behind the Humanitarian Label': Refugees, Repatriates, and the Rebuilding of America's Benevolent Image after the Vietnam War," *Diplomatic History* 39, no. 2 (2015): 223–44; Đình Trụ Trần, Jana K. Lipman, and Hoài Bắc Trần, *Ship of Fate: Memoir of a Vietnamese Repatriate* (Honolulu: University of Hawai'i Press, 2017).

9. "Désespoir chez les Saïgonais," *Le Nouvelliste*, April 11, 1975.

10. Veith, *Black April*, 495–46.

11. For an analysis of the reeducation camps' theory, policy, and practice, see Minh Hoang Vu, "Recycling Violence: The Theory and Practice of Reeducation Camps in Postwar Vietnam," in *Experiments with Marxism-Leninism in Cold War Southeast Asia*, eds. Matthew Galway and Marc H. Opper (Canberra: Australian National University Press, 2022), 219–39.

12. Tiziano Terzani, *Giai Phong! The Fall and Liberation of Saigon* (New York: St. Martin's Press, 1976), 107.

13. Kosal Path, *Vietnam's Strategic Thinking during the Third Indochina War* (Madison: University of Wisconsin Press, 2020). On the relationships between the United States and Vietnam, some insist on the United States continuing the war by other means. Edwin A. Martini, *Invisible Enemies: The American War on Vietnam, 1975-2000* (Amherst: University of Massachusetts Press, 2007). Others consider there was a genuine interest in normalizing relations but a firm disagreement on war reparations. Edward Miller, "Past Imperfect: Peacemaking, Legitimacy, and Reconciliation in US-Vietnam Relations, 1975-2020," in *Vietnam: Navigating a Rapidly Changing Economy, Society, and Political Order*, ed. Börje Ljunggren and Dwight H. Perkins, 400-402 (Cambridge, MA: Harvard University Press, 2023).

14. South Vietnam was involved in multiple ongoing projects. On the Mekong Project, see Jeffrey W. Jacobs, "Mekong Committee History and Lessons for River Basin Development," *Geography Journal* 161, no. 2 (1995): 135-48; P. K. Menon, "Financing the Lower Mekong River Basin Development," *Pacific Affairs* 44, no. 4 (1972): 566-79. Vietnam waited for the US opinion on a separate membership. Note for the file on a meeting between the secretary-general and US Ambassador Bennett on the question of the US attitude in the event that North Vietnam and the PRG both applied for membership to the United Nations, May 28, 1975, UNARMS/Kurt Waldheim Files/ S-0901/0005/14.

15. The formal refusal was on August 11, 1975, when Washington vetoed its admission.

16. André Gélinas, "Life in the New Vietnam," *New York Review of Books*, March 17, 1977.

17. Trương Như Tảng, *Mémoires*, 295.

18. Nguyễn Công Luận, *Nationalist in the Viet Nam Wars: Memoirs of a Victim Turned Soldier* (Bloomington: Indiana University Press, 2012), 519.

19. Gélinas, "Life in the New Vietnam."

20. A missionary expelled by the communist authorities claimed that from four hundred thousand to five hundred thousand underwent reeducation. Gélinas, "Life in the New Vietnam." Trần Tam Tỉnh, in defense of the new authorities, responded that there were around forty thousand. Trần Tam Tỉnh, "Vietnam," *Globe and Mail*, April 5, 1977. However, the Vietnamese representative in France contacted by the *New York Times Review of Books* claimed that there were fifty thousand.

21. Father Trần Hữu Thanh was not immediately arrested and met a foreign correspondent who witnessed the arrival of the PRG in Saigon. Terzani, *Giai Phong*, 261.

22. He published his memoirs later. Phanxicô Xaviê Văn Thuận Nguyễn and Bernard F. Law, *The Road of Hope: Thoughts of Light from a Prison Cell* (London: New City, 1997).

23. Van Canh Nguyen and Earle Cooper, *Vietnam under Communism, 1975-1982* (Stanford, CA: Hoover Institution Press, 1983), 170.

24. "Vatican Aide in Saigon Leaves under Criticism," *New York Times*, June 6, 1975; "15 jours d'actualité religieuse," *Informations Catholiques Internationales* 7 (1975): 25.

25. "Vietnam: Le Saint-Siège reconnait la réunification et va entretenir des relations diplomatiques avec Hanoi," *Informations catholiques internationales* 10 (1976): 38.

26. Terzani, *Giai Phong*, 256.

27. Nayan Chanda, "Vietnam's Parish of Resistance," *Far Eastern Economic Review*, February 27, 1977.

28. On the unity of the Church, see "Người Việt Nam công giáo," *Công giáo và dân tộc*, July 10, 1975; "Tình hình giáo hội công giáo miền Bắc," *Công giáo và dân tộc*, July 24, 1975. On Catholics' contribution to the August Revolution, see A. M. T., "Tình thương kitô giáo và cuộc đấu tranh cách mạng," *Công giáo và dân tộc*, July 31, 1975. On the war against French colonial rule, see T. B. C., "Người Việt Nam công giáo với cách mạng tháng tám," *Công giáo và dân tộc*, August 7, 1975. On the war against US invasion, see Nguyễn Thanh Long, "Sưu tầm, Mỹ và âm mưu chia đôi Việt Nam," *Công giáo và dân tộc*, November 21, 1975.

29. Trần Tam Tỉnh, "CIA lợi dụng tôn giáo, CIA lợi dụng các nhà truyền giáo Mỹ trong mưu đồ thống trị (viết theo ICI.)," *Công giáo và dân tộc*, December 7, 1975; Nguyễn Thanh Long, "Sưu tầm, Mỹ và âm mưu chia đôi Việt Nam."

30. Nguyễn Đình Đầu, "Giáo dân tìm hiểu: Có nên đặt người Việt Nam làm khâm sứ hay đại sứ tòa thánh không?" *Công giáo và dân tộc*, September 28, 1975.

31. Terzani, *Giai Phong*, 257.

32. Jean-Philippe Caudron, "Au Nord-Vietnam, peut-on servir Dieu et la patrie?" *Informations catholiques internationales* 8 (1975): 2–5.

33. Mai Thanh, "Phát Diệm quê ta," *Công giáo và dân tộc*, August 14, 1975. See also Nguyễn Thủy, "Trở lại vùng công giáo Hố Nai," *Công giáo và dân tộc*, September 21, 1975.

34. "Sud Vietnam: Les autorités soutiennent les catholiques progressistes," *Informations catholiques internationales* 9 (1975): 30.

35. "Vietnam-Sud: Les écoles catholiques nationalisées," *Informations catholiques internationales* 10 (1975): 28.

36. Bùi Đức Sinh, *Giáo hội công giáo Việt Nam, Phụ chương* (Calgary, AB: Veritas, 2000), 47.

37. "Linh mục Nguyễn Huy Lịch, Bề trên dòng Đa Minh chí Lyon," *Công giáo và dân tộc*, February 22, 1976.

38. "Seizure of Rebels in Saigon Is Reported," *New York Times*, February 15, 1976; "Three Are Now Reported Dead in Rebellion in Saigon Church," *New York Times*, February 16, 1976; "Saigon Now Says 3 Died in Clash," *Washington Post*, February 16, 1976; Ủy ban Mặt trận Dân tộc Giải phóng và Ủy ban Nhân dân Cách mạng thành phố Hồ Chí Minh, "Tuyên bố về một vụ phản nghịch vũ trang chống lại chính quyền cách mạng, phá hoại kinh tế và đời sống nhân dân," *Công giáo và dân tộc*, February 22, 1976.

39. "Villagers Arrested as Saigon Charges Church-Group Plot," *New York Times*, February 19, 1976.

40. "Vụ án Vinh Sơn và trách nhiệm của giáo hội công giáo," *Công giáo và dân tộc*, February 22, 1976.

41. Caudron, "Au Nord-Vietnam, peut-on servir Dieu et la patrie?"

42. Bùi Đức Sinh, *Phụ chương*, 49.

43. This is how Vietnamese Catholics turned into Catholic Vietnamese. Nguyen and Cooper, *Vietnam under Communism*, 172.

44. "Báo cáo của Bộ Chính trị tại Hội nghị lần thứ 24, Ban chấp hành trung ương đảng," in *Văn kiện Đảng*, 36: 291–369.

45. "Nghị quyết của Bộ chính trị số 248-NQ/TW, 16/1/1976," in *Văn kiện Đảng*, 37: 26.

46. Gélinas, "Life in the New Vietnam."

47. Nguyen, *South Vietnamese Soldiers*, 147–48. On the household registration system, see Andrew Hardy, "Rules and Resources: Negotiating the Household Registration System in Vietnam under Reform," *Sojourn* 16, no. 2 (2001): 187–212. On how personal and family documentation impacts self-representation to this day, see Ann Marie Leshkowich, "Standardized Forms of Vietnamese Selfhood: An Ethnographic Genealogy of Documentation," *American Ethnologist* 41, no. 1 (2014): 143–62.

48. Trương Như Tảng, *Mémoires*.

49. Leonard R. Sussman, "Saigon's Refugee Newsmen," *Christian Science Monitor*, July 18, 1975; Phạm Văn Liễu, *Trả ta sông núi*, vol. 3 (Houston: Văn Hoá, 2003), 26.

50. Government-funded publications, such as *Đời sống mới* (New Life), published by the US Department of Health, Education, and Welfare, and community-based newspapers both gave information about these aspects.

51. Vy Khanh Nguyễn, "Báo chí người Việt Nam tỵ nạn cộng sản ở Canada," 2012, accessed March 30, 2023, chinhnghia.com/baochitynancanada.asp.

52. One of them supported the Second International Assembly of Christians held in Québec. "Việt kiều Canada và Đại hội," *Công giáo và dân tộc*, November 1972.

53. "Sự cần thiết của một Hội Việt kiều," *Chân trời mới* 4 (1975): 1–2; Anh Việt Giang, "Sinh hoạt cộng đồng của Việt kiều tại Montréal trước và sau 30/4/1975," *Chân trời mới* 4 (1975): 3–5.

54. "Đặng Văn Quang, ông là ai?" *Chân trời mới* 1 (1975): 10; Robert Trumbull, "Canada Studying a Saigon General: Presence of Thieu Ex-Aide Stirring Controversy," *New York Times*, June 1, 1975; Bill Richards, "Viet General Upsets Canada," *Washington Post*, June 4, 1975.

55. "General Plans to Leave Canada of His Own Volition, MP says," *Globe and Mail*, June 3, 1975; Kinh-Luyen Huynh, "L'accueil des réfugiés vietnamiens et indochinois après la guerre du Vietnam par le Canada et les États-Unis (1975–1981)" (master's thesis, Université du Québec à Montréal, 2021), 85–86.

56. Huynh, "L'accueil des réfugiés vietnamiens," 57–58.

57. "Un Appel en faveur des populations du Sud"; "Destinés aux populations du Sud, les premiers secours arrivent à Hanoi," *Le Monde*, April 18, 1975.

58. "Un nouvel appel du comité Fraternité Vietnam SOS," *Le Monde*, April 24, 1975. On using the term *refugee*, see Micheline Droin, "Trois organismes œuvrent pour aider les réfugiés du Vietnam," *Le Soleil*, April 11, 1975.

59. Assemblée internationale pour le pansement des blessures de guerre et pour la reconstruction du Vietnam, *Destructions de la guerre sur le plan human et socio-économique* (Paris: Fraternité Vietnam, 1975). On other postwar humanitarian efforts, see Hang Thi Thu Le-Tormala, *Postwar Journeys: American and Vietnamese*

Transnational Peace Efforts since 1975 (Lawrence: University Press of Kansas, 2021), chap. 1.

60. Jim Forest, "After the War Was Over: Seeing What You'd Rather Not See," Jim and Nancy Forest, October 10, 2011, accessed June 9, 2022, https://jimandnancyforest.com/tag/joan-baez/.

61. Jean Lacouture, "A Bittersweet Journey to Vietnam," *New York Times*, August 23, 1976.

62. Jean Lacouture, "The Bloodiest Revolution," *New York Review of Books*, March 31, 1977.

63. Swarthmore College Peace Collection, "World Conference on Religion and Peace Records, 1967–1995, Historical Background," 2007, accessed February 25, 2024, https://archives.tricolib.brynmawr.edu/resources/scpc-dg-078.

64. Gélinas, "Life in the New Vietnam."

65. Pierre Castel, "Vietnam: Le temps de la liberté surveillée," *Informations catholiques internationales* 5 (1977): 27–28.

66. Trần Tam Tỉnh, "Vietnam"; Trần Tam Tỉnh, "Savoir lire l'Évangile: un défi pour l'Église au Vietnam," *Le Devoir*, December 10, 1976.

67. Trần Tam Tỉnh, *Dieu et César*; Trần Tam Tỉnh, *Thập giá và lưỡi gươm* (Hanoi: NXB Trẻ, 1978); Trần Tam Tỉnh, "Savoir lire l'Évangile"; Trần Tam Tỉnh, "Vietnam." Trần Tam Tỉnh declared that Vietnam might be the only socialist country where female congregations ran orphanages and rehabilitation centers for sex workers. Trần Tam Tỉnh, "Religieuses comblées au Vietnam," *Le Soleil*, November 21, 1978.

68. On Vandermeersch's journey as an antiwar activist, see Sabine Rousseau, *Françoise Vandermeersch: L'émancipation d'une religieuse* (Paris: Karthala, 2012).

69. Nguyen Thi Minh Tam, "Pourquoi le Père Gélinas ne répond pas à ses détracteurs," *La Presse*, May 31, 1977. See also Chanda, "Vietnam's Parish of Resistance," 13.

70. On restricting individual freedom, see Anh Việt Giang, "Quan điểm," *Chân trời mới* 1 (1975): 2; on arrests, see "Tin ngụy quyền Cộng sản bắt giám Thượng Tọa Trí Quang và Linh mục Trần Hữu Thanh," *Chân trời mới* 6–7 (1976): 6–7.

71. "Hà Nội, Thủ đô Việt Nam," *Chân trời mới* 5 (1975): 4; "Tin thống nhất đất nước," *Chân trời mới* 6–7 (1976): 6–7.

72. Anh Việt Giang, "Quan điểm."

73. "Quốc kỳ quốc ca," *Chân trời mới* 11 (1976): 5.

74. "Ý nghĩa cuộc đấu tranh của nhân dân Việt Nam," *Chân trời mới* 9–10 (1976): 12–14.

75. "Tổng hợp tin tức kháng chiến," *Chân trời mới* 9–10 (1976): 6. On the FULRO, see William Noseworthy, "Lowland Participation in the Irredentist 'Highlands Liberation Movement' in Vietnam, 1955–1975," *Aktuelle Südostasienforschung/Current Research on South-East Asia* 6, no. 1 (2013): 7–28.

76. Richards, "Viet General Upsets Canada"; "Growing Headache," *Daily Colonist*, May 29, 1975. On Nguyễn Hữu Chi, an evacuee who disclosed the existence of this network, see "Obituaries: Nguyen Huu Chi 1936–August 22, 2019," accessed June 28, 2023, https://ottawacitizen.remembering.ca/obituary/nguyen-chi-1076804156/; Carleton University, "Carleton University Mourns the Passing of Nguyen Huu Chi," August 26, 2019, accessed June 28, 2023, https://newsroom.carleton.ca/2019/carleton-university-mourns-the-passing-of-nguyen-huu-chi.

77. "Lễ kỷ niệm mừng chiến thắng 30/4/1975," *Chân trời mới* 11 (1976); "Lễ kỷ niệm một năm ly hương," *Chân trời mới* 11 (1976): 7.

78. Nguyễn Văn Bích, "Người Việt giỗ Tổ, Vietnamese Honor Hung Dynasty," *Chân trời mới-New Life* 2, no. 4 (1976): 5. Almost ten years later, the Việt Tân party, the organization supposed to lead the political struggle after the United Front overthrew the SRVN, chose this ceremony to celebrate its own national day. Duyen Bui, "Diasporic Nationalism: Continuity and Changes," in Peché, Vo, and Vu, *Toward a Framework*, 231–32.

79. Phạm Duy, *Một đời nhìn lại*, vol. 4, chap. 6.

80. Chen Jian, "China, the Vietnam War, and the Sino-American Rapprochement, 1968–1973," in *The Third Indochina War: Conflict between China, Vietnam, and Cambodia, 1972–1979*, ed. Odd Arne Westad and Sophie Quinn-Judge (London: Routledge, 2006); Chen Jian, *Mao's China & the Cold War* (Chapel Hill: University of North Carolina Press, 2001); Qiang Zhai, *China and the Vietnam Wars, 1950–1975* (Chapel Hill: University of North Carolina Press, 2000).

81. Lorenz Lüthi, *The Sino-Soviet Split: Cold War in the Communist World* (Princeton, NJ: Princeton University Press, 2008); Sergey Radchenko, *Two Suns in the Heavens: The Sino-Soviet Struggle for Supremacy, 1962–1967* (Redwood City, CA: Stanford University Press, 2009).

82. On the departure from the south, see UNICEF/UNHCR/UNIC Joint Representative for Australia and New Zealand, Sydney, to UNHCR Geneva, June 27, 1978, UNHCR/F11/2/60_600_SRVa. On the "privileged outsider" status in the DRV, see Han, "Spoiled Guests or Dedicated Patriots?" On their legal status, see Lili Song, "China and the International Refugee Protection Regime: Past, Present, and Potentials," *Refugee Survey Quarterly* 37 (2018): 139–61; Hungdah Chiu, "Current Developments: China's Legal Position on Protecting Chinese Residents in Vietnam," *American Journal of International Law* 74, no. 3 (1980): 685–93. On their resettlement, see Zhu Rong, "China and the Indochinese Refugees," in *Indochinese Refugees: Asylum and Resettlement*, ed. Supang Chantavanich and E. Bruce Reynolds (Bangkok: Institute of Asian Studies, 1988); Xiaorong Han, "From Resettlement to Rights Protection: The Collective Actions of the Refugees from Vietnam in China since the Late 1970s," *Journal of Chinese Overseas* 10 (2014): 197–219.

83. Consultative Meeting with Interested Governments on Refugees and Displaced Persons in South East Asia, Geneva, Draft Summary Report, December 11–12, 1978, UNHCR/F11/2/39_391_39d, para. 36.

84. Sydney to UNHCR Geneva, 1. Although Beijing claimed that Vietnam was discriminating against Chinese people, these measures did not target them but affected their livelihoods disproportionately. Alexander Woodside, "Nationalism and Poverty in the Breakdown of Sino-Vietnamese Relations," *Pacific Affairs* 52, no. 3 (1979): 381–409.

85. Consultation with interested governments on refugees and displaced persons in South East Asia, Background Note, November 29, 1978, UNHCR/F11/2/39_391_39d. The "land cases" included a cumulative total, on October 31, 1978, of 192,000 in Thailand and around 150,000 in Vietnam, for total cumulative departures of only 63,000. "Boat cases" totaled 72,722, for 34,000 departures.

86. Barry Wain, *The Refused: The Agony of the Indochina Refugees* (New York: Simon & Schuster, 1981).

87. On Southeast Asian states' lack of recognition of the 1951 convention, see Sarah Davies, "Saving Refugees or Saving Borders? Southeast Asian States and the Indochinese Refugee Crisis," *Global Change, Peace & Security* 18, no. 1 (2006): 3-24. On their use of the term "boat people" instead of "refugees," see Martin Tsamenyi, "The 'Boat People': Are They Refugees?" *Human Rights Quarterly* 5 (1983): 348-73.

88. Note for the file: Consultation with interested governments on refugees and displaced persons in South East Asia, November 10, 1978, UNHCR/F11/2/39_391_39a; Aide memoire, 29th Session of the Executive Committee of the High Commissioner's Programme, Consultations with Interested Governments, October 27, 1978, UNHCR/F11/2/39_391_39a.

89. The first countries of asylum were Indonesia, Japan, Malaysia, Philippines, Republic of Korea, Singapore, Socialist Republic of Vietnam, and Thailand. Hanoi initially refused to go but changed its mind hoping it could discuss the case of Kampuchean refugees fleeing the Khmer Rouges. V. Dayal, Confidential Memorandum to UNHCR Geneva, November 24, 1978, UNHCR/F11/2/39_391_39b; HICOM Hanoi to UNHCR Geneva, cable, December 7, 1978, UNHCR/F11/2/39_391_39c.

90. Consultative Meeting with Interested Governments on Refugees and Displaced Persons in South East Asia Geneva, Draft Summary Report.

91. Aide memoire, 29th Session of the Executive Committee; Socialist Republic of Vietnam, Announcement regarding the UNHCR Consultations on Indochinese Refugees, January 12, 1979, UNHCR/F11/2/39_391_39e.

92. "The USSR-Vietnam Treaty," *Executive Intelligence Review* 5, no. 48 (1978): 32. For a short analysis, see Céline Marangé, "Les Relations politiques de l'Union soviétique avec le Vietnam de 1975 à 1995," *Outre-mers* 94, nos. 354-355 (2007): 147-71.

93. On Hanoi's decision to overcome the economic crisis and diplomatic isolation, see Path, *Vietnam's Strategic Thinking*.

94. On the Third Indochina War, see David W. P. Elliott, ed., *The Third Indochina Conflict* (Boulder, CO: Westview Press, 1981); Nayan Chanda, *Brother Enemy: The War after the War* (New York: Harcourt, 1986); Westad and Quinn-Judge, *Third Indochina War*. On the military aspects of the conflict, see Nicholas Khoo, *Collateral Damage: Sino-Soviet Rivalry and the Termination of the Sino-Vietnamese Alliance* (New York: Columbia University Press, 2011). On reinforcing Deng Xiaoping's Four Modernizations, see Zhang Xiaoming, *Deng Xiaoping's Long War: The Military Conflict Between China and Vietnam, 1979-1991* (Chapel Hill: University of North Carolina Press, 2015).

95. Nguyen, "The Politics of the Southeast Asian Refugee Crisis." I borrow the expression "de facto" refugee from Gil Loescher, *The UNHCR and World Politics: A Perilous Path* (Oxford: Oxford University Press, 2001).

96. He gave an interview to a US veteran, David Butner, in November 1982 on his days in Saigon. See "50 ngày chót của VNCH," *Thức tỉnh* 95 (1982): 22-26.

97. "50 ngày chót của VNCH," 23.

98. "Tháng ngày sôi động," *Thức tỉnh* 1 (1978): 7-12.

99. Lê Minh Trực, "Nhân định đúng, hành động đúng, Thế nước, lòng dân, giữa khúc quanh lịch sử," *Thức tỉnh* 21 (1979): 10.

100. Vi Nhân, "Lá thư Liên minh," *Thức tỉnh* 3 (1978): 3–5.

101. Lê Minh Trực, "30.4.1978, Ngày phục quốc," *Thức tỉnh* 1 (1978): 5–6, 14.

102. Lê Minh Trực, "Nhân định đúng, hành động đúng, Địa Lĩnh nhân kiệt dân tộc VN sẽ đánh gục bọn CS quốc tế," *Thức tỉnh* 13 (1978): 13–15.

103. Lê Minh Trực, "Nhân định đúng, hành động đúng, Giờ hành động đã điểm," *Thức tỉnh* 29 (1979): 6–7.

104. "Người Việt ty nạn nghĩ sao trước họa diệt vong do bọn CSVN gây ra?" *Thức tỉnh* 20 (1979): 5–6.

105. "Những vấn đề của chúng ta: Phải chân Hoa Kỳ và Trung Cộng đành cúi đầu trước cuộc xâm lăng Miên của CSVN!" *Thức tỉnh* 40 (1979).

106. "Thư của Liên minh Hải ngoại Phục quốc Việt Nam gửi ông Kurt Waldheim, Letter of the Greater Overseas Alliance for National Restoration of Vietnam, February 20th, 1979," *Thức tỉnh* 21 (1979): 8.

107. Phạm Văn Liễu, *Trả ta sông núi*, 3: 95.

108. Phạm Văn Liễu, *Trả ta sông núi*, 3: 88, 114, 127, 144–45.

8. Breaking Free of the War

1. Cao Thi Bich Thuy, application, May 15, 1997, Families of Vietnamese Political Prisoners (hereafter cited as FVPPA)/box 4/folder 48.

2. This trend was particularly notable in the applications from A to L, in which applicants from the north comprised 70–80 percent. In the second half of the alphabet, the proportion of applicants from the south increases. An overall proportion of 50 percent is thus a conservative estimate. Calculations were made based on the archives available in Lubbock, Texas, in 2009, before digitization of the applications. Some applications were removed for confidentiality reasons before being uploaded online.

3. For figures counted by the UNHCR, see *The State of the World's Refugees 2000: Fifty Years of Humanitarian Action* (Geneva: UNHCR, 2000). The figures for land and boat departures as well as ODP come from Robinson, *Terms of Refuge*, appendix 2. It is important to add to that total the 140,000 people who fled in the immediate aftermath of April 1975 with the US Navy and did not go through any screening or UNHCR program. The estimate of 10 percent deaths among those who departed by boat comes from UNHCR, *The State of the World's Refugees*. But a high percentage may be more likely for the period 1978 to 1981, rather than the entire period from 1975 to 1995.

4. The percentage of the population is calculated using the total of 1,691,216, compared with a population of 48 million in 1975 (3.16%) or 74 million in 1995 (2.05%).

5. UNHCR, *The State of the World's Refugees*; Loescher, *The UNHCR and World Politics*. For a comprehensive analysis, see Robinson, *Terms of Refuge*. For individual case studies, see Jana K. Lipman, *In Camps: Vietnamese Refugees, Asylum Seekers, and Repatriates* (Berkeley: University of California Press, 2020); Astri Suhrke, *Indochinese Refugees: The Impact of First Asylum Countries and Implications for American Policy; A Study Prepared for the Use of the Joint Economic Committee, Congress of the United States* (Washington, DC: US Government Printing Office, 1980); Supang

Chantavanich and E. Bruce Reynolds, eds., *Indochinese Refugees: Asylum and Resettlement* (Bangkok: Institute of Asian Studies, 1988); Supang Chantavanich and Paul Rabe, "Thailand and the Indochinese Refugees: Fifteen Years of Compromise and Uncertainty," *Southeast Asian Journal of Social Science* 18, no. 1 (1990): 66–80. On resettlement in China, see Han, "From Resettlement to Rights Protection"; in France, see Karine Meslin, *Les réfugiés du Mékong: Cambodgiens, Laotiens et Vietnamiens en France* (Détours: Bourdeaux, 2020); in Canada, see Michael J. Molloy et al., *Running on Empty: Canada and the Indochinese Refugees, 1975-1980* (Montreal: McGill University Press, 2017); in Thailand, see Suteera Thomson, "Refugees in Thailand: Relief, Development, and Integration," in *Southeast Asian Exodus: From Tradition to Resettlement*, ed. Elliot L. Tepper (Ottawa, ON: Canadian Asian Studies Association, 1980). For an analysis of a longer history of US immigration policies, see Bon Tempo, *Americans at the Gate*.

6. On critical refugee studies, see Yến Lê Espiritu, "Toward a Critical Refugee Study," *Journal of Vietnamese Studies* 1, nos. 1–2 (2006): 410–33; Espiritu, *Body Counts: The Vietnam War and Militarized Refugees* (Berkeley: University of California Press, 2014); Mimi Thi Nguyen, *The Gift of Freedom: War, Debt, and Other Refugee Passages* (Durham, NC: Duke University Press, 2012). On other host countries and territories, see Evyn Le Gandhi Espiritu, *Archipelago of Resettlement: Vietnamese Refugee Settlers in Guam and Israel-Palestine* (Berkeley: University of California Press, 2022); on temporary camps across Southeast Asia, see Lipman, *In Camps*. For studies focusing on memory, see Nathalie Huynh Chau Nguyen, *Memory Is Another Country* (London: Bloomsbury, 2009); Nguyen, *New Perceptions of the Vietnam War* (Jefferson, NC: McFarland, 2015).

7. For a study analyzing historical change in self-representation, see Nguyen, *Becoming Refugee American*. See also Thanh Thuy Vo Dang, "Anticommunism as Cultural Praxis: South Vietnam, War, and Refugee Memories in the Vietnamese American Community" (PhD diss., University of California, 2008); on anticommunism, see Nguyen, "(Re)making the South Vietnamese Past." On the continuing importance of the Virgin Mary in the Vietnamese diaspora, see Thien-Huong Ninh, "The Virgin Mary Became Asian: Diasporic Nationalism among Vietnamese Catholic Refugees in the United States and Germany," in *Refugees and Religion: Ethnographic Studies of Global Trajectories*, ed. Birgit Meyer and Peter van der Veer (London: Bloomsbury, 2021), 68–86.

8. Nguyen, "(Re)making the South Vietnamese Past." This contributes to a recent trend in scholarship highlighting the connections and continuities of practices, ideas, and values in South Vietnam and Vietnamese America. Linda Ho Peché, Alex Thai Vo, and Tuong Vu, "Introduction," and Y Thien Nguyen, "Legacies and Diasporic Connectivity: Dialogues and Future Directions of Vietnamese and Vietnamese American Studies," in Peché, Vo, and Vu, *Toward a Framework*, 23-39. However, the experience is different where overseas Vietnamese have resettled outside the United States, as noted in Ivan Small, "Vietnamese Americans and Their Homeland: Transnational Advocacy Efforts and Diasporic Ties," in Peché, Vo, and Vu, *Toward a Framework*, 116–32.

9. On initiatives to make peace, see Le-Tormala, *Postwar Journeys*; on transnational movements and ideas, see Valverde, *Transnationalizing Viet Nam*.

10. Sergey Radchenko, *Unwanted Visionaries: The Soviet Failure in Asia at the End of the Cold War* (Oxford: Oxford University Press, 2014), 131; David W. P. Elliott, *Changing Worlds: Vietnam's Transition from Cold War to Globalization* (Oxford: Oxford University Press, 2014), 63-64. On the realization that there was no immediate payoff, see Elliott, *Changing Worlds*, 71. On the strategic and economic calculations, see Path, *Vietnam's Strategic Thinking*.

11. Elliott, *Changing Worlds*, 61-62. On Hanoi's eagerness to join ASEAN, see Carlyle Thayer and Amer Ramses, eds., *Vietnamese Foreign Policy in Transition* (Singapore: Institute for Southeast Asian Studies, 1999), 3.

12. Rafeeuddin Ahmed, Briefing Note to the UN Secretary-General on the International Conference on Indochinese Refugees, June 8, 1989, UNARMS/Javier Pérez de Cuéllar Files/S-1046/0012/0001. On the explanation that "all states" includes more participants than "all member states," see Confidential, Notes on a meeting held in the Secretary-General's office, January 24, 1989, UNARMS/de Cuéllar Files/S-1046/0012/0001; UNHCR to the UN Secretary-General, June 1, 19899, UNARMS/de Cuéllar Files/S-1046/0012/0001; UN Department of Public Information, Secretary-General's Statement to International Conference on Indochinese Refugees, press release, June 13, 1989, UNARMS/de Cuéllar Files/S-1046/0012/0001.

13. Elliott, *Changing Worlds*, 110.

14. Minh Hoang Vu, "Sortir du bourbier: Les méandres du Vietnam vers l'accord de paix de Paris, 1986-1991," in *Un triangle stratégique à l'épreuve: La Chine, les États-Unis et l'Asie du Sud-Est depuis 1947*, ed. Pierre Journoud (Montpellier, France: Presses universitaires de la Méditerranée, 2022), 219-38.

15. The historian Christopher Goscha declared that, from an ideological point of view, the Cold War ended in 1979, when Vietnam entered into a war against China and Cambodia and repudiated the myth of international communist solidarity. Christopher E. Goscha, "Vietnam, the Third Indochina War and the Meltdown of Asian Internationalism," in Westad and Quinn-Judge, *The Third Indochina War*, 152-86.

16. On the French reaction, see François Hourmant, *Le désenchantement des clercs, figures de l'intellectuel dans l'après-Mai 68* (Rennes: Presses Universitaires de Rennes, 1997).

17. Lê Minh Trực, "Nhân định đúng, hành động đúng, Thế nước, lòng dân, giữa khúc quanh lịch sử," *Thức tỉnh* 21 (1979): 11.

18. *Thức tỉnh* ran a series of articles on the armed conflict. Huỳnh Minh Đạo, "Những vấn đề của chúng ta: Trung lập hoá Đông Dương," *Thức tỉnh* 22 (1979): 9-12.

19. "Những vấn đề của chúng ta: Trung lập hóa Đông Dương," *Thức tỉnh* 32 (1979): 9-10.

20. "Ông Trương Như Tảng, Phát ngôn viên UBCNVN đứng đất Bắc khi kêu gọi đồng bào trong nước và hải ngoại hãy đứng lên đáng đổ CSVN," *Thức tỉnh* 90 (1982): 4-6.

21. Huỳnh Minh Đạo, "Thông qua đài phát thanh Bắc Kinh, ông Hoàng Văn Hoan chúc Tết và kêu gọi nhân dân đồng khởi lật đổ tập đoàn Lê Duẩn," *Thức tỉnh* 99 (1983): 6-9.

22. Tùng Anh, "Chống cộng sản hay chống Le Duẩn?" *Thức tỉnh* 109 (1984): 8–10.
23. Phạm Văn Liễu, *Trả ta sông núi, Tập 3*, 141.
24. Phạm Văn Liễu, *Trả ta sông núi, Tập 3*, 141–44.
25. Phạm Văn Liễu, *Trả ta sông núi, Tập 3*, 164.
26. Nguyen, "(Re)making the South Vietnamese Past," 74.
27. Huỳnh Minh Đạo, "Người Việt ở hải ngoại làm gì để phối hợp với nhân dân VN lật đổ CS Hà Nội?" *Thức tỉnh* 58 (1980): 9.
28. "Người Campuchea tỵ nạn biểu tình phản đối ký giả cộng sản Mỹ," *Thức tỉnh* 15 (1978): 22; "Khu bộ NSW của Liên minh hải ngoại Phục quốc Việt Nam tổ chức, Người Việt tỵ nạn ở Úc bao vây bọn CS Hà Nội đi dự hội nghị nghiệp đoàn," *Thức tỉnh* 40 (1979): 29; "Người Việt tỵ nạn tuyệt thực đòi nhân quyền tại Việt Nam," *Thức tỉnh* 15 (1978): 18–21; "Nhân ngày kỷ niệm 30 năm Liên hiệp quốc cộng Bản tuyên ngôn QT nhân quyền, Cộng đồng VN tỵ nạn khắp thế giới biểu tình đòi nhân quyền ở Việt Nam," *Thức tỉnh* 16 (1978): 18–23.
29. "Phe Cộng Hòa bảo thủ Mỹ đại thắng Reagan-Bush đắc cử Tổng thống, chiếm đa số Th. Viện, Hạ phe chủ bại," *Thức tỉnh* 62 (1980): 12–15; Đào Đăng Vỹ, "1981: Năm chuẩn bị sắp xếp lại bàn cờ thế giới," *Thức tỉnh* 65/66 (1981): 8–13; "Các học giả, chính khánh và các nhà ngoại giao thảo luận đã cho rằng Liên Xô không dám tấn công Ba Lan," *Thức tỉnh* 71 (1981): 16–17; "Người Việt tỵ nạn biểu tình tố cáo Đế quốc Liên Xô và tay sai CSVN," *Thức tỉnh* 72 (1981): 35, "Tranh đấu cho quyền lợi của người Đông Dương tỵ nạn tại Bắc California," *Thức tỉnh* 79 (1981): 31–33.
30. On the rapprochement between Washington and Beijing, see *How the Republic of China Views the Normalization of Relations between the US and the Chinese Communist Regime* (Taipei: World Anti-Communist League, China Chapter, 1978). On ethnic Chinese refugees, see Lo Shi-Fu, *The Reason of Exodus of Refugees from Vietnam and Its Consequences* (Taipei: World Anti-Communist League, China Chapter, 1980); on ASEAN, see Lo Shi-Fu, *Southeast Asia: Target of Moscow-Peiping Rivalry* (Taipei: World Anti-Communist League, China Chapter, 1980); *How the Republic of China Views the Normalization*; Chang Yao-Chiu, *Communist China's Strategy towards ASEAN Countries* (Taipei: World Anti-Communist League, China Chapter, 1986). On the prospects of another Chinese intervention, see "Đặng Tiểu Bình nói thẳng với ông K. Waldheim, Tổng thư ký Liên hợp quốc, Bắc Kinh: Phải dạy cho Hà Nội một bài học đích đáng thứ hai nữa," *Thức tỉnh* 25 (1979): 26.
31. Trương Như Tảng, *Mémoires*.
32. "Sau nhiều phiên họp liên tiếp, xét nét từng giai đoạn của tình hình Ủy ban Cứu nước Việt Nam, Phát động cuộc vận động QT ở các nước Tây Âu," *Thức tỉnh* 71 (1981).
33. Lê Minh Trực, "Đ. Dương chuyển mình nổi dậy," *Thức tỉnh* 62 (1980): 6–7.
34. "Các nhóm cũng như các chính khách VN đang tích cực vận động với Bắc Kinh, Các ông Nguyễn Cao Kỳ, Ngô Chí Dũng, Nguyễn Ngọc Huy đi Bắc Kinh," *Thức tỉnh* 74 (1981): 26. On Nguyễn Ngọc Huy, see François Guillemot, "An Intellectual through Revolution, War and Exile: The Political Commitment of Nguyen Ngoc Huy (1924–1990)," in Nguyen, *New Perceptions of the Vietnam War*, 41–71.

35. "Sihanouk tính chuyện 'cứu nước' nhưng cuối cùng lại tuyên bố hủy việc lập chinh phủ lưu vong, lập Mặt trận Đoàn kết Campuchea," *Thức tỉnh* 33 (1979): 31-32; "Pháp không cho Sihanouk hoạt động chính trị tại Pháp," *Thức tỉnh* 33 (1979): 32. *Thức tỉnh* also published a translation of the king's memoirs, Norodom Sihanouk, *My War with the CIA: The Memoirs of Prince Norodom Sihanouk* (New York: Parthenon, 1973), starting in issue 37. Norodom Sihanouk, "Cuộc chiến của CIA và tôi," trans. Nguyễn Đồng Tháp, *Thức tỉnh* 37 (1979).

36. "Người Việt tỵ nạn nghĩ sao trước họa diệt vong do bọn CSVN gây ra?" *Thức tỉnh* 20 (1979): 5-6.

37. "500.000 dân Miên chết dưới thời Lon Nol, Pol Pot giết 3 triệu rưỡi nhưng . . . Campuchea sẽ bị diệt chủng vì nạn đói khủng khiếp," *Thức tỉnh* 27 (1979): 21. An article in 1978 also insisted Lon Nol was the legitimate head of state because the Khmer Rouge had illegally taken over Phnom Penh. "Vẫn xưng danh Quốc trưởng Lon Nol họp báo đòi trục xuất phái đoàn CS Miên ra khỏi tổ chức Liên hiệp quốc," *Thức tỉnh* 11 (1978): 29, 32; "Sihanouk, Son Sann, Khieu Samphan sẽ họp tại Paris vào tháng 6/1981," *Thức Tỉnh* 69 (1981): 23; "Mặc dầu có nhiều sự bất đồng giữa ông hoàng Sihanouk và nhóm Khmer Đỏ, Nhưng thỏa hiệp đạt được giữa Sihanouk-Samphan," *Thức tỉnh* 71 (1981): 34-36; "Trước áp lực của tình hình, của khối ASEAN, 3 lãnh tụ khmer đã chấp thuận thành lập Mặt trận Đoàn kết Thống nhất," *Thức tỉnh* 78 (1981): 38-39; "Liên minh Giải phóng Đông Dương," *Thức tỉnh* 74 (1981): 4-5.

38. Lê Minh Trực, "Nhân định đúng, hành động đúng, Chánh phủ lâm thời quốc gia VN," *Thức tỉnh* 34 (1979): 7; Lê Minh Trực, "Nhân định đúng, hành động đúng, Bài học Sihanouk," *Thức tỉnh* 38 (1979): 6-8.

39. "Lời kêu gọi của Phong trào Hòa bình: Trung lập và tự do dân chủ tại Việt Nam," *Thức tỉnh* 42 (1980): 23.

40. Lê Minh Trực, "Nhân định đúng, hành động đúng, Một nước VN trung lập trong tương lai," *Thức tỉnh* 55 (1980): 6-9.

41. Lê Minh Trực, "Nhân định đúng, hành động đúng, Thế nước, lòng dân, giữa khúc quanh lịch sử."

42. Tô Văn criticized Võ Đại Tôn's armed front, which predated the Hoàng Cơ Minh's National Front. See Nguyễn Khắc Ngữ, *Đại cương về các đảng phái chính trị Việt Nam* (Montreal: Tủ sách nghiên cứu sử địa, 1989), 117.

43. Phạm Văn Liễu, *Trả ta sông núi*, 3: 293-95, 390-91.

44. See also Bui, "Diasporic Nationalism: Continuity and Changes," 224.

45. Dan Rather and Morley Safer, "Vietnam/Internal Conflict," *Evening News*, CBS, March 30, 1982.

46. Phạm Văn Liễu, *Trả ta sông núi*, 3: 206, 223, 232-33, 236, 296-97.

47. Phạm Văn Liễu, *Trả ta sông núi*, 3: 199, 223, 238.

48. For a recent analysis of this classic national history textbook, see Nguyễn Lương Hải Khôi, "Early Republican Concept of the Nation: Trần Trọng Kim and *Việt Nam sử lược*," in Tran and Vu, *Building a Republican Nation in Vietnam*, 43-60.

49. Mặt trận quốc gia thống nhất giải phóng Việt Nam, *Anh hùng nước tôi*, in lần thứ ba (San Jose, CA: Đông Tiến, 1988), 10.

50. According to the *Washington Post*, no group would call a meeting because the others would not join. This was the main reason why Don Bailey invited seventy-eight group leaders to meet in December 1982. Joanne Omang, " 'Little Saigons' in U.S. Foster Hopes of Toppling Hanoi: In Exile Enclaves, Hopes of Toppling Hanoi," *Washington Post*, January 16, 1983.

51. "Thư của nhóm chủ trương Thức tỉnh (Vùng dậy)," *Thức tỉnh* 109 (1984): 3.

52. "Tâm thư của ký giả Tô Văn gửi đồng bào trong và ngoài nước," *Thức tỉnh* 109 (1984): 4–5.

53. Samuel Moyn, *The Last Utopia: Human Rights in History* (Cambridge, MA: Harvard University Press, 2010).

54. Vy Khanh Nguyễn, "Báo chí người Việt Nam tỵ nạn cộng sản ở Canada," March 2013, accessed March 30, 2023, chinhnghia.com/baochitynancanada.asp.

55. "Chính đề Việt Nam," *Dân quyền* 1 (1978): 6.

56. "Phong trào Tranh đấu cho nhân quyền chi bộ Ottawa trình bầy với Hội Ân xá Quốc tế về hiện tình Việt Nam," *Dân quyền* 1 (1978): 6.

57. Tâm Việt, "Hồi ký, Tôi là ủy viên tuyên huấn chi Hội phụ nữ giải phóng," *Dân quyền* 2 (1978): 8–10.

58. The 1957 PEN International Congress recognized Vietnam's club for authors. See PEN Vietnam, "Lịch sử văn bút Việt Nam hải ngoại," *Viet Pen* (2023), accessed May 5, 2023, https://vietpen.org/lich-su-van-but-viet-nam-hai-ngoai. On another journalist association with a large proportion of northerners, see Phạm Trần, "Life and Work of a Journalist," 123–24.

59. Nguyễn Khắc Ngữ, *Đại cương về các đảng phái chính trị Việt Nam*, 114.

60. Trần Thanh Hiệp, *Dân chủ cho Việt Nam* (Fairfax, VA: Việt Thức, 2018).

61. "Nhận định đúng, hành động đúng, 3 vị trí phối hợp đấu tranh cứu nước," *Thức tỉnh* 86 (1982): 12–15.

62. Huỳnh Minh Đạo, "Cuộc cách mạng mới sẽ do nhân dân Việt Nam chủ động," *Thức tỉnh* 99 (1983): 3–5. The United States also limited to three hundred dollars the amount that could be sent to a person in the SRVN, which people circumvented by sending through third parties in France. See Small, "Vietnamese Americans and Their Homeland," 117.

63. As the historian Minh Hoang Vu states, the amount was greater for the inhabitants of the two largest cities—VNĐ 6,000 for people living in Hanoi and Ho Chi Minh City, and only VNĐ 4,500 for people anywhere else. See Minh Hoang Vu, "Return of the Prodigious Sons: Émigré Contributions to Vietnam's Economic Revival, 1985–1995" (paper presented at the Association for Asian Studies, 2021); Minh Hoang Vu, "Overseas Remittances in Vietnam's Reform Era," Nordic Asia Podcasts, 2021, accessed May 9, 2023, https://newbooksnetwork.com/overseas-remittances-in-vietnams-reform-era; Xã hội chủ nghĩa cộng hòa (Hội đồng bộ trưởng chính phủ), "Quyết định của Hội đồng bộ trưởng số 151-HĐBT ngày 31 tháng 8 năm 1982 về việc các gia đình có thân nhân định cư ở các nước ngoài hệ thống xã hội chủ nghĩa nhận tiền, nhận hàng do thân nhân của họ gửi về," 1982, accessed May 9, 2023, https://luatvietnam.vn/linh-vuc-khac/quyet-dinh-151-hdbt-hoi-dong-bo-truong-8819-d1.html; Xã hội Chủ nghĩa Cộng Hòa (Ngân hàng nhà nước), "Thông tư của Ngân hàng

nhà nước số 34-NH/TT ngày 10 tháng 2 năm 1983 hướng dẫn thi hành quyết định số 151-HĐBT ngày 31-8-1982 của Hội đồng bộ trưởng về việc các gia đình có thân nhân định cư ở các nước ngoài hệ thống xã hội chủ nghĩa nhận tiền, nhận hàng do thân nhân của họ gửi về," 1983, accessed May 9, 2023, https://vietlaw.quochoi.vn/Pages/vbpq-toan-van.aspx?ItemID=8848/.

64. Vu, "Return of the Prodigious Sons"; Vu, "Overseas Remittances"; Đặng Phong, *"Phá rào" trong kinh tế vào đêm trước Đổi mới* (Hanoi: NXB Tri thức, 2009).

65. Hue-Tam Ho Tai, "Introduction: Situating Memory," in *The Country of Memory: Remaking the Past in Late Socialist Vietnam* (Berkeley: University of California Press, 2001); Christoph Giebel, "Museum-Shrine: Revolution and Its Tutelary Spirit in the Village of My Hoa Hung," in Hue-Tam Ho Tai, *The Country of Memory*, 77–108.

66. Viet Stories: Vietnamese American Oral History Project, UC Irvine, accessed February 26, 2024, https://sites.uci.edu/vaohp/; Hearts of Freedom, accessed February 26, 2024, https://heartsoffreedom.org; and First Days Story Project, PBS, accessed February 26, 2024, https://www.pbs.org/wgbh/americanexperience/lastdays/firstdaysstoryproject/.

67. Alan Freeman, "Canada Connects with Viet Kieu," *Globe and Mail*, November 18, 1994.

68. Philip Shenon, "Homeland Offers Golden Promises: Vietnam; Twenty Years after Fleeing Communism and Poverty, Many Former Boat People Are Returning to Invest in a Fast-Growing Economy," *Globe and Mail*, November 18, 1993.

69. James Webb, "Not All the Wounds Have Healed," *Washington Post*, August 23, 1992; Small, "Vietnamese Americans and Their Homeland," 121–24.

70. Ivan Small, *Currencies of Imagination: Channeling Money and Chasing Mobility in Vietnam* (Ithaca, NY: Cornell University Press, 2019).

71. On how "China and Chinese emigrants were coproduced by the discursive and material history of departures, exchanges, and returns," see Shelly Chan, *Diaspora's Homeland: Modern China in the Age of Global Migration* (Durham, NC: Duke University Press, 2018), 8.

72. Tuan Hoang, "The Resettlement of Vietnamese Refugee Religious, Priests, and Seminarians in the United States, 1975–1977," *U.S. Catholic Historian* 37, no. 3 (2019): 99–122. The case of Dominicans in Alberta, Canada, is striking, as they managed to have their parish in Calgary, in Alberta, recognized as an extension of the Dominican Province of Vietnam. "Lịch sử—Phụ tỉnh Đa Minh Việt Nam hải ngoại," 2006, accessed May 9, 2023, daminhptvn.org/?page_id=33/; "Giới thiệu—Phụ Tỉnh Đa Minh Việt Nam Hải Ngoại," 2006, accessed May 9, 2023, daminhptvn.org/?page_id=33/; Tim Drake, "800 Years of Preaching the Gospel, Dominicans Celebrate Jubilee," *Catholic Digest*, November 5, 2016, accessed May 9, 2023, https://www.catholicdigest.com/amp/faith/201611-05800-years-of-preaching-the-gospel.

73. The priest completed a master's program at the Université de Montréal in 1956. Bùi Đức Sinh, "Aspects de l'évolution littéraire et scientifique au Vietnam" (master's thesis, Université de Montréal, 1956).

74. Bùi Đức Sinh, *Giáo hội công giáo Việt Nam, Phụ chương*, 5.

75. Bùi Đức Sinh, *Giáo hội công giáo Việt Nam* (Calgary, AB: Veritas, 1998).
76. Nguyễn, "Bắc di cư in the Diaspora."
77. Hội ái hữu Bùi Chu tại Hoa Kỳ, *Đặc san Bùi Chu, 1989: Kỷ niệm 141 năm thành lập giáo phận Bùi Chu từ 5-9-1848 đến 1989* (Garden Grove, CA: Hội ái hữu gia đình Bùi Chu tại Hoa Kỳ, 1989).
78. Hội ái hữu Bùi Chu tại Hoa Kỳ, *Đặc san Bùi Chu.*
79. Viet Stories, "Oral History of Ung Canh Bui," February 23, 2012, accessed June 15, 2022, https://calisphere.org/item/ark:/81235/d8r85d/.
80. Viet Stories, "Oral History of Dzung Bach," February 24, 2012, accessed June 15, 2022, https://calisphere.org/item/ark:/81235/d8kk2t.
81. Viet Stories, "Oral History of Dzung Bach"; Viet Stories, "Oral History of Paulette Nguyen," August 30, 2012, accessed June 15, 2022, https://calisphere.org/item/ark:/81235/d89183; Viet Stories, "Oral History of Antony LeDuc," October 23, 2012, accessed June 15, 2022, https://calisphere.org/item/ark:/81235/d8dn2z; Viet Stories, "Oral History of Nguyen Dinh Cuong," May 5, 2012, accessed June 15, 2022, https://calisphere.org/item/ark:/81235/d8s172/?order=0.
82. Trần Quy Phúc, application, FVPPA/box 58/folder 194, https://www.vietnam.ttu.edu/virtualarchive/items.php?item=1849104058000/.

Conclusion

1. Nu-Anh Tran, "The Neglect of the Republic of Vietnam in the American Historical Memory," in Vu and Fear, *The Republic of Vietnam*, 173–78; Thuy Vo Dang, "The Preservation and Production of Diasporic Knowledge: Oral History and Archival Contributions," and Quan Tue Tran, "Remembering War and Migration: Mapping the Contours of Diasporic Vietnamese Memoryscapes," in Peché, Vo, and Vu, *Toward a Framework*, 240–56.
2. Vo Dang, "Anticommunism as Cultural Praxis"; Nguyen, "(Re)making the South Vietnamese Past."
3. Recent works include Phi Hong Su, *The Border Within: Vietnamese Migrants Transforming Ethnic Nationalism in Berlin* (Redwood City, CA: Stanford University Press, 2022); Tam T. T. Ngo and Nga T. Mai, "In Search of a Vietnamese Buddhist Space in Germany," in Meyer and van der Veer, *Refugees and Religion*, 105–22; Janet Alison Hoskins and Thi Hien Nguyen, "Vietnamese Transnational Religions: The Cold War Polarities of Temples in 'Little Hanois' and 'Little Saigons,'" in *Transnational Religious Spaces: Religious Organizations and Interactions in Africa, East Asia, and Beyond*, ed. Philip Clart and Adam Jones (Berlin: De Gruyter Oldenbourg, 2020), 183–210.
4. On the clash between northern evacuees' interests and those of the population in the south, see Picard, "'They Eat the Flesh of Children.'"
5. Goscha, *Vietnam*, chap. 9.
6. I borrow this expression from Louis A. Wiesner, *Victims and Survivors: Displaced Persons and Other War Victims in Viet-Nam, 1954-1975* (New York: Greenwood Press, 1988).
7. Goodwin-Gill, "The Politics of Refugee Protection."
8. On the global war and its entanglement with regional conflicts, see Odd Arne Westad, *The Global Cold War: Third World Interventions and the Making of Our*

Times (Cambridge: Cambridge University Press, 2007); Lüthi, *Cold Wars*. On a long peace, see John Lewis Gaddis, "The Long Peace: Elements of Stability in the Postwar International System," *International Security* 10, no. 4 (1986): 99–142; John Lewis Gaddis, "The Cold War, the Long Peace, and the Future," *Diplomatic History* 16, no. 2 (1992): 234–46. For a rebuttal, see Paul Thomas Chamberlin, *The Cold War's Killing Fields: Rethinking the Long Peace* (New York: HarperCollins, 2018).

9. Heonik Kwon, *Ghosts of War in Vietnam* (Cambridge: Cambridge University Press, 2008); Kwon, *The Other Cold War*. On the subjectivity, see also Masuda, *Cold War Crucible*.

10. For a similar attempt to bridge the local to the global but on initiatives to make peace, see Le-Tormala, *Postwar Journeys*, 3–4.

Selected Bibliography

This is a list of the main archival funds and a selection of publications in the secondary literature. It is not an exhaustive bibliography of the literature, nor does it fully represent all of the works and documents I have consulted. For example, printed primary sources such as newspapers and other publications produced by the evacuees are not listed here but appear in full in the endnotes. This selection only serves as a guide for anyone interested in the history of the evacuees, the Vietnam wars, the Cold War, the Church's history, and population movements.

Primary Sources

Archives of the Archdiocese of New York, including the Francis Cardinal Spellman Collection
Archives nationales d'outre-mer (ANOM), including Haut Commissariat en Indochine (HCI); Fonds du Service du conseiller diplomatique (Consdiplo); and Fonds du Service de Protection de la Représentation civile française et du Corps expéditionnaire (SPCE)
Archives of the Comité international de la Croix-Rouge (CICR)
Archives of the Établissement de Communication et de Production Audiovisuelle de la Défense (ECPAD)
Archives of the Families of Vietnamese Political Prisoners Association (FVPPA)
Archives of the Foreign Relations of the United States (FRUS)
Archives of Michigan State University (MSU), including the Wesley Fishel Papers
Archives of the Service historique de l'armée de Terre (SHAT), including Archives de l'Indochine (série 10H); Archives du 2ème bureau (série 10T); and Archives du Service de documentation extérieure et de contre-espionage (série GR10R)
Đảng Cộng sản Việt Nam. *Văn kiện Đảng [Party Documents]*. Vols. 8–49 (from 1945 to 1989). Hanoi: NXB Chính trị quốc gia, 2000–2006.
Trung tâm Lưu trữ quốc gia 2 (National Archival Center 2) (TTLT2), including Phủ Thủ tướng (PThT; Office of the Prime Minister); Phủ Tổng thống Đệ nhất Cộng Hòa (PTTĐICH; Office of the Presidency, First Republic); Phủ Tổng thống Đệ nhị Cộng Hòa (PTTĐIICH; Office of the Presidency, Second Republic); Sưu tập liệu ảnh (Photographs collection); and Ủy ban Lãnh đạo Quốc gia (UBLĐQG; High National Council)

Archives of the United Nations High Commissioner for Refugees (UNHCR)
National Archives and Records Administration (NARA), including RG 49, US Foreign Assistance Agencies; and RG 472, US Forces in Southeast Asia
United Nations Archives and Records Management Section (UNARMS), including Fact-Finding Mission to South Vietnam; Javier Pérez de Cuéllar Files; and Kurt Waldheim Files

Selected Secondary Sources

Ahern, Thomas L., Jr. *CIA and Rural Pacification and South Vietnam*. Washington, DC: Center for the Study of Intelligence, CIA, 2001.
Alberigo, Giuseppe, and Joseph A. Komonchak, eds. *History of Vatican II*. 6 vols. Leuven, Belgium: Peeters, 1995.
Anderson, David. *Facing My Lai: Moving beyond the Massacre*. Lawrence: University Press of Kansas, 1998.
Andersson, Stefan, ed. *Revisiting the Vietnam War and International Law: Views and Interpretation of Richard Falk*. Cambridge: Cambridge University Press, 2018.
Ang Cheng Guan. *Ending the Vietnam War: The Vietnamese Communists' Perspective*. London: Routledge, 2003.
Applegate, Celia. *A Nation of Provincials: The German Idea of Heimat*. Berkeley: University of California Press, 1990.
Artaud, Denise. "La menace américaine et le règlement indochinois à la conférence de Genève" [The American Threat and the Indochinese Settlement at the Geneva Conference]. *Histoire, économie et société* 13, no. 1 (1994): 47–62.
Asselin, Pierre. *A Bitter Peace: Washington, Hanoi, and the Making of the Paris Agreement*. Chapel Hill: University of North Carolina Press, 2002.
Asselin, Pierre. "The Democratic Republic of Vietnam and the 1954 Geneva Conference: A Revisionist Critique." *Cold War History* 11, no. 2 (2010): 155–95.
Asselin, Pierre. "National Liberation by Other Means: US Visitor Diplomacy in the Vietnam War." *Past and Present* (2024): advance access.
Asselin, Pierre. *Vietnam's American War*. Cambridge: Cambridge University Press, 2018.
Assemblée internationale pour le pansement des blessures de guerre et pour la reconstruction du Vietnam. *Quelques orientations de la reconstruction du Viet-Nam* [Several Directions for Rebuilding Vietnam]. Paris: Fraternité Vietnam, 1975.
Atkinson, Stan. *The Village That Refuses to Die*. 1962. TVT, 56 min.
Biggs, David Andrew. "Canals in the Mekong Delta from 200 C.E. to the Present." In *Water Encyclopedia*, edited by J. H. Lehr and J. Keeley. 2005. https://doi.org/10.1002/047147844X.wh18.
Blanc, Marie-Eve. *Tương tế hội, La pratique associative vietnamienne, Tradition et modernité* [*Tương tế hội*, Vietnamese Associational Practices, Tradition and Modernity]. Aix-en-Provence: Université de Provence, 1994.
Blanchet, Marie-Thérèse. *La naissance de l'état associé du Viêt-Nam* [The Birth of the Associated State of Vietnam]. Paris: M. Th. Génin, 1954.
Blickle, Peter. *Heimat: A Critical Theory of the German Idea of Homeland*. Rochester, NY: Camden House, 2002.

SELECTED BIBLIOGRAPHY

Bon Tempo, Carl. *Americans at the Gate: The United States and Refugees during the Cold War*. Princeton, NJ: Princeton University Press, 2009.

Bourdeaux, Pascal. *Bouddhisme Hòa Hảo, d'un royaume à l'autre: Religion et Révolution au Sud Viêt Nam (1935-1955)* [Hoa Hao Buddhism, from One Kingdom to Another: Religion and Revolution in South Vietnam (1935-1955)]. Paris: Les Indes savantes, 2022.

Bradley, Mark Philip. *Imagining Vietnam and America: The Making of Postcolonial Vietnam, 1919-1950*. Chapel Hill: University of North Carolina Press, 2000.

Bradley, Mark Philip, and Viet Thanh Nguyen. "Vietnam: American and Vietnamese Public Diplomacy." In *Isolate or Engage: Adversarial States, US Foreign Policy, and Public Diplomacy*, edited by Geoffrey Wiseman, 110-39. Redwood City, CA: Stanford University Press, 2015.

Bridel, Renée. *Neutralité: Une voie pour le tiers monde?* [Neutrality: A Path for the Third World?] Paris: L'Âge d'Homme, 1968.

Broussole, Bernard, and Lucien Provençal. "L'évacuation des catholiques du Tonkin en 1954-1955" [The Evacuation of Catholics from Tonkin in 1954-1955]. *Bulletin de l'Association amicale Santé navale et d'Outre-mer* 125 (2013): 24–30.

Bùi Chí Thanh. "Công giáo (hoạt động chính trị sau cách mạng 1.11.1963)" [Catholics (Political Activities after the 1.11.1963 Revolution)]. PhD diss., ĐH Sài Gòn, 1971.

Bùi Diễm. *Gọng kìm lịch sử, Hồi Ký* [In the Jaws of History: A Memoir]. Paris: SudAsie, 2000.

Bùi Đức Sinh. "Aspects de l'évolution littéraire et scientifique au Vietnam" [Aspects of Literary and Scientific Evolution in Vietnam]. Master's thesis, Université de Montréal, 1956.

Bùi Đức Sinh. *Giáo hội công giáo Việt Nam* [The Catholic Church in Vietnam]. Calgary, AB: Veritas, 1998.

Bùi Đức Sinh. *Giáo hội công giáo Việt Nam, Phụ chương* [The Catholic Church in Vietnam: A Supplement]. Calgary, AB: Veritas, 2000.

Bui, Long T. *Returns of War: South Vietnam and the Price of Refugee Memory*. New York: New York University Press, 2018.

Bùi Văn Lương. "The Role of Friendly Nations." In *Vietnam: The First Five Years; An International Symposium*, edited by Richard W. Lindholm, 48-54. East Lansing: Michigan State University Press, 1959.

Campeau, Olivier. "La perception française de l'Inde durant la guerre d'Indochine, 1947-1954: une étude de cas du mouvement anticolonialiste sur la scène internationale avant Bandung" [French Perception of India during the Indochina War, 1947-1954: A Case Study of International Anticolonialism before Bandung]. Master's thesis, Université du Québec à Montréal, 2014.

Carter, James M. *Inventing Vietnam: The United States and State Building, 1954-1968*. Cambridge: Cambridge University Press, 2008.

Catton, Philip. *Diem's Final Failure: Prelude to America's War in Vietnam*. Lawrence: University Press of Kansas, 2002.

Catton, Philip. "'It Would Be a Terrible Thing If We Handed These People over to the Communists': The Eisenhower Administration, Article 14(d), and the Origins of the Refugee Exodus from North Vietnam." *Diplomatic History* 39, no. 2 (2015): 331-58.

Catton, Philip. "The Royal Navy's Vietnam War: H.M.S. Warrior and the Evacuation from North Vietnam, September 1954." *Historical Research* 83, no. 220 (2010): 358–77.
Césari, Laurent. *L'Indochine en guerres, 1945-1993* [*Indochina at War, 1945-1993*]. Paris: Belin, 1995.
Césari, Laurent. "Business as (Almost) Usual: The French Consulate General in Saigon during the Break of Diplomatic Relations between France and the Republic of Vietnam, 1965–1973." In *Consuls in the Cold War*, edited by Sue Onslow and Lori Maguire, 135–50. Leiden, The Netherlands: Brill, 2023.
Chakrabarty, Dipesh. "Remembered Villages: Representation of Hindu-Bengali Memories in the Aftermath of the Partition." *Economic & Political Weekly* 31, no. 32 (1996): 2143–45, 2147.
Chamberlin, Paul Thomas. *The Cold War's Killing Fields: Rethinking the Long Peace.* New York: HarperCollins, 2018.
Chan, Shelly. *Diaspora's Homeland: Modern China in the Age of Global Migration.* Durham, NC: Duke University Press, 2018.
Chanda, Nayan. *Brother Enemy: The War after the War.* New York: Harcourt, 1986.
Chang, Yao-Chiu. *Communist China's Strategy towards ASEAN Countries.* Taipei: World Anti-Communist League, China Chapter, 1986.
Chantavanich, Supang, and Paul Rabe. "Thailand and the Indochinese Refugees: Fifteen Years of Compromise and Uncertainty." *Southeast Asian Journal of Social Science* 18, no. 1 (1990): 66–80.
Chantavanich, Supang, and E. Bruce Reynolds, eds. *Indochinese Refugees: Asylum and Resettlement.* Bangkok: Institute of Asian Studies, 1988.
Chapman, Jessica. *Cauldron of Resistance: Ngo Dinh Diem, the United States, and 1950s Southern Vietnam.* Ithaca, NY: Cornell University Press, 2013.
Chapman, Jessica. "Staging Democracy: South Vietnam's 1955 Referendum to Depose Bao Dai." *Diplomatic History* 30, no. 4 (2006): 671–703.
Chen, Jian. *Mao's China & the Cold War.* Chapel Hill: University of North Carolina Press, 2001.
Chen, Jian. "China, the Vietnam War, and the Sino-American Rapprochement, 1968–1973." In *The Third Indochina War: Conflict between China, Vietnam, and Cambodia, 1972-1979*, edited by Odd Arne Westad and Sophie Quinn-Judge, 33–64. London: Routledge, 2006.
Chen, Jian. "China and the Indochina Settlement at the Geneva Conference of 1954." In *The First Vietnam War: Colonial Conflict and Cold War Crisis*, edited by Mark Lawrence and Frederik Logevall, 240–62. Cambridge, MA: Harvard University Press, 2007.
Chiu, Hungdah. "Current Developments: China's Legal Position on Protecting Chinese Residents in Vietnam." *American Journal of International Law* 74, no. 3 (1980): 685–93.
Collins, James Lawton. *The Development and Training of the South Vietnamese Army, 1950-1972.* Washington, DC: Department of the Army, US Government Printing Office, 1975.
Columban Fathers. *Those Who Journeyed with Us, 1918-2016.* St. Columbans, NE: Missionary Society of St. Columban, 2017.

Cooper, Chester. *The Lost Crusade: America in Vietnam*. New York: Dodd, Mead, 1970.
Curless, Gareth, and Martin Thomas, eds. *The Oxford Handbook of Late Colonial Insurgencies*. Oxford: Oxford University Press, 2023.
Dacy, Douglas. *Foreign Aid, War and Economic Development: South Vietnam, 1955-1975*. Cambridge: Cambridge University Press, 1986.
Đặng Phong. *Kinh tế miền Nam Việt Nam thời kỳ 1955-1975* [South Vietnam's Economy in 1955-1975]. Hanoi: NXB Khoa học xã hội, 2004.
Đặng Phong. *"Phá rào" trong kinh tế vào đêm trước Đổi mới* [Breaking the Walls of Economy on the Eve of Doi Moi]. Hanoi: NXB Tri thức, 2009.
Darcourt, Pierre. *De Lattre au Viet-Nam: Une année de victoires* [De Lattre in Vietnam: A Year of Victories]. Paris: La Table ronde, 1965.
Das, Veena. *Critical Events: An Anthropological Perspective on Contemporary India*. Oxford: Oxford University Press, 1995.
Davies, Sarah. "Saving Refugees or Saving Borders? Southeast Asian States and the Indochinese Refugee Crisis." *Global Change, Peace & Security* 18, no. 1 (2006): 3-24.
de Jaegher, Raymond. *The Enemy Within: An Eyewitness Account of the Communist Conquest of China*. New York: Doubleday, 1952.
de Jaegher, Raymond. *The Growth of the Free Pacific Association in Vietnam*. Saigon: Free Pacific Association, 1962.
Demmer, Amanda. *After Saigon's Fall: Refugees and US-Vietnamese Relations, 1975-2000*. New York: Cambridge University Press, 2021.
DeVido, Elise Anne. "'Buddhism for This World': The Buddhist Revival in Vietnam, 1920 to 1951, and Its Legacy." In *Modernity and Re-enchantment: Religion in Post-Revolutionary Vietnam*, edited by Philip Taylor, 250-96. Singapore: ISEAS, 2007.
Diocesan Committee for the Alberta Centennial Celebration. *Timeline: Celebrating Contributions of the Roman Catholic Diocese of Calgary to the Province of Alberta*. Calgary: Diocese of Calgary, 2005.
Đỗ Mậu. *Việt Nam máu lửa quê hương tôi* [Vietnam, My Homeland on Fire]. Westminster, CA: NXB Văn nghệ, 1993.
Đoàn Độc Thư and Xuân Huy. *Giám mục Lê Hữu Từ & Phát Diệm* [Bishop Lê Hữu Từ and Phát Diệm]. Saigon: Kim Studio, 1973.
Dommen, Arthur J. *The Indochinese Experience of the French and the Americans: Nationalism and Communism in Cambodia, Laos, and Vietnam*. Bloomington: Indiana University Press, 2002.
Donovan, John T. "The American Catholic Press and the Cold War in Asia: The Case of Father Patrick O'Connor, S.S.C. (1899-1987)." *American Catholic Studies* 115, no. 3 (2004): 23-49.
Dooley, Thomas A. *Deliver Us from Evil*. New York: Farrar, Straus, and Cudahy, 1956.
Dorais, Louis-Jacques. "Vietnamese Communities in Canada, France, and Denmark." *Journal of Refugee Studies* 11, no. 2 (1998): 107-25.
Elkind, Jessica. *Aid under Fire: Nation Building and the Vietnam War*. Lexington: University Press of Kentucky, 2016.
Elliott, David W. P. *Changing Worlds: Vietnam's Transition from Cold War to Globalization*. Oxford: Oxford University Press, 2014.

Elliott, David W. P., ed. *The Third Indochina Conflict*. Boulder, CO: Westview Press, 1981.
Elliott, Duong Van Mai. *The Sacred Willow: Four Generations in the Life of a Vietnamese Family*. Oxford: Oxford University Press, 1999.
Ély, Paul. *Mémoires: L'Indochine dans la tourmente* [Memoirs: Indochina in Upheaval], vol. 1. Paris: Plon, 1964.
Ernst, John. *Forging a Fateful Alliance: Michigan State University and the Vietnam War*. East Lansing: Michigan State University Press, 1998.
Espiritu, Yến Lê. "Toward a Critical Refugee Study: The Vietnamese Refugee Subject in US Scholarship." *Journal of Vietnamese Studies* 1, nos. 1–2 (2006): 410–33.
Espiritu, Yến Lê. *Body Counts: The Vietnam War and Militarized Refugees*. Berkeley: University of California Press, 2014.
Fall, Bernard B. "Commentary: Bernard B. Fall on Bùi Văn Lương." In *Vietnam: The First Five Years; An International Symposium*, edited by Richard W. Lindholm, 56. East Lansing: Michigan State University Press, 1959.
Fall, Bernard B. *The Two Vietnams*. New York: Praeger, 1963.
Fall, Bernard B. *Le Viêt Minh, La République démocratique du Viêt-Nam, 1945-1960* [The Viet Minh, the Democratic Republic of Vietnam, 1945-1960]. Paris: Armand Colin, 1960.
Fear, Sean. "The Ambiguous Legacy of Ngô Đình Diệm in South Vietnam's Second Republic (1967-1975)." *Journal of Vietnamese Studies* 11, no. 1 (2016): 1–75.
Fear, Sean. "Saigon Goes Global: South Vietnam's Quest for International Legitimacy in the Age of Détente." *Diplomatic History* 42, no. 3 (2018): 428–55.
Firestone, Bernard. "The U Thant–Stevenson Peace Initiatives in Vietnam, 1964–1965." *Diplomatic History* 1, no. 3 (1977): 285–95.
Firestone, Bernard. "Failed Mediation: U Thant, the Johnson Administration, and the Vietnam War." *Diplomatic History* 37, no. 5 (2013): 1060–89.
Fontaine, Darcie. "At the Crossroads of East and West: Christianity and the Legacy of Colonialism in North Africa." In *Decolonization and the Remaking of Christianity*, edited by Elizabeth Ann Foster and Udi Greenberg, 105–24. Philadelphia: University of Pennsylvania Press, 2023.
Fontaine, Darcie. *Decolonizing Christianity: Religion and the End of Empire in France and Algeria, 1940-1965*. Cambridge: Cambridge University Press, 2016.
Foster, Elizabeth Ann, and Udi Greenberg, ed. *Decolonization and the Remaking of Christianity*. Philadelphia: University of Pennsylvania Press, 2023.
Frankum, Robert B. *Operation Passage to Freedom: The United States Navy in Vietnam, 1954-1955*. Lubbock: Texas Tech University Press, 2007.
Furet, François. *Penser la révolution française* [Thinking about the French Revolution]. Paris: Gallimard, 1978.
Furet, François, and Mona Ozouf. *Dictionnaire critique de la révolution française* [A Critical Dictionary of the French Revolution]. Paris: Flammarion, 1988.
Gaddis, John Lewis. "The Long Peace: Elements of Stability in the Postwar International System." *International Security* 10, no. 4 (1986): 99–142.
Gaddis, John Lewis. "The Cold War, the Long Peace, and the Future." *Diplomatic History* 16, no. 2 (1992): 234–46.

Gandhi Espiritu, Evyn Le. *Archipelago of Resettlement: Vietnamese Refugee Settlers in Guam and Israel-Palestine.* Berkeley: University of California Press, 2022.

Garret, Martin. "Playing the China Card? Revisiting France's Recognition of Communist China, 1963–1964." *Journal of Cold War Studies* 10, no. 1 (2008): 52–80.

Gettig, Eric. "'Trouble Ahead in Afro-Asia': The United States, the Second Bandung Conference, and the Struggle for the Third World, 1964–1965." *Diplomatic History* 39, no. 1 (2015): 126–56.

Gheddo, Piero. *The Cross and the Bo-Tree: Catholics & Buddhists in Vietnam.* New York: Sheed and Ward, 1970.

Gibbons, William Conrad. *The US Government and the Vietnam War: Executive and Legislative Roles and Relationships, Part III.* Princeton, NJ: Princeton University Press, 1984.

Giebel, Christoph. *Imagined Ancestries of Vietnamese Communism: Ton Duc Thang and the Politics of History and Memory.* Seattle: University of Washington Press, 2011.

Giebel, Christoph. "Museum-Shrine: Revolution and Its Tutelary Spirit in the Village of My Hoa Hung." In *The Country of Memory: Remaking the Past in Late Socialist Vietnam*, edited by Hue-Tam Ho Tai, 77–108. Berkeley: University of California Press, 2001.

Gill, Jill K. *Embattled Ecumenism: The National Council of Churches, the Vietnam War, and the Trials of the Protestant Left.* DeKalb: Northern Illinois University Press, 2011.

Goodman, Allan E. *Politics in War: The Bases of Political Community in South Vietnam.* Cambridge, MA: Harvard University Press, 1973.

Goodwin-Gill, Guy. "The Politics of Refugee Protection." *Refugee Survey Quarterly* 27, no. 1 (2008): 8–23.

Goscha, Christopher E. *Historical Dictionary of the Indochina War (1945–1954): An International and Interdisciplinary Approach.* Copenhagen: NIAS Press, 2011.

Goscha, Christopher E. "Le premier échec contre-révolutionnaire au Vietnam: La destruction des partis nationalistes non-communistes devant le Viet Minh et la France en 1946" [The First Counterrevolutionary Failure in Vietnam: The Destruction of Non-Communist Nationalists Before the Viet Minh and France in 1946]. Dipl. d'études approfondies, Université de Paris VII, 1994.

Goscha, Christopher E. *The Road to Dien Bien Phu: A History of the First War for Vietnam.* Princeton, NJ: Princeton University Press, 2022.

Goscha, Christopher E. "Vietnam, the Third Indochina War and the Meltdown of Asian Internationalism." In Westad and Quinn-Judge, *The Third Indochina War,* 152–86.

Goscha, Christopher E. *Vietnam: Un état né de la guerre, 1945–1954* [Vietnam: A State Born out of the War]. Paris: Armand Colin, 2011.

Goscha, Christopher E., and Karine Laplante, eds. *L'échec de la paix en Indochine, 1954–1962* [The Failure of Peace in Indochina, 1954–1962]. Paris: Les Indes savantes, 2010.

Greenberg, Udi. "The Rise of the Global South and the Protestant Peace with Socialism." *Contemporary European History* 29 (2020): 202–19.

Grosser, Pierre. "Une 'création continue'? L'Indochine, le Maghreb et l'Union française" [A Work in Progress? Indochina, the Maghreb, and the French Union]. *Monde(s)* 12, no. 2 (2017): 71-94.

Grosser, Pierre. "La France et l'Indochine (1953-1956): Une 'carte de visite' en 'peau de chagrin'" [France in Indochina (1953-1956): A Calling Card Dwindling into Next to Nothing]. PhD diss., Institut d'études politiques, 2002.

Grossheim, Martin. "'1954 verlor der Vater seine Heimat, 1975 verlor der Sohn sein Vaterland,' Teilung, Flucht und Wiedervereinigung in Vietnam" ['A Father Leaves His Home Village, a Son Leaves His Homeland,' Partition, Flight, and Reunification in Vietnam]. In *Die geteilte Nation: Nationale Verluste und Identitäten im 20. Jahrhundert*, edited by Andreas Hilger and Oliver von Wrochem, 97-115. München, Germany: Oldenbourg Verlag, 2013.

Guillemot, François. "Autopsy of a Massacre: On a Political Purge in the Early Days of the Indochina War (Nam Bo 1947)." *European Journal of East Asian Studies* 9, no. 2 (2010): 225-65.

Guillemot, François. "Au coeur de la fracture vietnamienne: l'élimination de l'opposition nationaliste et anticolonialiste dans le Nord du Vietnam (1945-1946)" [At the Heart of the Vietnamese Fracture: The Elimination of Nationalist and Anticolonialist Opposition in Northern Vietnam (1945-1946)]. In *Naissance d'un Etat-Parti: Le Viet Nam depuis 1945*, edited by Christopher E. Goscha and Benoît de Tréglodé, 175-216. Paris: Les Indes savantes, 2004.

Guillemot, François. *Dai Viêt, indépendance et révolution au Viêt-Nam: L'échec de la troisième voie (1938-1955)* [Dai Viet Independence and Revolution in Vietnam: The Failure of the Third Path (1938-1955)]. Paris: Les Indes savantes, 2012.

Guillemot, François. "An Intellectual through Revolution, War and Exile: The Political Commitment of Nguyen Ngoc Huy (1924-1990)." In *New Perceptions of the Vietnam War: Essays on the War, the South Vietnamese Experience, the Diaspora and the Continuing Impact*, edited by Nathalie Huynh Chau Nguyen, 41-71. Jefferson, NC: McFarland, 2015.

Guillemot, François. *Viêt-Nam, fractures d'une nation: Une histoire contemporaine de 1858 à nos jours* [Vietnam, A Nation's Fractures: A Modern History from 1858 to the Present]. Paris: La Découverte, 2018.

Haas, Harry. *Vietnam: The Other Conflict*. London: Sheed and Ward, 1971.

Hammer, Ellen J. *A Death in November: America in Vietnam, 1963*. New York: E.P. Dutton, 1987.

Han, Xiaorong. "From Resettlement to Rights Protection: The Collective Actions of the Refugees from Vietnam in China since the Late 1970s." *Journal of Chinese Overseas* 10 (2014): 197-219.

Han, Xiaorong. "Spoiled Guests or Dedicated Patriots? The Chinese in North Vietnam, 1954-1978." *International Journal of Asian Studies* 6 (2009): 1-36.

Hansen, Peter. "Bắc Di Cư: Catholic Refugees from the North of Vietnam, and Their Role in the Southern Republic, 1954-1959." *Journal of Vietnamese Studies* 4, no. 3 (2009): 173-211.

Hansen, Peter. "The Virgin Heads South: Northern Catholic Refugees in South Vietnam, 1954-1964," PhD diss., Melbourne College of Divinity, 2008.

Hardy, Andrew. "Internal Transnationalism and the Formation of the Vietnamese Diaspora." In *State/Nation/Transnation: Perspectives on Transnationalism in the Asia-Pacific*, edited by Brenda S. A. Yeoh and Katie Willis, 218–37. London: Routledge, 2004.

Hardy, Andrew. "Rules and Resources: Negotiating the Household Registration System in Vietnam under Reform." *Sojourn* 16, no. 2 (2001): 187–212.

Harouel-Bureloup, Véronique. "L'action du CICR en Indochine" [The Work of the ICRC in Indochina]. *Grotius* (2010): 1–4.

Heineman, Kenneth J. *Campus Wars: The Peace Movement at American State Universities in the Vietnam Era*. New York: New York University Press, 1992.

Hershberger, Mary. *Traveling to Vietnam: American Peace Activists and the War*. Syracuse, NY: Syracuse University Press, 1998.

Ho Tai, Hue-Tam, ed. *The Country of Memory: Remaking the Past in Late Socialist Vietnam*. Berkeley: University of California Press, 2001.

Hoàng Chí Hiếu. *Đôi bờ giới tuyến (1954-1967)* [*On Both Sides of the Parallel (1954-1967)*]. Ho Chi Minh City: NXB Tổng hợp T.P. Hồ Chí Minh, 2014.

Hoàng Linh. *Tội ác của đế quốc Mỹ, Trong việc bắt ép đồng bào di cư vào Nam* [*The Atrocities of American Imperialists, Forcing Compatriots to Migrate to the South*]. Hanoi: NXB Sự thật, 1955.

Hoàng Văn Chí. *The Fate of the Last Viets*. Saigon: Hoa Mai, 1956.

Hoàng Văn Chí. *From Colonialism to Communism*. New York: Praeger, 1964.

Hoàng, Tuấn. "The August Revolution, the Fall of Saigon, and Postwar Reeducation Camps: Understanding Vietnamese Diasporic Anticommunism." In Péché, Vo, and Vu, *Toward A Framework*, 76–95.

Hoàng, Tuấn. "The Early South Vietnamese Critique of Communism." In *Dynamics of the Cold War in Asia*, edited by Tưởng Vũ and Wasana Wongsurawat, 17–32. New York: Palgrave Macmillan, 2009.

Hoàng, Tuấn. "The Resettlement of Vietnamese Refugee Religious, Priests, and Seminarians in the United States, 1975–1977." *US Catholic Historian* 37, no. 3 (2019): 99–122.

Hội ái hữu Bùi Chu tại Hoa Kỳ. *Kỷ yếu địa phận Bùi Chu: Kỷ yếu ghi nhớ 50 năm địa phận Bùi Chu được trao hoàn toàn cho hàng giáo VN (1936-1986)* [*The Almanac of the Diocese of Bùi Chu: 50 Years of Belonging Entirely to the Church of Vietnam (1936-1986)*]. Santa Ana, CA: Hội ái hữu gia đình Bùi Chu tại Hoa Kỳ, 1986.

Hội ái hữu Bùi Chu tại Hoa Kỳ. *Đặc San Bùi Chu, 1989: Kỷ niệm 141 năm thành lập giáo phận Bùi Chu từ 5-9-1848 đến 1989* [*The Bulletin of Bui Chu, 1989. Remembering 141 Years since the Creation of the Diocese of Bùi Chu from September 5, 1848, to 1989*]. Garden Grove, CA: Hội ái hữu gia đình Bùi Chu tại Hoa Kỳ, 1989.

Holcombe, Alec G. *Mass Mobilization in the Democratic Republic of Vietnam, 1945-1960*. Honolulu: University of Hawai'i Press, 2020.

Hoskins, Janet Alison, and Thi Hien Nguyen. "Vietnamese Transnational Religions: The Cold War Polarities of Temples in 'Little Hanois' and 'Little Saigons'." In *Transnational Religious Spaces: Religious Organizations and Interactions in Africa, East Asia, and Beyond*, edited by Philip Clart and Adam Jones, 183–210. Berlin: De Gruyter Oldenbourg, 2020.

Hourmant, François. *Le désenchantement des clercs, Figures de l'intellectuel dans l'après-Mai 68* [*The Disillusionment of the Wizards: Features of the Intellectual in the Post-May 1968 Era]. Rennes, France: Presses Universitaires de Rennes, 1997.

How the Republic of China Views the Normalization of Relations between the US and Chinese Communist Regime. Taipei: World Anti-Communist League, China Chapter, 1978.

Huynh, Kinh-Luyen. "L'accueil des réfugiés vietnamiens et indochinois après la guerre du Vietnam par le Canada et les États-Unis (1975–1981)" [The Reception of Vietnamese and Indochinese Refugees in Canada and the United States after the Vietnam War (1975–1981)]. Master's thesis, Université du Québec à Montréal, 2021.

Immerwahr, Daniel. Thinking Small: The United States and the Lure of Community Development. Cambridge, MA: Harvard University Press, 2015.

Jacobs, Jeffrey W. "Mekong Committee History and Lessons for River Basin Development." Geography Journal 161, no. 2 (1995): 135–48.

Jacobs, Seth. America's Miracle Man in Vietnam: Ngo Dinh Diem, Religion, Race and US Intervention in Southeast Asia, 1950-1957. Durham, NC: Duke University Press, 2005.

Jacobs, Seth. Cold War Mandarin: Ngo Dinh Diem and the Origins of America's War in Vietnam. Lanham, MD: Rowman & Littlefield, 2006.

Jammes, Jérémy. "Caodaism in Times of War: Spirits of Struggle and Struggle of Spirits." Sojourn 31, no. 1 (2017): 247–94.

Jammes, Jérémy. Les Oracles du Cao Dai: Étude d'un mouvement religieux vietnamien et de ses réseaux [Cao Dai Oracles: A Study of a Vietnamese Religious Movement and Its Networks]. Paris: Les Indes savantes, 2014.

Jentel, Marie-Odile, and Gisèle Deschênes-Wagner, eds. Tranquilitas, Mélanges en l'honneur de Tran Tam Tinh [Tranquilitas: Compositions in Honor of Tran Tam Tinh]. Québec: Hier pour aujourd'hui, 1994.

Journoud, Pierre. De Gaulle et le Vietnam [De Gaulle and Vietnam]. Paris: Tallandier, 2011.

Journoud, Pierre. "Des Savants français contre la guerre du Vietnam. De l'anti-impérialisme à la construction d'une paix positive" [French Scholars against the Vietnam War: From Anti-Imperialism to Building a Constructive Peace]. Bulletin de l'Institut Pierre Renouveau 44, no. 2 (2016): 87–102.

Journoud, Pierre, and Cécile Ménétrey-Monchau, eds. Vietnam, 1968-1976: La sortie de guerre [Vietnam, 1968-1976: Exiting a War]. Bruxelles: Peter Lang, 2011.

Karnow, Stanley. Vietnam: A History; The First Complete Account of Vietnam at War. New York: Viking Press, 1983.

Kauffman, Christopher J. "Politics, Programs, and Protests: Catholic Relief Services in Vietnam, 1954–1975." Catholic Historical Review 91, no. 2 (2005): 223–50.

Keely, Charles. "The International Refugee Regime(s): The End of the Cold War Matters." International Migration Review 35, no. 1 (2001): 303–14.

Kelley, Liam. "The Biography of the Hồng Bàng Clan as a Medieval Vietnamese Invented Tradition." Journal of Vietnamese Studies 7, no. 2 (2012): 87–130.

Khoo, Nicholas. Collateral Damage: Sino-Soviet Rivalry and the Termination of the Sino-Vietnamese Alliance. New York: Columbia University Press, 2011.

Kim, Monica. *The Interrogation Rooms of the Korean War: The Untold History*. Princeton, NJ: Princeton University Press, 2019.
Krouck, Bernard. *De Gaulle et la Chine: La politique française à l'égard de la République populaire de Chine, 1958-1959* [De Gaulle and China: French Policy and the People's Republic of China, 1958-1959]. Paris: Les Indes savantes, 2012.
Kumar, Aishwary. *Radical Equality: Ambedkar, Gandhi, and the Risk of Democracy*. Stanford: Stanford University Press, 2015.
Kwon, Heonik. *Ghosts of War in Vietnam*. Cambridge: Cambridge University Press, 2008.
Kwon, Heonik. *The Other Cold War*. New York: Columbia University Press, 2010.
Lam Giang. *Nói với quần chúng, Thực nghiệm biện chứng pháp* [Talking to the People, Implementing Dialectics]. Saigon: Ấn quang Nguyễn Văn Cửa, 1956.
Lam, Vinh-The. *The History of South Vietnam: The Quest for Legitimacy and Stability, 1963-1967*. London: Routledge, 2021.
Lansdale, Edward G. *In the Midst of Wars: An American Mission to Southeast Asia*. New York: Harper & Row, 1972.
Larkin, Bruce D. *China and Africa, 1949-1970: The Foreign Policy of the People's Republic of China*. Berkeley: University of California Press, 1971.
Lawrence, Mark Atwood. "Mission Intolerable: Harrison Salisbury's Trip to Hanoi and the Limits of Dissent against the Vietnam War." *Pacific Historical Review* 75, no. 3 (2006): 429-60.
Lê Bảo Hoàng. *Tác giả Việt Nam* [Vietnamese Authors]. Miami: Songvan Magazine xuất bản, 2005.
Le Thi Hoa, Marie. "L'Enseignement catholique aux prises avec les mutations de la société et de l'Église au Vietnam de 1930 à 1990" [Catholic Teaching and the Transformations of the Society and the Church in Vietnam from 1930 to 1990]. PhD diss., Paris Diderot, 2018.
Le Thi Hoa, Marie. "Le rôle des papes Jean XXIII et Paul VI dans la recherche de la paix au Việt Nam de 1963 à 1969" [The Role of Popes John XXIII and Paul VI in the Search for Peace in Vietnam from 1963 to 1969]. *Moussons* 32 (2018): 133-51.
Le-Tormala, Hang Thi Thu. *Postwar Journeys: American and Vietnamese Transnational Peace Efforts since 1975*. Lawrence: University Press of Kansas, 2021.
Leshkowich, Ann Marie. "Standardized Forms of Vietnamese Selfhood: An Ethnographic Genealogy of Documentation." *American Ethnologist* 41, no. 1 (2014): 143-62.
Li, Kevin. "Partisan to Sovereign: The Making of the Bình Xuyên in Southern Vietnam, 1945-1948." *Journal of Vietnamese Studies* 11, nos. 3-4 (2016): 140-87.
Lipman, Jana K. "'Give Us a Ship': The Vietnamese Repatriate Movement on Guam, 1975." *American Quarterly* 64, no. 1 (2012): 1-31.
Lipman, Jana K. *In Camps: Vietnamese Refugees, Asylum Seekers, and Repatriates*. Berkeley: University of California Press, 2020.
Ljunggren, Börje, and Dwight H. Perkins, eds. *Vietnam: Navigating a Rapidly Changing Economy, Society, and Political Order*. Cambridge, MA: Harvard University Press, 2023.

Lo, Shi-Fu. *The Reason of Exodus of Refugees from Vietnam and Its Consequences*. Taipei: World Anti-Communist League, China Chapter, 1980.

Lo, Shi-Fu. *Southeast Asia: Target of Moscow-Peiping Rivalry*. Taipei: World Anti-Communist League, China Chapter, 1980.

Loescher, Gil. *The UNHCR and World Politics: A Perilous Path*. Oxford: Oxford University Press, 2001.

Logevall, Fredrik. *Choosing War: The Lost Chance for Peace and the Escalation of War in Vietnam*. Berkeley: University of California Press, 1999.

Logevall, Fredrik. "De Gaulle, Neutralization, and American Involvement in Vietnam, 1963–1964." *Pacific Historical Review* 61, no. 1 (1992): 69–102.

Loicano, Martin. "Military and Political Roles of Weapons Systems in the Republic of Viet Nam Armed Forces, 1966–1972." PhD diss., Cornell University, 2008.

Lương Khải Minh. *Làm thế nào để giết một Tổng thống? Bút ký lịch sử* [*How to Kill a President? A Historical Memoir*]. Saigon: Đinh Minh Ngọc, 1970.

Lüthi, Lorenz. *Cold Wars: Asia, the Middle East, Europe*. Cambridge: Cambridge University Press, 2020.

Lüthi, Lorenz. "The Non-Aligned Movement and the Cold War, 1961–1973." *Journal of Cold War Studies* 18, no. 4 (2016): 98–147.

Lüthi, Lorenz. "Rearranging International Relations? How Mao's China and de Gaulle's France Recognized Each Other in 1963–1964." *Journal of Cold War Studies* 16, no. 1 (2014): 111–45.

Lüthi, Lorenz. *The Sino-Soviet Split: Cold War in the Communist World*. Princeton, NJ: Princeton University Press, 2008.

Mai Thảo. *Đêm giã từ Hà Nội* [*The Night I Left Hanoi*]. Saigon: Người Việt, 1955.

Malraux, André. *La Condition humaine* [*Man's Fate*]. Paris: Gallimard, 1933.

Marangé, Céline. "Les Relations politiques de l'Union soviétique avec le Vietnam de 1975 à 1995" [The Soviet Union's Political Relationships with Vietnam from 1975 to 1995]. *Outre-mers* 94, nos. 354–55 (2007): 147–71.

Mariani, Paul. *Church Militant: Bishop Kung and Catholic Resistance in Communist Shanghai*. Cambridge, MA: Harvard University Press, 2011.

Marr, David. *Vietnam, 1945: The Quest for Power*. Berkeley: University of California Press, 1997.

Marr, David. *Vietnam: State, War, and Revolution (1945–1946)*. Berkeley: University of California Press, 2013.

Martin, Jean-Clément. *La Terreur, vérités et légendes* [*The Terror, Truth and Legends*]. Paris: Perrin, 2017.

Martini, Edwin A. *Invisible Enemies: The American War on Vietnam, 1975–2000*. Amherst: University of Massachusetts Press, 2007.

Masuda, Hajimu. *Cold War Crucible: The Korean Conflict and the Postwar World*. Cambridge, MA: Harvard University Press, 2014.

Mặt trận quốc gia thống nhất giải phóng Việt Nam. *Anh hùng nước tôi* [*The Heroes of My Country*], 3rd ed. San Jose, CA: Đông Tiến, 1988.

Mayer, Arno. *The Furies: Violence and Terror in the French and Russian Revolutions*. Princeton, NJ: Princeton University Press, 2000.

Mazelaygue, R. P. *Mission dominicaine au Tonkin* [*The Dominican Mission in Tonkin*]. Lyon, France: Perroud, 1921.

McAllister, James. "'Only Religions Count in Vietnam': Thich Tri Quang and the Vietnam War." *Modern Asian Studies* 42, no. 4 (2008): 751–82.
McHale, Shawn. *The First Vietnam War: Violence, Sovereignty, and the Fracture of the South, 1945-1956*. Cambridge: Cambridge University Press, 2021.
McLeod, Mark W. "Nationalism and Religion in Vietnam: Phan Boi Chau and the Catholic Question." *International History Review* 14, no. 4 (1992): 661–80.
Mehta, Harish C. "North Vietnam's Informal Diplomacy with Bertrand Russell: Peace Activism and the International War Crimes Tribunal." *Peace and Change* 37, no. 1 (2012): 64–94.
Mehta, Harish C. *People's Diplomacy of Vietnam: Soft Power in the Resistance War, 1965-1972*. Newcastle upon Tyne: Cambridge Scholar Publishing, 2019.
Melman, Seymour, Melvyn Baron, and Dodge Ely. *In the Name of America: The Conduct of the War in Vietnam by the Armed Forces of the United States as Shown by Published Reports, Compared with the Laws of War Binding on the United States Government and on Its Citizens*. [New York]: Clergy and Laymen Concerned about Vietnam, 1968.
Menon, P. K. "Financing the Lower Mekong River Basin Development." *Pacific Affairs* 44, no. 4 (1972): 566–79.
Meslin, Karine. *Les réfugiés du Mékong: Cambodgiens, Laotiens et Vietnamiens en France* [*The Mekong Refugees: Cambodians, Laotians, and Vietnamese in France*]. Détours, France: Bourdeaux, 2020.
Meyer, Birgit, and Peter van der Veer, eds. *Refugees and Religion: Ethnographic Studies of Global Trajectories*. London: Bloomsbury, 2021.
Miller, Edward. "Buddhist Revival and the Politics of Nation Building: Reinterpreting the 1963 'Buddhist Crisis' in South Vietnam." *Modern Asian Studies* 49, no. 6 (2015): 1903–62.
Miller, Edward. *Misalliance: Ngo Dinh Diem, the United States and the Fate of South Vietnam*. Cambridge, MA: Harvard University Press, 2013.
Moïse, Edwin. *Tonkin Gulf and the Escalation of the Vietnam War*. Chapel Hill: University of North Carolina Press, 1996.
Molloy, Michael J., Peter Duchinsky, Kurt F. Jensen, and Robert Shalka. *Running on Empty: Canada and the Indochinese Refugees, 1975-1980*. Montreal: McGill University Press, 2017.
Morgan, Joseph G. *The Vietnam Lobby: The American Friends of Vietnam, 1955-1975*. Chapel Hill: University of North Carolina Press, 1997.
Moses, Dirk. "Partitions and the Sisyphean Making of Peoples." *Refugee Watch* 46 (2015): 36–50.
Moses, Dirk. "Partitions, Hostages, Transfer: Retributive Violence and National Security." In *Partitions: A Transnational History of Twentieth-Century Territorial Separatism*, edited by Arie M. Dubnov and Laura Robson, 257–95. Redwood City, CA: Stanford University Press, 2019.
Moses, Dirk. *The Problems of Genocide*. Cambridge: Cambridge University Press, 2021.
Moyar, Mark. *Triumph Forsaken: The Vietnam War 1954-1965*. Cambridge: Cambridge University Press, 2006.
Moyn, Samuel. *Christian Human Rights*. Philadelphia: University of Pennsylvania Press, 2015.

Moyn, Samuel. *The Last Utopia: Human Rights in History*. Cambridge, MA: Harvard University Press, 2010.
Mungello, David E. *The Catholic Invasion of China: Remaking Chinese Christianity*. Lanham, MD: Rowman & Littlefield, 2015.
Ngo, Tam T. T., and Nga T. Mai. "In Search of a Vietnamese Buddhist Space in Germany." In Meyer and van der Veer, *Refugees and Religion*, 105–22.
Nguyễn, Bắc. *Au coeur de la ville captive* [*Inside a Captive City*]. Translated by Philippe Papin. Paris: Arléa, 2004.
Nguyễn, Công Luận. *Nationalist in the Viet Nam Wars: Memoirs of a Victim Turned Soldier*. Bloomington: Indiana University Press, 2012.
Nguyen, Duy Lap. *The Unimagined Community: Imperialism and Culture in South Vietnam*. Manchester, UK: Manchester University Press, 2020.
Nguyen, Duy Tân Joëlle. "L'évolution du statut juridique du Viet-Nam et ses répercussions sur les principaux aspects du conflit" [The Evolution of Vietnam's Status and Its Consequences for the Main Aspects of the Conflict]. PhD diss., Université de droit, d'économie et de sciences sociales de Paris, 1975.
Nguyen, Duy Tân Joëlle. "La représentation du Viet-Nam dans les institutions spécialisées" [Vietnamese Representation in Technical Institutions]. *Annuaire français de droit international* 22 (1976): 405–14.
Nguyễn, Hữu Châu. *Les Reflets de nos jours* [*Reflections of Our Days*]. Paris: René Julliard, 1955.
Nguyễn, Joseph. "Bắc di cư in the Diaspora: Mapping a Vietnamese Catholic Refugee Identity." Master's thesis, Columbia University, 2022.
Nguyễn, Khắc Ngữ. *Đại cương về các đảng phái chính trị Việt Nam* [*An Overview of Political Parties in Vietnam*]. Montreal: Tủ sách nghiên cứu sử địa, 1989.
Nguyen, Lien-Hang T. "The Double Diaspora of Vietnam's Catholics." *Orbis* 39, no. 4 (1995): 491–501.
Nguyen, Lien-Hang T. *Hanoi's War: An International History of the War for Peace in Vietnam*. Chapel Hill: University of North Carolina Press, 2012.
Nguyen, Mimi Thi. *The Gift of Freedom: War, Debt, and Other Refugee Passages*. Durham, NC: Duke University Press, 2012.
Nguyen, Nathalie Huynh Chau. *Memory Is Another Country*. London: Bloomsbury, 2009.
Nguyen, Nathalie Huynh Chau. *New Perceptions of the Vietnam War*. Jefferson, NC: McFarland, 2015.
Nguyen, Nathalie Huynh Chau. *South Vietnamese Soldiers: Memories of the Vietnam War and After*. Santa Barbara, CA: Praeger, 2016.
Nguyen, Nathalie Huynh Chau. *Vietnamese Voices: Gender and Cultural Identity in the Vietnamese Francophone Novel*. DeKalb: Southeast Asia Publications, Northern Illinois University Press, 2003.
Nguyễn, Phanxicô Xaviê Văn Thuận, and Bernard F. Law. *The Road of Hope: Thoughts of Light from a Prison Cell*. London: New City, 1997.
Nguyễn, Phi-Vân. "Fighting the First Indochina War Again? Catholic Refugees in South Vietnam, 1954–1959." *Sojourn* 31, no. 1 (2016): 207–46.

Nguyen, Phi-Vân. "Ngô Đình Diệm and the Republic of Vietnam." In *Origins*, edited by Edward Miller and Lien-Hang Nguyen, 302–25. Vol. 1 of *The Cambridge History of the Vietnam War*. New York: Cambridge University Press, 2024.

Nguyen, Phi-Vân. "The Politics of the Southeast Asian Refugee Crisis, 1978–1979." *Journal of Cold War Studies* (forthcoming).

Nguyen, Phi-Vân. "Refugees in Violent Decolonizations." In *The Oxford Handbook of Late Colonial Insurgencies and Counterinsurgencies*, edited by Martin Thomas and Gareth Curless, 565–79. Oxford: Oxford University Press, 2023.

Nguyen, Phi-Vân. "Réfugiés, religion et politique: La signification du regroupement de 1954" [Refugees, Religion, and Politics: The Significance of the 1954 Evacuation]. In *Travail, migrations et culture au Viêt-Nam, du début du 19e s. à nos jours*, edited by Éric Guérassimoff, Thi Phuong Ngoc Nguyen, and Emmanuel Poisson, 185–204. Paris: Maisonneuve Larose, 2020.

Nguyen, Phi-Vân. "Les résidus de la guerre: la mobilisation des réfugiés du nord pour un Vietnam non-communiste, 1954–1965" [War Residues: The Mobilization of Norther Refugees for a Non-Communist Vietnam, 1954–1965]. PhD diss., Université du Québec à Montréal, 2015.

Nguyen, Phi-Vân. "Le saccage de l'ambassade de France à Saigon en juillet 1964, Les réfugiés du Nord face à la double menace de neutralization" [The July 1964 Sack of the French Embassy in Saigon]. *Revue historique des armées* 276 (2014): 57–68.

Nguyen, Phi-Vân. "A Secular State for a Religious Nation: The Republic of Vietnam and Religious Nationalism, 1946–1963." *Journal of Asian Studies* 77, no. 3 (2018): 741–71.

Nguyen, Phi-Vân. "Victims of Atheist Persecution: Transnational Catholic Solidarity and Refugee Protection in Cold War Asia." In Meyer and van der Veer, *Refugees and Religions*, 51–67.

Nguyen, Phi-Vân. "Vietnamese Catholics' Search for Independence, 1941–1963." In *Decolonization and the Remaking of Christianity*, edited by Elizabeth Foster and Udi Greenberg, 51–66. Philadelphia: University of Pennsylvania Press, 2023.

Nguyen, Phi-Vân. "The Vietnamization of Personalism: The Role of Missionaries in the Spread of Personalism in Vietnam, 1930–1961." *French Colonial History* 17 (2017): 103–34.

Nguyen, Phuong Tran. *Becoming Refugee American: The Politics of Rescue in Little Saigon*. Champaign: University of Illinois Press, 2017.

Nguyễn, Quang Hưng. *Katholizismus in Vietnam von 1954 bis 1975* [Catholicism in Vietnam from 1954 to 1975]. Berlin: Logos, 2003.

Nguyễn, Thế Anh. "Le bouddhisme dans la pensée politique du Viêt-Nam traditionnel" [Buddhism in Traditional Vietnamese Political Thought]. *Bulletin de l'École française d'Extrême-Orient* 89 (2002): 127–43.

Nguyễn, Tuấn Cường. "The Promotion of Confucianism in South Vietnam (1955–1975) and the Role of Nguyễn Đăng Thục as a New Confucian Scholar." *Journal of Vietnamese Studies* 10, no. 4 (2016): 30–81.

Nguyen, Van Canh, and Earle Cooper. *Vietnam under Communism, 1975-1982*. Stanford, CA: Hoover Institution Press, 1983.

Nguyễn, Văn Vĩnh. *Savings and Mutual Lending Societies (Ho): A Translation of an Article from a Series by Nguyen Van Vinh on Vietnamese Customs and Institutions*. New Haven, CT: Yale University Southeast Asia Studies, 1949.

Nguyễn, Xuân Tuấn. "Báo chí Việt Nam nhìn dưới khía cạnh kinh tế" [The Economic Dimension of the Vietnamese Printed Press]. PhD diss., Học Viện Quốc Gia Hành Chánh Sài Gòn, 1971.

Nguyen, Y Thien. "Legacies and Diasporic Connectivity: Dialogues and Future Directions of Vietnamese and Vietnamese American Studies." In Peché, Vo, and Vu, *Toward A Framework*, 23–39.

Nguyen, Y Thien. "(Re)making the South Vietnamese Past in America." *Journal of Asian American Studies* 21, no. 1 (2018): 65–103.

Nguyen, Y Thien. "When State Propaganda Becomes Social Knowledge." In Tran and Vu, *Building a Republican Nation in Vietnam*, 202–30.

Nguyen-Marshall, Van. *Between War and the State: Civil Society in South Vietnam, 1954-1975*. Ithaca, NY: Cornell University Press, 2023.

Nguyen-Marshall, Van. "Student Activism in Time of War: Youth in the Republic of Vietnam, 1960s–1970s." *Journal of Vietnamese Studies* 10, no. 2 (2015): 43–81.

Nguyen-Marshall, Van. "Tools of Empire? Vietnamese Catholics in South Vietnam." *Revue de la société historique du Canada* 20, no. 2 (2009): 138–59.

Nhị Hồ. *Điệp viên giữa sa mạc lửa* [*A Spy in a Desert of Fire*]. Hanoi: NXB Công an nhân dân, 2002.

Ninh, Thien-Huong. "The Virgin Mary Became Asian: Diasporic Nationalism among Vietnamese Catholic Refugees in the United States and Germany." In Meyer and van der Veer, *Refugees and Religion*, 68–86.

Ninh, Xuân Thao. "L'État du Viêt-Nam dans ses rapports avec la France (1949–1955)" [The State of Vietnam and Its Relationships with France (1949–1955)]. PhD diss., Université de Bordeaux, 2019.

Noseworthy, William. "Lowland Participation in the Irredentist 'Highlands Liberation Movement' in Vietnam, 1955–1975." *Aktuelle Südostasienforschung/ Current Research on South-East Asia* 6, no. 1 (2013): 7–28.

Nutt, Anita Lauve. "Regroupment, Withdrawals, and Transfers—Vietnam: 1954–1955 Part I." Rand Memorandum RM-6163-ARPA (Santa Monica, CA: RAND, 1969).

Olsen, Mari. *Soviet-Vietnam Relations and the Role of China: Changing Alliances*. London: Routledge, 2006.

Oyen, Meredith. *The Diplomacy of Migration: Transnational Lives and the Making of U.S.-Chinese Relations in the Cold War*. Ithaca, NY: Cornell University Press, 2016.

Parrel, Fernand. "De l'emploi des armes spirituelles ou 43 ans de vie missionnaire au Viet-Nam" [Of the Use of Spiritual Weapons or 43 Years of Missionary Life in Vietnam]. Unpublished manuscript, 1974.

Parrel, Fernand. "Syndicalisme au Vietnam" [Unionism in Vietnam]. *Revue des missions étrangères de Paris* 149 (1967): 38–43.

Paterson, Pat. "The Truth about Tonkin." *Naval History* 22, no. 1 (2008). https://www.usni.org/magazines/naval-history-magazine/2008/february/truth-about-tonkin.

Path, Kosal. *Vietnam's Strategic Thinking during the Third Indochina War*. Madison: University of Wisconsin Press, 2020.

Peché, Linda Ho, Alex Thai Vo, and Tuong Vu, ed. *Toward a Framework for Vietnamese American Studies*. Philadelphia: Temple University Press, 2023.

Pelley, Patricia. *Postcolonial Vietnam: New Histories of the National Past*. Durham, NC: Duke University Press, 2002.

Pergande, Delia T. "Private Voluntary Aid in Vietnam: The Humanitarian Politics of Catholic Relief Services and CARE, 1954–1965." PhD diss., University of Kentucky, 1999.

Peterson, Glen. "The Uneven Development of the International Refugee Regime in Postwar Asia: Evidence from China, Hong Kong and Indonesia." *Journal of Refugee Studies* 25, no. 3 (2012): 326–43.

Phạm Bá Trực. *Kính chúa yêu nước, Đoàn kết giáo lương* [For the Love of God and the Country, Uniting Catholics and Non-Catholics]. Hanoi: Ủy ban Liên Việt toàn quốc, 1954.

Phạm Duy. *Một đời nhìn lại* [Looking Back at a Life], 4 vols. Midway City, CA: PDC Musical Production, 1989.

Phạm Huy Khuê. *Sự thật trên một chuyến tàu di cư Mỹ* [The Truth aboard an Evacuating American Ship]. Hanoi: NXB Văn nghệ, 1955.

Phạm Ngọc Chi Committee of Aid for Resettlement of the Refugees from North Vietnam. *Refugees of North Vietnam: The Refugees Fled for the Sake of Their Faith*. Saigon, n.p.: 1955.

Phạm Văn Liễu. *Trả ta sông núi* [Give Us Back Our Homeland]. Vols. 2–3. Houston: Văn Hoá, 2003.

Phan Thị Xuân Yến. *Ban thống nhất trung ương trong cuộc kháng chiến chống Mỹ cứu nước (1954–1975)* [The Central Committee for Unification in the War of Resistance and National Salvation against the United States (1954–1975)]. Ho Chi Minh City: NXB Tổng hợp T.P. Hồ Chí Minh, 2011.

PhaoLô Lê Đắc Trọng. *Chứng từ của một giám mục: Những câu chuyện về một thời* [A Document from a Bishop: Stories of a Time]. San Diego: Nguyệt san Diễn đàn giáo dân, 2009.

Picard, Jason A. "'Fertile Lands Await': The Promise and Pitfalls of Directed Resettlement, 1954–1959." *Journal of Vietnamese Studies* 11, nos. 3–4 (2016): 58–102.

Picard, Jason A. "'Renegades': The Story of South Vietnam's First National Opposition Newspaper, 1955–1958." *Journal of Vietnamese Studies* 10, no. 4 (2015): 1–29.

Picard, Jason. "'They Eat the Flesh of Children': Migration, Resettlement, and Sectionalism in South Vietnam, 1954–1957." In Tran and Vu, *Building a Republican Nation in Vietnam*, 143–63.

Pinto, Roger. "La France et les États d'Indochine devant les accords de Genève" [France and Indochinese States before the Geneva Agreements]. *Revue française de science politique* 5, no. 1 (1955): 63–91.

Porter, Gareth. "The Myth of the Bloodbath: North Vietnam's Land Reform Reconsidered." *Bulletin of Concerned Asian Scholars* 5, no. 2 (1973): 2–15.

Pouvatchy, Joseph. "Les Vietnamiens au Cambodge, étude d'une minorité étrangère" [The Vietnamese in Cambodia: A Study of a Foreign Minority]. PhD diss., Université de Paris VII, 1975.
Qiang, Zhai. *China and the Vietnam Wars, 1950-1975*. Chapel Hill: University of North Carolina Press, 2000.
Quinn-Judge, Sophie. "Giving Peace a Chance: National Reconciliation and Neutral South Vietnam, 1954–1964." *Peace and Change* 38, no. 4 (2013): 385–410.
Quinn-Judge, Sophie. *The Third Force in the Vietnam War: The Elusive Search for Peace, 1954-1975*. London: I.B. Tauris, 2017.
Radchenko, Sergey. *Two Suns in the Heavens: The Sino-Soviet Struggle for Supremacy, 1962-1967*. Redwood City, CA: Stanford University Press, 2009.
Radchenko, Sergey. *Unwanted Visionaries: The Soviet Failure in Asia at the End of the Cold War*. Oxford: Oxford University Press, 2014.
Randle, Robert F. *The Settlement of the Indochinese War*. Princeton, NJ: Princeton University Press, 1969.
Reilly, Brett. "The Origins of the Vietnamese Civil War and the State of Vietnam." PhD diss., University of Wisconsin–Madison, 2018.
Reilly, Brett. "The Sovereign States of Vietnam, 1945–1955." *Journal of Vietnamese Studies* 11, nos. 3–4 (2016): 103–39.
République du Viêt-Nam, Secrétariat d'Etat à l'économie nationale. *Enquêtes démographiques au Vietnam en 1958* [*Demographic Surveys in Vietnam in 1958*]. Saigon: Institut national de la statistique, 1958.
Robinson, Courtland. *Terms of Refuge: The Indochinese Exodus and International Response*. New York: Zed Books, 1998.
Rousseau, Sabine. "Des chrétiens français face à la guerre du Vietnam" [French Christians before the Vietnam War]. *Vingtième siècle, Revue d'histoire* 47 (1995): 176–90.
Rousseau, Sabine. "Christianisme français et engagement politique à travers les guerres d'Indochine et du Vietnam (1945–1975)" [French Christianism and Political Activism during the Indochina War and the Vietnam War (1945–1975)]. *Chrétiens et sociétés* 7 (2003): 75–98.
Rousseau, Sabine. *La Colombe et le napalm: Des Chrétiens français contre les guerres d'Indochine et du Vietnam, 1945-1975* [*The Dove and the Napalm: French Christians against the Wars in Indochina and Vietnam, 1945–1975*]. Paris: CNRS, 2002.
Rousseau, Sabine. *Françoise Vandermeersch: L'émancipation d'une religieuse* [*Françoise Vandermeersch: The Liberation of a Nun*]. Paris: Karthala, 2012.
Saint Martin, Amaury de. "La contribution de la SAM (Société Auxiliaire des Missions) auprès du monde catholique vietnamien entre 1945 et 1975" [The Contribution of SAM (The Auxiliary Society of Missions) to Vietnamese Catholics from 1945 to 1975]. In *Vincent Lebbe et son héritage*, edited by Arnaud Join-Lambert, Paul Servais, ShenChung Heng Shen, and Éric de Payen, 145–68. Louvain-la-Neuve, Belgium: Presses Universitaires de Louvain, 2017.
Sao Mai. *Trại di cư Pa Gốt Hải Phòng, Phóng sự điều tra* [*The Camp of the Pagoda: Investigation Reportage*]. Hanoi: NXB Văn nghệ, 1955.
Sardesai, D. R. *Indian Foreign Policy in Cambodia, Laos, and Vietnam, 1947-1964*. Berkeley: University of California Press, 1968.

Schama, Simon. *Citizens: A Chronicle of the French Revolution.* New York: Knopf, 1989.
Schwenkel, Christina. *Building Socialism: The Afterlife of East German Architecture in Urban Vietnam.* Durham, NC: Duke University Press, 2020.
Shaplen, Robert. *The Lost Revolution: The U.S. in Vietnam, 1946-1966*, rev. ed. New York: Harper & Row, 1966.
Sheehan, Neil, Hendrick Smith, E. W. Kenworthy, and Fox Butterfield. *The Pentagon Papers: The Secret History of the Vietnam War; The Complete and Unabridged Series as Published by the New York Times.* New York: Bantam Books, 1971.
Sihanouk, Norodom. *My War with the CIA: The Memoirs of Prince Norodom Sihanouk.* New York: Parthenon, 1973.
Słowiak, Jarema. "The Role of the International Commission for Supervision and Control in Vietnam in the Population Exchange between Vietnamese States during the Years 1954-1955." *Prace Historyczne* 146, no. 3 (2019): 621-35.
Small, Ivan. *Currencies of Imagination: Channeling Money and Chasing Mobility in Vietnam.* Ithaca, NY: Cornell University Press, 2019.
Small, Ivan. "Vietnamese Americans and Their Homeland: Transnational Advocacy Efforts and Diasporic Ties." In Peché, Vo, and Vu, *Toward A Framework*, 116-32.
Smith, Andrew F. *Rescuing the World: The Life and Times of Leo Cherne.* Albany: State University of New York Press, 2002.
Song, Lili. "China and the International Refugee Protection Regime: Past, Present, and Potentials." *Refugee Survey Quarterly* 37 (2018): 139-61.
Stewart, Geoffrey. *Vietnam's Lost Revolution: Ngô Đình Diệm's Failure to Build an Independent Nation, 1955-1963.* New York: Cambridge University Press, 2017.
Stur, Heather Marie. "'Hiding Behind the Humanitarian Label': Refugees, Repatriates, and the Rebuilding of America's Benevolent Image After the Vietnam War." *Diplomatic History* 39, no. 2 (2015): 223-44.
Stur, Heather Marie. *Saigon at War: South Vietnam and the Global Sixties.* Cambridge: Cambridge University Press, 2020.
Su, Phi Hong. *The Border Within: Vietnamese Migrants Transforming Ethnic Nationalism in Berlin.* Redwood City, CA: Stanford University Press, 2022.
Suhrke, Astri. *Indochinese Refugees: The Impact of First Asylum Countries and Implications for American Policy; A Study Prepared for the Use of the Joint Economic Committee, Congress of the United States.* Washington DC: US Government Printing Office, 1980.
Tá Chung. *Duy vật với duy thực* [Materialism and Realism]. Bùi Chu: Sao Biển, 1946.
Tan, Mitchell. "Spiritual Fraternities: The Transnational Networks of Ngô Đình Diệm's Personalist Revolution and South Vietnam's First Republic, 1955-1963." *Journal of Vietnamese Studies* 14, no. 2 (2019): 1-67.
Taylor, Keith. *The Birth of Vietnam.* Berkeley: University of California Press, 1983.
Tertrais, Hugues. *La Piastre et le fusil: Le Coût de la guerre d'Indochine, 1945-1954* [The Piaster and the Rifle: The Cost of the Indochina War, 1945-1954]. Paris: Institut de la gestion publique et du développement économique, 2002.
Terzani, Tiziano. *Giai Phong! The Fall and Liberation of Saigon.* New York: St. Martin's Press, 1976.

Thakur, Ramesh. *Peacekeeping in Vietnam: Canada, India, Poland, and the International Commission*. Edmonton: University of Alberta Press, 1984.
Thakur, Vineet. "An Asian Drama: The Asian Relations Conference, 1947." *International History Review* 3 (2018): 673–95.
Thayer, Carlyle, and Amer Ramses, ed. *Vietnamese Foreign Policy in Transition*. Singapore: Institute for Southeast Asian Studies, 1999.
Thomson, Suteera. "Refugees in Thailand: Relief, Development, and Integration." In *Southeast Asian Exodus: From Tradition to Resettlement*, edited by Elliot L. Tepper, 69–80. Ottawa, ON: Canadian Asian Studies Association, 1980.
Tô Huy Rúa, ed. *Thư tịch báo chí Việt Nam* [*An Anthology of Vietnamese Newspapers*]. Hanoi: NXB Chính trị quốc gia, 1998.
Toner, Simon. "Imagining Taiwan: The Nixon Administration, the Developmental States, and South Vietnam's Search for Economic Viability, 1969–1975." *Diplomatic History* 41, no. 4 (2017): 772–98.
Toner, Simon. "'The Paradise of the Latrine': American Toilet-Building and the Continuities of Colonial and Post-Colonial Development." *Modern American History* 2 (2019): 299–320.
Topmiller, Robert J. *The Lotus Unleashed: The Buddhist Peace Movement in South Vietnam, 1964-1966*. Lexington: University Press of Kentucky, 2006.
Tourison, Sedgwick. *Secret Army, Secret War: Washington's Tragic Spy Operation in North Vietnam*. Annapolis, MD: Naval Institute Press, 1995.
Trần Anh Dũng, ed. *Hàng giáo phẩm công giáo Việt Nam (1960-1995)* [*The Hierarchy of the Catholic Church in Vietnam*]. Paris: Mission catholique vietnamienne, 1996.
Trần, Đình Trụ, Jana K. Lipman, and Hoài Bắc Trần. *Ship of Fate: Memoir of a Vietnamese Repatriate*. Honolulu: University of Hawai'i Press, 2017.
Tran, Khanh. *The Ethnic Chinese and Economic Development in Vietnam*. Singapore: ISEAS, 1993.
Trần, Mỹ Vân. *A Vietnamese Royal Exile in Japan, Prince Cường Để (1882-1951)*. London: Routledge, 2005.
Tran, Nu-Anh. "Contested Identities: Nationalism in the Republic of Vietnam (1954-1963)." PhD diss., University of California, Berkeley, 2013.
Tran, Nu-Anh. *Disunion: Anticommunist Nationalism and the Making of the Republic of Vietnam*. Honolulu: University of Hawai'i Press, 2022.
Tran, Nu-Anh. "The Neglect of the Republic of Vietnam in the American Historical Memory." In Vu and Fear, *The Republic of Vietnam*, 173–78.
Tran, Nu-Anh. "South Vietnamese Identity, American Intervention, and the Newspaper *Chính Luận* (Political Discussion), 1965-1969." *Journal of Vietnamese Studies* 1, nos. 1–2 (2006): 169–209.
Tran, Nu-Anh. "Will the Real Caravelle Manifesto Please Stand Up? A Critique and a New Translation." *Journal of Vietnamese Studies* 18, no. 3 (2023): 1–55.
Tran, Nu-Anh, and Tuong Vu, eds. *Building a Republican Nation in Vietnam, 1920-1963*. Honolulu: University of Hawai'i Press, 2023.
Trần Tam Tỉnh. *Dieu et César: Les Catholiques dans l'histoire du Vietnam* [*God and Caesar: Catholics in the History of Vietnam*]. Paris: Sud-Est Asie, 1978.
Trần Tam Tỉnh. *Peace in Vietnam: A Roman Catholic Vietnamese Priest Looks at the War*. Translated by Peter Weldon. Québec: Thế hệ, 1968.

Trần Tam Tỉnh. *Pour la paix au Vietnam* [For Peace in Vietnam]. Québec: Thế hệ, 1968.
Trần Tam Tỉnh. *Thập giá và lưỡi gươm* [The Cross and the Sword]. Hanoi: NXB Trẻ, 1978.
Trần Tam Tỉnh. *Tôi về Hà Nội* [I Return to Hanoi]. Paris: Cộng đồng Việt Nam, 1975.
Trần Thanh Hiệp. *Dân chủ cho Việt Nam* [Democracy for Vietnam]. Fairfax, VA: Việt thức, 2018.
Tran, Thi Liên. "The Catholic Question in North Vietnam: From Polish Sources, 1954–1956." *Cold War History* 5, no. 4 (2005): 427–49.
Tran, Thi Liên. "Les catholiques vietnamiens pendant la guerre d'indépendance (1945–1954) entre la reconquête coloniale et la résistance communiste" [Vietnamese Catholics during the War of Independence (1945–1954), Between Colonial Reconquest and Communist Resistance]. PhD diss., Institut d'études politiques, 1996.
Tran, Thi Liên. "The Challenge for Peace within South Vietnam's Catholic Community: A History of Peace Activism." *Peace and Change* 38, no. 4 (2013): 446–73.
Tran Thi Liên, Claire. "The Role of Education Mobilities and Transnational Networks in the Building of a Modern Vietnamese Catholic Elite (1920s–1950s)." *Sojourn* 35, no. 2 (2020): 243–70.
Trần Văn Tuyên. *Hội nghị Genève 1954, Hội ký* [The Geneva Conference in 1954: A Memoir]. Saigon: Chim đàn, 1964.
Trương, Như Tảng. *Mémoires d'un Vietcong* [The Memoir of a Vietcong]. Paris: Flammarion, 1985.
Tsamenyi, Martin. "The 'Boat People': Are They Refugees?" *Human Rights Quarterly* 5 (1983): 348–73.
Turley, William S. *The Second Indochina War: A Concise Political and Military History*, 2nd ed. Lanham, MD: Rowman & Littlefield, 2009.
Turpin, Frédéric. *De Gaulle, les gaullistes et l'Indochine* [De Gaulle, the Gaullists, and Indochina]. Paris: Les Indes savantes, 2005.
Turse, Nick. *Kill Anything That Moves: The Real American War in Vietnam*. New York: Metropolitan Books, 2013.
UNHCR. *The State of the World's Refugees 2000: Fifty Years of Humanitarian Action*. Geneva: UNHCR, 2000.
US Department of State. *Aggression from the North: The Record of North Viet-Nam's Campaign to Conquer South Viet-Nam*. Washington, DC: US Government Printing Office, 1965.
Ủy Ban Liên Lạc Công giáo toàn quốc. *Báo cáo kỷ niệm 5 năm ngày thành lập Ủy Ban liên lạc công giáo yêu tổ quốc, yêu hòa bình toàn quốc* [A Report on the Fifth Anniversary of the National Liaison Committee for Catholics Loving Their Homeland and Peace]. Hanoi: Đồng tiến, 1960.
Vaïsse, Maurice. "De Gaulle and the Vietnam War." In *The Search for Peace in Vietnam, 1964–1968*, edited by Lloyd C. Gardner and Tet Gittinger, 162–65. College Station: Texas A&M Press, 2004.
Valverde, Kieu-Linh Caroline. *Transnationalizing Viet Nam: Community, Culture, and Politics in the Diaspora*. Philadelphia: Temple University Press, 2012.

Van Dijk, Boyd. "Internationalizing Colonial War: On the Unintended Consequences of the Interventions of the International Committee of the Red Cross in South-East Asia, 1945–1949." *Past and Present* 250, no. 1 (2021): 243–83.

Veith, George J. *Black April: The Fall of South Vietnam, 1973-1975*. New York: Encounter Books, 2012.

Veith, George J. *Drawn Swords in a Distant Land: South Vietnam's Shattered Dreams*. New York: Encounter Books, 2021.

Vidal-Naquet, Pierre. *L'Affaire Audin* [*The Audin Affair*]. Paris: Éditions de Minuit, 1958.

Việt Nam Cộng Hòa, ed. *Con đường chính nghĩa độc lập, dân chủ, Hiệu triệu và diễn văn quan trọng của Tổng Thống Ngô Đình Diệm, quyển I, từ 16-6-1954 đến 7-7-1955* [*The Just Cause, Independence, and Democracy: Speeches and Important Announcements of President Ngô Đình Diệm, vol. 1, from June 16, 1954, to July 7, 1955*]. Saigon: Sở báo chí thông tin Phủ Tổng thống, 1956.

Việt Nam Dân Chủ Cộng Hòa. *Đồng bào bị cưỡng bức vào Nam trở về tố cáo giặc* [*Compatriots Forced to Migrate to the South Return to Denounce the Aggressor*]. Hanoi: NXB Sự thật, 1955.

Vo, Alex Thai. "From Anticolonialism to Mobilizing Socialist Transformation in the Democratic Republic of Vietnam, 1945–1960." PhD diss., Cornell University, 2019.

Vo, Alex Thai. "Nguyễn Thị Năm and the Land Reform in North Vietnam, 1953." *Journal of Vietnamese Studies* 10, no. 1 (2015): 1–62.

Vo Dang, Thanh Thuy. "Anticommunism as Cultural Praxis: South Vietnam, War, and Refugee Memories in the Vietnamese American Community." PhD diss., University of California, 2008.

Vũ Bằng. *Bốn mươi năm nói láo* [*Forty Years Lying*]. Saigon: Phạm Quang Khải, 2011.

Vũ Đình Trắc. *Công giáo Việt Nam trong truyền thống văn hóa dân tộc* [*Vietnamese Catholics in Popular Culture*]. Orange, CA: Thời điểm công giáo, 1996.

Vu, Minh Hoang. "Recycling Violence: The Theory and Practice of Reeducation Camps in Postwar Vietnam." In *Experiments with Marxism-Leninism in Cold War Southeast Asia*, edited by Matthew Galway and Marc H. Opper, 219–39. Canberra: Australian National University Press, 2022.

Vu, Minh Hoang. "Sortir du bourbier: Les méandres du Vietnam vers l'accord de paix de Paris, 1986–1991" [Getting Out of the Quagmire: The Winding Road to the Paris Peace Agreement, 1986–1991]. In *Un triangle stratégique à l'épreuve: La Chine, les États-Unis et l'Asie du Sud-Est depuis 1947*, edited by Pierre Journoud, 219–38. Montpellier, France: Presses universitaires de la Méditerranée, 2022.

Vu, Tuong. *Vietnam's Communist Revolution: The Power and Limits of Ideology*. Cambridge: Cambridge University Press, 2017.

Vu, Tuong, and Sean Fear, ed. *The Republic of Vietnam, 1955-1975: Vietnamese Perspectives on Nation Building*. Ithaca, NY: Cornell University Press, 2019.

Vương Kỳ Sơn. *Di cư 54, Triệu người muốn sống* [*The Migration of 1954: A Million Want to Live*]. New Orleans: Lĩnh Nam, 2009.

Vương Văn Đông. *Binh biến 11/11/1960* [*The November 11, 1960, Putsch*]. Westminster, CA: Văn Nghệ, 2002.

Wain, Barry. *The Refused: The Agony of the Indochina Refugees.* New York: Simon & Schuster, 1981.
Wall, Irwin M. *France, the United States, and the Algerian War.* Berkeley: University of California Press, 2001.
Wehrle, Edmund. "'Awakening the Conscience of the Masses': The Vietnamese Confederation of Labour, 1947–1975." In *Labour in Vietnam*, edited by Anita Chan, 13–45. Singapore: ISEAS, 2011.
Westad, Odd Arne. *The Global Cold War: Third World Interventions and the Making of Our Times.* Cambridge: Cambridge University Press, 2007.
Westad, Odd Arne, and Sophie Quinn-Judge, eds. *Third Indochina War: Conflict between China, Vietnam and Cambodia, 1972–1979.* London: Frank Cass, 2006.
Wiesner, Louis A. *Victims and Survivors: Displaced Persons and Other War Victims in Viet-Nam, 1954–1975.* New York: Greenwood Press, 1988.
Woodside, Alexander. "Nationalism and Poverty in the Breakdown of Sino-Vietnamese Relations." *Pacific Affairs* 52, no. 3 (1979): 381–409.
World Council of Churches. *The Uppsala Report 1968: Official Report of the Fourth Assembly of the World Council of Churches. Uppsala, July 4th-20th 1968.* Uppsala, Sweden: World Council of Churches, 1968.
Wu, Albert. *From Christ to Confucius: German Missionaries, Chinese Christians, and the Globalization of Christianity, 1860–1950.* New Haven, CT: Yale University Press, 2016.
Yacoobali-Zamindar, Vazira Fazila. *The Long Partition and the Making of Modern South Asia.* New York: Columbia University Press, 2007.
Yang, Dominic Meng-Hsuan. *The Great Exodus from China: Trauma, Memory, and Identity in Modern Taiwan.* Cambridge: Cambridge University Press, 2021.
Zhang, Xiaoming. *Deng Xiaoping's Long War: The Military Conflict Between China and Vietnam, 1979–1991.* Chapel Hill: University of North Carolina Press, 2015.
Zhou, Taomo. *Migration in the Time of Revolution: China, Indonesia, and the Cold War.* Ithaca, NY: Cornell University Press, 2019.
Zhu, Rong. "China and the Indochinese Refugees." In *Indochinese Refugees: Asylum and Resettlement*, edited by Supang Chantavanich and E. Bruce Reynolds, 80–102. Bangkok: Institute of Asian Studies, 1988.
Zinoman, Peter. "Reading Revolutionary Prison Memoirs." In *The Country of Memory: Remaking the Past in Late Socialist Vietnam*, edited by Hue-Tam Ho Tai, 21–45. Berkeley: University of California Press, 2001.
Zubovich, Gene. *Before the Religious Right: Liberal Protestants, Human Rights, and the Polarization of the United States.* Philadelphia: University of Pennsylvania Press, 2022.

Index

Note: *Italicized* page numbers refer to figures.

1917 Bolshevik revolution, 10
1951 Refugee Convention, 8
1954 evacuation, 1, 4–5, 7–8, 10–11, 30–32, 33–43, *43*, 55, 57–59, 61, 68, 118, 137–38, 155, 158, 177–79, 186n1, 198n50
1975 departure, 136–38, 144–50, 155–57

Adams, Eddie, 146
Affaire des piastres, 29, 119
Afghanistan, 160
Afro-Asian countries, 88–89, 94
Algeria, 94, 101; Algerian War, 89, 111, 227–28n84
Allende, Salvador, 112
Ấn Quang pagoda, 129
Anh Hợp, 47
Anh hùng nước tôi (*The Heroes of My Country*), 167
anticommunism: Catholics and, 91, 105, 134, 143, 196n15; evacuees and, 4–5, 8, 126, 185n17; National Unified Front and, 157; new Christianity and, 122–25; Nguyễn Viết Khai and, 116; noncommunists and, 26; Phan Huy Quát's and, 95; post–Cold War period and, 172–73; PRG and, 148–50; in RVN, 75–76; Sino-Vietnamese War and, 161; strategies for, 163–68; tensions in Southeast Asia and, 159; Tết Offensive and, 106; *Thức tỉnh* and, 156; Trần Tam Tỉnh and, 111; in Vietnam, 169; Vietnamese diaspora and, 176–79. *See also* communism (and communists)
antiwar movement, 109–10, 115, 118–19, 122–27. *See also* peace movement
Article 14(d), 31–32
Asian People's Anti-Communist League, 37, 164

Associated State of Vietnam (ASVN), 3, 11, 17–18, 20–25, 27–29, 58, 93, 188n21, 199n71. *See also* Vietnam
Association of Confucian Studies (Hội Khổng học), 87
Association of Northern Vietnamese (Hội Bắc Việt tương tế), 87, 207n32
Association of Southeast Asian Nations (ASEAN), 164
Association of the Bùi Chu Family, 173
asylum, applications for, 158, 243n2
atheists, 36, 101. *See also* communist atheism
Atkinson, Sean, 166
August Revolution, 12, 14, 16, 47, 68

Bắc Phong, 170
Bắc tiến (March to the north), 48, 87–88
Bailey, Don, 168, 248n50
Bandung Conference, 49, 89, 94, 220n110
Bảo chính đoàn (Primary Defense Corps), 58, 205n12
Bảo Đại, King, 12, 16–17, 24, 27, 30, 44, 51–54, 62
Ben Bella, Ahmed, 94
Bình Xuyên, 51–52, 204–5n8
Black April, 149
Black Panthers, 112
"boat people" crisis, 8, 137–38, 147, 151–53, *152*, 242n89
Buddhists, 13, 54, 75, 77–83, *78*, 91–92, 95, 101, 103, 105–6, 114, 122, 129, 134, 147, 222n26
Bùi Chu diocese, 13, 15, 22–23, 25, 30–31, 41, 173–74
Bùi Diễm, 63, 93, 106
Bùi Đức Sinh, 172
Bùi Thị Xuân High School, 173
Bulganin, Nikolai, 46–47
Bửu Hội, Prince, 52

277

Cà Mau peninsula, 31
Cái Sắn project, 59
Cambodia, 8, 12, 17, 32, 89, 118, 120, 139–40, 146–47, 159–60, 164–65, 167–68
Cambodian-Vietnamese War, 3–4, 137–38, 150, 152–53, *154*, 156, 160
Cân lào (Personalist Revolutionary Labour Party), 52, 57, 68, 78–80, 82, 87
Canada, 42, 110–14, 145–46, 149
Cao Đài (Great Đạo of the Third Era of Universal Salvation), 13–14, 16, 27, 51, 54, 57, 129, 149
Cao Minh Chiếm, 100
Caravelle Manifesto, 73–74
cartoons, political, 45–47
Catholic Action, 23
Catholic Bloc (Khối công giáo), 84
Catholic Church: anticommunism and, 91, 104–5, 178; Buddhists and, 105–6; cease-fire agreements and, 102–4; communism and, 124–25; corruption and, 130–32, 134; criticism of Vietnamese Catholics and, 15; in DRV, 64–65; DRV independence and, 14; in East Asia and, 20–25, *24*; evacuation of clergy and, 41–42; evacuees and, 180–82; Legion of Mary and, 191n58; political stance in Vietnam and, 83–86; in post–Cold War Vietnam, 172–73; PRG and, 141–43, 147, 240n67; refugees and, 36–37; in RVN, 69–71; Second Vatican Council and, 101; in Vietnam, 72–73; Vietnam War and, 126–27
Catholic National Liaison Committee, 64
Catholic Relief Services, 82
Catholics: 1954 evacuation and, 2, 5, 10–11, 30–31, 41–43, 57, 186n1; 1975 remaining in Vietnam, 138; anticommunism and, 64–65, 178, 196n15; antiwar movement and, 97–98, 122–23; assistance to evacuees and, 62; communism and, 15, 73–74, 92, 124–25, 187n15; Congress of the Evacuation and, 54; counterrevolution and, 79–82; criticism of PRG and, 147; Đặng Sỹ trial and, 83; DRV and, 40–41, 103–4, 126–28, 198n49; as evacuees, 37, 182; in France, 110–11; Hồ Chí Minh and, 14; instability in South Vietnam and, 85–86; lack of autonomy and, 58–59; march to the north and, 88; nationalist parties and, 13; Ngô Đình Cẩn and, 82; Paris Peace Accords and, 107–9; personalism and, 26; Phan Huy Quát and, 94–95; political alliances and, 27; post–Cold War period and, 172–73; PRG and, 141–43, 149; protests in RVN and, 92; purge committees and, 83–84; in Québec, 111–13; remittances and, 171; riot in Thanh Bồ-Đức Lợi and, 91; in RVN, 69–71; support for war and, 114–15; transnational networks and, 129; US and, 88; in Vietnam, *24*, 72–73; violent protests and, 77–78, *78*
Catton, Philip, 31
cease-fire agreements, 2–3, 32, 38–39, 42–44, 50, 53–54, 86–91, 93–94, 102–3, 108–9, 179–80. *See also* Geneva Conference (1954); Geneva Conference (1962); Paris Peace Accords
Central Intelligence Agency (CIA), 75, 118–19, 122, 125
central Vietnam, 80–81, 91, 105, 120. *See also* Democratic Republic of Vietnam (DRV); Republic of Vietnam (RVN); Vietnam
Cha bỏ quê, con bỏ nước (A Father Leaves His Home Village, a Son Leaves His Homeland), 1
Chakrabarty, Dipesh, 47
Chân Tín, 123, 129, 132
Chân trời mới (New Horizons), 145, 148
Chiêu hồi program, 83
China, 2–4, 12, 16–17, 21, 38–39, 45–47, 58, 71–72, 88–89, 91, 94, 101, 103–5, 137, 162, 191n58. *See also* People's Republic of China (PRC)
Christians, 101–3, 105, 112, 114, 122–27, 128
Chúng tôi muốn sống (We Want to Live), 63, 208n43
Citizens' Front of Religions (Mặt trận Công dân các tôn giáo), 105–6, 225–26n58
civil servants, 18, 23, 138
civilians: 2, 11, 25–26, 31–32, 33–36, 42–44, *60*, 194n2, 195n11, 201n95
clergy, 21, 23, 41–43, *43*, 102. *See also* missionaries; priests
Cochinchina, 12, 14, 16, 199n71
Cold War: during 1980s, 159–63, 245n15; anticommunism and, 178–80; in Asia, 3–4, 11, 17; Cambodian-Vietnamese War and, 153; communist countries and, 150; complexity of, 55; end of, 173–75; evacuees and, 2–3, 6–8, 9, 44, 158; Geneva Conference and, 32; human

rights and, 181–82; Bảo Đại and, 16; literature and, 47–49; nationalists and, 28; political ideology and, 5; Vietnam and, 6–7, 45, 89, 99, 117, 169
Collins, Lawton, 40
colonialism, 3, 17–18, 45, 50–54, 89–90, 126, 170. *See also* decolonization
Commisariat Général (COMIGAL), 34, 36–37, 49, 55, 57, 61, 195n6, 204–5n8
Committee for the Defense of Peace, 99–100, 221–22n15, 222n24
Committee for the People's Salvation, 91–92
communism (and communists): 1954 evacuation and, 4–5, 31, 33–35, 59, 183n8, 184n10; 1963 Revolution and, 79–80, 83; anticommunism and, 92, 176–79; in Asia, 3; Bình Xuyên and, 51; Cambodian-Vietnamese War and, 152–53; Catholics and, 11, 20–25, 70–73, 83–84, 91, 97–98, 141–43, 147, 189–90n43; China and, 39; Cold War and, 16–17, 162; Committee for the Defense of Peace and, 100; corruption and, 131–32, 134; DRV and, 14, 68; evacuees and, 6–8, 36–38, 49–50, 55, 56–57, 64, 96, 114–15, 128; First Indochina War and, 2–3; France and, 28, 110–11; Hồ Chí Minh and, 13; ICC and, 54; journalists and, 44; LLĐĐK and, 93–94; march to the north and, 87–88; Marxism and, 144, 161; nationalists and, 14–15, 28; new Christianity and, 122–25; noncommunists and, 25–26; overseas Vietnamese and, 155–57; Paris Peace Accords and, 107–9, 130; partitioning and, 45–46; peace movement and, 116–17; Phạm Văn Huyến and, 204–5n8; Phan Huy Quát and, 95; political cartoons and, 46–47; political instability and, 88; PRC and, 160; public opinion and, 191n67; rebellion against, 163–68; religion and, 102–6; RVN and, 135; Sino-Vietnamese War and, 161; South Vietnam and, 53, 85–86; in Soviet Union, 64; SRVN, PRC, Soviet Union, and, 150; Tết Offensive and, 106; US and, 98–99; Vietnam and, 30, 138, 140, 169–70. *See also* anticommunism
communist atheism, 22, 36, 72, 101–2. *See also* atheists
Confucianism, 104
Công giáo và dân tộc (*Catholics and the Nation*), 141–43, 232n43

Congress (US), 31, 98, 118, 138
Congress of the Evacuation (Đại hội di cư), 54
Convention for the Prevention and Punishment of the Crime of Genocide, 102
Cornell University, 118
Corps expéditionnaire français en Extrême-Orient (CEFEO), 12, 17, 29–30, 42, 51, 53
corruption, 117, 119, 130–32, *133*, 134–35, 145, 149
Cultural Revolution, 103–4
Cường Để, Prince, 27
Czechoslovakia, 113–14

Đại Việt (Nationalist Party of Greater Vietnam), 13, 18, 27, 58, 74–75, 80–81, 92
Dân chủ mới (*New Democracy*), 86, 119–20
Dân đen (*The Masses*), 50
Dân nguyện (*The Popular Will*), 47
Dân quyền (*Civic Rights*), 170
Dân Việt (*The People of Vietnam*), 55, 67
Danang, Vietnam, 77, 99
Đặng Sỹ, 82–84, 214n26, 214–15n32
Đặng Văn Quang, 145
Đạo binh Đức Mẹ (*Legion of Mary*), 25, 27
Das, Veena, 55
Day of National Unity, 49, 52
de Gaulle, Charles, 89, 112
de Jaegher, Raymond, 36–37, 81, 111
de la Rochejaquelein, Henri, 38
de Lattre de Tassigny, Jean, 17, 21–22
decolonization, 11–14, 20–21, 23–24, 28, 45. *See also* colonialism
Decree 007, 129
Deliver Us from Evil (Dooley), 37
Đêm giã từ Hà Nội (*The Night I Left Hanoi*; Mai Thảo), 47–48, 201n94
Democratic Republic of Vietnam (DRV): 1954 evacuation and, 30–31, 35, 42–44; Afro-Asian Conference and, 94; alternative states to, 16–17; anticommunism and, 64–69, 176–78; areas under control of, 18, *19*; ASVN and, 20; "boat people" crisis and, 8; Bửu Hội and, 52; Catholics and, 10–11, 22–25, 111, 125–27, 142, 189–90n43, 198n49, 211n90; Christianity and, 102–5; defectors and, 123; end of Vietnam War and, 139; evacuees and, 4, 7, 117; First Indochina War and, 11, 15–16; Geneva Conference and, 29–30, 32;

Democratic Republic of Vietnam (*continued*) independence and, 12–14; intellectuals in, 100–101; isolationism of, 180; nationalists and, 14–15, 38–39, 47; Ngô Đình Cẩn and, 82; Nixon and, 117–18; northern Vietnamese and, 46; Paris Peace Accords and, 107–9; partitioning and, 2–3; PRG and, 128, 144; propaganda and, 40–41; religion and, 114; Russell Tribunal and, 102; South Vietnam and, 53–54, 77–78; SVN and, 34; Tết Offensive and, 106; US and, 99. *See also* central Vietnam; Vietnam

denunciation campaigns, 3, 23, 25, 64
Department of Defense (US), 118
diaspora, Vietnamese, 4–5, 159, 176, 184n10, 185n17. *See also* Vietnamese, overseas
Diệm, Ngô Đình. *See* Ngô Đình Diệm
Diên Hồng assembly, 129–30, 234n72
Dieu et César (*God and Caesar*; Trần Tam Tỉnh), 147
diplomacy, 6, 8–9, 163–68, 171
Đỗ Mậu, 86–87
Đối diện (*Face to Face*), 123–24, 128–29, 232n38, 234n69. *See also Đồng dao* (*In Unison*); *Đứng dậy* (*Rise Up*)
Đổi mới (Renovation) reform, 158, 171–72
Đồng dao (*In Unison*), 129, 234n69. *See also Đối diện* (*Face to Face*); *Đứng dậy* (*Rise Up*)
Đồng minh Hội (ĐMH), 13
Dooley, Thomas A., 37
Đứng dậy (*Rise Up*), 129, 132, 134, 234n69. See also *Đối diện* (*Face to Face*); *Đồng dao* (*In Unison*)
Đường sống, 73
Dương Văn Minh, 80–81

Easter Offensive (1972). *See* Spring Offensive (1972)
economy, 2, 97, 130–32, 140, 158, 171, 175, 237n14
Elliott, Dương Văn Mai, 136–37, 230n10
Ély, Paul, 30
Esprit, 26
ethnic minorities, 15–17, 88, 148–49, 151. *See also* minority groups
Europe, 27, 64, 67
evacuees: 1954 evacuation and, 30–35, 57–59, 60, 61, 194n2; 1975 departure and, 8, 136–38, 144–50, 155; Afro-Asian Conference and, 94; anticommunism and, 4–5, 65–67, 69, 159–63, 177–79, 185n17; Buddhists and, 78; Catholics and, 10–11, 24–25, 58–59, 69–71, 104–6, 126; cease-fire and, 86–87, 89–91; Cold War and, 6–7; communism and, 76, 122–25; counterrevolution and, 79–82; defined, 8–9; Diệm and, 50–52, 56–57, 74–75; DRV and, 40–41, 142; international support and, 35–38, 180–81; march to the north and, 67–68, 87–88, 96; media and, 63; minority groups and, 185n19; native land and, 61–63; ODP and, 158; Paris Peace Accords and, 107–9; partition and, 47–50; peace movement and, 114–15, 116–17; PRG and, 128–29; propaganda and, 6, 39–41, 118–19; purge committees and, 83; remittances and, 171; return to Vietnam and, 174–75; significance of, 44–47; SRVN and, 150; Tết Offensive and, 106; Third Indochina War and, 157; Trần Tam Tỉnh and, 110; US and, 88, 99; Vietnam War and, 98–99, 179–80; Vietnamese people, 53–55. *See also* migrants; refugees
Experimenting the Dialectic (*Thực nghiệm biện chứng pháp*), 50

Falk, Richard, 102
Families of Vietnamese Political Prisoners Association (FVPPA), 158, 174
famine (1945), 99–100
film industry, 63, 208n43
First Indochina War (1946–1954), 1–3, 7, 11, 21–32, 70, 93, 124, 156, 177, 181. *See also* Second Indochina War (1955–1975); Third Indochina War (1978–1991)
First International Assembly of Christians in Solidarity with the Vietnamese, Laotians, and Cambodians, 125, 127
Fishel, Wesley, 75
flooding (1964–1965), 99
For Vietnam, 75
foreign intervention, 4, 6, 53–54, 79, 88, 91, 93–94, 97–99, 101–2, 114–15, 141–42. *See also* international support
Forest, Jim, 146
France: 1954 evacuation and, 4, 30–31, 33–34, 38–42; 1963 Revolution and, 79; Afro-Asian Conference and, 94; ASVN and, 17, 20; August Revolution and, 47; Catholic Church and, 21–25; cease-fire and, 89–91; Christians in,

125–26; colonialism and, 170; Diệm and, 52–53; DRV and, 12–14; evacuees and, 7, 57–58, 180; First Indochina War and, 3, 11, 15–17; Geneva Conference and, 29–30; partitioning and, 45; Phan Huy Quát and, 95; in southern Vietnam and, 51–52; SVN and, 35–36; Trần Tam Tỉnh and, 110–11; Vietnamese independence and, 27–29, 32, 192n79
Free Pacific Association, 36, 81
French Indochina, 12, *19*
French Union, 17, 28–29, 51, 192nn75–76
Friends of Overseas Vietnamese, 157
From Colonialism to Communism (Hoàng Văn Chí), 118–19, 230n9
Front de Libération du Québec (FLQ), 112

Gélinas, André, 147–48
General Student Association (GSA), 86–87, 90, 92. *See also* students
Geneva Conference (1954), 3, 11, 29–32, 38, 45, *46*, 51–52, 62, 86–87, 89–90, 93, 108–9, 128, 156. *See also* cease-fire agreements
Geneva Conference (1962), 88–89. *See also* cease-fire agreements
Geneva Conference (1979), 153. *See also* cease-fire agreements
Germany, 174, 176–77
Gheddo, Piero, 134
Giai phẩm (*Masterpieces*), 64–65
Giáp, Võ Nguyên. *See* Võ Nguyên Giáp
Gió Việt (*The Wind of Vietnam*), 18, 20
Greene, Graham, 41
Guam, 138–39, 145

Hà Nội, 65, 69
Hà Thành Thọ, 47
Hà Tĩnh Province, 70, 123
Hải Dương, Vietnam, 32, 66
Hải Hồng, 151, *152*
Hải Ninh, 16
Haiphong, Vietnam, 25, 30, 41–42
Hajimu, Masuda, 55
Hamilton, Marianne, 127
Hammer, Ellen, 75
Hanoi, Vietnam, 3, 30, 32
Hanoi University Student Corps, 50
Hemispheric Conference to End the War in Vietnam, 112, *113*
Hiền Lương Bridge, 100
Hindus, 47

History of the Catholic Church (Bùi Đức Sinh), 172
Hồ Chí Minh, 3, 12–14, 16–17, 30, 32, 40, 46–47, 54, 65, 67, 90, 102, 150, 166–67, 180
Ho Chi Minh City, Vietnam, 139. *See also* Saigon, Vietnam
Hồ Chí Minh Trail, 78, 99, 117
Hồ Nai village, 116, 124
Hòa bình (*Peace*), 95
Hòa Hảo (Supreme Harmony), 13–14, 16, 27, 51, 54, 57, 92, 129
Hoàng Cơ Bình, 38, 92, 109
Hoàng Cơ Minh, 157, 162–63, 165–67
Hoàng Cơ Thụy, 109
Hoàng Quỳnh, 15, 74, 84, 92, 105–9, 120, 130–32, 134–35, 138, 141, 214–15n32
Hoàng Văn Chí, 118–19, 230nn9–10
Hoàng Văn Hoan, 161
Hội tương tế Nghệ Tĩnh Bình, 70
Hong Kong, 16, 25, 151
human rights advocacy, 102, 110, 169–70, 181–82
humanitarian assistance, 6, 137, 153
Hùng kings, 87, 149, 216n56, 241n78
Hungary, 64
Hương Khê, 134
Huỳnh Phú Sổ, 13
Huỳnh Tấn Phát, 148

imperialism, 112–14
India, 2, 42, 47, 183n3
Indochina, 3, 89
Informations catholiques internationales, 147
insurgencies, 51, 73–74
intellectuals, 26–28, 38, 53, 63–65, 73–74, 100, 111–13, 119, 146–47, 207n40
International Committee for the Red Cross (ICRC), 36, 135
International Control Commission (ICC), 42–43, 52, 54, 65, 68, 89, 199n63
international support, 28, 35–36, 49, 59, 109–14, 140, 146, 153, 156, 180, 195n11. *See also* foreign intervention
International Voluntary Service, 124
interzone IV, 18, 20, 22, 53, 123
interzone V, 31, 71, 178
interzones (*liên khu*), 18, *19*
Ivens, Joris, 113

Jacqueney, Theodore, 147
Japan, 12, 27, 47, 91, 165
John XXIII, Pope, 72, 101, 111, 127, 134
Johnson, Lyndon B., 78–79, 96, 98, 106

journalists (and journalism), 44, 52, 68, 119–20, 129, 156, 168, 170, 207–8n41. *See also* newspaper industry

Kahin, George McTurnan, 118
Kennedy, John F., 78–79, 88, 96
Khieu Samphan, 164
Khmer Rouge, 3, 139, 146–47, 152, 156, 159–60, 164
Khrushchev, Nikita, 64, 89
King, Martin Luther, Jr., 112
Kinh people, 37
Kissinger, Henry, 134
Kommunismus, 113
Korea, 16, 23, 25, 28, 89, 174; Korean War and, 2
Kwon, Heonik, 55

La Vang church, 72–73
labor activists, 27, 57, 107
Lacouture, Jean, 146–47
land reform, 3, 18, 23, 64–65, 118–19
Làng Nghi, 70
Laos, 3, 12, 17, 32, 88–89, 118, 163, 165–67
Lê Duẩn, 72, 162, 168; clique of, 159, 161
Lê Hữu Từ, 14–15, 22–24, 30, 58, 75, 93, 131
Lê Quảng Luật, 58
Legion of Mary, 21, 25, 191n58
Lemaître, Henri, 141
Liên Việt, 23, 144
literature, 47–49, 62, 65–67
Lodge, Henry Cabot, 88
Logevall, Fred, 96
Lửa sống (*The Fire of Life*), 44
Lực lượng Đại đoàn kết (LLĐĐK; the Greater Solidarity Movement), 84, 88, 91–95, 106, 108–9
Lukács, György, 113
Luyện thép, Cơ quan ngôn luận Nghệ Tĩnh Bình (*Hardening Steel*), 70, 116, 123

Mai Thanh, 142
Mai Thảo, 47–49
Malraux, André, 48, 201n94
Mao Zedong, 46
Marxism. *See* communism (and communists)
Melman, Seymour, 102
Mendès-France, Pierre, 32
Michigan State University, 36, 59
migrants, 8–9, 34, 61, 151. *See also* evacuees; refugees

minority groups, 185n19. *See also* ethnic minorities
missionaries, 21, 23–24, 71–72, 101, 126, 134, 138, 143, 237n20. *See also* clergy; priests
Montagnard Country of South Indochina (Pays montagnard du Sud-Indochinois), 15–16
Montréal, Québec, 112, 145, 170
Monument of Remembrance (Đền kỷ niệm), 45
Mounier, Emmanuel, 26
Movement for the Defense of Peace, 53, 100
Moyn, Samuel, 102
Muslims, 47, 101, 222n26
mutual aid associations, 62, 70
Mỹ Lai massacre, 119

Naïdenoff, Georges, 10
National Assembly, 14, 216n51
National Catholic Welfare Council, 36, 209–10n72
National Day of Shame (Ngày quốc hận), 62, 106, 109, 149
National Liberation Front (NLF), 3, 72, 74, 84–85, *85*, 97, 102–3, 106, 111, 117–18, 140, 143–44, 170, 178
National Red Cross Leagues, 99
National Unified Front for the Liberation of Vietnam (Mặt trận Quốc gia Thống nhất Giải phóng Việt Nam), 157, 163, 165–67
nationalists, 13–15, 18, 20, 25–29, 38–39, 45, 47, 50, 75, 107–9, 162, 180–82
native land (*quê hương*), 62
Neuhaus, Richard, 146
neutrality, 92–94, 165
New Economic Zones, 139–41, 149
New Left, 113
New York Times, 31, 118
newspaper industry, 63, 68–69, 129, 207–8n41. *See also* journalists (and journalism)
Nghệ An Province, 65, 70, 123
Nghệ Tĩnh Bình region, 70, 71, 123
Nghiêm Xuân Thiện, 45, 92, 177
Ngô Bá Thành, 100, 132
Ngô Đình Cẩn, 73, 81–82
Ngô Đình Diệm: assassination of, 3, 77–81, 96; Catholics and, 40–41, 58–59; CIA and, 122; communists and, 72; coup attempts and, 74–76; critics of, 73–74;

evacuees and, 5, 34–36, 51–55, 57–59, 61–62, 180; France and, 50–52; Hoàng Văn Chí and, 119; march to the north and, 67–68, 67; nationalists and, 38–39; NLF and, 111; personalism and, 26–27; as prime minister, 30; Procession of the Sacred Land and, 56–57; US and, 88
Ngô Đình Luyện, 81
Ngô Đình Nhu, 26, 52, 57, 59, 68, 75, 77, 80–81
Ngô Đình Thục, 26–27, 73, 75, 81–83
Nguyen, Joseph, 173
Nguyen, Nathalie Huynh Chau, 235n2
Nguyen, Y Thien, 159
Nguyễn Bá Tòng High School, 209–10n72
Nguyễn Cao Kỳ, 77, 92, 95, 98, 145, 164
Nguyễn Chánh Thi, 74
Nguyễn Công Luận, 48, 140
Nguyễn Đình Thi, 125, 138, 141–42, 146, 147, 232n43
Nguyễn Hữu Thọ, 100, 148
Nguyễn Khánh, 81, 84, 87, 92
Nguyễn Lạc Hóa, 24–25, 58, 166
Nguyễn Mạnh Tường, 65
Nguyễn Ngọc Loan, 145–46
Nguyễn Quang Minh, 143
Nguyễn Thị Liên, 20, 27
Nguyen Thi Minh Tam, 148
Nguyễn Tôn Hoàn, 75, 81
Nguyễn Trung Trinh, 95
Nguyễn Văn Bình, 75, 106, 130, 138, 143, 211n90
Nguyễn Văn Hình, 51
Nguyễn Văn Thiệu, 77, 92, 95, 98, 116, 120, 129, 131–32, 134, 148, 155, 169
Nguyễn Văn Thuận, 141
Nguyên vẹn hình hài (*An Unscathed Body*), 149
Nguyễn Viết Khai, 70–71, 116, 123–24, 129, 177
Nhân dân (*The People*), 119, 146
Nhân văn (*Humanities*), 64–65
Ninh Bình Province, 142, 174
Nixon, Richard, 7, 108, 117–18, 122, 162, 180
Norodom Sihanouk, 89, 164–65
North Vietnam. *See* Democratic Republic of Vietnam (DRV)
November 1, 1963, Revolution, 79–87, 88
Nu Anh Tran, 119
Nùng people, 16, 58

O'Connor, Patrick, 37, 80, 82–83, 103, 125
Office for Northern Vietnam (Bắc Việt Vụ), 61
Operation Passage to Freedom, 35–36
Operation Rolling Thunder, 93
Orange County, California, 173
Orderly Departure Program (ODP), 137, 152, 158–59, 243n3
Ordinance 50, 59
Osservatore Romano, 23, 31, 71

Pacem in Terris: encyclical (Pope John XXIII), 101; conferences, 101, 112
Paris, France, 90–91
Paris Peace Accords, 3, 106–9, 120, 129–30, 135, 156, 234n73. *See also* cease-fire agreements
Paris Peace Agreement (1991), 160
Parrel, Fernand, 99
partition, 1–2, 6–7, 34–35, 38, 45–51, 55, 61–62, 86, 183n3
Paul VI, Pope, 101, 103–5, 127
Pax Christi, 99
peace movement, 97, 101–15, 116–17, 122, 125, 130, 228n97. *See also* antiwar movement
peasants, 20, 37
PEN International, 170, 248n58
Pentagon Papers, 118, 125, 229–30n8
People's Army of Vietnam (PAVN), 29–30, 43, 49, 65, 117, 120, 124, 129, 135, 138–40, 152–53, 160
People's Republic of China (PRC), 3, 7, 17, 21, 23–25, 117, 122, 150–53, 154, 156, 159–64, 180, 241n84. *See also* China
People's Republic of Kampuchea, 152
personalism, 26–27, 69–70, 72, 99
Phạm Bá Trực, 14, 23
Phạm Duy, 1, 149–50, 157
Phạm Huy Thông, 53
Phạm Ngọc Chi, 23, 58, 75
Phạm Văn Đồng, 14, 54
Phạm Văn Huyến, 18, 20, 49, 57, 99–100, 177, 204–5n8, 222n19
Phạm Văn Liễu, 61, 74, 144–45, 156–57, 162, 165–66, 204–5n8
Phạm Văn Tấn, 41
Phan Huy Quát, 92–95, 99
Phan Khắc Sửu, 93, 95
Phan Quang Đán, 90
Phát Diệm diocese, 13–15, 22–23, 25, 30–31, 41, 58, 131, 189–90n43. *See also* Lê Hữu Từ
Phnom Penh, Cambodia, 90–91, 139–40
Phú Lâm temple, 109
Pius XII, Pope, 21–22

Poland, 4, 42–43, 64, 105, 163
political ideology, 4–5, 7–8, 43–44, 49–50, 160–63, 169–70, 177, 183n8, 185n7
Porter, Gareth, 118–19, 230n10
Pour la Paix au Vietnam (*Peace in Vietnam*; Trần Tam Tỉnh), 114
press, freedom of, 129, 148
priests, 126–27, 130–32, 134, 138, 142–43, 147, 233n58. *See also* clergy; missionaries
Procession of the Sacred Land, 44–45, 47, 56
propaganda, 6, 11, 39–41, 45–47, *46*, 52, 58, 63, 69, 118–19, 126–27, 147–48, 198n50
Protestants, 21, 112, 125
protests, 52, 54, 77, 80–84, 90, 101–2, 112
Provisional Revolutionary Government of the Republic of South Vietnam (PRG), 128, 139–40, 141–43, 146–49. *See also* Republic of Vietnam (RVN)
public opinion, 35, 75, 109–10, 117, 120, 146–48, 150, 163, 179, 191n67
purge committees (Ủy ban Thanh trừng), 83–84

Quách Thị Trang, 81
Quakers, 101–2
Quan điểm (*Perspective*), 45, *46*
Quảng Trị Province, 120
Quê mẹ (*The Motherland*), 123
Québec, Canada, 110–14, 125–27, 129, 145
Quỳnh Lưu uprising, 64–65, 69–70

rapprochement, 89, 101–6, 117, 164
Reagan, Ronald, 159, 163
rectification, 18, 114
Red River delta, 13, 30
reeducation campaigns, 136, 139–40, 143–44, 147, 149, 168, 237n20
Refugee Problem in the Republic of Vietnam, The, 57, 204n6
refugees: 1975 departure and, 155–57; "boat people" crisis and, 151–53, *152*, *154*; cease-fire and, 179; from China, 58; defined, 8; evacuees as, 57; new Cold War and, 159–61; ODP and, 158–59, 243n3; peace movement and, 110; Vietnam and, 1–2, 137, 174–75; war criminals and, 145. *See also* evacuees
religion (and religious freedom), 10–11, 27, 54, 64, 94–95, 97–98, 102–6, 108–9, 126, 141–43, 147–48
Remembrance Monument (Đền ký niệm), 62

remittances, 171–72, 248–49nn62–63
Republic of China. *See* China; People's Republic of China (PRC)
Republic of Vietnam Armed Forces (RVNAF), 53, 65–67, 74, 80, 105, 120–22, 138–39, 143–44, 148–49, 158, 177–79, 208n58
Republic of Vietnam (RVN): 1954 evacuation and, 34–35; 1963 Revolution and, 79–83; anticommunism and, 68–69, 73; Black April and, 149; Catholics and, 10, 69–72, 83–84, 127, 172; cease-fire and, 88–90; corruption in, 116–17, 130–32, *133*; creation of, 3; Diệm and, 53; evacuees and, 4–5, 9, 57–58, 61–62; lack of democratic freedoms in, 75–76; ODP and, 158; Paris Peace Accords and, 107–9; PAVN and, 135; Phan Huy Quát and, 93–95; political instability in, 77–78, 85–88; PRG and, 128–29; reunification and, 61; Tết Offensive and, 106; Thiệu and, 92; US and, 114, 120–22; Vietnamese Armed Forces Overseas and, 157; Vietnamese diaspora and, 177. *See also* central Vietnam; Provisional Revolutionary Government of the Republic of South Vietnam (PRG); Vietnam
resettlement, 36–38, 57–61, *60*, 67, 137, 140–41, 151–53, 155, 158–59, 209n61
reunification, 40, 49, 61, 67–68, 86–87
Russell, Bertrand, 102
Russell Tribunal, 102

Safer, Morley, 166
Saigon, Vietnam, 1–3, 17, 30, 45, 51, 54, 135, 138–40. *See also* Ho Chi Minh City, Vietnam
Salisbury, Harrison, 103, 224n38
Sáng tạo (*Creation*), 48
Santa Ana, California, 155
Sartre, Jean-Paul, 102
Schweizer, Albert, 113
Scott, James, 122
Second Indochina War (1955–1975): 1963 Revolution and, 80–84; antiwar movement and, 103–5, 112–15, 116, 122–23; Catholics and, 97–98; cease-fire and, 88–91; as civil war, 128, 156; communists and, 84–88; end of, 3, 135; evacuees and, 7–8, 136–37, 181; Phan Huy Quát and, 92–93; political instability and, 77–79; RVN and, 93–94;

Tết Offensive and, 106; Trần Tam Tỉnh and, 110–11; US and, 96, 98–99, 102, 117–18, 220n110; war profiteering and, 119. *See also* First Indochina War (1946–1954), Third Indochina War (1978–1991)

Second International Assembly of Christians in Solidarity with the Vietnamese, Laotians, and Cambodians, 125, 127

Second Republic of Vietnam (RVN), 92, 97–98. *See also* Republic of Vietnam (RVN)

Second Vatican Council, 83, 101, 103–4, 134

Secret Service (US), 118

self-criticism, 18, 114–15

self-defense militias, 14, 65, 74, 80, 106, 163

self-immolation, 75, 101–2, 146

Service for Migration to New Lands, 68

seventeenth parallel, 1–3, 9, 11, 32, 58

Sino-Vietnamese War, 3–4, 161–62

Sleepless Night (Đêm không ngủ), 86, 90

socialist reforms, 17–18, 22, 25–26, 137, 139–40. *See also* communism (and communists)

Socialist Republic of Vietnam (SRVN): 1976 election and, 144; anticommunists in, 163–68; "boat people" crisis and, 151–52; Cambodian-Vietnamese War and, 152–53; communists and, 155–56; human rights and, 169–70; humanitarian crisis in, 154; Lê Duẩn and, 162; new Cold War and, 159–60; opening of borders and, 172–74; postwar crises in, 150–51; PRC and, 161–63, 241n84; refugees from, 158–59; remittances and, 171, 248–49nn62–63; unification of Vietnam and, 137; Vietnamese diaspora and, 176–77

soil, 44–45, 56, 62, 87, 216n60

Sơn Mỹ village, 119

Sống đạo (Living the Faith), 105, 122–23

South Vietnam. *See* Republic of Vietnam (RVN)

Southeast Asia, 76, 89, 151–53, 159–60

Southeast Asia Collective Defense Treaty, 98

Soviet Union, 3, 16–17, 28, 32, 46–47, 64, 89, 91, 94, 113–14, 117, 150, 152–53, 156, 160–62, 188n21

Special Commissariat for Civic Action, 71

Spellman, Cardinal Francis, 36, 58, 82, 97, 103, 125, 209–10n72

Spragens, John, 124

Spring Offensive (1972), 120–21, *121*, 129

Stalin, Joseph, 16, 64, 180

State of Vietnam (SVN), 29–30, 32, 34–36, 38, 40, 44–45, 49, 54, 128, 192n81

State of Vietnam's Armed Forces (SVNAF), 17, 29, 39, 49, 51

strategic hamlets program, 73–75

students, 49–50, 52–53, 86, 90–92, 112–13, 125, 228n97. *See also* General Student Association (GSA)

Témoignage chrétien (*Christian Witness*), 111

Tết Offensive, 106, 109–12, 117, *121*, 122, 145–46

Thailand, 166

Thanh Bồ-Đức Lợi (Danang neighborhood), 77, 91

Thanh Hóa Province, 65, 68

Thế hệ (*Generation*), 112, 126

Thích Nhất Hạnh, 146–47

Thích Quảng Liên, 91, 222n24

Thích Tâm Châu, 106

Thích Trí Quang, 105, 148

Thiệu, Nguyễn Văn. *See* Nguyễn Văn Thiệu

Third Indochina War (1978–1991), 153, 156, 157

Thời luận, 45, 73, 87

Three-Self Patriotic Church, 21

Thức tỉnh (*Awakening*), 155–56, 161–62, 164–65, 168, 171

Tiananmen Square protests, 160

Tin Bắc (*News of the North*), 65, 68

Tin Việt Nam (*News of Vietnam*), 161

Tinh thần (*Esprit*), 26, 57

Tô Văn, 68, 95, 144, 155, 162, 163, 168, *169*, 177, 209n64

Tôn Thất Dương Kỵ, 100, 222n19

Tonkin Gulf resolution, 98

Topmiller, Robert, 91

Trần Đình Trụ, 139

Trần Hữu Thanh, 131–32, 134, 141, 148, 237n21

Trần Lệ Xuân, 52, 73, 81–82

Trần Quý Phúc, 174–75

Trần Tam Tiệp, 170

Trần Tam Tỉnh, 98, 110–14, 125–29, 142–43, 147–48, 177, 240n67

Trần Thanh Hiệp, 49, 170

Trần Thị Liên, Claire, 104

Trần Trung Dung, 59

Trần Văn Tuyên, 93, 128, 138, 177

286   INDEX

transnational networks, 109–15, 124–27, 129, 159, 182
Trịnh Như Khuê, 41, 141
Trương Bá Cẩn, 129
Trương Như Tảng, 140, 144, 161–62, 164
Tự do dân chủ (Democratic Freedom), 91–92
Tự do (Freedom), 73

U Thant, 89
United Front for the Liberation of Oppressed Races (FULRO), 148–49
United Kingdom, 12, 14, 32, 153
United Nations High Commissioner for Refugees (UNHCR), 36, 151–53, 154, 243n3
United Nations (UN), 17, 29, 49, 57, 80, 135, 140, 160, 188n21
United States: 1954 evacuation and, 4, 11, 31, 34, 59; 1975 departure and, 138, 144–46; Cambodian-Vietnamese War and, 153, 156; Catholics and, 128; Cold War and, 16–17, 28; communism and, 6, 103; Diệm and, 27, 75; DRV and, 40; evacuees and, 7, 37–38, 119, 180; France and, 89; Geneva Conference and, 32; imperialism and, 113–14; Khmer Rouge and, 159–60; Mỹ Lai massacre and, 119–20; Ngô Đình Cẩn and, 82; overseas Vietnamese and, 168; Paris Peace Accords and, 107–8, 129; peace movement in, 110, 112, 125–27; protests against, 101–2; refugees and, 159; RVN and, 77–89; RVNAF and, 53; Spring Offensive and, 120–22; SRVN and, 150; SVN and, 35–36; Tết Offensive and, 106; Vietnam and, 96, 140, 237n14; Vietnam War and, 3, 53–54, 79, 88, 91, 93, 97–99, 112, 117–18, 139; war crimes and, 102, 105
Université de Laval, 110–12, 129
US Congress. See Congress (US)
US Operations Mission (USOM), 35, 59, 63

Vandermeersch, Françoise, 148
Vidal-Naquet, Pierre, 111, 227–28n84
Việt Bắc, 18, 25
Việt Cộng, 45, 47, 70, 73–74, 200n91. See also Việt Minh
Việt Minh, 1, 3, 11–16, 18, 20–23, 27, 38, 47, 53, 61, 63, 70–71, 180, 200n91. See also Việt Cộng

Việt Nam dưới thời đại Mỹ (Vietnam in the American Era), 122
Việt Nam Quốc dân Đảng (VNQDĐ; Vietnamese Nationalist Party), 13–14, 18, 27, 51, 74–75, 80, 92
Việt Nam sử lược (A Brief History of Vietnam; Trần Trọng Kim), 167
Vietnam: 1954 evacuation and, 8–9, 33–35; Catholic Church and, 20–25, 72–73, 101; central Vietnam and, 91–92; Cold War and, 6; Diệm and, 27; displacement in, 1–3; evacuees and, 6–7, 54–55, 136–37, 182; foreign intervention and, 4–5; France and, 27–28, 192n76; Geneva Conference and, 29–30; independence and, 12, 51–53; nationalists in, 13–14; partitioning of, 30–32, 46–49; population of, 171–72; reunification and, 44–45, 56–57, 86–87, 117, 137, 144, 174–75; socialist reforms in, 139–40; two states and, 25; uncertainty in, 139; unity of, 17; US and, 96, 119–22; wars against China and Cambodia and, 3–4. See also Associated State of Vietnam (ASVN); central Vietnam; Democratic Republic of Vietnam (DRV); Republic of Vietnam (RVN); Socialist Republic of Vietnam (SRVN)
Vietnam War. See Second Indochina War (1955–1975)
Vietnam Workers' Party (VWP), 17–18, 64, 72, 119, 128, 139–40
Vietnamese, overseas, 169; anticommunism and, 162–68; assimilation and, 145; Bùi Chu diocese and, 173; cease-fire and, 90–91, 98; in Canada, 110–14, 228n91; Catholics and, 129; evacuees' exile in 1975 and, 137; PRG and, 148–49; refugee crisis and, 155–57; remittances and, 171–72, 248–49nn62–63; return to Vietnam and, 174–75; SRVN and, 176–77; transnational networks and, 124–25, 159. See also diaspora, Vietnamese
Vietnamese Armed Forces Overseas, 157
Vinh diocese, 22, 42–43, 64, 70, 123
Võ Nguyên Giáp, 15, 30, 119
voter eligibility cards, 144
Vương Văn Đông, 74

Wałęsa, Lech, 163
war crimes, 102, 145

war profiteering, 119, 130–31, 145
Week of National Shame (Tuần quốc hận), 87, 216n60
World Council of Churches, 101, 112
World Refugee Year (1959), 57, 204n6
World War II, 12
Wu, Albert, 21

Xây dựng (*To Build*), 95, 97, 104, 106, 122

Yalta Conference, 12
Yu Pin, Paul, 103–4
Yugoslavia, 105

Zhou Enlai, 30, 122

Studies of the Weatherhead East Asian Institute, Columbia University

Selected Titles

(Complete list at: weai.columbia.edu/content/publications)

Afterlives of Letters: The Transnational Origins of Modern Literature in China, Japan, and Korea, by Satoru Hashimoto. Columbia University Press, 2023.

Republican Vietnam, 1963-1975: War, Society, Diaspora, edited by Trinh M. Luu and Tuong Vu. University of Hawai'i Press, 2023.

Territorializing Manchuria: The Transnational Frontier and Literatures of East Asia, by Miya Xie. Harvard East Asian Monographs, 2023.

Takamure Itsue, Japanese Antiquity, and Matricultural Paradigms that Address the Crisis of Modernity: A Woman from the Land of Fire, by Yasuko Sato. Palgrave Macmillan, 2023.

Rejuvenating Communism: Youth Organizations and Elite Renewal in Post-Mao China, by Jérôme Doyon. University of Michigan Press, 2023.

From Japanese Empire to American Hegemony: Koreans and Okinawans in the Resettlement of Northeast Asia, by Matthew R. Augustine. University of Hawai'i Press, 2023.

Building a Republican Nation in Vietnam, 1920-1963, edited by Nu-Anh Tran and Tuong Vu. University of Hawai'i Press, 2022.

China Urbanizing: Impacts and Transitions, edited by Weiping Wu and Qin Gao. University of Pennsylvania Press, 2022.

Common Ground: Tibetan Buddhist Expansion and Qing China's Inner Asia, by Lan Wu. Columbia University Press, 2022.

Narratives of Civic Duty: How National Stories Shape Democracy in Asia, by Aram Hur. Cornell University Press, 2022.

The Concrete Plateau: Urban Tibetans and the Chinese Civilizing Machine, by Andrew Grant. Cornell University Press, 2022.

Confluence and Conflict: Reading Transwar Japanese Literature and Thought, by Brian Hurley. Harvard East Asian Monographs, 2022.

Inglorious, Illegal Bastards: Japan's Self-Defense Force During the Cold War, by Aaron Skabelund. Cornell University Press, 2022.

Madness in the Family: Women Care, and Illness in Japan, by H. Yumi Kim. Oxford University Press, 2022.

Uncertainty in the Empire of Routine: The Administrative Revolution of the Eighteenth-Century Qing State, by Maura Dykstra. Harvard University Press, 2022.

Outsourcing Repression: Everyday State Power in Contemporary China, by Lynette H. Ong. Oxford University Press, 2022.

Diasporic Cold Warriors: Nationalist China, Anticommunism, and the Philippine Chinese, 1930s–1970s, by Chien-Wen Kung. Cornell University Press, 2022.
Dream Super-Express: A Cultural History of the World's First Bullet Train, by Jessamyn Abel. Stanford University Press, 2022.
The Sound of Salvation: Voice, Gender, and the Sufi Mediascape in China, by Guangtian Ha. Columbia University Press, 2022.
Carbon Technocracy: Energy Regimes in Modern East Asia, by Victor Seow. The University of Chicago Press, 2022.

www.ingramcontent.com/pod-product-compliance
Lightning Source LLC
Chambersburg PA
CBHW030525230426
43665CB00010B/765